the
Herods

the
Herods

Murder, Politics, and the Art of Succession

Bruce Chilton

Fortress Press
Minneapolis

THE HERODS
Murder, Politics, and the Art of Succession

All Scripture quotations are the work of the author. All rights reserved worldwide.

Cover image: Photo by William Krause on Unsplash
Cover design: Landerholm

Print ISBN: 978-1-5064-7428-1
eBook ISBN: 978-1-5064-7429-8

CONTENTS

PREFACE

THE HERODIAN DYNASTY was complex, conflicted, and compelling; so is the considerable scholarship that approaches the vivid figures responsible for its emergence and demise. I would not have taken up the issue of the Herodians' impact on governance without considerable encouragement, moral support, and practical help from many colleagues. An afternoon's conversation with Joan Bingham brought vividly alive the interest that Herod the Great, always the center of the narrative, could evoke in acute readers. A series of experimental forays, guided by Gail Ross and Ken Wapner, led to the conclusion that the issue of governance was much larger than Herod himself (big though he was) and that the arc of the dynasty needs to be traced for its political impact to be assessed.

Just as this finding came home to me, I was finishing my study of the resurrection of Jesus, another topic whose complexity is a challenge.[1] The editor, Carey Newman, exerted a catalytic influence on my address of the issues involved and my approach to presenting them. In the case of the Herodians, Carey's contribution has been even greater, as we have devised a way to coordinate the moving parts of the Herodian machine. In deciding how to anticipate readers' interests, as well as where to explain more and where to leave matters for inference, I have been greatly helped by Francis Karagodins, a student at Bard College, as well as by Carey. Francis read the proofs of *Resurrection Logic*, showing editorial skills in the process, so it was natural to involve him earlier on in the composition of *The Herods: Murder, Politics, and the Art of Succession*. Library staff at Bard College have provided me with unfailing support, even during the worst days of the pandemic in New York State. The director, Betsy Cawley, provides an example of how institutions, however stressed, need not fail under the pressure of events.

In taking on authorly accountability for the inevitable faults that works of history are heir to, I am heartened that I have no responsibility whatever for the lapses of Josephus, the principal source for all work of this kind. These are so striking that a scholarly literature, some of it cited here, has developed to account for all his apparent *bêtises*. Typically, the problem is addressed by considering his perspective first and then applying that analysis to what Josephus says.[2] Here I prefer to analyze his individual assertions of fact before coming to an assessment in regard to his aims (which appears in the epilogue). Since he was himself a political player and militant leader near the end of the events he narrates, his actions—like those of the Herodians he both admired and criticized—shaped his preferred theory of governance at least as much as his theory guided his actions. Power (like the resurrection) generates its own characteristic logic, in the first century as in the twenty-first.

Bruce Chilton

FEAST OF AIDAN OF LINDISFARNE

INTRODUCTION

IN AUGUST 2000, I went swimming for the first time in the Mediterranean Sea at the beach in Tel Aviv. On an oppressively hot and humid day, signs posted in Hebrew on jetties along the beach cautioned against going in the water and warned that there was no lifeguard. Still, the weather was too stifling to ignore the lure of the impressive waves that crushed in. Because I grew up on Long Island, I have a long-standing habit both of appreciating opportunities to swim and of ignoring signs. In any case, there were some other swimmers that day already in the water, none of whom seemed to struggle.

The Mediterranean Sea has a different taste from the Long Island Sound or the Atlantic Ocean; the salt itself stings more on the tongue and the water is warmer. The waves that day were more distinctive still. Because the Mediterranean is long and relatively narrow and Tel Aviv sits on its eastern end, a storm far out of sight can whip up the impressive breakers that had drawn me into the water, and they are funneled toward the beach. In addition, the drop from the beach into the water is steeper than in the case of the Atlantic Ocean (and more like the Long Island Sound, with its smaller waves). As I found, once in the water, this makes for a strong shear of forces, with the waves' tops pressing into the beach and an undertow dragging the broken waves back out. It did not take long for me to become much cooler, invigorated, but also quite tired, and I made my way back on foot through town.

The Herodian dynasty rolled through the lands of territorial Israel like a series of breakers. Herod the Great; his father, Antipater; Herod's sons, Archelaus, Antipas, and Philip; his extraordinarily lucky grandson, Agrippa I; and his great-grandchildren, Bereniké and Agrippa II were all forces unto themselves, breakers that threatened what stood in their way. Yet they also were part of a single dynastic complex, whose force is explicable not only in terms of their talent and ambition and drive (all of which remain astonishing) but also on the basis of Rome's projection of its might, sometimes blatantly and to the point of violence, sometimes cloaked in the claims of legitimacy of local rulers like the Herodians who did their bidding. The breakers on the eastern end of the Mediterranean are absorbed back into the sea from which they emerged, and the Herodian dynasty by the end of the first century CE was submerged within the Roman imperium that had largely produced it. But in the caesura between their appearance and disappearance, the Herodians made their influence felt on their subjects, among whom were formative figures in the emergence of Judaism and Christianity.

Until his death in 4 BCE, Herod the Great ruled lands that included territories that once made up the kingdoms of Judea and Israel. Although he exercised his monarchy over a rich, strategically crucial territory, his royal title did not derive from heredity. His family came from the people of Idumea, ancient antagonists of the Israelites. Herod and his dynasty framed the basis of their authority at the same time that they ruled, wielding power ruthlessly to maintain and extend their hold on their often fractious, sometimes fiercely rebellious subjects.

Yet Herod ruled not as an outsider but on the basis of a family commitment to Judaism going back to his grandfather and his father. Three generations had served the priestly dynasty of the Maccabees that had submitted Idumea to their rule, helping implement the Maccabean version of what loyalty to the Torah required. Herod's father, Antipater, rose not only to manage affairs on behalf of his priestly masters but to become a pivotal military leader. He inaugurated a new lineament of power: alliance with Rome in the persons of Pompey and Julius Caesar. In the crucible of civil war among Romans as the First Triumvirate broke up and international war between Rome and Parthia became ambient, Antipater managed to leave his sons with the prospect of a dynasty. With a dexterity that became a dynastic trait, Antipas managed to secure just enough stability to secure a position of governance within the volatile changes of political and military conditions.

Antipater achieved success, not by compromise, but by choosing sides and then ferociously standing by his choice.[1] He ruled Idumea on behalf of the Maccabees, preferring their priestly theocracy to the

Hellenizing regime of the Seleucids to the east. That choice involved supporting the Maccabean monarchy over the objections of Jewish groups such as the Essenes. Their reaction to both Maccabean and then Herodian hegemony helped shape their characteristic theology of divine rule. As Antipater set about establishing a dynasty for his family, however, the Maccabees themselves fell into internecine civil war. Antipater remained loyal to the high priest Hyrcanus, whose victory ultimately depended on the incursion of the Romans under Pompey. That great general became the first example among many of Rome's alliances with Antipater and his successors.

Herod inherited the twin pillars of loyalty to Judaism and loyalty to Rome that became the basis of Herodian rule. He was Antipater's second son, born after and subordinate to Phasael, the finest diplomat of the family. Herod inherited his father's audacity and dash, alongside more skill in horsemanship than any of his relatives. But he sorely lacked judgment in the first phase of his career, a trait made all the more obvious by a relentless ambition that never left him. As long as Antipater and Phasael guided him, the worst results of his deficiency in judgment could be contained. Antipater's policy of loyalty to the Romans brought the family into an alliance with Julius Caesar, whose cousin—named Sextus Caesar—developed a particular liking for the extravagant young Herod. While Antipater had turned down the title of king offered to him by Julius Caesar (and ruled instead as procurator), Herod acted arrogantly after his brilliant campaign to subjugate Galilee by ordering the immediate execution of the rebel leader Hezekiah. That brought him into conflict with the Sanhedrin in Jerusalem, which claimed capital jurisdiction. When Herod came to appear before that body in the temple, many in the Pharisaic faction feared that they faced a pretender to the royal title. Pharisees did not come into existence because of or in spite of Herod, but their view of how God intended governance developed during generations of Herodian rule.

For all his ambition, Herod would never have chosen the path he actually took to become a king: his father's death by assassination put a series of unlikely events in motion. He learned to use subterfuge to exact revenge on his father's killer and also resorted to the politics of marriage in the manner of Rome by arranging a marriage with a young Maccabean princess. Another member of that family, however, a would-be high priest named Antigonus, allied with the Parthians to expel the Romans as well as Phasael and Herod from their governance of the land of Israel. Phasael, in fact, committed suicide in Parthian custody, and Herod was brought to the brink of defeat. But he made his way to Rome, where the royal diadem was bestowed on him by Antony and Octavian before the Senate. Herod had elevated Antipater's opportunism into a political masterstroke. That in theory made him king of the Jews, a status that became a reality on the ground after the grisliest fighting of his long career.

During Herod's time, Roman power itself took its imperial form. As Octavian ruled, of course, he took the title Augustus, in keeping with his devotion to his adoptive father's cult of "the divine Julius." Imperial power was a theocratic assertion as well as a dominant military, economic, and political force. Herod framed a version of theocratic ambition all his own: he had married the Maccabean princess named Mariamme in order to produce heirs who would rule with both Rome's sanction and the temple's mandate. He deliberately crafted a dynastic claim grounded in Roman might and Israelite theocracy. That unlikely hybrid was the key to the Herodians' surprising longevity in power during the most chaotic century in the political history of Judaism in the land of Israel. Herod's dynastic ambition peaked when he consummated his marriage to Mariamme, producing heirs who were literally Maccabean royalty. His marriage to his princess happened as Antony's liaison with Cleopatra became fully public—and evidenced no less passion. Cleopatra, however, coveted Herod's lands and his friendship with Antony. When Octavian emerged as the victor after Actium, Herod also triumphed despite his relationship with Antony. The transition to empire only strengthened Herod's hand—and his good standing with Augustus.

By then, however, Herod's suspicion of Maccabees in his own entourage had put him on a murderous course, which saw him assassinate or execute his own relations, including Mariamme's brother and Mariamme herself. Herod ultimately ordered Mariamme killed by strangulation, and their relationship exemplifies Herod's resort to intrigue and violence as well as the self-consuming hybris he brought to every aspect of his rule. Once her sons had grown, she herself was dispensable, but Herod ordered the execution of even those sons for alleged conspiracy. In any case, his total of ten wives had provided ample progeny. Increasingly, he ruled as an imperial client, collided with his Pharisaic opposition, and, as he approached death, confused his own legacy with vicious executions and a series of contradictory wills that named different sons as his successors.

Despite the chaos Herod produced at the end of his life, his dynastic project survived him, becoming a controlling political reality within his territories until the end of the first century CE. None of this worked out smoothly, and one of the two main purposes of this book is to relate a complicated history in a coherent way. Recent scholarship has detailed Herod's personal tragedy and has also shown how his entire family developed and tailored his project of governance within the changing politics of Rome, Judea, Galilee, and international Judaism. Herod and his offspring knew how to play the politics of God, and here their narratives are woven together instead of being treated as separate topics (as in the specialist literature, which is cited). They played a ruthless game, eliminating enemies as they went—Jews and gentiles, Egyptians and Parthians, distant relations and close family. Their violence and their sophistication complemented one another, as they consolidated the power of their dynasty by means of military prowess and political skill and projected their dominance by resorting to public spectacle, massive projects of building and charity, and their appropriation of the traditional symbols of Israelite power.

This was the epoch of Herod the Great: a period extending from the emergence of his father, Antipater, as a governor and ending with the deaths of Bereniké and Agrippa II, Herod's great-grandchildren. As the Herodians negotiated an always explosive set of forces, defining movements in Judaism emerged, each with its own conception of political theology. Essenes, Pharisees, Sadducees, priestly nationalists, revolutionaries, Christians, and ultimately Zealots all held their particular views of *theokrateia*, a term that the general and historian Josephus invented to explain the different strands of his religion. In every case, they framed their theocratic perspective within a Herodian environment, to which they adapted; whether that adaptation was positive or negative, the demand for some response, cooperative or resistant, proved inexorable. The Herodians appropriated elements from some theocratic models, resisted others, and unleashed genocidal violence against opponents who invoked a divine warrant for their own revolutionary programs.

Herod's son Archelaus, in an attempt to imitate his father's final phase of governance, became a model of Herodian cruelty. Herod's first son by his Samaritan wife Malthaké, Archelaus was designated to inherit the royal title by the terms of the dying king's last will. He pressed the dynastic claim to monarchy by organizing a magnificent funeral for his father, flaunting his own status as Herod's rightful heir. But his own brother, Antipas, contested the will and was supported in his challenge before Augustus himself by Herod's sister, Salomé, and even Malthaké, mother of both Archelaus and Antipas. Worse, factions among the Pharisees and Sadducees hardened in their opposition, until militant resistance to both Archelaus and Rome emerged. Archelaus responded by means of the undiscriminating use of force, often unleashing disproportionate devastation against opponents, real and imagined. Augustus, who had supported Archelaus out of loyalty to the memory of Herod, wearied of the persistent rebellions in Judea and finally exiled Archelaus and ordered direct Roman rule by means of a prefect within Judea proper while Archelaus's brothers, Antipas and Philip, continued to rule as tetrarchs of their territories, Galilee and Gaulanitis.

Whether a given Herodian ruler was cruel or generous, effective or useless, gifted or limited, their subjects could not ignore them. Yet those who study Judaism and Christianity today typically treat them as a matter of "background," when in fact the Herodians were in the foreground of political power. Various models of theocracy that have long been recognized, from the Essenes' *War of the Sons of Light against the Sons of Darkness* to Jesus's vision of the kingdom of God, were not abstract assertions but living alternatives to Herodian power. Tracing the relationship between the Herodian project and political theologies within Judaism and Christianity is the second main purpose of this book.

The Herodians have exerted an outsized influence compared to the territory and forces they commanded because strands of Judaism long survived them. Among these survivals, of course, Christianity also emerged, and each of the key figures within that movement—Jesus, James (the brother of Jesus), and Paul among them—dealt with a different inflection of Herodian power. For this reason, Herod's successors—above all his sons, Archelaus, Antipas, and Philip; his grandson, Agrippa I; and his great-grandchildren, Agrippa II and Bereniké—were all vital influences on the emergence of Christianity. The competitors and victims of the Herodian project are as fascinating as the Herodians themselves; many of them contributed to models of governance that exercise influence until this day.

No Herodian pursued advancement toward the dynastic end more persistently than Antipas. Disappointed in his attempt to be named king of Judea in a hearing before Augustus to adjudicate Herod the Great's will and again after Archelaus was deposed, Antipas contented himself with shoring up his position as tetrarch of Galilee and Perea. With stolid effectiveness, he rebuilt Sepphoris after the occupation of Judas the Galilean and made a marriage alliance with the king of Nabataea. After Augustus's death and the accession of Tiberius, Antipas's ambition burned anew. He married Herodias, daughter of Herod's son Aristobulus and therefore a Maccabean heiress. She was already married to Antipas's brother Philip, and the union was criticized by John the Baptist. Just as Antipas eliminated John in Machaerus, he sought to dispose of John's disciple Jesus in Galilee. He only achieved the latter aim in Jerusalem, however, by means of a strategic alliance with the prefect of Jerusalem, Pontius Pilate. With John and Jesus dealt with and his brother Philip dead, Antipas seemed secure in his reach for the royal title, provided the aging Tiberius would reward decades of loyal service yoked with smoldering ambition.

Agrippa I, grandson of Herod the Great and son of Aristobulus, formed an intimate friendship with Caligula, Tiberius's heir by adoption. When Tiberius died, Agrippa suddenly became the Herodians' golden boy. Caligula named his friend to Philip's former tetrarchy, but as *king*. When Antipas petitioned Caligula to be named a king of his own tetrarchy, false charges by Agrippa instead ensured that the emperor banished Antipas altogether. With that, Agrippa I became king of Galilee and Perea as well. The new king used his influence on behalf of Judaism and was a key figure in convincing Caligula to rethink and delay his order to set up a statue of himself in the temple. Only Caligula's assassination, however, spared Jerusalem this "abomination of desolation" (Mark 13:14). In the transition to Claudius as emperor, Agrippa proved himself useful and was rewarded with the inheritance of the whole realm of Herod the Great, again as king. Lavish spending, skillful diplomacy, and (like Claudius) selective persecution of minorities such as Jesus's followers earned Agrippa admiration and broad success. His single greatest misfortune was his health, however, and his premature death threw Judea into confusion. Amid a rising tide of rebellion, Claudius resorted to the appointment of procurators (rather than prefects), whose increased authority was nonetheless inadequate to the rising tide of revolt.

The turbulence of the period after Agrippa I as well as a concern for his son's inexperience prevented Claudius from appointing Agrippa II in his stead. The reticence was shown to be justified, because when Agrippa II did finally come into power over parts of Herod and Agrippa I's old realm, he administered it tentatively, merely as a Roman client. In stark contrast, there was nothing tentative about his sister, Bereniké. Twice married by the time of Agrippa I's death, she and her sister Drusilla continued to forge marriages to advance the dynastic cause. But no spouse was as interesting to Bereniké as her brother, and—despite rumors of incest—she left a third husband to rejoin Agrippa II's court. In that setting, she and her brother attempted to moderate legal action against the apostle Paul, but neither that prosecution nor the extralegal execution of James could be prevented.

The temple occupied a position at the center of controversy and increasingly saw violence. The last procurator before open war with Rome broke out, Gessius Florus, overreacted while Agrippa II was in Egypt on a diplomatic mission—a crucial moment when revolt might have been averted. But Bereniké stood in the eye of the storm in Jerusalem, undertaking a Nazirite vow, and she attempted to mitigate the procurator's tactics. Even with Agrippa II's belated arrival and his support of his sister's approach, the revolt came. When it did, Bereniké and Agrippa alike supported the general Vespasian and his son Titus, both of whom acceded to the position of emperor as their Flavian dynasty came to power. Bereniké began an affair with Titus that was no passing liaison and became the basis of speculation from Jerusalem to Rome that the Herodian dynasty would join with the Flavians to shape a new settlement for the empire as a whole. Bereniké, the most prominent figure in her generation of the Herodians, brought the dynastic ambition to its most extensive aspiration.

At the same time, the surprising resonance between, on the one hand, the Herodians and their apologists and, on the other hand, Roman conceptions of providential governance emerge at the close of the narrative. Bereniké, certainly the most religious and perhaps the most ambitious of all the Herodians, consummated her affair with the Roman general Titus as he besieged the Second Temple. When he became emperor, she was his consort; however controversial that relationship, she brought her family and Judaism itself to the verge of a completely new form of power. Bereniké embodied not only the Herodians' passion to rule but also their challenging insistence that religion and politics—far from separable—are embedded with one another. Although they pursued their ambition with characteristic audacity and a unique set of resources, talents, and opportunities, the dynasty also brought out of their subjects and their collaborators a common quest for *theokrateia* that is the topic of the epilogue.

1

ANTIPATER

A NOBLE IDUMEAN MERCENARY
FOUNDS A DYNASTY

Antipater, father of Herod the Great, navigated the conflicting forces of his time by choosing sides and then fiercely standing by his choices. He ruled Idumea on behalf of the Maccabees, preferring their priestly theocracy to the Hellenizing regime of the Seleucids. That choice involved supporting the Maccabean monarchy over the objections of Jewish groups such as the Essenes. As Antipater set about establishing a dynasty for his family, however, the Maccabees themselves fell into internecine civil war. Antipater remained loyal to the high priest Hyrcanus, whose victory ultimately depended on the incursion of the Romans under Pompey. That great general became the first example among many of Rome's alliance with Antipater and his successors.

The founder: *Loyal, adept, generous, fearless; gifted commander of eclectic forces*

Setting

A ROCKY, RED-CLAY kingdom stretched south of Judea from the Sinai Peninsula to beyond the Dead Sea; Israelites had called it Edom (which means "red" in their language). Despite close trading and ethnic relationships between the two nations, Edom warred frequently with Israel. Biblical legend had it that the people of Edom descended from Esau, the slightly elder of the patriarch Isaac's two sons. The book of Genesis says that at his birth, Esau was red or ruddy like his land, and also hairy (Gen 25:25): a born outdoorsman.

Esau's younger twin brother, Jacob[1]—who is also given the name Israel as an adult (Gen 32:28)—tricked Esau out of his birthright as Isaac's principal heir. Genesis recounts the trick in two different ways, each derived from its own source. In one, Esau returns from hunting so famished that he is willing to trade anything for the vegetable stew that his domesticated younger brother has prepared. Jacob agrees to give him some at the price of his privileged position as the firstborn son of Isaac. Esau consents, exchanging his birthright for a vegetable stew that had been made—in the story's etiological flourish—from red lentils (Gen 25:29–34).

In the second source, the account of Jacob's appropriation of Esau's birthright is more dramatic and complicated (Gen 27:1–40). Isaac, blind and aware that he is dying, intends to bless his firstborn son, thereby giving Esau preeminence over all the family. An endowment of that kind implies preference, and Isaac makes it clear that his favoritism is grounded in Esau's status as a hunter, a man of fields rather than flocks. He sends Esau to hunt for the game meat he likes to eat so that he can relish a meal from the prey as he bestows the blessing.

Isaac's wife, Rebecca, however, shows partiality in her own way: her favorite son is Jacob. She overhears the conversation between Isaac and Esau, and once Esau leaves for the hunt, she arranges with Jacob to prepare a meal from young goats, seasoned as if it were game. Jacob becomes nervous: since his build is not at all like his brother Esau's, he fears even the blind Isaac will recognize the deception. But Rebecca clothes Jacob in Esau's garments, putting goatskin on his hands and neck, and Jacob presents himself and his meal to Isaac. The deception reaches its ironic peak when Isaac speaks words that would signal his deep paternal recognition of and attachment to Esau. He eats, smells the disguised Jacob in his animal skins, and says, "The smell of my son is like the smell of a field that the Lord has blessed" (Gen 27:25–27). So Jacob receives the blessing intended for Esau, including the promise that his brothers will do obeisance to him, and all because Esau smelled like a goat.

The narrative continues with Esau's ongoing and understandable rage as well as Jacob's long and guileful history; the fraught relationship between the brothers portends succeeding centuries of border skirmishes between Edom and Israel. Genesis conveys a deep sense of jealous suspicion between the brothers, and the stories more accurately convey the social reality of how Edom and Israel interacted than they give information about their progenitors Jacob and Esau. As Genesis puts the matter, Esau was a man who hunted in the open field, while his young brother preferred pastoral life in the shelter of tents (Gen 25:27). The two lifestyles never fully converged, and on the contrary, they often conflicted, as the people of Edom retained renown for hunting, mobility, and outdoor prowess, while Israel—itself named after Jacob's byname, "striver with God" (Gen 32:28)—made its way as an agricultural and increasingly sedentary nation. The horse became as emblematic of Edom[2] as the courtyarded farmhouse was of Israelite society.

The legendary blessing that Isaac gave to Jacob, mistakenly or not, took generations to approach accomplishment. The Davidic monarchy might have seemed to realize the promise in the nation Israel, but after the time of David and his son Solomon, the country was divided into Israel in the north, with its capital in Samaria, and Judah (or Judea, *Ioudaia* in Greek) in the south, with its capital in Jerusalem. The internecine war between the two states only came to an end when the northern kingdom, which had taken the name Israel, was destroyed by the Assyrian Empire in 722 BCE. In the south, Judah barely survived Babylonian deportation in 586 BCE and eked out a limited autonomy under the hegemony of Cyrus the Persian and then Alexander the Great and his successors. Only a part of the land David and Solomon had conquered and a fraction of the people that claimed descent from Jacob remained: Israel had been reduced to the ancient clan of Judah. Their name is the reason people in the ancient world came to think of their religion as "Judaism" (from the Greek term *Ioudaïsmos*). The people of Judea, the *Ioudaioi*, were the only widely recognized inheritors[3] of the blessing that Isaac had bestowed on Jacob.

Neither Israel nor Edom could contend against the great imperial powers that surrounded and dominated them. Egypt, Assyria, Babylonia, Persia, and the Hellenistic empires of Alexander the Great and his successors took the territory they desired when it pleased them.[4] By the second century BCE, the territories of Jacob's and Esau's progenies were caught between two empires, each founded by one of Alexander's generals: the Ptolemaic dynasty ruled from Egypt and the Seleucid dynasty from Antioch. Although Edom and Judea had been kingdoms in their own right, their national existence had been overcome by imperial hegemony. Judea held on to a centralizing focus of power—the temple in Jerusalem—while Edom reverted to prenational competition among rival warrior leaders and trading interests. In any case, neither Israelite nor Edomite ambition played a dominant role in the region. The Ptolemies to the west and the Seleucids to the east overwhelmed old rivalries in tides of new power.

In Egypt, Alexander's general Ptolemy had established a dynasty that concentrated the command of the territory in its hands. The rulers took on the trappings of new pharaohs, and they harnessed the fertility of the Nile to secure an agricultural preeminence within the Mediterranean Basin. In the Near East, a general named Seleucus seized power in order to pursue the program of Alexander the Great. That involved rapid conquest and the imposition of Greek language and culture— worship, dress, and art, all under a military aegis—known as Hellenization. While the Ptolemies' strategy was to clothe their dynasty in the indigenous legacy of the pharaohs, their counterparts in the Seleucid dynasty, without recourse to the pretense that they ruled under traditional authority, relied on violence within their vast and diverse territory, which reached from Afghanistan to Turkey under Antiochus III. To govern this sprawling range of peoples required stunning displays of military dominance and an insistence on the superiority of the Seleucids' variant of Hellenistic civilization.

The Maccabees

EDOM AND JUDEA soon became pawns in the clash of the Ptolemaic and Seleucid empires. During the second century BCE, the Seleucids pressed their distinct military advantage. Aware of the fragility of their regime in political terms, over the years, they incorporated advanced techniques of war, including the most expensive. Hannibal, the great general from Carthage and renowned in the use of elephants in war, had personally pledged his military acumen to the Seleucids.[5] Armored and equipped with a platform to carry archers and lancers, each beast was surrounded by supporting cavalry. An elephant could be deployed as a shield for infantry and as a mobile siege engine that could be directed against its target to crush gates, walls, and retreating soldiers.

Conquest served the Seleucids as a means to consolidate an already extensive commercial influence so that the Mediterranean would be their western portal for trading links that reached deep into Asia. In addition, the rise of the Parthian Empire in ancient Iran made westward expansion a Seleucid imperative in order to compensate for losses to Parthia to the east. In that effort, Edom appeared a minor annoyance; some of its ancestral lands had already been consumed, and what remained posed little obstacle to Seleucid expansion. Judea was only the rump of the once much larger kingdom of Israel, invaded and parceled out in a series of imperial invasions from the Assyrians in the eighth century to Alexander the Great in the fourth century.[6]

The Seleucid ruler Antiochus IV pressed on with the final annexation of the reduced inheritances of Jacob and Esau into the Seleucid Empire. Taking the name Epiphanes—a Greek term that means "revealed one," since he held himself to be a divinity manifest—he pursued a policy of Hellenizing the territories he occupied. His campaign reached such an extreme that he converted the temple in Jerusalem to the worship of Zeus in 167 BCE, complete with the sacrifice of swine's flesh on the altar; concurrently, he outlawed Judaism.[7] He started this program in person by entering and plundering the temple himself when he returned from a campaign against Ptolemaic Egypt, leaving it to his general Apollonius to implement his wishes for conquest and domination. Then he returned to his magnificent palace in Antioch, the Syrian city that had replaced Seleukia as the capital of the Seleucid Empire. Meanwhile, Apollonius and his more than twenty-two thousand mercenary troops put Antiochus's policy into effect. They were paid to obliterate Judaism in Jerusalem and were allowed at the same time to take from their victims what profit they wished. This complex of tyranny—from the desecration of the altar to the ruin of individual Israelites—is the horror that the book of Daniel calls "an abomination that desolates" (Dan 9:27; 11:31).

Antiochus's tactics of state terror shaped contemporaneous Judaic literature and later remembrance. His soldiers hunted women who had consented to their infant sons' circumcision on the eighth day in accordance with the Torah. Apollonius's troops patrolled the city and entered homes, free to strip infants to look for evidence of what was considered to be their parents' religious crime. They killed circumcised babies with the stroke of a sword and hung the corpses around the necks of their mothers, who were marched through the city and displayed on the city walls around Jerusalem. Crowds looked on as these women were pushed to their deaths off parapets from heights of up to a hundred feet. Some of the onlookers, horrified yet defiant, fled Jerusalem to embrace the continued practice of circumcision as a means of passive resistance against the Seleucid tyranny. Others, either opposed or indifferent to Judaism, saw the killings as collateral damage in the advance of the Seleucid's Hellenistic empire. But whether in horror or admiration, the crowd looked on, because it was a crowd, and the Seleucid general understood the art of spectacle. Apollonius perfected the policy of coercing religion into service of the empire.[8]

Apollonius acted under Antiochus's orders to set up a statue of Zeus within the temple, a blatant display of idolatry. As a matter of course, he arranged for the slaughter of pork, Zeus's preferred meat according to Hellenistic theology, and Seleucid priests, protected by Apollonius's troops, herded swine through the city and into the slaughter yard just north of the altar in the temple. Pursuing his program with the zeal of a fundamentalist and the bloodlust of a thug, Apollonius forced the consumption of pork on the population of Jerusalem; his soldiers gave their victims the choice of either eating swine's flesh or being hacked to death.

An old scribe named Eleazar said he would rather die and receive the reward for his soul that God would bestow in the next life than betray what he called the "holy laws" of Judaism that he had upheld for some ninety years (2 Macc 6:28). His torturers punished him with blows and cuts designed to inflict pain rather than death, but neither their vicious cruelty nor their offers of clemency caused the old man to waver before he died. He even turned down the option of pretending that food which he had prepared himself was the pork offered to Zeus (2 Macc 6:21–25). In his mind, even the pretense of disobedience of the Torah, under threat of death or not, was a form of treason against God. A literature of Judaic resistance celebrated Eleazar's recalcitrance. Stories of such courage, multiplied in the rich canon of martyrdom from the Judaism of this period (no doubt idealized and exaggerated), gave birth to a religious revolution that had not been seen before. The scale of Judean resistance, with a program of martyrdom animated by the belief in the resurrection of the righteous, was unanticipated and irresistible.

The vital center of and leadership for the Judaic revolution was a family of priests that came to be known as the Maccabees. They were of provincial background, from Modi'in, and mounted a resistance to attempts by Antiochus's officers to compel the population there to offer idolatrous sacrifice. Combining direct, physical combat with a zeal for the Torah, the Maccabean resisters killed an Israelite on the verge of sacrificing to Zeus, murdered the officer who had supervised the act, and destroyed the altar set up in Modi'in (1 Macc 2:1–28). The Maccabees did not pause to consider that they were taking on the heirs of Alexander's general, Seleucus, when they fought the Seleucid dynasty. They were confident that the honor of God would always prevail against the oppressor, however powerful he might be.

The Maccabees celebrated a warrior from their family called Eleazar (nicknamed Avaran), who cut his way through a phalanx in order to eviscerate a Seleucid siege elephant from beneath. He died under the weight of the beast, and they said, "He gave his life to save his people and to win for himself an everlasting name" (1 Macc 6:43–46, 44).[9] The episode depicts the tactical resourcefulness of the Maccabees in using guerilla tactics and conveys how the theology of martyrdom was weaponized in their asymmetrical warfare. They trained willing recruits and employed mercenaries, pushing back against the Seleucid forces with every means at their disposal. Three years of sanguine strife pitted an organized insurgency against an increasingly disorganized imperial force and culminated in the Maccabees' rededication of the temple to the worship of the God of Israel. Their name—and that of Eleazar Avaran—seemed to them eternal at the time. Their historical memory has indeed survived the demise of their dynasty and has done so out of all proportion to the power and influence they wielded in their time.

Their victory is celebrated still with the powerful legends of Hanukkah (which means "[re]dedication"). Traditions of the Talmud, a text produced centuries after the Maccabees rededicated the temple, tell the story that the rebels found a single vial of oil that had not been defiled by the Seleucids and that it alone sufficed to illuminate the temple lamps during the eight days of purifying sacrifice necessary to rededicate the polluted temple (Talmud Bavli, *Shabbat* 21a).[10] The Maccabean leaders of the resistance relied less on the miraculous means of legend and more on *themselves* as God's agents, and they destroyed the Seleucids' abominations with unquenchable zeal. Their magnificent and violent campaign was headed by a leader called Judas Maccabeus—Judas the "Hammer"—and he gave this name[11] to the movement and the family as a whole.

The sacerdotal dynasty turned quickly from resistance to stabilization and finally to conquest; over several decades, their regime absorbed more territory than any previous sovereign of Israel, even David and Solomon. The new regime annexed Samaria and Galilee in the north and Iturea and Perea on the eastern side of the Jordan River. In that policy of extension, they overran Edom, now called Idumea in Greek, which had already been pushed west as compared to ancient Edom with the growing power of the Nabataean kingdom.[12] Caught between the greater powers of Judea and Nabataea, Idumea chose the Maccabees, accepting the requirement of conversion to Judaism and the compulsory circumcision of male infants on the eighth day that conversion involved.

The Maccabees nonetheless amounted to only a minor power, no more than a petty kingdom compared to vast, powerful empires that had exerted hegemony before and would again. But they controlled a strategic region in their rule over some three million people within a total landmass just over the size of New Hampshire, some nine thousand square miles. Their conquests followed three interlocking lines of attack. Their coordination of these strategies helps explain the Maccabees' remarkable success.

First and foremost, the Maccabean campaign of martyrdom against the Seleucids had galvanized the loyalty of the faithful.[13] For this reason, most of those who wanted to see their religion triumph were willing to overlook the Maccabees' defects (which feature later in this narrative) and join in a popular uprising to demand obedience to the Torah of Moses, a common denominator among the various factions of Judaism. Maccabean propaganda produced books included today in the Apocrypha. The Maccabees saw young Eleazar Avaran, together with the aged scribe who refused to eat pork and many other heroic people, men and women, as examples of righteousness. By taking on the pain of a martyr's death, the righteous assured that God would restore the bodies they were willing to give (2 Macc 7).[14] The broad appeal of that promise gave the Maccabean revolt its impetus and mainstreamed the attraction of martyrdom within the religions of the West. This deliberate emphasis on resurrection was a fresh departure within the Israelite tradition, but one with a powerful influence on Judaism, Christianity, and Islam. Maccabean theology far outlasted Maccabean power.

Lands that had long been under gentile sway, such as Galilee, were reconverted to Judaism, and the Samaritan temple was destroyed[15] as the public conventions of Judaic practice emerged as the second line of conquest. That muscular extension of obedience to the Torah brought with it a popular enthusiasm for pursuing its implications at every level. Practices such as keeping the Sabbath, obeying laws of purity in food and sexuality, and the circumcision of male children[16] all became requirements, demanded by public opinion and the conventions of power and endorsed by the Maccabean high priest besides. Squads of loyalists saw to religious obedience and easily turned violent when any resistance was encountered. Failure to obey the Torah could mean expulsion from a community or death, and in either case, the Maccabees' local cohort could claim the additional property and wealth that came their way when a resister fled or was killed. Piety under the Maccabees conferred wealth, sustained social status, and justified violence. Sanctioned public aggression was always their most potent weapon, and the brutal power of the mob proved so effective that it too, like their theology, long survived the Maccabees' regime.

The Maccabees ruled in a way that religiously inspired movements of resistance sometimes do: by absorbing the imperial ethos of their oppressors. In fact, their success resided in their capacity to find a modus vivendi with the powers that surrounded them, including the Seleucids.[17] Part of the Seleucid religious campaign against Judaism had involved compelling people to join in processions to honor the god Dionysus (2 Macc 6:7). The Maccabees turned the Dionysian hope of rebirth into the promise of *physical* resuscitation for the righteous.[18] The Maccabean dynasty inherited and transformed other Seleucid traits, as frequently occurs when religion rises to resist the onslaught of an occupying power. The impulse to imitate the oppressor who is to be overcome was in no way, however, unique to the Maccabees. Much as Christianity absorbed the language, the taste for hierarchy, and the patriarchy of the Roman Empire even during its long period of persecution and Islam framed its conception of jihad in response to the Crusaders' onslaught upon Muslims as infidels,[19] so the Maccabees came to imitate the Seleucids. In strife between two cultures, one takes on successful or advantageous traits of the other, so that the Maccabees came to boast military methods that Seleucid soldiers had taught them by painful experience. The imperial aspirations of their foes appealed to the Maccabees, and they recruited into their forces some of the mercenaries employed formerly by the Seleucids. They also inherited the Seleucids' devotion to Hellenization,[20] the most effective instrument of hegemony for several centuries before, and adopted the use of Greek, the language of hegemony since Alexander the Great. Divine sanction for rule featured strongly in the

Hellenistic fashion of governance. From the claim that Zeus was the true father of Alexander the Great[21] to Antiochus IV's appropriation of the title *Epiphanes*, monarchy assumed the attributes of power from beyond this world. The king was to engage in conquest, judge his people, and propitiate the divine realm. The Maccabees draped their hegemony in the mantle of the high priesthood that served what Judaism recognized as the only temple in which God took pleasure.

That Hellenistic ethos formed their third line of conquest. They spoke Greek, ruled through a military bureaucracy oiled with the skill of mercenaries, and aspired to a combination of religious and political power as remorseless as that of Antiochus IV. Maccabean zeal emerged as the counterpoint to Hellenistic zeal, less extensive in territory yet more intense in passion. The new kingdom proudly understood itself as a theocracy, the term used by the later historian and apologist Josephus with the explanation that it is a form of government "placing all sovereignty and authority in the hands of God."[22]

The Maccabees offer a clear precedent for theocratic rebellion down to the time of the Iranian Revolution. They forged their religion into a weapon, forcing those they conquered to accept male circumcision as relentlessly as Antiochus IV had attempted to extirpate it. But they were also flagrant in denying the biblical promise of a Davidic ruler (2 Sam 7) and took the power and ultimately the title of kings for themselves without any pretense of descent from David. Although their priestly genealogy did not put them in the ranks of those qualified for the highest roles, they also usurped the high priestly succession, even accepting appointment to that office by a pretender to the Seleucid throne.[23] Their willingness to make treaties with gentile regimes also meant that they came to relax requirements of purity to the point that many practitioners of Judaism, such as the group that inhabited Qumran and produced the Dead Sea Scrolls, attacked the Maccabees as interlopers, false kings, and wicked priests. Among the challenges they faced, the most troubling from the Maccabean point of view was the religious challenge to their legitimacy. But against traditionalist opposition, the Maccabees commanded resources of wealth, military dominance, and state propaganda, all deployed in the interests of state Judaism.

For the next century, the Maccabees remained firmly in power by paying off local warlords to help subdue any sporadic recalcitrance. Among their favored commanders was Antipater,[24] a talented and effective Idumean mercenary who had a knack for ingratiating himself to power and for timing a change of patrons. Several volatile factors—not least the challenge to the Maccabees' religious legitimacy—gave Antipater the room to maneuver amid the conflicting claims of priests, kings, generals, and eventually an emperor-in-waiting; he came to exert much more power than could have been expected for a man who began as a local and marginal figure.

The Essenes

AMONG THE MANY groups and movements that competed for influence or struggled simply to survive during the rule of the Maccabees, the Essenes were the most distinctive—and the most radical in their political theology. Generations of resistance to the dominion of superior foreign powers from a time long before the Maccabees produced a mentality of denying the authority of those who ruled and anticipating a final judgment by God that would replace human arrogance with divine justice. By the time Judas Maccabeus had led his successful rebellion against the Seleucids, the Essenes already populated many cities in the region, reaching as far north as Damascus and as far west as Alexandria. They had settled in those locations once Judeans had been permitted by Cyrus the Persian to depart from Babylonia in 539 BCE. Cyrus celebrated his own policy of toleration in an inscription from that period, which details how he sanctioned the return to their lands by many peoples taken captive during the time of the Babylonian Empire, which he had overthrown. He even authorized returning captives of various religions to rebuild their temples and reestablish worship according to their traditional practice. Some Judeans were so enthusiastic about Cyrus's rule that they called him the Lord's "messiah" (Isa 45:1).[25] But the attitude of the Essenes toward all forms of government and toward the attempt to restore the temple that Cyrus endorsed differed strongly from that of most of their contemporaries' and indeed defined their movement more than any other factor.

Cyrus had specifically sanctioned a rebuilding of the temple, but a plan for how to replace the edifice the Babylonians destroyed in 586 BCE needed to be devised. Prophetic and priestly forces allied to support a descendant of David named Zerubbabel in completing the task. Yet as the Second Temple took shape, disputes concerning its validity and purity became routine. In fact, the Israelite religion of this period—known as Second Temple Judaism—is characterized by an apparent paradox. Widespread agreement *that* sacrifice could be offered uniquely in Jerusalem provoked disputes concerning *how* sacrifices should be prepared and presented there. Precisely because the temple was venerated as the only one in the world that God desired, it attracted a fierce competition among sacrificial partisans who believed that theirs was the one way to serve God in the one place that he had chosen for worship. The Essenes brought a distinctive and self-isolating program to the Judean worldview of sacrifice.

Before Cyrus's edict of toleration, in Babylonia, many of the exiles from Jerusalem and Judea after 586 BCE adapted to the customs and even the language of their new land. They followed God's advice as given by Jeremiah, to "seek the peace of the city to which I have sent you into exile" (Jer 29:7). To the Essenes, however, assimilation was not a divine imperative at all. They objected, for example, to the use of the Babylonian names of months within the calendar of sacrifice. Their fellow exiles accepted the new nomenclature and even incorporated it within the text of the Hebrew Bible, which was edited during the period of exile. In rejecting that practice, the Essenes also departed from their contemporaries in another, more fundamental way.

The Essenes opposed any veneration of the moon, which was associated with the Babylonian goddess Ishtar, by devising a calendar governed solely by the sun, the symbol of Yahweh. This was a radical reaction, since the traditional calendar of the First Temple had also been calculated on the basis of the moon's phases. The Essene movement was not conservative; it stood for a change in a central dimension of sacrifice.[26] A calendar in antiquity was more than a method of keeping time. Its dedicated purpose was to regulate the sacrificial rhythm that animated a given religion; in fact, from the point of view of a sacrificial religion, the presentation of offerings at the correct times of the year kept the world and its seasons intact.[27] For Israel, that meant recollecting Passover with the Exodus, Weeks or Pentecost with the giving of the Torah, and Sukkot or Tabernacles with the wilderness period prior to coming into the land of Canaan.

During the period in Babylonia, however, when there was no temple and there could be no sacrifice, the Essenes and the Judean exiles remembered what should be done without actually doing it. Independently of the controlling authorities of their time, whether gentile or Judaic, they also curated the texts that have come down to us in the Hebrew Bible and the Dead Sea Scrolls, so that the conflict between the lunar calendar[28] of most Judeans and the solar calendar of the Essenes is evident. By remembering the feasts at times that differed from the rest of the Judean community, the Essenes set themselves apart; eventually they established communal settlements of their own or established exclusive neighborhoods within larger Judean communities.

After their period of self-isolation during the Babylonian exile, Essenes experienced Cyrus's policy of permitting Judeans to return to their land more as a challenge than as a vindication. The new temple that Zerubbabel built did not coincide with their vision of how sacrifice was to be offered. The calendar, of course, was wrong from their point of view; moreover, Essene teaching in regard to the arrangement of the temple and the proper means of butchering and carving up animals for sacrifice did not agree with the practices of the priestly establishment that saw to the erection of the Second Temple at the end of the sixth century BCE.[29] None of these matters was a marginal concern, and the Essenes were convinced of the truth of their minority position.

Essenes looked to the memory of the "Teacher of Righteousness," whom they idealized. His influence on the Essene program made him a principal guide, but this community (the *yachad*, as they designated themselves) also looked to angels for guidance.[30] As they understood it, in special congregations such as the famous settlement at Qumran that kept purity, God sent his angels from the divine court in order to reveal his ways and his purposes for Israel and humanity as a whole. Essene dietary purity involved stricter rules than those widely kept for keeping food kosher. Sexual ethics were also more stringent than the Judaic norm, and at least some Essenes maintained celibacy in order to prepare themselves for contact with angels.

Those angels had another providentially determined purpose: to be the ultimate military and moral support of the Essenes. When God is referred to in the Hebrew Bible as "Yahweh of hosts" (or "Lord of hosts" in the convention of the King James Version), the "hosts" are massive contingents of heavenly armies. For the Essenes, that was not merely a matter of imagery. Their expectation was that the angels of God would join with Essene forces in a final "war of the sons of light against the sons of darkness."[31] Everyone else who disagreed with them was in the dark, even the leadership in Jerusalem. The Essenes and their angelic counterparts would begin the eschatological war by taking the temple as their own, destroying all enemies in Judea and in the world, until the Essene *yachad*, true Israel, exercised sole sovereignty. The only question was when the battle would commence; until then, readiness was the fundamental principle of Essene ethics.

It may well have been the case that Essenes joined in the resistance campaign when Judas Maccabeus took up arms against Antiochus IV. The Maccabees, of course, wanted to restore the Second Temple, while the Essenes longed for a complete change in the practice and layout of sacrifice in Jerusalem, but the Seleucid blasphemy revolted all sides of Judaic opinion. The Maccabees unified their people better when they opposed the Seleucids than when they ruled in their own right. For the Essenes especially, Judas and his successors were arrogant. They assumed the high priesthood without being, in the sense of adhering to the Essene view of the covenant God had made with his people, true descendants of Zadok (see Ezek 44:15), and although not of the line of David, they claimed to be kings. In both regards, the problem from the Essene point of view was not merely genealogical. They saw the sons of Zadok as those who would always keep the purity and the calendar they insisted upon and anticipated a Davidic "messiah of Israel" capable of taking up leadership in the ultimate struggle of the sons of light against the sons of darkness. They came to oppose the Maccabees' root and branch, even calling their most magnificent and powerful rulers the "Wicked Priest."[32]

The Maccabees responded to Essene theology with marketing. They encouraged the dissemination of the picture of the high priest as glorious in the sanctuary that he had fortified, "like the morning star among the clouds, and the moon when it is full" (Sir 50:6). Language of that kind, of course, was exactly the sort of Babylonian worship imagery, redolent of the veneration of the lunar goddess Ishtar, that the Essenes detested. The Maccabees were in the best position to mount spectacle, but to retain their position, they required force, not only propaganda. For this reason, they turned to the Idumean warrior and mercenary, Antipater.

Antipater in the Maccabean Hegemony

ANTIPATER WAS AN Idumean clan chief; each clan knitted families together by the remembrance of common ancestors in Edom, much as in the case of the "tribes" of Israel. The chief saw to arrangements of planting and harvesting, of shepherding herds and timing their movements from pasture to pasture, and of hunting in accordance with the seasonal movements of antelope and Mesopotamian fallow deer; he sealed the approval of marriages within the clan and conducted relations with other clans as well as commercial arrangements with traders.[33] Antipater's family and clan had been converted at the time of the Maccabean takeover of Idumea; he proved a loyal ally of his Judean masters and had already mastered relations within the mixture of cultures and peoples in the territory that the Maccabees wished to rule. A skilled horseman whose tactics in the hunt could be used to the advantage of the military, like his father, he even bore the name of one of the greatest generals of Alexander the Great. The very name Antipater, whether given at birth or appropriated over time as a sign of victory in battle, flagged an affinity with the rising tide of Hellenism apparent during the entire period and from well before the rise of the Maccabees.

Antipater's wife was a noblewoman from Nabataea named Cypros; a relative of the king of Nabataea,[34] she enabled Antipater to develop a strategic friendship. The Nabataeans were an Arabian people who had pushed the Idumeans to the west in their struggle against the Seleucids. At their peak, they ruled a centralized kingdom from their fabled capital in Petra, then and now an architectural marvel, all the way north to Damascus, covering a greater landmass than the present kingdom of Jordan. Over time they profited from the Maccabean insurrection against the Seleucids and looked for lucrative accommodations with their neighbors, Idumea included. Antipater was in a perfect position to accommodate at once to Maccabean rule and to the fierce independence of the Nabataeans, who shared with the Idumeans a devotion to their ancestral clans.

Cypros bore four sons—Phasael, Herod, Joseph, and Pheroras, all of them circumcised in obedience to the Torah—as well as a famously strong-willed daughter named Salomé. His connections, military prowess, and social status qualified Antipater to serve as governor of Idumea under the aegis of the Maccabees in their newly expanded kingdom. By fully embracing Judaism and accepting circumcision for his sons in the covenant with Abraham, Antipater became the most powerful Idumean under the Maccabees and made himself the founder of a dynasty.[35]

Antipater's second son, Herod, eventually overshadowed everyone in the family, including his father. For this reason, the dynasty is now called "Herodian" rather than "Antipatrid." But none of Antipater's progeny could have come into their renown apart from his unexpected successes, remarkable talent, and seemingly limitless courage. His effectiveness as a mercenary derived in significant measure from the ethic of warfare instilled by his Idumean ancestors and the characteristics they handed on to their progeny. Wars over territory between clans, collective defense against common invaders and commercial competitors, and above all unrivaled expertise in the use of the horse in battle all made the Idumeans ready and resourceful warriors, so superb in their skills that they became indispensable to the Maccabean regime.

Yet at the same time, the Idumeans (as descendants of Edom) fell under a suspicion that undermined their standing among the Maccabees and their supporters—namely, that the Idumean acceptance of Judaism had been a convenience, an act of fealty amounting to no more than an acknowledgment of their Maccabean conquerors. Those Idumeans who did not flee the new rulers and remained in their land abandoned Qos, the ancestral god of fertility and divine wisdom that they had served for generations, in order to serve the God of Israel. And the clan images of Qos and other protective gods in the Canaanite tradition that had featured in Edomite culture now fell under the Israelite prohibition of the worship of idols. Conversion also included the compulsory circumcision of males, turning the recent campaign of Antiochus IV into its mirror image. Yet precisely because the Maccabees intensified the demand for consistent loyalty to the Torah, no Idumean—not even Antipater or his sons—could escape suspicion among Judeans that their conversion was an expedient means of advancement. Moreover, dealing with traders from adjacent lands meant that Idumean troops compromised almost any understanding of Judaic purity. Antipater developed a flexible standard of how loyal to Judaism his fellow Idumeans had to show themselves to be in order to maintain sound relations with the Maccabean regime.

No matter how questionable their cultural standing, Antipater and his sons enforced the rule of law, which for the Maccabees meant public acknowledgment of the Torah. Their theocracy required that God's mandates should be maintained throughout the entire territory of the expanded Judean kingdom, which included, on the east side of the River Jordan, Gaulanitis,[36] Galaaditis, Perea, and Moabitis and, on its west side, Galilee, Samaria, Judea, and Idumea, with an annexed territory that reached to the Mediterranean Sea. From there the Maccabees established ports and exerted a sphere of influence that reached Egypt to the south and Damascus to the north. For a century, they remained firmly in power by bribing local warlords to help subdue any local resistance and provide for the loyal practice of Judaism. For all Antipater's sub-Judean pedigree, he was the linchpin of a military operation that kept the Maccabees in power within their recently annexed southern territory, and at the same time, he benefited Idumea as a whole with relative peace and the commerce that came from good order and rational relations with surrounding powers.

Since Idumea had been compressed over several centuries as a result of occupation as well as by the territorial pressure exerted by Nabataea and then by Judea, it remained about half the size of Judea, although it occupied a strategic location. With Egypt to the southwest,

Nabataea to the east and south, and Judea directly north, lucrative trade routes crisscrossed the territory. Policing them so as to prevent theft and assure the Maccabean margin of profit became Antipater's dominant concern. The Maccabees had conquered two towns in the center of this domain, Adora and Mareshah (each of them quite near to Judea),[37] and furnished them with rough fortresses of stone and mudbrick. As an agent of the Maccabees, Antipater used these centers as well as a Maccabean fortress at Machaerus on the east side of the Jordan River in order to maintain a highly mobile program of patrol and—when necessary—attack on horseback.

The ancestral recourse to horses had for generations enabled Idumean chiefs to organize hunts for game and to eliminate the threat of predators, whether animal or human. Archers, swordsmen, and lance men, all with the advantage of height when mounted, swirled in on their prey from several directions at once. Their tactics were so well practiced as to seem instinctive, and they knew how to confuse their victims by closing in on them from multiple directions. In the case of human adversaries, that meant a squad of twenty or thirty mounted cavalry could break up and defeat a larger body of armed men, killing enough of their number to force a retreat and make survivors wary of further engagement.[38] Antipater brought to bear in battle a flexibility and apparent omnipresence of which the Maccabean infantry, superior in numbers and force but notoriously sluggish in the field, could only dream.

Accountable to his Maccabean masters for profit, Antipater commanded a degree of autonomy, largely because he enjoyed latitude where it concerned the means he used. His troops could count on his generosity when they seized property; when they restored what had been stolen or commandeered what had belonged to those who resisted the Maccabees, they could be assured of their proportional share. And the relatively high status of soldiers permitted them to hunt at will in any part of the territory in which they operated; they enjoyed the status of minor nobility wherever they went. Just as they could override the authority of local chiefs when it concerned what could be pillaged, so they made their own rules when it came to the amount of game they hunted—gazelle, roe deer, and Arabian oryx as a matter of preference.

Skills with horse and bow and arrow at once served the Maccabean state, Antipater's standing, and personal enjoyment in a regime of legal piracy.

As long as the Maccabees remained in power, however, Antipater and Idumean leaders as a whole had few prospects except for local power under Maccabean hegemony. Only a weakening within the Maccabees, combined with the emergence of a new power in the region, could change the equation in which Antipater was a minor variable. Both changes occurred, and Antipater rose to an unexpected level of power.

What the Maccabees lacked in traditional authority, they tried to compensate by raw military power and the trappings of dominion that they derived from their alliances with foreign rulers. Recourse to mercenaries such as Antipater came as a matter of course. But with their willingness simply to assert their superiority over others—and to cloak that assertion with the claims of religious legitimacy—there emerged a strong tendency among the Maccabees to dispute with one another over supremacy. Those who put law and custom at the service of ambition create perfect conditions for competitive flux within their own ranks.

As part of a rapid establishment of international connections, the Maccabees entered into an alliance of mutual defense with the Roman Republic. Even before it became an empire, Rome probed east; the rich fertility of Egypt and its wheat beckoned. That prize might have seemed unattainable at the height of Seleucid power, but the house of Antiochus had proven fractious, and conflict among contenders to the throne after his death in 164 BCE[39] made a once formidable dynasty into a minor force. This internal instability was all the more inopportune with the increase of Parthian power to the east of the Seleucids. Although Maccabean propaganda had portrayed their victory in epic terms, their ascendency would have been impossible but for the military and political breakdown of the Seleucid regime. The Maccabees implicitly acknowledged their delicate position by combining forces with the Romans, who were happy to seal their hegemony over Egypt and use Judea (with its new Maccabean extensions, including Idumea) as a buffer state between themselves and the Parthian empire.

Judea and Rome entered into a treaty, conceived of as a pact of mutual assistance but formalizing Roman preeminence:[40]

May it go well for the Romans and the nation of the Judeans
on sea and dry land forever, and may sword and enemy be kept
far from them. If war comes first to Rome or to any of their
allies in all their dominion, the nation of the Judeans shall ally
as the moment demands with a full heart. To those who war
they shall not give or supply grain, arms, money, or ships, just
as Rome decides; and they shall keep their obligations without
taking anything. In the same way, if war befalls the nation
of the Judeans first, the Romans shall ally with a will, as the
moment demands. And to the combatants grain, weapons,
money, and ships shall not be given, as Rome decides. They
shall keep their obligations without deceit.

The text of the treaty, even as embedded in the First Book of Maccabees, assumes Roman priority. The recognition of that power differential only grew over time. Yet Rome had accepted the legitimacy of the Judean state and therefore recognized that what they came to call "the religion of the Judeans" (*religio Iudaeorum*) was compatible with Roman law.[41]

The Roman recognition of Judaism, which came as a matter of course with the right of the people of Judea to form communities of custom at home and abroad, ran contrary to the usual practice in a crucial respect. Acknowledgment of Rome's ancestral gods by citizens and subjects, including those newly conquered, amounted to the norm. Because those who practiced Judaism did not accept the gods of Rome, take part in civic processions that they regarded as idolatrous, work on the seventh day of the week, or eat ordinary Roman food, they were often subject to contempt, sometimes even to violence, within Rome's territories. Legally, however, they were allies, and their practices were to be tolerated. Some of those among the Maccabean aristocracy might have wished to accommodate more with the Romans and further embrace Hellenism. The clearest indication of that is the continued practice of "epispasm," a medical procedure designed to make a circumcised male appear to have a foreskin so that he could participate naked in athletic contests without appearing grotesque to Greco-Roman sensibilities.[42] But a state grounded in revolutionary Judaism could scarcely trade away a principal covenantal marker of the people of Israel, and the Maccabees did not do so.

Occurring as it did at a moment before Roman dominance had been achieved, the treaty gave Judaism a unique place within the Republic and consequently within the empire at a later stage. Western law inherited the understanding that a people and their religion might be treated, if not as equals with the citizens that grounded power within their traditional beliefs, then as partners with the state. Judaism became a legal, protected practice and, to that extent, a tolerated religion, although Rome was far from attempting a policy of general toleration. Centuries later, Christianity would achieve a similar privilege under Constantine, opening the door to its eventual position as Rome's official religion. In the waning days of Seleucid power, the Maccabees enjoyed the confidence that they could call on military support from an army of increasing range and force and that their establishment of worship in the temple was a matter of Roman law.

The Maccabees had already adopted the use of the phalanx (line after line of infantry in block formation) in addition to their resort to guerilla tactics; now their growing infantry mimicked the system of Roman legions.[43] That involved further training so deployment during battle could be varied in formation: the triple line, the wedge, and the enveloping maneuver had to become second nature to all troops, whether mercenaries or not. Maccabean forces may have amounted to a hundred thousand men in all, and they copied Roman hierarchies of office and uniform. The arms of their allies—dagger, sword, and spear—also replaced their earlier usage of the long and clumsy pike.

At the apex of the Maccabean hierarchy, the reigning high priest ruled the temple as its most holy officiant at the same time as he governed Judea as the country's monarch. A linen headdress and a golden plate mounted above his forehead designated him in contrast to every other person on earth as "holy to Yahweh"; a blue robe with golden bells and tassels at its hem also distinguished his person.[44] Beneath the robe, a breastplate shone with precious stones, on which the names of the twelve clans of Israel were inscribed. He and he alone could intercede for Israel on the Day of Atonement, making his solitary entrance into the holy of holies on the Temple Mount; on any day he chose, he could take up his place on the throne the Maccabees had installed in their palace adjacent to the temple in order to command that troops be committed to battle.

The perennial difficulty the Maccabees faced was that their very right to the high priesthood came under severe challenge. The Essenes, of course, would not accept them, because their distinctive calendar and view of the covenant and sacrifice made the Maccabees appear to be obvious interlopers, beset by foreign influences. In addition, however, the Maccabees' recourse to warfare along with their assumption of Hellenistic language and customs—including lavish symposial feasts with abundant wine—put them in the position of being unfit to offer sacrifice in the eyes of many pious practitioners of Judaism. They were impure, and none more so than the heavy-drinking Alexander Yannai (who reigned until 76 BCE and is typically referred to by historians under the Latinized name Alexander Jannaeus). At the major feast of Sukkot, when the autumn harvest was celebrated, a mob pelted Alexander Yannai with the lemons that featured in the procession. He was beaten back from performing his duties, and a riot broke out in the temple. Supported by his mercenaries, he allegedly killed six thousand of the militants.[45] When the insurgency persisted, he had eight hundred captives crucified; they were forced to look on as their wives and children were put to the sword. Only the death of Alexander Yannai brought an end to the strife. His wife, Salomé Alexandra, accommodated a faction of the insurgents who came to be called the Pharisees[46] by seeing to it that ritual arrangements accorded with their views of how purity should be kept and sacrifice offered.

These accommodations proved effective as Seleucid power waned and Judea prospered as a centralized Maccabean state. The treaty with the Romans and Antipater's semiautonomous cooperation made the arrangement complex, and as a family, the Maccabees needed to be united in purpose in order to maintain their hegemony. Instead, disunity at the highest level proved disastrous within a century of their remarkable victory over the Seleucids.

Between 67 and 63 BCE, two Maccabean brothers, Hyrcanus II and Aristobulus II, went to war with one another for the throne of

Judea and for the high priesthood. Antipater, showing a reflex of loyalty deep in his character, supported Hyrcanus, the elder brother who had acceded lawfully to the combined office.[47] Aristobulus, a shameless interloper, put himself at the head of a mercenary cohort to dethrone his brother and take power himself; his only argument, apart from personal ambition, was that his dynamism made him fitter for office than the notoriously passive Hyrcanus. Victorious in a battle that took place at Jericho, Aristobulus offered his brother a prosperous retirement in Jerusalem in exchange for giving up his royal claim.

But Antipater correctly read Aristobulus's character as that of a person who could never be trusted. Advising Hyrcanus to resist, despite the temptations of a quiet life, Antipater with Hyrcanus made the journey across the wilderness from Jerusalem to Petra to secure the help of the king of Nabataea, Aretas III, who sent soldiers in aid of Hyrcanus.[48] Yet continued bloodshed in and around Jerusalem failed to settle the matter; the brothers' forces were evenly matched, and each outbid the other in an attempt to secure the loyalty of troops whose motivation was like that of most mercenaries.

The warring brothers then angled for favor with a potential ally more powerful than Nabataea. During the course of hectic negotiation, both offered considerable advantages to the Roman general then active in the east, whose name was Pompey, to intervene in Jerusalem. Caravans from both priestly contenders made their way to Damascus from the Jordan Valley, each of them claiming to be custodians of gold and silver in the treasury of the temple weighed out by talents, units of seventy pounds.[49] That and more would come Pompey's way, he knew, if he reacted prudently and exploited his advantages. Hyrcanus and Aristobulus appeared personally before the general, each to make his case.

Hyrcanus, backed by Antipater, set out his argument before Pompey in the modest, somewhat pedantic terms of legal precedent. Antipater had counseled him not to flaunt the royal prerogatives that might legitimately be claimed and to avoid causing offense to Pompey, who although a general, commanded resources to which most kings could never aspire. Antipater was silent at this juncture, but he observed. He saw the tough, cosmopolitan troops bivouacked in Damascus and noted in particular the heavy weapons designed to mount a siege: battering rams, catapults, massive crossbows that threw javelins, and towers fitted with drawbridges. Aristobulus, on the other hand, was impressed more by his own standing than by the might of the Romans, and he dressed up for the session before the general as if he were already a king, flowing purple robe and diadem contrasting with Pompey's tight-fitting breastplate and protective helmet and with Hyrcanus's priestly garments.[50] He followed Hyrcanus in inviting Pompey to settle the fratricidal civil war, but he did so with the confidence of a man who believed he had already won, and he made the fatal mistake of alternatively attempting to buy Pompey off and mounting armed resistance to his advance.

Pompey could not resist the opportunity and made his way to Jerusalem with a magnificent and overwhelming show of force. By this stage, Pompey—now already known as "the Great"—had emerged as the most powerful general the Roman Republic had ever known. His most recent campaigns included the suppression of piracy in the Mediterranean and the conquest of Armenia. The Senate, although deeply jealous of his fame, had provided him with a total force of over a hundred thousand soldiers. From his stronghold in Damascus, Pompey marched down the Jordan Valley in an awesome display of military might. A single Roman legion at the time numbered around five thousand men;[51] Pompey easily commanded four legions for the Judean incursion, not including the supply of caravans for provisions, tents, and entertainment (culinary, sexual, and theatrical) that followed interventions of infantry. Although the cavalry supported the troops, its function was ancillary to the magnificent squads of uniformed soldiers—light infantry and armored troops, differentiated according to their experience in battle— which were kept in cohorts and lines by their centurions, pushing through the dust that their feet threw up as they maintained formation in mobile but impregnable squares.

The army was a moving city, some thirty-five thousand strong in all, that consumed whatever it needed or wanted as it approached the threshold of Jerusalem. Hyrcanus put up no resistance whatever; Antipater had assessed the situation and the extraordinary might of the Roman force, and he concluded that the best course was to seek an even closer alliance with Judea's strongest ally. The compliant Hyrcanus was more than happy to agree. Antipater and a few chosen horsemen rode out ahead of the Roman march, scouting on behalf of Pompey to identify any possible opposition and at the same time absorbing what a trained military eye and mind could learn by watching the advance of a sophisticated new army.

Aristobulus sealed his fate with characteristic arrogance by attempting to reinforce fortresses ahead of Pompey's advance. Antipater claimed in messages to Pompey that Aristobulus intended to attack the Romans, an assertion that was more creative than accurate. Realizing he had been outmaneuvered, in a last, pathetic gamble, Aristobulus gave Pompey yet another bribe and promised him safe passage into the Holy City. The offer was welcome because Jerusalem boasted sturdy walls—not yet the massive defenses that Herod the Great would later build, but stone barriers reaching twenty or thirty feet that might check even Roman momentum. Aristobulus failed in his reversal of tactics because his own people did not follow his lead and attempted to resist Pompey's entrance into the city. But they were only a fraction of the populace and diluted any effectiveness they might have brought to bear in concurrent battles with Hyrcanus's forces and troops loyal to Antipater. Pompey's siege engines broke through the walls of the city within three months. He entered Jerusalem—going to the point of taking a tour through the temple[52]—and formally claimed it and its territories for Rome.

The fractious brothers' foolish dispute had given Rome riches that only a long and difficult war could otherwise have achieved. Judea—including the acquisitions of the Maccabees in Idumea, Galilee, and lands east of the Jordan River—now became Roman property, with titles and proceeds of abundant estates assigned to wealthy oligarchs in Rome. Pompey did not repeat Antiochus's error, refusing to attempt any change of the temple's god. He left it to his Maccabean clients under Hyrcanus to sort out the conduct of the worship of their ancestral and legal deity in the temple but under the aegis of Rome. What had been until recently an ambitious new Judean state with an inheritance of ancient traditions became occupied territory whose inhabitants had somehow to reconcile their proud ancestry with the unexpected intervention of military and economic dominance from across the Mediterranean Sea. Reaction to the Romans was always ambivalent, but it is notable that the rabbis came to compare Rome to Esau,[53] the brother and antagonist of Jacob.

Antipater, the minor Idumean retainer of the Maccabees and actual descendant of Esau, reacted to this regime change by welcoming Pompey before, during, and after his campaign. Pompey secured Antipater's man Hyrcanus in the role of high priest,[54] while Aristobulus was displayed as a prisoner in a triumphal parade in Rome, prominently marching in chains along with other captives but in the most prominent position. Antipater saw in Rome a completely new order of military accomplishment. Although he did not abandon his Maccabean protectors, he also served Pompey, even before the Jerusalem campaign, and had made himself useful during the march to unalloyed victory. Having seen what the Romans could do, he never abandoned them, no matter how complicated the demands of his loyalty became.

An alliance *against* the Romans would have been suicidal, leaving Idumea's western border a frontier to be defended when Rome's power at sea (especially after Pompey's successful operation against Cilician pirates) was undisputed. Egypt to the south increasingly aligned with Rome, and the Dead Sea provided Idumea with a natural barrier on the east. Even as Parthia replaced the Seleucids as a regional power east of the Dead Sea, Antipater never seems to have considered shifting his allegiance in that direction. After all, the Nabataeans were a considerable force in the area east of the Dead Sea, a buffer between Idumea and Parthia under any circumstances. Altogether it was much more straightforward to ally with Rome against Parthia than with Parthia against Rome and merely to seek accommodation with Nabataea. This proved a winning strategy for most of the lifetime of the Herodian dynasty, and it derived from Antipater.

The Romans for their part admired Antipater's ability to deal with other local chieftains, enter into amicable relations with Nabataea, recruit new officials, and most importantly, collect taxes—the lifeblood of Roman power. Antipater became the new regime's man on Idumean ground. The high priest Hyrcanus continued in his office in Jerusalem, but now under Roman protection—and, therefore, Antipater's. This ceremonial role, however, no longer gave him the mandate as king that his Maccabean predecessors had exercised. Antipater began to fill the royal vacuum of power left by the de facto demotion of Hyrcanus as all the lands that the Maccabees had ruled learned to reckon with the overwhelming implications of Roman hegemony.

2

HEROD'S DEBUT

THE LURE OF KINGSHIP

Herod, Antipater's second son, was born after and subordinate to Phasael, the finest diplomat of the family. Herod inherited his father's audacity and dash, alongside more skill in horsemanship than any of his relatives, but he lacked judgment in the first phase of his career. As long as Antipater and Phasael guided him, the worst results of this flaw could be contained. Antipater's policy of loyalty to the Romans brought the family into alliance with Julius Caesar, whose cousin—named Sextus Caesar—developed a particular liking for the extravagant young Herod. While Antipater had turned down the title of king offered to him by Julius Caesar (and ruled instead as procurator), Herod acted arrogantly after his brilliant campaign to subjugate Galilee by ordering the immediate execution of the rebel leader Hezekiah. That brought him into conflict with the Sanhedrin in Jerusalem, which claimed capital jurisdiction. When Herod came to appear before that body in the temple, many in the Pharisaic faction feared that they faced a pretender to the royal title.
Young Herod: *Muscular, striking, physically overwhelming, volatile, and fiercely ambitious*

Caesar and Antipater in the Conquest of Egypt

ROME GREW MORE powerful, even as the politics of the late Republic descended into internecine violence. The statesman and intellectual Cicero gave Pompey, known already as "the Great," the nickname "our Jerusalemite."[1] His victory inflated his influence such that he vied with the Senate to become the pivot of Roman decision-making, especially when he joined in the First Triumvirate with Julius Caesar and Crassus. By a tortuous path of alliance, betrayal, and stunning projections of power, their collaboration changed Rome from being a republic, to becoming a dictatorship, to finally emerging after their deaths as an empire.

Among the triumvirs, Crassus owed his position more to his wealth than to his military prowess, having seemed indecisive in dealing with the slave revolt under Spartacus.[2] But after Pompey's triumphal procession in Rome in which he displayed Aristobulus as his captive, Crassus attempted to advance his own image as a warrior. Leading an army of some fifty thousand soldiers in order to compensate for his reputational deficit, he marched against the Parthians at Carrhae in Mesopotamia. With the Seleucid regime in disarray, Rome had long since understood that their principal foe in the east was Parthia. Although Crassus's military aim was sensible and his army sufficient to the purpose, he lost to a much smaller force in 53 BCE, owing to the effectiveness of the Parthian cavalry. He was killed in battle, and a lieutenant named Cassius held on to what remained of Roman Syria. Dealing with Parthia became an improvised operation, and Roman generals and politicians were a good twenty years away from calling the Mediterranean Sea *Mare Nostrum*, or "Our Sea,"[3] with any degree of conviction.

Absent Crassus, Pompey and Caesar found themselves increasingly at odds.[4] The aristocratic Optimates in the Senate supported Pompey, while the Populares favored Caesar. Crossing the Rubicon in 49 BCE with his troops, Caesar made an illegal claim to the direct military rule of Rome that challenged Pompey's ambition as well as his military pride, and civil war began. In 48 BCE, the two surviving generals of the triumvirate met in battle at Pharsalus in Greece. Caesar's tactical acumen overcame a disadvantage in numbers, and Pompey fled to Egypt. There, a brother and sister were locked in battle over which one of them would inherit the Ptolemaic throne. Forces loyal to the brother, the boy king Ptolemy XIII, assassinated Pompey and presented his head to Caesar, who condemned the treachery and was in any case inclined to support the other Ptolemaic contender, Cleopatra VII (known to this day simply as Cleopatra). Caesar's involvement with her was comprehensive: he and Cleopatra carried on a liaison, according to Plutarch from their first meeting,[5] and they forged a political and military alliance between Rome and Egypt that long survived their affair.

In the midst of dizzying shifts in power and alliance, Antipater pivoted deftly. He intervened in Egypt with thousands of troops—pressing west on horseback all the way from Idumea with his own troops as well as affiliated forces he convinced to join him[6]—in order to augment Caesar's forces in Egypt and to offer the mobility of which he was the master. In the volatile fighting among rival groups of Romans, Ptolemies, and disaffected Egyptian soldiers and mercenaries, the Idumean's capacity to strike quickly with light but concentrated force offered a key tactical advantage. Even as he fought in a bloody campaign, Antipater also engaged in propaganda under Hyrcanus's name to endorse Caesar's reputation for the favorable treatment of Judeans.[7] Antipater had sided with Rome, and now he chose the last surviving member of the triumvirate as his patron.

The battle against Pompey had been brutal and casualties so high that Caesar had to contend with a shortage of able troops. Antipater's force was therefore critical, but—more crucially—opposition to Caesar in Egypt collapsed after the sad death of Ptolemy XIII. Ptolemaic practice, following that of the Pharaohs, had paired in marriage Cleopatra, who was eighteen, with her younger brother, who was then only eleven years old. Pharaonic nuptials were held to perpetuate those of Osiris and his sister Isis, the divine pair at the base of Egypt's dynastic mythology.[8] Isis was said to have revived Osiris from the dead, and he became king of the underworld while his Pharaonic successor ruled the two kingdoms of Egypt. But Ptolemy, the putative groom whose actions were coached by his advisers, found himself three years later at the head of an army against Cleopatra and her forces to make himself sole ruler of Egypt. His army faltered in battle against the combined opposition of Caesar and Cleopatra, and he drowned in the Nile during a disorganized retreat. Victorious and no longer challenged by an effective military foe, Caesar and Cleopatra carried on their affair, and Cleopatra bore a son, whom she named Caesarion.[9]

Caesar's Man in Judea

ANTIPATER, BY MEANS of his astute decision to support Caesar as well as his physical prowess in battle, enhanced his position well beyond the status he had already achieved under the Maccabees. He played a key role in reordering Egypt under a new regime, especially until more Roman troops could be secured to serve under Caesar. Antipater rose in Caesar's esteem, but the family of Hyrcanus's old rival, Aristobulus, made an effort to poison the relationship between the Idumean chief and Rome's new de facto dictator.

Caesar passed through Syria, always the center of Roman power in the Near East, in a majestic victory procession in 47 BCE. It was a show of force centered in Damascus but a spectacle that involved appointing governors of whose personal loyalty Caesar was certain. Antipater had every reasonable expectation of preferment. But Hyrcanus's brother Aristobulus had a son named Antigonus, who made a claim for his own appointment to office. He appeared before Caesar in Damascus and complained about his treatment by Pompey, having been taken prisoner in Rome with his father. This criticism of Pompey was strategic because the same Pompey—Caesar's newly slaughtered rival—had also accepted Antipater's support and had confirmed Antipater in power under the high priest by choosing Hyrcanus over Aristobulus. Moreover, Pompey's agents had later poisoned Antigonus's father because he had allied himself with Caesar at an early stage in the civil war.[10] Antigonus confronted Caesar, then, with the competing claims between himself, the son of Caesar's early supporter, and Antipater and Hyrcanus, who were the protégés of Caesar's former rival.

Antigonus's argument was pressed with skill, but he acted in a way that showed the same counterproductive egotism that had upended his father's relationship with Pompey. He made his case immodestly, as if his family's suffering during a Judean and then a Roman civil war justified his personal claim to power. In particular, Antigonus attempted to force a decision on the basis of his putative moral superiority to Antipater.[11] He accused Antipater of willful violence and personal profiteering under the cloak of service to Rome.

At this time, Antipater carried wounds and bruises from his combat in Egypt that covered his torso and arms, and he stripped off his clothing to reveal them.[12] His loyalty to Caesar, he said, needed no words of proof, unlike that of Antigonus, decades junior to Antipater, who stood beside him dressed in immaculate linen and displaying only his attitude of entitled ambition instead of the proof of scars. Even more to the point, Antipater accused Antigonus of sedition against Rome on the grounds that proved to be well founded—because he persistently negotiated with the Parthians in order to undermine Roman rule.

In a single moment, Antipater mastered a volatile situation with theatrical assurance grounded in sure military and political calculations. His grand gesture was an early manifestation of the Herodians' gift for public spectacle calculated to serve the state and their own interests. He could not have known that one day, his son Herod would stand before the Roman Senate to receive the diadem of rule from the hands of Mark Antony and Octavian,[13] but he would readily have seen the family resemblance with his own command of astute public spectacle. With audacity, Antipater combined in the face of trial a total commitment to his own position together with a fierce loyalty to his allies. At many points in his life and in the lives of his descendants, the capacity to invest an action with complete dedication turned even difficult situations to one's advantage, making survival and advancement possible even under adverse conditions.

Whether under Pompey or Julius Caesar, Rome had no interest in turning the high priesthood in Jerusalem over to Antigonus or anyone in his family who might foment revolt. Maccabean militancy had proven its intransigence in the past; elevating an ambitious Maccabee would only encourage nationalistic dreams and might be a costly mistake. Caesar denied Antigonus's claim to be high priest in the temple. That role more deservedly belonged to his uncle Hyrcanus, who, although also a

Maccabean, was a manageable character who could safely be named *eth-narch*, or "ruler of the people."[14] Julius Caesar knew how to steer a middle course between humiliating the Judean nation and permitting them autonomy. The Maccabean royal family would be present in the temple in the person of Hyrcanus, Antipater's ally, but without power. Power belonged to Julius Caesar because his ambition to be dictator of Rome came with a desire to dictate the affairs of Syria and its coastal region, which Romans came to call Palestine after the Philistines who once lived there. For this purpose, Caesar governed by means of surrogate rulers in the territories that he had taken from his former triumvirs. With Crassus and Pompey both dead, Caesar had no intention of sharing power again. The loyalty of his regional surrogates, therefore, would always be a pressing concern.

Caesar saw in Antipater an ideal surrogate and gave him the governance of Judea as well as Idumea. He even granted Antipater the right to select his own title. Showing a prudent reserve that characterized Antipater and tempered his intensity, he did not ask to be called Judea's "king." In the question of rank, he deferred to Caesar, who named Antipater the "procurator"[15] of Judea. The extent of this realm was reduced from what the Maccabees had ruled because some northern territories had been assigned directly to the Roman province of Syria. Judea itself was subsidiary within this jurisdiction, since Damascus was the fulcrum of military operations and the authority of Rome. Antipater made a well-informed choice in foregoing any royal title so as to avoid resentment in Judea in regard to his family pedigree as well as any suggestion of rivalry with the authority of Caesar. In any case, with the designation as procurator came Roman citizenship and personal exemption from taxes. Antipater emerged at the head of a new and potent—though dependent—dynasty that was founded on a mutual regard between him and Caesar. That allegiance proved remarkably durable well beyond the lives of both men.

Although relative latecomers to Judaism, Antipater's family ruled the Judean homeland on Rome's behalf. With his sons, who had been born within Judaism,[16] administering the religiously sensitive Jerusalem and Galilee, Antipater could see to his affairs in Idumea and maintain local alliances, above all with the Nabataeans. The family seemed set to enjoy prosperity and power as long as Roman rule also prospered. Antipater's sons reaped the benefits of their father's determined but disciplined ambition as soon as he became procurator. He appointed Phasael, his eldest son, commander of Jerusalem and its region and his second son, Herod, commander of Galilee. Among his many virtues, Antipater's generosity made the life of a dynasty possible; had he not shared power as he did early in his rule, dynastic succession would have been out of the question. The brutal politics of the region would bring Antipater down by assassination; he had placed his sons, however, to continue and even extend his inheritance.

Jerusalem, Religious Politics, and the Sanhedrin

FATHER AND SONS shared power, although as long as he lived, Antipater wielded the underlying authority, grounded in his Roman appointment, within the regional areas for which Phasael and Herod took responsibility. Each of the three men boasted a strong personality, but familial loyalty assured their coordination, and they provided for effective government. The father had won his scars because he delighted in battle, fighting alongside his foot soldiers and cavalry, and his swordsmanship was famous. Phasael fought along with him and showed an instinctive gift for diplomacy that permitted him to maintain peace in Jerusalem amid the competing interests of Rome, the Maccabees, and the great crowds of pilgrims that made their way to the temple for major feasts, all the while remaining ready for a Parthian attack. Like his father, he combined stalwart courage in battle with a natural disposition to permit others to take public positions of prominence, such as the weak but serviceable Hyrcanus. Herod, very much the junior of the partnership, inherited more of his father's horsemanship than his diplomacy, but he proved ideally suited for policing an upsurge of restive criminality in Galilee.

Phasael's appointment ensconced the dynasty within Jerusalem, and that city, whose preeminence was assured in the Scriptures of Israel, became a pivot of power in the region as a whole. Its politics became the politics of Judaea and of Judaism beyond the borders of Judaea; Roman policies both advanced this process and over time were themselves influenced by events in Jerusalem. The Romans had inadvertently established a new force of Judaic influence: a body known in the history of Judaism as the Sanhedrin or the Great Sanhedrin. Initially a committee set up by the Romans for local administrative purposes in several Judean centers, in Jerusalem, the committee's engagement centered on the temple as the most important public institution, and—owing to the temple's influence—the impact of this Sanhedrin's decisions reached far beyond Jerusalem.

Part of Rome's settlement policy allowed prominent cities or towns within certain regions to adjudicate their own affairs, to an extremely limited extent in regard to military policy but sometimes quite broadly where local governance was concerned, albeit always in consultation with Rome.[17] The arrangement was an inheritance of Hellenization under Alexander the Great, and the Greek term *sunedrion* (Aramaized as *sanhedriyn*) designated the local council. In the case of lands once controlled fully by the Maccabees, Roman rule eventually provided for five councils to be set up:[18] in Jerusalem, Gadara, Amathus, Jericho, and Sepphoris. This regional arrangement, intended to distribute and designate authority that depended on Rome's legate in Damascus, in fact only enhanced Jerusalem's prestige in contrast with the other distinctly provincial centers. With Roman occupation, Judea was no longer a political state, but it remained the cultural and religious epicenter for the practice of Judaism, and Jerusalem enjoyed an unquestioned privilege.

The Jerusalem Sanhedrin's rising influence, then, grew as an inadvertent consequence of Pompey's conquest. Governance of Judea lay in Roman hands and yet allowed for a degree of consultation. The factor that united Judean loyalty and survived the effective removal of sovereignty was devotion to the temple, which came to be a potent force in governing the country. In fact, because Judaism was already practiced throughout the Mediterranean world and the Near East, the temple attracted loyalty in lands well beyond Judea so that the Jerusalem Sanhedrin exerted influence beyond its technical power in political terms. It came to be known as "the Sanhedrin" as a result of its link to the sacrificial center of Judaism.

Judaism was by no means unusual in the understanding that its deity desired regular sacrifice and enjoyed devoted offering. Sacrifice was characteristic of Near Eastern and Mediterranean religions as a whole; the practices involved precede recorded history. The presentation of animals, grain, oil, and wine throughout the year was more than a symbol of commitment: it amounted to a contractual bond between Yahweh and his people. In the book of Exodus, Moses calls sacrifice "the blood of the covenant" (Exod 24:8), joining Israel with God in an intimate relationship.

In the earliest phase of Israel's worship, which reaches back to the Iron Age long before a central temple existed, sacrifice was offered at multiple sites, conducted by prophets and military leaders as well as by priests in the succession of Moses's brother Aaron. But as the worship of Yahweh competed with that of other deities, a vigorous prophetic critique during the eighth century BCE developed against any form of sacrificial practice outside of Jerusalem. By the following century, the book of Deuteronomy quoted Moses as mandating that even Passover—which had been a household sacrifice—had to be offered in the temple.[19] A single God was to be acknowledged in the one place on earth that he chose; increasingly, worship in that city was seen as the only legitimate form of devotion. After the disaster of the First Temple's destruction by the Babylonian Empire in 586 BCE, prophets in exile announced the restoration of what scholars would come to call the Second Temple.

According to the vision of many of Israel's prophets, the restored temple was to be of a higher purity than the first. Only priests in the line of Zadok would govern the operation (Ezek 44:15), and every sacrifice, even if that meant suppressing local Passover practices, was to be offered in the temple (Deut 16:2), the place chosen by God "to make his name dwell there." This phrase, repeated throughout the book of Deuteronomy, is attributed to Moses, and with that attribution, the claim is made that the Deuteronomic Moses is more genuine than that of Exodus,[20] who required *household* sacrifice at Passover (Exod 12:1–10) rather than the centralized sacrifice in Jerusalem that became characteristic of Second Temple Judaism.

In this prophetic program, the temple was to be the unique place of Israel's sacrifice and therefore a pilgrimage center where Deuteronomy demands that every male Israelite should appear three times a year, at Passover, Pentecost, and Tabernacles (Deut 16:16–17). As a practical matter, this new requirement could never have been honored completely. The great feasts involved corresponded to times of harvest, when adult males were needed in the fields, and after the exile in Babylonia, the Judaic Diaspora extended through the Mediterranean Basin and east of Babylonia, so that a pilgrimage to the temple might require traveling over a thousand miles. But the formation of the written Bible and its translation into Greek and Aramaic ensured that those who practiced Judaism recognized Jerusalem's scriptural status as the place God had uniquely chosen for worship. It drew tens of thousands of pilgrims for the major feasts, attracted financial support from synagogues throughout the Diaspora, and provided the common sacrificial focus of the differing kinds of Judaism that had emerged in the historic land of Israel and beyond. The period between the temple's restoration late in the sixth century BCE and the Roman arson that destroyed the edifice in 70 CE is therefore known as that of Second Temple Judaism, in which the Sanhedrin featured centrally.

Even groups such as the Essenes, who contested the very architecture of the temple and the conduct of worship there, saw the site as the sole place where Yahweh was to be offered the sacrifices that he demanded. Attempts to erect sacrificial centers in Egypt—most famously by a Maccabean priest who had been frustrated in his attempt to rule in Jerusalem[21] and by a colony of mercenaries at Elephantine[22]—are notable as exceptions whose influence remained marginal. Such efforts did not succeed in undermining the preeminence of Jerusalem, which reinforced the view among those who disapproved of the Maccabean administration that the best course of opposition was to change the conduct of worship in the temple that the Torah authorized rather than attempt to establish pristine worship in an unsanctioned place.

Among those who disputed Maccabean legitimacy, the Essenes appear to have been the most persistent and most prominent. Despite adhering to a separate calendar, their distinctive understandings of purity, and an emphasis on the line of Zadok (understood as those Zadokites who adhered to their way),[23] those Essenes who resided in or made the pilgrimage to Jerusalem could nonetheless enter the temple as acknowledged Israelites. For those who lived in communities such as the one at Qumran, on the other hand, participation of this kind was at best infrequent. Yet for Essenes residing near the temple, it was possible to adhere to the strictures of the "community" (the *yachad*) while joining, if selectively, in public worship. It is notable that one of the portals into the city was called "the gate of the Essenes."[24] As a group, the Essenes framed their entire style of life around the pure administration of a divinely willed order in the temple and adjusted with varying degrees of acceptance of and distance from the temple as it stood.

Roman administration established a *sunedrion* on the ground, in Jerusalem or elsewhere, as a customary government of management and adjudication, but always within the higher authority of Rome. When that local, subsidiary government included the operation of the temple, new forces were set in motion that made the Jerusalem *sunedrion* into the "Great Sanhedrin" of later rabbinic literature. The forces that allowed for this were both centripetal and centrifugal. On the one hand, the sacrificial uniqueness of the temple drew diverse practitioners, from Essenes to wealthy philo-Roman aristocrats, so that the *sunedrion*'s importance was established along with the axiom of Jerusalem's centrality. On the other hand, practices in Judaism were conflicting and sometimes altogether at odds. Once the Maccabees in their recourse to the trappings and language of Hellenistic majesty had called their own priestly and royal court a *sunedrion*; now the Maccabean high priest (Hyrcanus at this time) still chaired the body the Romans had set up, but the Romans saw to it that local magistrates, prominent property owners, and influential religious factions were represented, however varied their perspectives.

The proportional seats among those represented on the *sunedrion* at any given time cannot be known,[25] but incidental references to its constituents throughout the period of the Herodian dynasty make clear the presence of Maccabees and their supporters, local scribes whose literacy made them useful as judges, wealthy patrons, priests outside the Maccabean family who tolerated their power without quite approving of it, and even Essenes—together with another kind of group altogether.

As the Jerusalem *sunedrion* came into being under Roman rule, a group known as the Pharisees became deeply influential in the governance of the temple, and more than any other single group, they were responsible for the memory centuries later of the "Great Sanhedrin" as the principal arbiter of administration in the temple and Jerusalem as well as among pious practitioners of Judaism everywhere. Among those who confronted the Maccabees in Jerusalem when they were at their most powerful, no group was more aggressive than the Pharisees. Unlike the Essenes and those who supported the temples in Elephantine and Leontopolis, the Pharisees did not consider withdrawal from Jerusalem as an option. They wanted worship in the temple, the one place God had selected for his name to dwell, to conform to their view of the Torah. When the conduct of sacrifice seemed inappropriate, they were well known to react vehemently.

The reputation of the Pharisees for vehemence, in fact, predated the Roman control of Judea. They began as a movement for scrupulous ritual performance, a concern that the growing importance of the temple during the period reinforced. They saw themselves—and others described them—as exact in their accordance with the laws of Moses, which they believed came down to them not only in writing but also in the oral traditions of their movement.[26] During the pilgrimage Feast of Tabernacles, the most lavish sacrifice of the year, the Maccabean priest-king named Alexander Jannaeus (or Alexander Yannai, the father of Hyrcanus II and Aristobulus II, the two brothers whose rivalry opened Jerusalem up for Pompey's taking) made his way in procession to the temple. The Pharisees present, already skeptical of his suitability for the high priesthood in view of his reputation for heavy drinking and violence,[27] became outraged at his ritual performance. Their view of the Torah was that in addition to the written text of the Five Books of Moses, Moses had initiated an oral tradition that also demanded obedience. It required pouring a massive libation of water on the altar of the temple during the feast so that it ran down the steps of the sanctuary and cleansed the whole edifice and purified its functioning. The conception was that water poured there was pleasing to God, who enjoyed the newly established purity of his dwelling and would show this by bestowing seasonable rainfall during the following year. Here was an evocative ritual enactment of the temple's central importance, and popular support for the Pharisaic teaching ran high.

Alexander Jannaeus, however, was of no mind to take advice in regard to his high priestly function. As far as he was concerned, water was not to be poured *upon* but rather *at the base of* the altar, since sacrifice had already guaranteed the purity of the immediate place where it was offered. In the way of religious partisans, the Pharisees portrayed his ritual preference in the most prejudicial terms and claimed that he had poured the water *on his own feet*, as if cleansing himself.[28] They spread their false account through the thousands gathered in the temple for the greatest yearly sacrifice, and an excited, outraged mob went into action. Zeal for worship often made pilgrims willing participants in protest, direct action, or riot during the Second Temple period,[29] and Alexander Jannaeus was to become familiar with the resourceful force of holy violence.

The Feast of Tabernacles celebrates the harvest and makes intercession to God for the rains necessary for the next year's harvest. In addition to the priestly ritual of pouring water, all those present—priests and lay participants alike—carried in their procession a tied-up bundle of seasonal leaves and lemon called an etrog. The leaves of palm, myrtle, and willow are of little use to any mob, but lemons make fine projectiles. Alexander Jannaeus, on one of the holiest occasions of the year, retreated from the temple under a hail of lemons.

Although the tableau is inescapably comic, the consequence was not. Hundreds of rioters were killed that day when Alexander released his troops into the temple. Presumably, he had them at the ready in order to put down any resistance to his own ritual practice. Josephus's estimate that six thousand people were put to death in the melee might well be exaggerated, but it is clear that Jannaeus heightened fully armed policing arrangements in the temple and pursued the Pharisees relentlessly even after the riot.[30] On another occasion, he ordered eight hundred of his enemies crucified while their wives and children were killed before their eyes and he feasted and drank copiously with his concubines.

At the end of his life, however, for all his violent arrogance and drunkenness, Jannaeus allowed the Pharisees to exert influence on the administration of the temple. He and his family would continue to exercise the high priesthood and associated royal prerogatives, but the Pharisees' views on how the ritual should be performed and how purity would be assured were to be accommodated. He never repeated his willful rejection of the Pharisaic teaching of purity and advised his wife, who succeeded him in power, to make peace with the Pharisees. They had won their place on the Maccabean council and naturally carried that membership into the Roman Sanhedrin. By that time, the power of the Maccabean high priest (Hyrcanus II, whom we sometimes simply know as Hyrcanus) was limited. He no longer wielded royal power, which had been co-opted by the Romans, and even in the case of ritual in the temple, he needed to act in accordance with the Sanhedrin and the increasingly confident Pharisees within it.

The growth of Pharisaic influence related directly to the increased importance of the Sanhedrin and to the curtailment by Rome of the high priest's military power and ruling authority. Administratively, however, the new Roman government did not rely on the proximity of its own army alone to supervise the territorial inheritance of Israel. Instead, they turned to their trusted ally in the region: Antipater. His preferment by the new masters of Judea did nothing to allay skepticism among religiously minded Jews at seeing an Idumean entrusted with power over them. But the will of Rome prevailed. Hyrcanus held on to every royal privilege he could, but he saw his military powers (apart from a remnant of his army) assigned to Antipater and his sons. Even in Jerusalem, Hyrcanus had to depend on Phasael's arrangements for defense, and the fractious Sanhedrin demanded its say as well. The Maccabees, whose sole remaining office was the high priesthood, would never fully accept a settlement that made them secondary to an Idumean family and beholden to the Sanhedrin. They might acknowledge the status quo, but they would never like it, and some of them came sporadically to open revolt. Latent insurgency also persisted far beyond Maccabean ranks, and crime often cloaked itself in the mantle of nationalism. Brigands—loosely organized bands of thieves and extortioners known as *lêstai* in Greek—plagued Roman Palestine.

Herod's Campaign in Galilee

ALTHOUGH ROME OCCUPIED the position of an overlord, the contest between Caesar and Pompey had produced uncertainty and raised expectations among some in the new and expanded Judea that Roman rule in the historic territories of Israel might be overthrown. After all, by this time, seemingly greater empires—Assyrian, Babylonian, Persian, and Greek—had come and gone; the claim that Rome might also be uprooted was attractive to all who yearned for self-rule. In a well-known rabbinic comparison, Rome amounted to no more than clotted seaweed in the Mediterranean,[31] nothing like the great land powers that had already been seen out of Israel's history.

When his father appointed him prefect of Jerusalem, the most powerful political position within Judea proper, Phasael did not interfere with the Sanhedrin, chaired by the high priest of the time, the apparently docile Maccabean Hyrcanus. No harm threatened in letting him play his ceremonial role and convene the Sanhedrin for its parliamentary controversies concerning local privileges and religion. Antipater fully agreed with his son and remarked frequently that Hyrcanus was too sluggish to worry his Idumean masters. Here was a Maccabean with whom they could do business while remaining firmly in charge of events.

Young Herod, twenty-seven years old when he assumed command in Galilee,[32] figured as a junior partner in the dynastic succession, but he made a stunning impression. Taller than average for an Idumean of his time, his black hair and beard framed dark eyes, and his handsome head crowned an athlete's body.[33] Having grown up in his father's entourage, he knew the people Antipater knew—whether subjects or clients—and had a working knowledge of several of their languages, which he spoke with greater facility than Antipater or even Phasael. Neither the Aramaic dialects of Judea and Galilee nor the Koine Greek that the Roman Empire had adopted as its lingua franca posed an obstacle to him, although his accomplishment was strictly at a practical level of communication rather than as a trained speaker. Nonetheless, on several key occasions, his ability to give powerful speeches in those tongues—to those under his command, within the temple, before emperors, and once before the Senate in Rome[34]—allowed for his success. His mother, Cypros, came from a noble family in Nabataea, the Arab nation that bordered Idumea, and she showed as deep an affinity for Herod's driving ambition as Antipater did for Phasael's instinctive diplomacy.

Herod's office as governor of Galilee came to him apart from any merit; that fact and his natural assumption of an attitude of dominance did not at first endear him to his subjects or his troops. His powerful physique compounded the impression he made on people, whether to appeal or to threaten. His reputation as a wrestler and an archer attracted those looking for a strong leader and those who admired the Greco-Roman culture of physical sport. Naked wrestling contests between young contestants always proved popular in public games, and Herod entertained his troops, both pagan and Jewish, by taking on promising opponents. Later in his career, he would found games in honor of the emperor Augustus,[35] an act of loyalty that also reflects a lifelong passion for sport. As a young man, he was quick, lithe, and cunning, though his victories in wrestling bouts naturally fell under the suspicion that they owed more to his unearned status than to his native skill.

His preeminent physical prowess, however, quickly emerged as beyond dispute and much more than a matter of display.[36] Herod was a consummate horseman, and his entourage regaled listeners with his command of steeds as he negotiated the scrublands, thickets, isolated copses, and rugged hills of Galilee. Always dressed correctly for the hunt, the Idumean prince rode his Arabian mounts daily and frequently enjoyed equestrian pursuit. Supported by footmen and guided by trained dogs, Herod and his privileged company gave chase not only to foxes, the common nuisance to agricultural production in Galilee, but to wild asses, jackals, wolves, boars, bears, and even lions. Galilee in this period was not yet denuded of forests, and Herod could indulge in his beloved pastime to his heart's content, all the while directing his teams of footmen, mounted hunters, and dog handlers with ease in staccato Aramaic, Greek, and his native Idumean, as occasion demanded.

The fitness required to ride the hunt for hours at a time before the heat of the day set in was prodigious. Saddles had long been current, but they were designed more for the health and endurance of the horse than for the comfort of the rider. A wooden frame distributed the rider's weight and was packed and wrapped with wool, blankets, and sometimes leather. Bridles had changed little since the Iron Age, but stirrups were not yet current.[37] Riders kept their stability by the strength of their legs rather than by any reliable technical aid. A rider's affinity with his mount developed through direct contact, as the pressure of his legs on the horse's flanks brought the animal to just the right point of balance beneath him. Herod's enthusiasm for the hunt, which might seem to have been an indulgence and his facility in the sport an incidental matter, proved vital to his success as a commander of legions and provinces.

On the borderland between Galilee and Syria, a local warlord named Hezekiah had for years mounted raids on villages and towns, extorting payment for "protection" while pillaging caravans and even picking off small numbers of Roman soldiers as targets of opportunity. Rome had, after all, claimed authority over Galilee fewer than twenty years earlier, and although Caesar's victories offered the prospect of stability for those who supported him, his own survival and Rome's continued hegemony were far from assured.

Hezekiah had neither sympathy for nor loyalty toward Caesar. The motivation of his anti-Roman stance was a matter of controversy in his own time. Josephus, writing as a pro-Roman Jewish historian over a century after Hezekiah's death, dismissed him as a mere thief (a *lêstês* in Greek). But while Josephus legitimated Rome's assertion of sovereignty in regard to anyone who opposed it, Hezekiah claimed that he used direct and even criminal methods to oppose the newly regnant Caesareans in the name of the Galilean hope of God's kingdom. In Galilee, where there was no priesthood (Maccabean or otherwise) that might resist Rome, only God's direct rule—governance by Israel's divine king—seemed to offer an alternative to increasing oppression from the latest in a long line of invaders.[38] The same traits that made Hezekiah a criminal in Josephus's estimate made him appeal to the Galileans, who believed that God's governance should replace that of Caesar.

Confiscatory economic policies complicated Roman pretenses to legitimacy. In addition to political as well as military authority and the right to tax, the new governors had asserted *ownership* of Galilean lands on behalf of landlords who lived in Rome. Rent was now to be paid for property that had been in local hands for generations, before there had been any understanding of legal ownership.[39] The Jews of Galilee, many of them settling in that region during the territorial expansion of the Maccabees in the second century BCE, did not accept these claims of foreign dominion easily. Farm was annexed to farm in imitation of *latifundia* (Latin "estates"), although on a smaller, local scale in order to increase productivity, regardless of the claims of individuals and communities. Rome had seemed to nullify the biblical promise of the land to Abraham and his progeny; Roman hegemony appeared a poor substitute for a legitimate government in accordance with God's promises to the people of Israel. Insurgents such as Hezekiah wanted to replace Rome's rule with what they called "the kingdom of God," by which they meant the direct implementation of everything God had promised in the prophecies of the Hebrew Bible.

The same Hezekiah who was a "chief criminal" (*arkhilêstês*) from the perspective of Rome proudly asserted his purpose as a leader who bore the name of an ancient Judean king in the time of Isaiah. For those keen to see Rome's occupation overthrown, Isaiah and other prophets during the eighth century BCE spoke to their condition and forecast the victory of their aspirations. Nothing less was at stake than the liberation of God's people and the vindication of God's purposes.

Herod, regardless of his relative inexperience, needed to address this challenge, a necessity that in any case suited his temperament.[40] Although he governed Galilee, he was dependent on his father and his brother for men and arms as well as for the legitimacy they gave his operations. Herod also needed to coordinate any military campaign with the regional commander for Rome and governor of Syria,[41] Julius Caesar's cousin, Sextus Caesar.

Sextus Caesar was anxious about Hezekiah's raids. A skilled propagandist as well as a guerilla leader, Hezekiah chose victims, less in established centers of Judaism than on the Syrian frontier,[42] which he could claim aligned with the interests of Rome. He had sufficient strength to attack small towns and villages openly and to exert enough control to select targets of wealth and oppression for his onslaughts. If the young governor Herod wanted to make life difficult for the prominent *arkhilêstês* and his thugs, so much the better for Sextus. Such thieves undermined the authority of Rome by interfering with the payment of taxes and preventing Roman landlords from their collection of rents from Galileans.

Sextus might well have doubted how successful Herod would be in a campaign against Hezekiah, but complete victory was not necessary in any case. From Sextus's point of view, brigands were a threat that needed to be contained, but eliminating them would have amounted to more trouble than it was worth. But despite Sextus's view, the religious resonance of Hezekiah's raids registered as a concern for Herod because he understood that Hezekiah appealed to direct rule by God rather than Caesar, the Maccabean Hyrcanus, or the Idumean family that served Hyrcanus. Still, to Sextus, criminal activity was only a generic problem. Experienced commanders acknowledged that tranquility was an unrealistic aim in newly conquered lands, although if the right balance could be struck in the control of criminality, that might make Sextus attractive to his subjects. Rome's interest would be adequately served if Herod could merely reduce the harassment of Hezekiah and his horde. Sextus's principal concern in terms of strategy was not the complete pacification of Galilee but containment of the growing threat of the Parthian Empire to the east.

Sextus found his interests engaged enough to offer some troops to complement Herod's force of Idumeans and mercenaries from Judea and Galilee, but at that stage, Herod's entire army probably amounted to less than five thousand, considerably less than armies of similarly sized regions in lands occupied by Rome. Even if he took to the field with most of all the forces within his command, the difficulty of inflicting serious damage on Hezekiah's three thousand highly mobile insurgents[43] was daunting.

Hezekiah's experience in battle against troops practiced in the conventions of Rome, whether Roman themselves or Maccabean, had prepared him to meet the arrival of superior forces formed in a "wedge," a configuration favored by Roman officers during an attack in the open.

Infantry were set up in that shape, protected by cavalry on the flanks under the command of an officer in accordance with usual tactics.[44] Reports of this massive and relatively slow movement from informants or even dust arising from the Roman march were enough to warn Hezekiah, who had the guerilla's choice to flee, try an opportunistic attack, or push expendable forces toward the Romans and then retreat. Provided he was camped so as to have a good sight of all angles of possible attack and could move quickly, he would indefinitely continue his lucrative career of putative insurgency and constant exploitation.

Herod, however, proved himself to be as wily as a guerilla leader. At this early stage in his military career, he showed the kind of resourcefulness that enabled him consistently to exceed expectations. Although factors seemed to be against his winning a complete victory against Hezekiah, that is just what he achieved, largely because his tactics departed from Roman military doctrine. Lacking the scale of all the troops that Sextus Caesar had at his disposal, he in effect reversed Roman military practice. Instead of supporting infantry with cavalry on the flanks, his cavalry was the main force, smaller in number than infantry but swift and lethal. They were also armed differently, with swords rather than the typical Roman javelins, because their purpose was not to defend flanks from attack but to advance and kill. Infantry, instead of serving as the principal force of attack, became like footmen in the hunt, waiting for prey to be forced into the open and taken.

In a series of raids into Galilee, Herod defied the odds apparently against him in routing Hezekiah's force. Some of the hapless captives were stripped of their weapons, flogged, and sent home on bare feet. Women in the camps were routinely raped; although Herod attempted to avoid that practice, soldiers and especially mercenaries involved in conquest expected their due. In any case, Herod's attention focused on the capture of Hezekiah and other leaders of his quasi-religious criminal militia.[45] His brilliant tactics, perhaps more instinctive than planned, had netted him his leading adversaries alive, and Herod made examples of them.

Charging Hezekiah and his lieutenants with murder, theft, and extortion under rough military justice, after a quick trial, Herod in the climax of his triumph had them publicly beheaded. He and his charger had been everywhere during the campaign, and each battle saw him giving directions in the field: wielding his sword, and sometimes his bow, against the enemy at the same time. Protected by a leather cuirass and greaves like a centurion, he appeared fearless, his legs gripping his mount through long trousers in the Persian style that the Romans found barbaric but Asians had long known enhanced a rider's mastery of his mount. Herod's dress, crowned with a turban-shaped helmet tied beneath his chin to protect him from a vagrant blow,[46] was incongruous and might have aroused scorn had he not been victorious. His charismatic example encouraged his troops to vary the angle and target of attack from moment to moment and so to be innovative in their tactics as well as in their dress and equipment. Instinctive talents honed during the hunt found their military purpose as he pressed the tactical advantage of swirling attack from unpredictable directions.

Local reaction to this decisive counterinsurgency made Herod's unanticipated success even greater. Villagers and townspeople, after years of Hezekiah's pillaging and empty promises of liberation from the Romans, had come to see the brigand and his followers as crude highwaymen. Herod was celebrated as the "restorer of peace" as well as of rightful possessions and the scourge of thieves.[47] Galilee, it seemed, could enjoy the prosperity of its naturally fertile lands. Produce could be used to pay Roman taxes and rents, in contrast to when Hezekiah's extortions came without warning and unattached to any predictable benefits.

Phasael imitated his younger brother's exploits, and crime control proved as popular in Jerusalem—and as pleasing to the Romans—as Herod's counterinsurgency in Galilee. The judicious use of force, violent when necessary, made the reputations of Antipater and his two sons and commended their regime to rulers and ruled alike, and among gentiles as well as practitioners of Judaism. The dynastic sword of Antipater and an Idumean family had largely restored order to the territory of the Maccabees, eliminating the predations of Parthia and Hezekiah alike.

In all, Herod seemed very much his father's son: quick, brave, smart, and loyal to Rome. The trait that he did not share with Antipater and Phasael, however, was a taste for diplomacy. That flaw, which Herod never overcame, would put at risk his own rise to power and indeed Antipater's entire regime.

Hybris

WITHIN THE SANHEDRIN in Jerusalem, jealousy roiled against Antipater and his sons. To some extent, that was just because they were successful,[48] but the family faced up to other underlying factors of skepticism. Once, a king from the house of David had ruled the land of promise, but for centuries, other hegemonies had taken the mantle of power. Pharisees in particular believed that any pretenders to the throne that God had promised to David needed nonetheless to accede as much as possible to the demands of the Torah: this stricture included the Maccabees and certainly Antipater along with his sons. Since the Pharisees believed that their oral Torah (quite aside from what was written) represented God's will, tension and controversy with the ruling power, whether Judaic or not, was inevitable. It had broken out with Alexander Jannaeus and lurked as a constant possibility in Pharisaic relations with the family of Antipater, especially since their Idumean descent could not be denied.

Moreover, the Idumeans' every success in governance under-scored the failure of Hyrcanus, the aging high priest, to hold on to the scepter that was his by right in the minds of those who, for reasons of ambition, nostalgia, or piety, supported Maccabean claims. Despite having been restored to the power he wielded as a result of Antipater's political acumen and military intervention, Hyrcanus nursed jealous grievances against the Idumean dynasty that made him more danger-ous to them than some of their overt enemies.

Herod offered the Sanhedrin its best target of opportunity within Antipater's clan as the youngest and most impetuous scion in the fam-ily. Cornering and capturing the rebel leader Hezekiah, he had taken to himself the authority to put Hezekiah on trial and execute him, not merely to kill him in battle. Execution, Pharisaic members of the San-hedrin argued, was a royal prerogative, to which neither Herod nor any-one in his family could claim any right; absent a king, the only Jewish authority that could legitimate an execution was the Sanhedrin itself.[49]

Those on the Sanhedrin who favored a restoration of fully Maccabean rule could only agree with the Pharisees that Herod had exceeded any reasonable understanding of his authority.

Hyrcanus himself did not make this argument, although he would have been its beneficiary, since he presided over the Sanhedrin. In this case, as in many others during his life, he attempted to have events do their work for his benefit. He let the Pharisee Shemaiah argue that the Sanhedrin should charge Herod with murder for beheading Hezekiah, while relatives of Hezekiah's slain partisans in Jerusalem pressed Hyrcanus to arraign Herod. Far from the predations of Galilean brigands, Hezekiah and his band seemed to many opponents of the Romans in Jerusalem a noble if crude weapon against Caesar's rule and on behalf of the kingdom of God.[50] Young Herod was now summoned onto unfamiliar terrain in a political battle that neither his father nor his older brother had anticipated and that he was himself unsuited to fight.

Antipater, Phasael, and Sextus Caesar improvised a solution to the problem once it arose, and they advised Herod wisely.[51] Herod agreed with them to appear before the Sanhedrin in Jerusalem, but he traveled according to Antipater's specification with a light bodyguard: large enough to offer protection but too small to amount to a threat to seize the city. At the same time, Sextus had a letter delivered to Hyrcanus requiring the high priest to have the Sanhedrin acquit his protégé of any charge and definitively to set aside the accusation of murder.

The Sanhedrin convened in the temple, not yet the huge edifice whose remains still dominate modern Jerusalem but already the greatest building in the city. In a room called the Chamber of Hewn Stone near the altar, members of the council met and considered their business. The charge against Herod was then their principal concern.

As he strode through the perimeter of the temple into the Chamber of Hewn Stone, young Herod progressively shed members of his bodyguard. Some of them awaited him outside the whole temple area; some walked with him through the great court of the temple, where thousands of people congregated; a smaller number, Israelites all, accompanied him into the interior court near the altar. Inside the chamber, only his first officer stood with him. Smoke from incense and the smell of flesh, grain, and evaporated wine and blood rose from the altar of burnt offering and filled the adjacent room that was set aside for meetings of the Sanhedrin.

Although Herod's military contingent was not a threat, it represented a powerful presence that his impressive physique and reputation in warfare underscored. He seemed from the outset more a warrior than a penitent in his appearance before this jury of the most prominent authorities of Judaism.

All might nonetheless have proceeded as Antipater and Phasael had planned but for Herod's choice of attire. Athletic and fluent in his movements, cheers of support and shouts of protest—both cried out in surprise—accompanied his decisive progress through the great court and into the special session of the Sanhedrin. Herod had dressed not only to awe but also to make a claim: his robe was purple, the color of the monarchy.

Although he wore no diadem on his head, the symbolic wreath of Rome's conferral of monarchy, he had his hair arranged as if prepared for the bestowal of this explicit symbol of royal power. He dressed for the title his own father had refused to claim in order to deliberately vex Hyrcanus, other partisans of the Maccabees, the Pharisees, and all those who most disputed any sort of royal pretension by Antipater's dynasty. Ignoring the tenor—although not the particulars—of his father's advice, Herod stood before the Sanhedrin as a king in waiting. Even in relation to his father and elder brother and apart from the issue of legitimate kingship according to Judaic tradition, Herod's arrogance was palpable.

Once in the meeting with the Sanhedrin, Herod's commanding presence silenced most of his critics. Shemaiah, however, remained fearless. He told his colleagues that their silence shamed them: failing to deal with Herod's lawlessness would only give him license to increase his power and to turn on the Sanhedrin itself one day, as well as on the high priest (who had no choice but to honor Sextus's request): "This man, whom you now wish to release for Hyrcanus's sake, will one day punish you."[52]

Herod appeared before the Sanhedrin in Jerusalem with an Idumean warlord's mercurial passion, but he had also learned a Roman officer's rigorous discipline, both through observation of his father and by direct experience of combat alongside the trained forces of Rome. Like many Roman generals, he enjoyed war and reveled in its spoils, which he assumed came to him by the right of his victory. Yet his dependence on his father and brother, as well as on Sextus Caesar, found no acknowledgment in his public demonstration of his personal command.

When he adopted the royal pretensions of a Near Eastern prince, Herod's gestures may well have been more flamboyant than serious. Yet royalty in the Near East claimed to embody the power of entire civilizations and the favor of their gods. Kings had for millennia claimed the designation "God's son," a title that Roman emperors eventually arrogated to themselves. It had no place in Israelite life except in reference to the Davidic king. Members of the Sanhedrin could not know how far young Herod wanted to take his military and royal pretensions. Shemaiah's words goaded at least some of the Sanhedrin into pursuing charges of murder against Herod, to the great pleasure of Hezekiah's supporters in Jerusalem.

Hyrcanus dithered: accounts are not even clear whether he acquitted Herod or adjourned temporarily.[53] He needed to honor Sextus Caesar's order to have Herod acquitted of any charge, but Shemaiah was a respected Pharisee who appealed broadly to a constituency that included many of those who opposed Roman rule. Rather than let a debate play out in the meeting of the Sanhedrin and putting himself in the position of having to overrule discussion, Hyrcanus adjourned the session; that night, he urged Herod to flee from further legal proceedings in Jerusalem. In that way, the high priest hoped to appease Herod and Shemaiah and stay on the right side of Sextus Caesar.

Herod did depart Jerusalem and made his way to Damascus, the seat of Sextus Caesar. For the first time in an official setting, the depth of rage in Herod's personality revealed itself, provoked by Hyrcanus's failure to deliver the acquittal that should have come. As he recounted to Sextus what he saw as an affront to both Rome and his own status, Herod outlined his plan: to raise a proper army, take Jerusalem by siege, and supplant the Sanhedrin.

The scale of this proposal was far bigger than Herod's police action against Hezekiah and his brigands; it would have involved the deployment of thousands of soldiers and the construction of siege works to surround a city that even Pompey did not immediately reduce to submission in 63 BCE. The operation would require Roman support in an incursion into Phasael's territory and offered virtually no benefit apart from assuaging Herod's pride.

Sextus Caesar had affection for Herod; despite being only a few years his senior, he spoke of loving him as a son.[54] Rather than simply rejecting this impossible scheme out of hand, he deflected Herod's passion in a productive direction by appealing to his ambition. In a gesture of confidence in Herod that also implicitly warned the Sanhedrin, Sextus extended the territory of Herod's governance. Now he ruled Samaria as well as Galilee, together with the region north of the Sea of Galilee until Mount Hermon, within what came to be known as Gaulanitis. Doubling his territory also meant doubling the military resources at his disposal; a mere display of temper had won ground and power for himself and his family.

Sextus wished not only to mollify the young governor but also to encourage him to keep up his campaign against insurgents. Herod's tactics had proven lucrative for Rome and its local administration, strategically helpful, and politically beneficial in Galilee; Sextus wanted to see his ward's policing style extended into Samaria and beyond the Sea of Galilee. But Sextus had no taste for internecine war among his Jewish subjects, and he did not see the Sanhedrin or Hyrcanus as a plausible threat to Roman interests. Herod had no backing and no permission to conduct an operation against Jerusalem.

Yet nothing in his exchange with Sextus prohibited Herod from indulging in a massive bluff with the new forces at his command. He departed Damascus with a greater endorsement for his rule than he could ever have anticipated, and he marched at the head of an army. As he headed south, following the valley north of the Sea of Galilee, rumors of his planned revenge against the Sanhedrin in Jerusalem—and particularly Hyrcanus—circulated in Judea and Samaria. They grew so severe that Phasael and Antipater intervened, traveling north to counsel Herod against the project.

But their intervention was probably a matter of show; the younger son already knew that, although he enjoyed Sextus's blessing, a campaign against Jerusalem could not be countenanced. The rumors had been only that, albeit skillfully nurtured by Herod—perhaps even with the help of Phasael and Antipater. The whole family showed that they were masters of propaganda as well as of intrigue and war. The maneuver was a feint, even though the rage it expressed ran deep and would break out over the years against individuals as well as adversarial movements.

When Herod reached the Sea of Galilee, he headed away from the southern route to Jerusalem and turned west, proceeding to Sepphoris, a garrisoned city that accommodated the Roman force as well as his own local Jewish administration. His display of force at the head of an army had been a parade, not an expedition, and it stamped Sepphoris as the epicenter of Herodian as well as of Roman power in Galilee.

Hyrcanus's failure to govern the Sanhedrin had flirted with disaster, but Herod's choice of dress had incited the Pharisees to a point where even an effective chair of proceedings probably could not have controlled the outcome. Herod had moved beyond a victory in the field against Hezekiah to making tacit claims about himself that were out of keeping with Antipater's and Phasael's policies. Yet an abiding loyalty to his family during this period is confirmed by the birth of Herod's first son, whom he named Antipater after his father, who was nearly sixty at the time.

The mother was Doris, Herod's recent bride whose family came from Jerusalem. Although the kind of influence he wanted over that city lay beyond his reach, he had at his disposal the means to develop a palace compound in Sepphoris of Galilee, converting the local military headquarters into his capital. Before the age of thirty, Herod had produced his own heir within a dynasty of growing power; he had extended his own territory, influence, and prestige; and he had secured the protective affection of Sextus Caesar and, through him, that of the dictator of Rome. His flash of anger against the Sanhedrin could be seen as a remnant of youthful arrogance, but Sextus, Antipater, and Phasael together proved more than sufficient to keep Herod in check. His successes were impressive, and he seemed set to enjoy their rewards.

3

KING HEROD

MURDER, POLITICS, ROMAN ENDORSEMENT, AND WAR

For all his ambition, Herod would never have chosen the path he actually took to become king: his father's death by assassination put a series of unlikely events in motion. He learned to use subterfuge to exact his revenge on Antipater's killer and also resorted to the politics of marriage in the manner of Rome by arranging to wed a young Maccabean princess. Another member of that family, however, a would-be high priest named Antigonus, allied with the Parthians to expel the Romans as well as Phasael and Herod from their governance of the land of Israel. Phasael, in fact, committed suicide in Parthian custody, and Herod was brought to the brink of defeat. But he made his way to Rome, where the royal diadem was bestowed on him before the Senate by Antony and Octavian. That in theory made him king of the Jews, but his authority only became a reality on the ground after the grisliest fighting of his long career.
Herod the king: *Resourceful, resilient, remorseless, and heroic*

Death, Revenge, and the Parthian Threat

JULIUS CAESAR HAD bestowed citizenship on Antipater, and Sextus Caesar had shown an almost indulgent affection for Herod. But although a secure relationship between Caesar's family and Antipater's remained, competing Roman commanders plotted to reshape the Near East and take power for themselves. Armies within Roman rule often developed a sense of loyalty to their commanders that transcended other allegiances, even to Rome; vendettas among semiautonomous legions pursued their course on behalf of the dead as well as the living. Under threat, Caesar could offer only limited protection to his friends. Some of Pompey's former officers sought for a new base of power, and while Caesar was still attempting to consolidate his power, Syria seemed to them ripe for the taking.

One of Pompey's lieutenants, Caecilius Bassus, led a mutiny against Sextus Caesar in Syria, colluding with some of Sextus's own soldiers to kill him.[1] In 46 BCE, he put himself at the head of a Roman army and pursued an alliance with the Parthians. In a stroke, Antipater's family lost its principal Roman sponsor in the area, and the Near Eastern region seemed poised to slip away from Rome's hegemony. Bassus's arrangement shifted the strategic balance of the two largest contending military forces in the Near East in favor of Parthia by removing Sextus Caesar and aligning himself with Rome's principal military competitor. He provided the Parthians with the prospect of a new geographical advantage of a power base in the pivotal region of Syria. Julius Caesar understood that his position had been directly undercut.

Some Roman officers during this period, smarting from real or imagined slights to their dignity or supporting factional interests (such as Pompey's, even after his death), believed that they could harness the wealth and power of the East—including the spice trade, local mercenaries, agricultural abundance, and the mining of precious metals—in order to master politics back in the Senate (as in Caesar's case). Other prominent figures who attempted or would attempt to parlay Eastern wealth to their own advantage include Pompey, Crassus, Antony, and Octavian. Bassus's ambition might have been realized, although his attempt to set himself apart from Rome was inherently risky. The gambit of mounting an army to rival Rome's could only succeed by going beyond the squabbles of the Roman military establishment and securing international alliances. Bassus's belief that he could secure independent power for himself in this way proved unrealistic. Yet even as he was unable to harness the promise of Parthian might as much as he had thought, he positioned himself to inflict irreparable harm on Rome.

Julius Caesar dispatched Roman troops to attack Bassus at Apamea on the Orontes River in Syria in 45 BCE. Keenly aware of the threat that Bassus posed, Antipater ordered both Phasael and Herod into the fray in favor of the Romans. Apamea was to be a pivotal battle in determining the character of the region, whether it was to be Parthian or Roman. Bassus was a renegade commander who in effect stood in for Parthian hegemony, and Apamea was his stronghold. While others in Judea went to war on behalf of Bassus, Antipater and his sons stood by Rome without demur. Confrontation between the global powers, Rome and Parthia, took the form of a civil war in the historic territory of Israel.

Antipater's loyalty to the Romans passed through a crucible of death, civil war, and defeat. On the fifteenth day of March in 44 BCE, Julius Caesar lay dead in Rome, cut up by dozens of senators' knives. The Roman historian Suetonius reports that Jews distinguished themselves during the funeral rites for the depth of their grief.[2] They flocked to the forum to mourn Caesar's passing with prayer and fasting, the tearing of their garments, and the self-imposition of ashes. Caesar had shown himself their friend in regard to the practice of their religion and in developing a fairer system than most rulers for the collection of taxes, under which monies collected for the support of the temple in Jerusalem could be sheltered from seizure.[3]

Cassius, one of the conspirators on the Ides of March, had acquired the governance of Syria after Crassus's death, and he used that position to buttress his standing in Rome. Within larger Syria fell the lesser but prosperous lands of Antipater and his sons in Judea and adjacent areas. In order to raise funds for ceaseless battles with the warring Roman factions that fought a series of proxy skirmishes throughout the territories of Rome after the assassination of Caesar, Cassius imposed taxes on ancestral Judean lands with a vengeance; Antipater and his sons loyally set about collecting them, but their subjects became increasingly restive. Antipater would even give Cassius payment from his personal wealth in order to cover a shortfall in tax income.[4]

In his zeal to enhance his revenue, Cassius also accepted tribute from Bassus to end the siege of Apamea, the center of the last of resistance from that quarter.[5] That arrangement left Bassus, a notorious traitor to Rome, in his position of local command. Lifting the siege without conquest, moreover, meant that the promise of booty was denied to the soldiers of Phasael and Herod. They had pressed the battle at Apamea on behalf of Rome and were so committed to Cassius as Rome's representative that they collected new taxes, yet Cassius did not return their loyalty. More a senator than a commander (and more a conspirator than a senator), he apparently did not understand that he was building resentment among the Judean and Idumean troops when he should have committed himself to raising morale and coordinating his military forces and commanders by means of able leaders such as Phasael and Herod. In terms of loyalty to Rome and resistance to any inroads Parthia might make, Antipater's family showed itself more Roman than Cassius.

By coming to terms with Bassus, Cassius had made an even more serious error. Internecine disputes in Rome as well as confrontations between Roman armies in Syria and an evident lack of reliable leadership from the Senate made Rome's policy in regard to Parthian expansion appear indecisive. With armies and politicians divided against themselves in the ongoing repercussions of Julius Caesar's assassination, the capacity to exert a unified force remained in question. The Parthians would soon—and sensibly—test Roman resolve and capacity as a result. Within that context, Cassius's amnesty to Bassus, the most senior commander to have negotiated with Parthia, represented a threat to the hegemony of the Roman Empire in the East.

Parthian intrigue extended even into the court of Hyrcanus. By this stage, the aging but wily high priest lent an ear within his entourage to Malichus, an aristocratic Judean who believed that the new power balance could be manipulated to restore the fortunes of the Maccabees and to free Israel of dependence upon Roman rule. By removing Antipater and his house, Malichus argued, Hyrcanus might join the Parthians in expelling the Romans and establish both priestly and royal power in his hands and in those of his heirs. The aim was nothing less than the restoration of Maccabean rule, albeit under Parthian aegis. Although Antipater believed that Hyrcanus was unintelligent and sluggish, events from this time show that he was cunning and voracious, full of appetite and yet without the character to state and achieve any aim except through intermediaries.

Hyrcanus allowed Malichus to organize a coup d'état against Antipater; because the Idumean now commanded superior forces to Hyrcanus's and Malichus's, stealth was required. To succeed, Malichus needed to lure Antipater into assassination with a minimum of force rather than risk open battle. Caesar's death might well have encouraged Malichus and Hyrcanus to believe that the coup might succeed, and they would select means even more underhanded than those deployed in Rome on the Ides of March.

Raising taxes for Cassius had been a bruising exercise; Antipater and his sons had succeeded, while Malichus as—tax officer for Hyrcanus—came up short, lacking the will and perhaps the ability to comply with Roman demands. The delay prompted Cassius to consider moving against Malichus. After all, he had the powerful police force of Hyrcanus's little army at his disposal and should have at least attempted to harvest funds for Rome. Cassius saw the shorting of the tax as a sign of disloyalty, and in this case, Cassius was right. Malichus was building credentials among nationalistic Judeans for resistance to Rome in order to prepare the way for a Parthian-backed resurgence by the Maccabees.

In an act of characteristic and public generosity, Antipater personally covered the expenses that fell short in paying the tax,[6] concerned to avoid Roman action against the court of Hyrcanus and unaware that Malichus had allied himself to the Parthians.[7] Hyrcanus joined Antipater, at least as far as appearances went, by helping pay from his private funds the shortfall in Malichus's collection. The high priest indulged in his inveterate duplicity by giving Antipater some of his money and Malichus his soldiers as well as approval for Antipater's assassination.

Malichus owed Antipater and Hyrcanus gratitude for their sub-vention, and—claiming he wanted to assure security for a proper, public recognition for all that the family of Antipater had done for him—he concentrated the high priest's army in Jerusalem. In effect, however, this move with forces that should have been collecting funds all along in any case meant his troops outnumbered Phasael's soldiers locally and therefore enhanced Malichus's authority. But Malichus ostentatiously flattered Antipater as the necessary bulwark of Judean authority and power, and Antipater assured Cassius (through his officers on-site) that all was well in the city in respect to cooperation among the forces of Judea. Antipater's trust in Malichus, however, would cost him his life.[8] His generosity toward his sons had been an act of political genius; his indulgence of Malichus proved suicidal.

To seal a show of grateful unity, Malichus offered Antipater a ban-quet of thanks in Jerusalem, hosted in the high priestly palace of Hyr-canus. Many courses were served during the banquet, including fish and lamb and beef; the sauces were distinguished, prepared from reduced wine (white and red) and flavored with quinces and in some cases honey. Hon-eyed wine was served at the start of the meal; thereafter, rounds of vintages made their way, chosen to accompany the course of food that was served. Over a hundred invited guests reclined on the couches provided for a sym-posium in the Greco-Roman fashion, with slaves serving the copious pro-visions as well as providing entertainment in the form of music and dance and poetry, all to honor Antipater. He ate and drank as a warrior, content that the only troublesome player within the Maccabean power structure, Malichus, was fully reconciled to his Idumean rule under Roman pro-tection. In the company of the high priest, surrounded by his officers as well as the dignitaries from Jerusalem, Antipater could feel secure in the knowledge that, disorganized insurgents apart, he had at his command a cohesive force to offer in the service of Rome. He was at the pinnacle of his power, with competent heirs ready in the wings.

Perhaps Antipater laughed more heartily that night than he usu-ally did. Manic laughter would be consistent with the symptoms he suffered after the feast. The sumptuous banquet had given Malichus his opportunity to execute his plans.[9]

Somewhere among the extravagant plates and cups, Malichus had arranged for poison to be administered to Antipater. As he left the banquet with some of his officers, he dizzied and fell in the street a few hundred paces from the high priestly palace where he had been feted and lapsed into a coma until his breathing and heartbeat stopped. The timing and range of his symptoms suggest that *atropa belladonna* (also called deadly nightshade and devil's herb), well known among Roman apothecaries, caused his death.[10] Malichus had struck by stealth, applying Roman poison in Roman cuisine, in what was now an internecine war that could not be controlled and that once again pitted the interests of Rome against the interests of Parthia. Antipater's sons came to the evident conclusion that Malichus had assassinated their father and that he acted in collusion with Parthia.

Herod prepared for an open war, gathering his forces for an assault on Jerusalem. This drive, sanctioned by his father's murder, was not planned as the feint he had indulged in to spite the Sanhedrin three years earlier. But the city was well protected, and Malichus had concentrated Hyrcanus's soldiers there as part of his conspiracy against Antipater. What they lacked in instinct for attack, they made up for in training, and their capacity to defend Jerusalem—their dedicated purpose—could not be doubted.

Phasael, as grieved by his father's death as Herod, was also careful in his protection of Jerusalem, and he restrained his younger brother from an assault. Phasael understood that any victory in a siege of Jerusalem at this time would be Pyrrhic. The cost in life and treasure on both sides would be overwhelming, and the Romans would likely conclude that their collaborators in Judea were in the process of dissipating in civil war any usefulness they might once have offered. The genius of Julius Caesar's support of Antipater had been that the Idumean delivered more loyalty and coherence than Roman commanders without his local knowledge would be capable of, and experience had shown that Roman officers all too easily developed their own agendas. Antipater's dynasty would not survive, however, unless his sons could deliver on the promise of coherent and concentrated loyalty to Rome against Parthia.

Phasael knew that the only plot against Malichus that Cassius would support would be by stealth.[11] By avoiding a siege of Jerusalem and months of open warfare, a semblance of control over the situation might be achieved. For Cassius, the prospect of a return to Maccabean hegemony—and now with Parthian backing—was unthinkable. Yet at the same time, committing Roman arms to a protracted struggle could weaken his position in Rome. So he abetted Phasael and Herod but offered his merely tacit approval and logistical support for a clandestine operation. Herod agreed, but only on the condition that he could arrange the assassination. Herod was learning how, in the Roman style, to turn his instant passion into a controlled lethal conspiracy.

Herod met Malichus on the neutral ground of Tyre on the Mediterranean coast, ostensibly for their reconciliation under Roman auspices. Herod, Malichus, and their retinues made their way into the city from the port while a servant ran ahead to announce their arrival for an official reception. That, in any case, was Herod's explanation for the servant's hurried departure ahead of the main party. In fact, the servant alerted a group of Roman officers whom Cassius had put at Herod's disposal.[12] Malichus might have been pleased initially at so distinguished a committee of greeting to guide him to the reception. But they greeted Malichus in the same way that Cassius and his companions had greeted Julius Caesar on the Ides of March.

Malichus was left dead from multiple dagger wounds. Hyrcanus announced his ignorance of the scheme to ally with the Parthians and kill Antipater, while Herod was learning not only to fight but also to think like a Roman. He and Phasael had won control of Jerusalem again, not by siege, but because the army Malichus once commanded now fell to their control. With a successful conspiracy, Herod had killed his father's killer and solidified his favor with Rome.

The vengeance was sweet, but any sense of triumph could only be fleeting. Cassius departed from the scene; he headed west to combat the Second Triumvirate of Antony, Octavian, and Lepidus. He was defeated by Antony's forces at Philippi and committed suicide in 42 BCE.[13] Turmoil in Rome and civil war in Roman territory seemed yet again to presage a major shift of power in the Near East. Galilee and Judea saw a number of priestly insurgents, some using Hyrcanus's forces (with or without his overt permission) and some mounting independent campaigns in order to establish the old Maccabean settlement under Parthian auspices.

Quite aside from the instability of his power base in Rome, Herod knew that his position in the esteem of his subjects was tenuous. A strategy was necessary for both him and his brother to co-opt the loyalty that tended naturally to the Maccabees. Herod found one, and his solution shimmered with arrogant brilliance and revealed the full extent of his political ambition.

Herod proposed marriage to a young but very prominent Maccabean princess of the time, Hyrcanus's granddaughter Mariamme. That finessed the problem of dealing with the ever unreliable high priest. Herod, however, was already married to Doris, by whom he had fathered his firstborn son; still, polygamy was not forbidden by the Torah, and in any case, he had some time to act, since Mariamme was only twelve years old. He could agree to a betrothal and wait. The consummation of the marriage would be delayed;[14] for the moment, he hoped that the agreement to marry was leverage enough on the house of Hyrcanus. In political terms, Herod's proposal reflected the tactical ingenuity that was beginning to rival his military skill. But more importantly, the arrangement revealed his dynastic ambition, which exceeded the expectations that Antipater had long nurtured. Any children of a marriage between Herod and Mariamme would combine the lineage of the Idumean mercenaries with that of the Maccabean priests in a new—and therefore potentially royal as well as priestly—succession.

As in the case of his appearance before the Sanhedrin, however, Herod had miscalculated in terms of immediate politics; the betrothal had no discernably positive impact on public opinion. Antony, the new Roman master of the region, received a delegation of Judean leaders who complained that Phasael and Herod aimed to usurp governance from Hyrcanus. The complaint in itself was inconvenient, and all the more so because—at least in Herod's case—it was well founded. His marriage with Mariamme was a brazen play for power, and Herod silenced the complainants only by paying Antony a bribe.[15] Herod never fully grasped that his ancestry as an Idumean, from the perspective of many people in Judea, disqualified him from governance. He also did not know—and could not have known—that Antigonus, the same Maccabean pretender who had opposed the appointment of Antipater in audience with Julius Caesar, was maneuvering for power again in the wake of Antipater's death.

Antigonus's present stratagem took a different direction from his earlier attempt to appeal to the Romans to supplant both Hyrcanus and the Idumeans and to install himself as the fresh and vigorous face of Maccabean rule. He had tried and failed to induce his Roman patrons to favor him, and for that reason, he found alternative means of support as well as new patrons. Antigonus fomented the religious nationalism of those who supported the Maccabees and called for revolt *against* Rome, appealing to the promise—articulated in 2 Maccabees 7—of resurrection for those who died as martyrs in the priestly cause. To this supernatural promise, he added the earthly means of forging an alliance with the Parthians. Violent zeal was soon to rise against both the Romans and the incipient Idumean dynasty in order to set up a new Maccabean kingdom under Parthian aegis and patronage.[16] Antigonus was a Maccabean who boasted all the aggression that Hyrcanus seemed to lack, and he planned to eliminate the old high priest in order to supplant him in the temple and to rule as Israel's Maccabean king.

The Roman triumvirate of Antony, Octavian, and Lepidus,[17] meanwhile, having united in its early phase with keen pragmatism, embraced the Idumean dynasty as a counterweight to Parthia. Antony came east to confirm Phasael and Herod in power. Recalling his experience years earlier as an officer in Egypt, where Antipater had aided Julius Caesar in the bloody campaign against Ptolemy, Antony believed that the Idumean brothers could serve Rome's interests as a bulwark against the Parthians.[18] Herod made this policy all the easier to settle because he freely bribed Antony's officers with gifts of silver as they arrived to take over from Cassius's administration. The silver had been confiscated from private wealth, however, and the mounting degree of opposition Herod faced from his subjects became clear when a delegation from Judea met Antony in Antioch. They protested so zealously against Herod's arbitrary governance that Antony, never known for his temperance or patience, considered giving an order to have them killed.

On this occasion, Herod pleaded for leniency. As in the case of his marriage to Mariamme, his governing passion was to achieve legitimacy in the eyes of his subjects, and with that aim in mind, he was willing to countenance their criticism in the short term. Hyrcanus, bereft of other options, supported Herod in his plea to spare the lives of the protesters. The high priest seems to have become content with retaining his sacred office, even if bereft of military might, while awaiting an opportunity to acquire the full range of powers that the Maccabean dynasty had once exercised.

Although Herod convinced Antony to spare demonstrators' lives on that occasion, when Antony proceeded to Tyre, a protesting crowd accosted him again, this time a thousand strong. In the face of a virtual riot, Antony ordered his troops out with daggers; they killed hundreds of protestors and jailed the wounded. Even the imprisoned delegation cried out against their Idumean masters, and Antony had all their throats cut. Antigonus had succeeded in awakening the nationalism with an attendant call to martyrdom that had brought the Maccabees to power during the previous century, and neither Phasael's probity nor Herod's diplomatic nuptials could overcome the hostility between Judeans and Idumeans.

Antony named Phasael and Herod as Rome's tetrarchs. The term means "ruler of a quarter," but it was applied to those who shared the governance of Roman territory in various proportions. By sanctioning the brothers to preside over their father's realms, with neither of them inheriting his title or his singular authority over their dominions as a whole, Antony appeared judicious, but his heart and his mind were elsewhere in any case. On his way to Antioch, he had already received Cleopatra in Tarsus in Asia Minor. She sailed up the River Cydnus clad as the goddess Aphrodite and invited the triumphant general to winter in Alexandria.[19] His hurried appointment of Phasael and Herod reflected his concern to establish a viable front against the Parthians but also to settle the administration of Judea quickly. Egypt was to be his new fulcrum of power as well as the crucible of his passion.

Antony's formal reason for leaving Syria so quickly was to repair his relationship within the triumvirate by marrying Octavian's sister (whose name was Octavia). But according to rumors among the ranks of his soldiers as well as in the bazaars of Egypt—and disastrously for him, the marketplaces of Greece and Rome—his erotic interest in fact lay in Egypt. A well-founded report had it that when Cleopatra made her way to Antony in Tarsus up the Cydnus River, he received her impersonation of Aphrodite as if he were the god Bacchus.[20] In his case no less than in Cleopatra's, however, sexuality was not only a primal force unto itself but an instrument in the service of power. Both Antony and Cleopatra saw in their union the promise of a third force in the struggle between Rome and Parthia—namely, a counterweight combining the stability and wealth of Egypt with the riches and commerce of the East, which they would take with the troops at their disposal: Roman, Egyptian, and—they trusted—Judean. Their passion went beyond their affair; it embraced a global play for dominance. Taking his cue from Plutarch and Josephus, Shakespeare portrays Antony and Cleopatra as slaves to passion; it would be truer still to say that desire for dominion was an aphrodisiac. Their blindness was induced as much by politics as by sex, and it hid from them the catastrophic consequences that their actions would provoke, to some extent because their relationship became an occasion for public prurience.

Antony's haste to depart Syria and join Cleopatra in Egypt meant he did not visit Damascus inland. Given Damascus's strategic location as the headquarters of Rome's military operations, that proved a costly mistake.[21] Military arrangements against the Parthians needed to be secured at that point in order to assure the martial integrity of Roman Syria. This was not the first of Antony's errors when it came to his attention to priorities when Cleopatra was involved, and this blunder might easily have undermined Roman power for a generation.

Acting on his new Maccabean stratagem, the high priestly contender Antigonus made common cause with the Parthian crown prince named Pacorus in order to take power from Rome and the Idumean dynasty. Antigonus, because of the popular backing he had been able to garner, joined with Pacorus to pose the greatest threat to Roman power in the region since the time of the Seleucids.[22] Phasael and Herod, recently bereaved of their father and each in titular control of only quadrants of their father's realm, would need to step into the vacuum of Roman authority that Antony's decampment to Egypt had produced, and they needed to do so against a combined force that exceeded their capacity.

Theoretical Monarch

ANTIGONUS COULD OFFER Pacorus little in exchange for Parthian backing except for what a renewed Maccabean dynasty might command if the alliance proved victorious. In an agreement that revealed the aspiring high priest's heartless cynicism, Antigonus promised Pacorus one thousand talents, a vast weight of precious metal equivalent to the tax income of all Judea, and five hundred women from the nobility of Jerusalem for the Parthians to use as they would. Capturing Jerusalem and the temple would provide him with all the resources he might need for this wildly extravagant bribe.[23] While Antigonus expected his followers to fight to the death without regard for benefit in this world, his alliance involved disposing of their wealth as well as of their freedom and their honor in order to pursue his personal and dynastic interests.

All Pacorus had to do was see to the removal of Hyrcanus, Phasael, and Herod. The Parthians at the same time made it clear that they would back Antigonus only to the extent that profit was clearly visible on the horizon. Allowing themselves latitude to abandon Antigonus in the event that course of action favored their interests, they nevertheless put an armed force at his disposal, which they ensured would fight under his banner, not theirs. Deniability was seen as a diplomatic advantage long before the growth of the modern nation-state, and Pacorus was in this regard a masterful diplomat. His recourse to duplicity in the midst of concurrent military campaigns seems to have been automatic,[24] to an extent not even his opponents realized.

The indirect Parthian conquest of Judea and Galilee began on the foundation of these cynical calculations by both Pacorus and Antigonus, with Antigonus besieging Jerusalem. Neither he nor the small army that he commanded could do more than inflict damage and death.

Possession of the city lay beyond their reach, largely because Antigonus on the one hand and Phasael and Herod on the other disposed of evenly matched forces, which fought skirmishes in and around the city even as pilgrims made their way in and out of the temple. The siege became a shambles, bringing ruin to both sides and inflicting damage on the city, its inhabitants, and its visitors, with neither side gaining ground.[25] Antigonus now imposed the kind of internecine bloodletting on the Holy City that Phasael had twice avoided by warning Herod against a siege.

Antigonus resolved on a way to end the stalemate, carefully arranged in advance with Pacorus, and the result entailed ever more harm for his countrymen. Pacorus's officer (also—however confusingly—named Pacorus) appeared in Jerusalem with a contingent, all given safe passage by Phasael. Concealing the Parthian alliance with Antigonus, he claimed that Parthia could serve as an honest broker between Rome's Idumean governors and the new Maccabean contender. Pacorus's officer proposed a negotiated settlement to the siege, with the Parthian satrap in Syria Barzaphranes as the immediate arbiter in the dispute. The result of any such negotiation, however, would have been a foregone conclusion, since the Parthians would always side with Antigonus and against the Idumeans. At the same time, the proposal made Parthia, rather than Rome, the arbiter of governance.[26] In effect, the crown prince Pacorus and the officer Pacorus wanted Barzaphranes to exercise the same sort of role that Pompey once assumed in the dispute between Hyrcanus and Aristobulus.

Meanwhile, Hyrcanus saw an opportunity in encouraging a new Parthian power broker in order to diminish the controlling authority of the Idumeans and the ultimate power of the Romans. A successful negotiation might in his mind provide him with enhanced sway while reducing Herod's and Phasael's; the tight coordination between Antigonus and Pacorus escaped him, to the point that he supported the proposal of Parthian mediation and even volunteered to accompany the delegation.[27] The counsel of Malichus, even after the death of that unscrupulous advisor, inclined him to believe that Parthia would align more with his interests than did the Romans and their Idumean clients.

Events proved that Hyrcanus's expectation of support from Parthia was disastrously misguided. By this stage, the Parthians used Antigonus as their cat's-paw and their agent. Hyrcanus was the sitting high priest and thought that his position would guarantee him a fruitful alliance when Parthia replaced Rome as the principal power in the region. His dream was that Parthia would find in favor of neither the Idumeans nor Antigonus and instead install Hyrcanus as the rightful inheritor of the Maccabean mantle. In all Hyrcanus's maneuvers, loyalty to his Idumean protectors seems never to have factored into his calculations, and he failed to appreciate the Parthian commitment to Antigonus. Lacking as he was in fidelity, he was quite consistent in his capacity to betray his allies. In any case, neither the crown prince nor the officer Pacorus would show any regard for the niceties of hierarchical succession in the temple, so that in welcoming Parthian intervention, Hyrcanus courted the death of his hopes.

While Hyrcanus's agreement to the mediation provided by Parthia was as characteristic of his behavior and character as it was ill judged, Phasael's response comes as a surprise. He also accepted the arrangement, a decision that would ruin him and very nearly destroy the prospects of Idumean power.[28] Although Phasael's passion for Jerusalem was no doubt the controlling factor in his agreement to negotiate, it is not clear what his political calculations were. He may have feared that Roman influence in the region would not, after all, prevail. Since the epic defeat of Crassus, the Parthians had proven resilient in resisting the advance of Roman hegemony, and in fact the Arsacid dynasty would endure until the third century, to be replaced by the Sassanian dynasty rather than by Rome.[29] The absence of Antony and the presence of a Parthian army on the ground in Syria might conceivably have made Phasael think that an accommodation with the Parthians, without betraying Rome, could be a necessary course. He also might genuinely have hoped that bringing an end to the contention with Antigonus would bring peace to Jerusalem. Giving up power to Antigonus was out of the question for him, but he could offer the Parthians lucrative opportunities for trade—using Judea as a gateway to the Mediterranean and Egypt—in exchange for accepting the status quo of Idumean dominance that Antipater had established.

Whatever Phasael's calculations, they were complex. In this case, Herod's disinclination for subtlety served him well and saved his life.

He refused to depart from Jerusalem with Phasael or to have his troops stand down during the negotiation. His inveterate and headstrong distrust proved wiser than Phasael's temperance, although he acceded to his brother's decision to the extent of refraining from attack and permitting the meeting in Syria with their adversaries to go on without him. Herod remained in Judea while Hyrcanus and Phasael made their way to Damascus.

The crown prince Pacorus's duplicity was shown to be consummate and perfectly executed by his officer Pacorus. On the way to the Parthians' headquarters, both Hyrcanus and Phasael were taken prisoner as soon as they reached Galilee. Antigonus immediately took the opportunity to guarantee that Hyrcanus would no longer be a competitor: he removed his uncle's ears,[30] a mutilation that prohibited Hyrcanus from serving as a high priest according to the Torah (Lev 21:16–24), since a priest's body had to be whole and without serious defect in order for him to minister.

Two accounts of Antigonus's barbarism remain in historical sources. In one, he orders a soldier to cut off Hyrcanus's ears; in another, he does the deed himself, and with his teeth no less.[31] Even if the second version is propaganda, the emergence of the rumor in his own time reflects the assessment of Antigonus's character among his contemporaries.

Despair seized Phasael, less from the immediate danger he confronted as a prisoner than from the recognition of his dreadful error in attempting to negotiate with Antigonus under Parthian protection. Above all, he feared what Antigonus might extort from his brother as long as he remained a hostage. The belated consideration also dawned on him that having consorted with the Parthians (albeit under their false pretenses), he had vitiated the claim he might make for the continued support of Rome. Herod was now the last best hope for the survival of the dynasty that Antipater had constructed; for him to succeed, he needed to be free of fear concerning what the Parthians might do to his brother, and he required full Roman cooperation.

Although Phasael was chained hand and foot in a guarded room, he could still move, and an unbarred window looked out into a ravine. He threw himself headlong to his death, smashing his skull on the rocks beneath his cell. He acted for his brother's sake and the survival of his family's power, but even so, he must have known at the time of his death that Herod's prospects remained dim.

Herod was still grieving for his father and, before news of Phasael's death came to Jerusalem, fearful for the fate of his elder brother. Without the benefit of the counsel of either, he confronted a seemingly impossible military situation. Although he could rely on his own army for support, his troops were sequestered in Jerusalem by the combined forces of Antigonus and the officer Pacorus, an army that now enjoyed open Parthian support and the promise of as many reinforcements as might be needed. The Parthians declared that Antigonus was in complete charge of Jerusalem as high priest of the temple *and* king;[32] they flaunted their own client dynasty, much as the Romans had done with the families of Antipater and Hyrcanus, although Antigonus boasted Maccabean descent as well as growing power on the ground. Control of the forces of Hyrcanus, including the policing unit that kept order in the temple and the conventional troops he had used for tax collection and the defense of the city, passed in his absence—and after his mutilation—to the alliance of Antigonus and the Parthians. Antigonus had become the master of the city. To Rome's horror and the shame of her appointees—including Herod—Antigonus and the Parthians won widespread support from much of the local populace and throughout Judea, many of whom had resented Roman rule for the past two decades and had never accepted Herod's pretensions to legitimacy.

Jerusalem had been lost, and Herod needed to take it back so that the badly damaged Idumean dynasty that he now headed would endure. Although the thought of retreat did not come naturally to Herod, he also resisted the Maccabean impetus to martyrdom. He chose to escape from Jerusalem with members of his family in the hope of regrouping and—with Roman support—returning to crush Antigonus and Pacorus. Commandeering a few thousand loyal soldiers, he also took those who would likely be harmed by Antigonus, including hundreds of noblewomen who rightly feared what the Parthians would do with and to them unless they escaped. Other supporters had already been dispatched to Idumea in advance, and the Maccabean fort at Masada, well stocked to withstand a siege, was prepared to receive escapees. Although complex and difficult to execute, this withdrawal was planned to be orderly and tactical.

Herod departed at night to make good his own escape; he showed good organization at the outset, but his eclectic company proved impossible to manage.[33] Wagons had to be used for a caravan of civilians as well as soldiers, despite the rocky, rutted roads that led from Jerusalem and harrying attacks from those of the local populace who resented Idumean rule. This made for a much clumsier cavalcade than Herod typically commanded under battle conditions. Despite the awkwardness, he forced speed on the contingent to put distance between himself and Antigonus's forces before dawn. In the night, however, wagons overturned on the rough, pitted road that led out of Jerusalem to the south, and Cypros, Herod's mother, was badly injured.

In the confusion, Cypros was reported as dying, and Herod lifted his sword to kill himself. He seemed, at thirty-three years old, to be at the end of an intensely eventful but short course of life. The impending death of his mother—so soon after other grievous losses—as well as the seeming impossibility of his tactical position at last brought him to despair. Only the pleas of his men stopped him from committing suicide. It turned out that Cypros revived, but by dawn, the caravan had traveled only to a large hill near Bethlehem, and the far superior force serving under Antigonus and the Parthians closed in on Herod in pursuit.

The Parthians had reinforced Antigonus's infantry with cavalry of a kind that posed an especial threat to Herod. Since the time of Crassus's defeat at Carrhae, two types of mounted configurations featured in the tactics of Parthia: heavily armed cataphracts and archers. The cataphract involved armoring both horse and rider, making for a living tank.[34] Speed was evidently deficient in comparison to less encumbered horses, but since their purpose was action against infantry, that was not a drawback as long as cataphracts were not required to compete directly against light cavalry. In any case, the addition of lightly armed mounted archers gave Parthian cavalry both speed and reach. In any direct engagement, Herod's cavalry would fall victim to the added reach of these mounted archers,[35] and his infantry would be chewed up by cataphracts in support of foot soldiers.

Herod had no intention of direct engagement, however. Even in despair, his sense of the battlefield and the resources of his soldiers did not leave him, and he devised tactics that overcame his disadvantage in both numbers and force. His aim was retreat, and he knew the ground better than his adversaries, and although Parthian riders were unsurpassed, Herod's cavalry were nimble and accustomed to improvisation. In addition, Antigonus's commanders had trouble synchronizing with the Parthians. Cavalry and infantry were uncoordinated in their maneuvers because the Parthian commanders under the officer Pacorus insisted on exercising their autonomy. That division of command proved a telling weakness.

The overwhelming superiority of the pursuers was in their well-trained foot soldiers. This Herod was able to overcome—and more than overcome—by taking advantage of terrain he knew well. At a small mountain seven and a half miles south of Jerusalem that he later named Herodium, he divided his caravan, one part heading east and the other west around the circular, steep-sided promontory.[36] The leaders of the pursuing force assumed that Herod's troops would continue to diverge farther and farther from one another on the other side of the hill, employing the classic tactic of the division of formations during a forced retreat. They sped in pursuit of what they took to be fleeing civilians and soldiers, calculating that the caravan had already faltered and was likely in disarray.

But Herod had gathered his forces *together* on the far side of the hill and took them up the slope; they were in fact lying in wait on the other side of the mount and used the advantage of height to attack their pursuers, who were not expecting an assault. All his cavalry plunged in against the enemy on their flank, and every trained foot soldier followed in hand-to-hand combat. The cataphracts fell victim to Herod's swifter cavalry, and even the effectiveness of the mounted archers was neutralized: they were trapped between their own forces and the charging cavalry and infantry of Herod and so were robbed of the room to maneuver that they required to be effective. Antigonus's commanders could not hold their force together, especially since the Parthian cavalry rode off while Herod's foot soldiers ran in to kill their unmounted opponents and to seize supplies. It was a rout; Herod's courageous ambush had defeated the forces of both the Maccabean pretender and the Parthian prince.

However unexpected and brilliant, this triumph was merely tactical; victory in the skirmish had allowed for what was an evacuation in force rather than a decisive battle in itself. Herod had bought enough time and supplies (some already in his caravan, some pillaged from the enemy) to send many of his supporters into Idumea, a safe haven for his partisans, while he brought members of his family to Masada, the most secure fortress under his command. Yet the retreat remained a retreat for all its consummate execution, and the fortress at Masada could not hold out indefinitely. Herod needed to gather those loyal to him, acquire resources for battle, and quickly press an attack against Antigonus and his Parthian backers. Combat was no longer a matter of ambition; it was about his family's survival.

Herod turned to his kinsmen in Nabataea. They also were Arabs, his own mother was a Nabataean princess, and the royal house had long benefited from loans from Antipater and Herod. But as he approached the border, royal messengers from the Nabataean court met Herod with the news that their king was acceding to a Parthian demand not to receive Herod.[37] He had run out of resources in his own region.

Crossing back to the west, he reached Egypt, where Cleopatra, seeing a formidable but impoverished warrior, offered him a command in her forces. With Antony in Rome in an attempt to keep his relations with Octavian in working repair, she understood that she and Antony would need compliant rulers in the localities they hoped to master in a new alliance.

Herod declined Cleopatra's invitation and sailed for Rome.[38] Herod's motivation for turning down Cleopatra's offer of a position was that he did not wish to be an Egyptian vassal. He knew that Rome was his mainstay. The Romans had given him support during all the changes in leadership they went through, his father's house had served them with tenacity as well as success, and his Idumean sense of loyalty made him turn to this ancestral alliance rather than to the Siren of the Nile.

The journey across the Mediterranean was difficult and storm ridden as well as expensive, but Herod arrived in Rome and explained his plight to Antony. The experienced soldier saw Herod as his best agent for removing Antigonus—the new Maccabean obstacle to Roman control—and simultaneously repelling the Parthian influence from the eastern lands. Octavian agreed with Antony, and together they presented Herod to the Roman Senate, recommending that he should be given the title of king. Rome made its choice with a deliberate, public act of state: only the Senate, not the Parthians, would appoint the king of the Jews.[39] In promoting Herod, at the same time, the Romans thwarted Maccabean ambitions for the royal title—definitively, as matters proved.

The decree of Herod's kingship was deposited in the capitol, and the new king walked between Octavian and Antony to observe the solemn Roman official sacrifices (including offerings of swine) on the way. On this occasion, any scruple about honoring Judaism—specifically in the rejection of foreign gods and their idols—was eclipsed by considerations of state and of family ambition. Herod had been granted just the title his father never dared to ask because the Parthians had forced Rome's hand. Although Octavian's role was crucial in swaying the Senate, Antony remained Herod's special friend in Rome, and he put on a lavish banquet for the new king; the diadem, for which his coiffure had long prepared a place, was his and his family's.[40]

Although Herod's success in Rome was spectacular, it was largely symbolic and a sign of Roman desperation. They had named Herod their client king in a mere week, and for good reason.[41] After all, their options were limited, and removing Parthian hegemony over Judea was imperative. Making Herod king was a calculated gamble.

King of the Jews

THE ROMAN GENERAL in Syria, Ventidius, vigorously backed Herod following his appointment as king. He and his commanders went into battle against the Parthians directly, pushing them back to their own lands and out of their military occupation in Syria.[42] That left Herod with the task of dealing with Antigonus.

Although the challenge was considerable, the mercenary forces at Antigonus's disposal had raped and pillaged their way into the enmity of many of their Jewish subjects, despite Antigonus's Maccabean pedigree and nationalistic appeal, making it more likely that Herod would succeed. Any priestly cachet that Antigonus might have claimed had been discredited by his conduct. Herod found many willing recruits as he made his way through Galilee, his established base of power,[43] using Roman funding to gather his own mercenary army of Jews and gentiles.

Coordinating with the autonomous Roman force did not always go smoothly,[44] however, and when Antigonus's army attacked the Roman officer Silo at Joppa, Herod had to save him rather than the reverse. Joppa was the port city of Jerusalem, and with that secured, Herod marched to Masada and saw to the release of his family.

Jerusalem was his next object, and he converged on it with Silo, who had every reason to be grateful to Herod. Even though preliminary attacks from defending forces inside the city by javelins, arrows, swords, and even hand-to-hand combatants commenced, Herod ordered his troops to announce in loud shouts in front of the walls that his intention was to secure the welfare of the city. Antigonus's response was that Herod, an Idumean and half Jew,[45] had no right to kingship. In this anti-Idumean propaganda, Antigonus found allies in the Pharisees. Although they were by no means natural supporters of the Maccabees, they saw Herod's siege of Jerusalem as an attempt to usurp the authority that rightly belonged to the house of David.[46] Some of the same teachers who had protested Herod's execution of Hezekiah encouraged a fierce and violent response to his siege.

Provisioning became a problem for the Romans, and Herod solved that by taking Jericho as his garrison; it became a base from which to arrange for the supply of troops in the environs of Jerusalem. But Herod did not immediately press a siege against Jerusalem itself; instead, he seized garrisons in Idumea and Galilee as well as Samaria while the Romans under Silo wintered in Lydda. Matching his strategy to his strengths and minimizing his reliance on the great but relatively cumbersome might of the Roman infantry, Herod rode out on a mobile, nimble campaign that made it difficult for Antigonus to know which fortress or town to defend at any given time.

Having defeated Hezekiah's insurgents in Galilee at the outset of his rule, Herod showed that he had learned their methods and could adapt them to general warfare. When entire towns seemed to resist, Herod imposed enormous fines and in some cases killed large segments of their populations.[47] He had subdued Galilee once; during this campaign against Antigonus, he brought that program to its dreadful conclusion.

Insurgents in Galilee nonetheless found a way to resist Herod's scorching counterinsurgency. Some had retreated to caves in a cliff near Arbela, west of the Sea of Galilee, after Herod's forces made one of their characteristic forays against them on horseback. It was impossible to deal with the insurgents from below because they had the advantage of height as well as the protection of the caves. Herod improvised; he deployed men from the cliff above the caves by lowering them on wooden crates with winches and chains. Armed with grappling hooks, javelins, bows, swords, axes, and flammable naphtha, they attacked as they descended; they pulled the enemy out of their caves—setting fires inside the caves—and hurled their adversaries over the cliff, some of them in flames. Herod would use all means necessary to expunge the insurrection. If he did not prevail by attracting loyalty or extending mercy, inspiring fear would have to be enough.

As Herod watched the cleaning-up operation at the caves of Arbela, he saw a man, described at the time as old but probably more worn than aged. With him were his seven sons as well as his wife. Herod offered them a safe passage.[48] But the man, reviling Rome's appointed king for his baseness, killed each of his sons and his wife and pushed their corpses off the cliff before he turned his sword on himself.

In any case, by this stage, the focus of Herod's operation was not hearts and minds in Galilee but the land of territorial Israel and especially the Holy City of Jerusalem. Take that, he believed, and the submission of the country would follow. The operation would require more dedicated Roman support than Herod had enjoyed before, and he particularly wanted to assure that Roman troops did not indulge in the pillaging and raping that had turned many Jews against Antigonus and the Parthians. To coordinate the campaign, Herod traveled all the way to the Euphrates, where Antony had besieged Samosata.[49] With a small force, Herod was able to help troops that wanted to reach Antony by way of reinforcement, contributing to Antony's strength.

The consultation with Antony secured what Herod needed, but he also heard the news that his brother Joseph had been killed in battle near Jericho with Antigonus's general, Pappus. To complete the humiliation, Pappus had cut off Joseph's head, sending it to Herod's sole surviving brother, Pheroras.[50] Pheroras had paid a rich ransom for Joseph's entire corpse, intending to provide for a decent burial according to the Torah; instead, Antigonus and Pappus took the money and sent the grotesque token of defilement.

Thirst for vengeance pushed Herod into a headlong confrontation with Pappus and Antigonus. Roman forces at his disposal bolstered his strength: the equivalent of over two entire legions was now under his unified command. He gathered his forces at Jericho and survived a collapse of the roof of the building in which he banqueted with his closest supporters. Not a person was injured. Rumors of Herod's invincibility fueled the keenness of his troops.[51] Antigonus countered the impending attack by sending Pappus north into Samaria in the hope of staging assaults there that would draw his opponent's soldiers away from Jerusalem.

Antigonus had clearly learned from Herod's diversionary tactics, but he had not mastered them. Inadvertently, by dividing their forces in this way, Antigonus and his general had given Herod all the opportunity he needed to conclude the conquest of his kingdom on behalf of Rome. Herod proceeded to raid the area around Jericho, pressing Pappus to return from Samaria. To lure him down, Herod wasted entire villages that had supported Antigonus, killing men, women, and children. In his hasty return to confront the disaster, Pappus camped in the town of Jeshanah in a narrow valley, a catastrophic choice of bivouac.

Herod's troops, emboldened by the sense that momentum was on his side, resentful of Parthian behavior, and drunk on the blood they themselves had shed, took the high ground around Pappus. Their crushing onslaught concluded with their use of siege engines to bring down buildings full of Pappus's forces. The sight of layer upon layer of corpses beneath collapsed roofs was long remembered as the ghastliest image of the three-year war.[52] The action broke the morale of all but Antigonus's most ardent zealots.

Yet Herod had suffered an injury to his side, caught by a javelin in the space between the front and back of his leather cuirass, and an unlikely blizzard canceled all thought of an immediate march on Jerusalem. A skilled aide cleansed the wound with wine and water on the field and wrapped linen around his torso. A healthy scab formed, but by the end of the battle, the inevitable stiffness set in. With an immediate advance on Jerusalem unfeasible, Herod felt weary. Heavy snow had fallen, and his men sought out protection for themselves and their horses without receiving orders to do so. On this occasion, Herod did not resist his troops' instinct for self-preservation, nor did he choose to enter combat with the elements themselves. Instead, he took a long bath.[53]

Warm-water baths were one of Rome's gifts to the Near East, as to its territories generally. Although plumbing was well out of the reach of most people, wealthy families and military installations enjoyed the luxury of the furnace, terracotta pipes, and large basins that were a signature of Roman ease. Military bathhouses were more serviceable than elegant, chambers of natural stone sealed with a view to containing heat. Herod commandeered the bathhouse in Jeshanah, and his men stoked a fire and assured the water supply from a cistern.

A single attendant in the bathing chamber verified that the king's wound was dry and kept above the surface of the water, and he applied herb-infused olive oil to encourage healing. Herod eased his body in the hot water and drank from time to time from a cup of deep red wine. As he began to doze, he and the attendant saw the unexpected.

An enemy soldier ran into the chamber, sword drawn. The attendant started to make for his weapon, but Herod forestalled him silently. The king, always ready to face his adversaries and gauge their intents, saw that the soldier was running in panic, not for attack, from farther inside the basement complex. The soldier continued his flight through the chamber and out of the bathhouse. A second soldier followed, and a third, all bent on escape, not attack. Herod had nearly slept through the easiest occasion for assassination he had ever offered to his enemies.

The pace of the campaign moderated; Herod took his time and bathed in victory with the kind of ease he had indulged in the bathhouse at Jeshanah. Pappus was already dead, but Herod had his head cut off and sent it to his brother Pheroras. That bit of vengeance accomplished, he advanced to Jerusalem and planned an invasion from the quarter of the temple, the same approach as Pompey's. He consummated his marriage to Mariamme, whom he had ensconced in Samaria; if she produced heirs, he could claim a dynasty that combined Maccabean lineage, the only virtue that Antigonus offered, with military prowess and Roman support. Herod was on the cusp of full power as king; all that was required was to complete the siege of Jerusalem.[54]

Mariamme was no longer a girl, and her grace during adolescence prompted public admiration. The young princess appeared thin and sculpted, her features more striking than beautiful but complementing the angular elegance of her figure. Herod had little conscience about sending Doris off to comfortable exile in one of his fortresses while he consummated his marriage to Mariamme. In the ten years of their marriage, Mariamme would bear five children: three sons and two daughters. Herod made no secret of his sexual enjoyment of his new bride, news that he trusted would come to Antigonus's ears.

Antigonus faced a more palpable threat from Herod than what was, from his point of view, the defilement of his niece. The Roman governor of Syria, Sossius, joined Herod in the siege of Jerusalem, which lasted for five vicious months. Herod himself attempted to mitigate damage and also to ingratiate himself with the nobles of Jerusalem by news of his marriage to Mariamme. He was successful on neither front.

Antigonus signaled that he wished to hold out until the end as the only legitimate Maccabean high priest and king. Sossius's troops wreaked vengeance on their victims, young and old, and even Herod's men were not to be restrained, once they had the example of unchecked Roman retribution before their eyes.[55] Herod came into real power in Jerusalem over the bodies of thousands of people who were slain, injured, and raped. Once the worse fighting around the temple was over, however, he did manage to preserve arrangements for sacrifice and to buy the peace of those parts of the city that had not been directly involved in fighting by imposing a tax, which Sossius agreed to accept in lieu of plunder.

Despite his call for the people of the city to resist to the end, Antigonus presented himself in person to Sossius, threw himself at the Roman conqueror's feet, and pleaded for mercy. Sossius burst into laughter at Antigonus's cowardice, called him "Antigone," and had him put in chains for dispatch to Antony,[56] who had come to Antioch to preside over Rome's latest Near Eastern conquest.

Antony proved cooler than Sossius but also crueler, ordering the so-called king to be crucified. This punishment, said the Roman historian Dio Cassius, had been inflicted on no other king at Roman orders.[57] The peculiar cruelty was deliberate; Antony had Antigonus whipped as he was crucified and then beheaded. Parthia's hope of proxy dominance in Jerusalem came to a humiliating end.

Antony acted in character by dishonoring Antigonus as he did but also in response to the gift of silver that Herod offered him by melting his own plate down. Confiscatory taxes in Jerusalem quickly made up for the expense. Herod judged that his impoverished state and low esteem in the city would be a short-term hardship and wanted to encourage Antony to discredit all that Antigonus stood for. His calculation was accurate, and in any case, his desire for bloody vengeance would not be denied.

In 37 BCE, with the violence of a monarchy that now went far beyond symbol, Herod—still only thirty-seven years old—had made the Roman title "king of the Jews" a military reality. He had earned the right to wear the diadem, the elegant band of silk around his head that distinguished a client king of Rome. From an early stage, he incorporated the diadem into the coins he minted proudly,[58] and no doubt he also wore the symbol-laden ribbon as much as possible. In a pool of blood, Herod claimed the power that would cause him to be remembered as "Herod the Great."

❧ 4 ❧

MARIAMME

POWER WEDDED TO—AND THEN DIVORCED FROM—MACCABEAN LEGITIMACY

Herod's dynastic ambition peaked when he consummated his marriage to Mariamme, producing heirs who were literally Maccabean royalty. His marriage to his princess happened as Antony's liaison with Cleopatra became fully public—and evidenced no less passion. Cleopatra, however, coveted Herod's lands and his friendship with Antony. When Octavian emerged as the victor after Actium, Herod prospered despite his relationship with Antony. The transition to empire only strengthened Herod's hand and his good standing with Augustus. But by then, Herod's suspicion of Maccabees in his own entourage had put him on a murderous course, which saw him assassinate or execute his own relations, including Mariamme's brother, and ultimately Mariamme herself. Once her sons had grown, she herself was dispensable, but Herod ordered the execution of even those sons for alleged conspiracy. In any case, his total of ten wives had provided ample progeny. Increasingly, he ruled as an imperial client, collided with his Pharisaic opposition, and, as he approached death, disrupted his own legacy with vicious executions and a series of contradictory wills that named different sons as his successors.

Herod in decline: *Suspicious, jealous, conniving, homicidal*

Marital and Priestly Strategies

HEROD'S MARRIAGE WITH Mariamme the Maccabee, the seventeen-year-old niece of Antigonus, signaled the magnitude of his ambition and desire. The Idumean king's political and sexual union with the young Maccabean princess focused and inflected his actions. On coinage that he issued, he impressed the anchor symbol of the Maccabees, and his title as king also featured prominently.[1] He even struck some coins with a double cornucopia, to represent the union of two great families as well as to iterate an earlier symbol of prosperity that the Maccabees had popularized.

As part of his program of suborning the Maccabees to his ends, Herod arranged for the return of Hyrcanus—worn, disfigured, and finally broken—from Parthian custody in Babylonia.[2] Owing to his mutilated ears, there was no hope of his serving again as high priest, and that suited Herod perfectly. Hyrcanus would return to Jerusalem and the care of his family, exercising only limited influence within the temple, while another man—younger, healthier, and more compliant with Herod's wishes—would officiate in the highly public role of high priest.

For this purpose, Herod chose Ananel, a priest whom Herod brought in from Babylonia along with a group of teachers whose immigration he had supported. Herod's motive and program were to place many of them on the Sanhedrin in order to offset any factions that developed against him,[3] but not before he had purged that body of Antigonus's supporters. After assuming power, he swiftly had them slain. Then he filled the council's ranks with the compliant Babylonian immigrants who owed their high status to Herod's intervention.

Yet one of the Pharisees who had opposed him at the time he appeared before the Sanhedrin after his execution of Hezekiah was spared; Herod felt that this teacher, named Shemaiah, had been honest in his opposition and prophetic in his prediction that Herod would one day punish the Sanhedrin that had failed to discipline him.[4] The king embraced support from any quarter, even if indirect and unintended. His cruelty was often vicious yet pragmatic and alloyed with sporadic and unexpected generosity.

Despite what Herod's rise to monarchy cost the Maccabees in terms of both effective rule and ritual status, Mariamme's support of her husband seems to have been deep as well as genuine, at least in the early years of their marriage. She bore a son named Alexander the year after their wedding and a second son named Aristobulus shortly after that. A united Idumean-Maccabean dynasty was in place genealogically, and the name of the first son evoked the great Macedonian conqueror as well as a principal high priest (Alexander Jannaeus) of the days when the Maccabees reached the apogee of their power. The second son, interestingly, bore the same name as Hyrcanus's vibrant challenger at the time of Pompey's incursion. The couple's ambition was hegemonic as well as sacerdotal. Daughters named Sampsios and Cypros (after Herod's mother) added to the dynastic quiver,[5] and since there was from the second century BCE a precedent among the Maccabees for women to rise to power in Israel, these children—male and female—represented the hope of a return to national glory and the achievement by Jerusalem's royal couple of a commanding lineage.

Cleopatra

HEROD AND MARIAMME were married in the same year, 37 BCE, as Antony and Cleopatra commenced their governing partnership in Egypt.[6] Contemporaries regarded both union as triumphs of passion, but each of them was at the same time an exercise in statecraft. Mariamme remained a Maccabee by loyalty and strategy as well as by birth. She alone had secured the possibility of renewing Maccabean dominance over Israel by means of complementing Herod's dynastic ambition and Rome's hegemony. As time went on, she became increasingly aware of her importance and would advocate for the Maccabean side of her connubial contract with Herod.

Yet the ambitions of Herod and his young wife seem less grandiose when compared to the global passions of Antony and Cleopatra. Although Cleopatra's erotic accomplishments were celebrated—and greatly exaggerated by detractors ancient and modern—her hold over Antony went beyond their sexual liaison. Egypt was a prized conquest for the Romans, to which Cleopatra added a skilled diplomatic corps, experienced military commanders, and the active wish to acquire territory to the east. If Antony could hold Asia Minor and Syria, Cleopatra would provide all that was needed to enhance the forces at the disposal of Rome and then to drive into the Parthian sphere of influence.

Antony and his Egyptian consort needed resources, however, to carry out their strategy, and Antony steadily damaged his own reputation in Rome, not least because marriage to a non-Roman woman was not recognized. But Antony also embraced Cleopatra's son, named Caesarion, whose father was none other than Julius Caesar. At a magnificent parade in Alexandria, Antony and Cleopatra (dressed as the goddess Isis) appeared seated on thrones, together with Caesarion on a throne beneath theirs, with the title "King of Kings." In effect, Antony was arguing that Caesarion had a better claim to succeeding Julius Caesar than Octavian did, to the great advantage of Cleopatra, whose natural son, already heir to Egypt, could in the event of Antony's conquest of Rome be put in the succession of power there.[7]

Antony's relationship with Cleopatra became well known, and he abandoned his legal wife, Octavia—the sister of Octavian—in favor of a liaison that had been a matter of scandal for several years. In response to this insult to his family honor, Octavian decided to read publicly, during a meeting of the Senate, a will Antony had made out. To do so, Octavian broke the terms of the deposit of wills with the vestals in Rome, and he enumerated the terms of Antony's testament selectively. He stressed that Antony provided for his body to be transported to Cleopatra at his death, even if he died in Rome, and that he had already transferred property and money to Cleopatra and the children he fathered with her.[8] If Octavian's interpretation were true, the will would have meant that Antony expatriated his Roman wealth to his foreign family in the east, implicitly designating Cleopatra and his children by her as heirs of Roman power in Egypt. By publishing the arrangement, Octavian answered the insult to Octavia by means of a war of political propaganda. On that field of battle, Octavian proved invincible, and Antony's decision to divorce Octavia in 32 BCE undermined his position further in the court of public opinion in Rome.

A choice between Octavian and Antony imposed itself on Rome's ruling classes in the capital and the farthest provinces, including Herod and Mariamme. Antony remained their patron and friend, and they showed him the loyalty that they owed. In this respect, Herod followed the precedent of Antipater in his unwavering devotion to Rome.

That loyal preservation of friendship proved costly in the short term, however, and as Antony's fortunes waned, association with him eventually threatened to be lethal. Yet Cleopatra pursued the advantages of her position as consort. She coveted some of the cities and fertile territories on the perimeter of Herod's rule—in particular, the palm grove in Jericho. The barter involved was intense, and Herod proved skillful in appealing against her to Antony, but his patron was in a defensive posture that made him less decisive over time; Cleopatra issued continuous demands, while Herod did his best to deflect them without being able to initiate his own projects of aggrandizement.[9] She insisted, for example, that Antony use Herod's influence and force in order to press her territorial demands on Nabataea. At first, Herod had no aversion on Cleopatra's behalf to force mineral rights (especially bitumen) out of his Nabataean kinsman Aretas, who had refused him refuge when he was pursued by Antigonus. That made benefiting Cleopatra somewhat more agreeable, but not if it led to a costly and protracted land war to his southeast; such a campaign did not feature in his desire to consolidate power over his own territory. Using a diplomatic dexterity that grew more impressive over time, Herod negotiated with the Nabataeans on Cleopatra's behalf. He acquired the exclusive right to bitumen from the Dead Sea for her and also ceded some of his own land, hoping that would satisfy her wants.

But Cleopatra's desires went further. She coveted Judea itself—nothing short of the acquisition of Herod's land. Antony would not accede to that, but she found another way at least to slink toward her ends. According to her agenda, Herod could play only an ancillary role in her grand alliance with Antony. Comprehensive royal status, anything like parity with the likes of Cleopatra, was to be denied him. Moreover, Cleopatra used Herod's family against him, stirring up intrigue inside his court. She undertook to set the Maccabean and Idumean sides of his marital alliance against one another so as to rupture the foundation Herod had laid for his exquisite ambition.

At the outset of her campaign, Cleopatra needed only to exploit a difference that had already emerged. Mariamme had a younger brother, near enough in age that they appeared like twins to many people. She loved her brother Aristobulus so much that she had used the same name for her second son. The same traits that made Mariamme appear handsome as a woman made her sixteen-year-old brother seem beautiful as a boy. Mariamme, probably at the prompting of her mother, Alexandra, asked Herod to depose Ananel as high priest and to put her brother Aristobulus in his place.

Mariamme's request reflected a natural loyalty to her family; there is no indication that she wished to reduce Herod's standing. In light of later events, Alexandra's motivations, however, seem much less straightforward.[10] Herod, even though as yet unaware of his mother-in-law's aims, denied Mariamme's request out of his protective instinct for the perquisites of his dynasty. He understood that having a high priest in place who was of pure Maccabean blood would always reflect negatively on the Idumean descent of his family. At the time of his contest with Antigonus, that Maccabean pretender had denounced Herod to the Romans as "an Idumean—that is, a half-Jew."[11] That opinion cut to the core of Herod's amour propre and undermined his dynastic pretensions. His refusal to name a new Maccabean purebred to the high priesthood, even if he was Mariamme's brother, came as naturally to him as Mariamme's familial loyalty came to her, but it set in motion one of Cleopatra's most insidious schemes.

Having disposed of Mariamme's uncle Antigonus and marginalized her grandfather Hyrcanus, Herod would not willingly put any Maccabean in the high priesthood who was not part of his own dynasty. The temple could await his newborn son Alexander, who would rule as both high priest and king. If not fully convinced, Mariamme was at least acquiescent, because Herod's policy would make her line the sole dynastic power in Israel,[12] the single guarantee of the prosperity symbolized by the double cornucopia stamped by both the Maccabees and Herod on their coins.

Mariamme's mother, Alexandra, however, saw a uniquely Maccabean future—beginning with her son Aristobulus. She persisted in her advocacy of Aristobulus's appointment as high priest, taking the case to Antony and adding her plea that the biological connection between Aristobulus and his sister Mariamme should be honored by granting them both high status. She commissioned portraits of her two children for Antony, as if the natural pairing in power were Aristobulus and Mariamme rather than Herod and Mariamme. Alexandra sent this elaborate calling card to Antony by means of Cleopatra, who needed no encouragement to act against Herod's interests. Cleopatra had one of Antony's staff sent to Jerusalem, with the request that Aristobulus should visit the Roman general in Egypt. The historian Josephus, quick to sexualize motives, portrays Antony (reputedly bisexual) as eager for a liaison with Aristobulus and Herod as aghast at the proposition.[13] But the underlying issue was power. If Aristobulus could win Antony's favor as the legitimate candidate for the high priesthood, Herod's power would be diminished, and the desires of both Cleopatra and Alexandra would be accommodated. Confronted with Antony's invitation, Herod needed to confront a serious political threat.

In one of the deftest political maneuvers of his rule, Herod made a tactical and uncharacteristic retreat.[14] His willingness to overrule his innate tendency toward confrontation shows how delicate his position was in his own estimate. When Mariamme renewed her request on behalf of her brother, Herod agreed. Young Aristobulus was high priest, but solely on Herod's appointment, and as high priest, he should not leave Jerusalem to accept an invitation to visit Antony in Egypt. Bound by his office to stay in Judea, Herod's watchful eye would remain on him. Years of experience with the Romans had taught Herod to act by diplomatic indirection. Antipas and Phasael would have been gratified to see this capacity to temper his volatile nature, even when an issue as close to his heart as his wife was involved.

Alexandra reacted so crassly, however, that Herod abandoned his newfound diplomatic touch. She decided to take leave of Herod's jurisdiction (and his spies) and to take her son with her. She hid herself and Aristobulus in coffins so that they could be smuggled out of Jerusalem as corpses. They were carried by hand outside the city gates, as if for burial; from there they would then be taken in a cavalcade to make their way to Cleopatra. But Herod's network of spies and informants was more effective than Alexandra imagined, and his soldiers broke the coffins open to retrieve Aristobulus and his mother.[15] He was thoroughly embarrassed but nonetheless carried on in his new and exalted office as high priest; he was good looking, vain, enamored of splendid clothing, and (to judge by his agreement to his mother's escape scheme) not terribly intelligent. When installed, he enjoyed a rapturous reception in Jerusalem at the Feast of Tabernacles, the most magnificent feast of the year. Resplendent in sacerdotal vestments, which under the Maccabees had been the symbols of royal power as well as high priestly intercession, his grace and youth seemed to some observers to promise a return to a single authority, religious and temporal, in the Holy City.

Herod could not abide Alexandra's conspiracy, Cleopatra's interference, or the highly visible and physically attractive alternative to his own rule that young Aristobulus represented. Addressing himself to Alexandra's behavior and its consequences, Herod in this instance, as in every other case thereafter of what he regarded as a betrayal, insisted on violence, albeit in this case by duplicitous means. All that remained of his diplomatic finesse was the indirection of his vengeance. Events conspired to make Jericho the site of his retribution.

King Herod came to be called great most of all because he was a builder on a monumental scale.[16] His initial projects, in keeping with his budgets, were relatively modest, but even so, they set a precedent for projecting power and affording elegance and luxury to Herod and his family. War had damaged many cities and fortresses; once he became king on the ground as well as by Roman law, Herod set about restoring fortresses and providing for royal accommodation. He also built a palace for himself near the Maccabean mansion in Jericho. The basic structure was of mudbrick, but the enormity of the edifice marked his claim to grandeur alongside that of Mariamme's family, which enjoyed a separate palace. The Jericho compound, accommodating the Herodian-Maccabean brood and featuring a pool for respite from the heat,[17] hosted a decisive and deadly turn in Herod's reign.

Mariamme's mother, Alexandra, invited Herod to Jericho for a banquet at which Aristobulus would also be present. In the heat of the day, Herod made a flattering show of concern for Aristobulus and suggested the young man might swim in the pool with the servants who routinely accompanied their royal masters, lest the heat distress him. Such pools were symbols of wealth, and Herod saw to their upkeep and extension in many of his buildings.

But Aristobulus thought it out of keeping with his position as high priest to disrobe before the eyes of the servants. He had also heard the rumor that Antony had invited him for an audience because the bisexual Roman general found him physically attractive. In the way of many sixteen-year-old males of that time and place, he did not want to be attractive to men, but he also wanted to get into the pool. He decided to wait until dark to swim with the servants. Once unencumbered of clothing and qualms about decorum and after feasting in the palace, he frolicked in the cooling water with the other bathers, a relief from heat even as the sun went down and all the more enjoyable for the delay. Much dunking and holding under water, the rough play of fit adolescents, was enjoyed by all, including some Herodian soldiers who had joined the company. One or more of them held Aristobulus under water, but not merely for sport.[18] Their instructions were to kill.

Mariamme would never forgive Herod, whose responsibility in the assassination became evident when he took no action against his soldiers. Alexandra became crazed with outrage,[19] and Cleopatra set about a campaign of retribution. At her insistence, Antony summoned Herod to appear at Laodicea, the principal port of Syria. There was little chance that Antony would part with his protégé over the drowning, but Herod could not judge how much influence Cleopatra might exert over her paramour. By this stage, he understood all too well that she wanted him either removed or reduced as Judea's king to make way for what she planned as the new eastern extension of her empire.

At this time, his young sons by Mariamme, Alexander and Aristobulus, were Herod's principal heirs and his best prospect for a combined Herodian-Maccabean succession. All other options were to be eliminated. Before he departed for his interview with Antony, Herod gave instructions to his sister Salomé's husband, Joseph, that if he should come to harm, Joseph was to kill Mariamme.[20] Joseph thought of the order as motivated by Herod's jealousy, whose passion for Mariamme defied any doubt. Joseph, in an act of folly that cost him his life, told Mariamme about the arrangement, confident that she would see it as a reflection of Herod's love for her. But Herod was increasingly running his family as a police state, constantly on guard against conspiracy. Eliminating Mariamme in the case of death would foreclose the possibility of her entering into a subsequent marriage and giving birth to potential usurpers of his sons' inheritance. In any case, Mariamme saw nothing to like in what Joseph told her and fumed at the king when he returned from his interview with Antony safe, sound, and largely unchastened. She rejected her husband's professions of love, and Herod executed Joseph as a matter of course, suspicious that his disclosure betrayed sexual intimacy with Mariamme.

Although Mariamme has entered popular imagination as a loyal and abused wife,[21] her own ambition clearly factored into the poisonous relations of the Herodian court. She came to hate her husband as much for taking her prospective power as for drowning her brother. She nonetheless produced heirs for the fractured, strange, and yet prosperous dynasty.

By playing on the cleavage between Herod and his Maccabean in-laws, Cleopatra had weakened the king enough, on the argument that his fissiparous court might prove militarily unreliable, that she could suggest to Antony that cities to the east of the Jordan River—and even Jericho to its west—should fall under her dominion. These were enormously profitable enterprises that brought in not only taxes but also revenues from state-owned date farms and spice and metal exchanges; Herod was so determined to hold on to Jericho and she was so insistent on having title to it that he agreed to lease it back from Cleopatra.

Herod met personally with the queen of Egypt while she was on a state visit to Jerusalem to consummate this arrangement, which—according to Herod's court reporter—Cleopatra offered to advance to the point of intimacy. The queen, in her midthirties and four years younger than Herod, was no longer as lithe as she had been in her youth.

But her features remained striking, framed by a distinctive coiffeur of waves pulled back to accentuate her features. Any wayward distribution of flesh in her expanding figure was managed by a cunning, layered approach to clothing. Garment covered garment so that Cleopatra could conduct a conversation with her fabled linguistic brilliance as if it were a dance of veils. By a single seduction, she could lay claim to Jericho and sow further discord in the house of Herod.

More clothing was discarded than replaced during Cleopatra's meeting with Herod, and she sent her servants away one by one. Herod also reduced the size of his entourage, but—despite his considerable sexual experience—he seems at first to have ignored the queen's sortie. Perhaps he did not believe that a queen of pharaonic lineage could be available to him sexually. At last, however, in the unmistakable sign of sexual readiness that a woman could give throughout the Roman world, Cleopatra unclipped her hair from the back and let the tresses fall to her neck and shoulders. Her desire for the East included the prospect of bedding the not unattractive Herod.

Still captivated by his young yet now obdurate wife and constantly loyal to Antony, Herod felt cornered. Refusing Cleopatra would bear consequences, but sealing their arrangement with sexual intercourse would make him her vassal. Herod negotiated the proposed rent for his lease of Jericho and suggested she call in a servant to help her rearrange her long hair. Although he deflected her advances, Herod later wrote in his memoirs that he had consulted with advisers about taking advantage of the situation:[22] Should he act prior to her departure from Jericho and have her killed? He decided against the idea, but not out of any liking for the puissant Egyptian queen.

Now the lines of battle between Cleopatra and Herod were drawn. She wanted to extend Egyptian hegemony to the east in order to profit from trade. He wanted to preserve—and even extend—his own territory. Both of them needed Antony, both wanted revenge after their misfired tryst, and each needed Roman power to deal with the Parthians.

Dramatic though the break between Herod and Cleopatra was, the final breach within the Second Triumvirate put every other crisis in its shadow. When Antony broke his alliance with Octavian by divorcing his sister in the wake of his sexual, military, and political alliance with Cleopatra and so made known his ambition for an eastern power base to rule the entire Mediterranean, Roman armies laid waste to each other as well as to territories they had conquered in a vicious civil war. Vast armies mustered for what would prove the final confrontation at Actium in Greece. Even in the midst of this decisive conflict, Cleopatra did not forget her vendetta against Herod.

Herod remained a loyal supporter of Antony, but Cleopatra kept him from the central confrontation with Octavian at Actium. That was to be the terrain of the ultimate battle between the forces of Antony and Octavian, as the growing number of troops there presaged. With the mighty navy at her disposal and Antony's incomparable experience in the field, Cleopatra and her consort seemed to be in a commanding position, and she behaved accordingly. She insisted in her consultations with Antony that Herod should be marginalized: sent to pursue a campaign to the east, in Nabataea, designed to punish the Nabataean king for his failure to pay tribute to her. Her military influence grew considerably, diluting some of Antony's strategic sense and tactical experience.

Herod rode out to meet the Nabataeans with his customary vigor and a well-trained army. He was not prepared, however, for the extent of Cleopatra's treachery, and he also did not exert the control he should have over his thousands of forces.[23] His soldiers, emboldened by their initial success against the Nabataean troops, pursued their fleeing enemies to the point that they permitted their lines to thin out. At just that moment, one of Cleopatra's generals named Athenion—nominally present with his army in support of Herod—attacked Herod's stretched-out flank. The ambush routed Herod's force; many of his soldiers were killed or wounded, while those who stayed whole simply fled. Forced into bloody retreat, he authorized his troops to attack Nabataean civilian stores in order to survive.

Two further disasters followed Herod's spectacular military failure.[24] The first was a major earthquake that devastated urban areas and cost some thirty thousand lives. The second was the battle of Actium and its aftermath; politically, that proved even more seismic than the earthquake.

At Actium, across the sea from Italy on Greece's western shore, Antony had amassed his army for what he thought was to be his final assault on Rome. Octavian evidently could not permit the buildup, which looked to seal his defeat at the hands of his more experienced opponent. Rather than risk a direct attack, however, Octavian harried Antony's lines of supply. Cleopatra's fleet of huge ships, together with Antony's, were supposed to guarantee the means to break out and secure supplies as well as to serve as transport to Italy for their forces.[25] Agrippa, Octavian's brilliant admiral, nonetheless managed with his lighter, more maneuverable craft to keep the combined fleet of Antony and Cleopatra bottled up in their anchorage at Actium.

The Roman ships were much smaller than those of Antony and Cleopatra; Agrippa's vessels maneuvered to avoid a direct collision while pursuing a constant harassment designed to force their opponents to remain close to their base. Antony's commanders set their larger ships into ranks, but they permitted the center to be thinned in response to attacks at the flanks. Cleopatra and her commanders interpreted that thinning as a breach in the line of defense, and they took the opportunity to break out and set sail in retreat. Antony and many of his vessels followed; technically, they had defeated Agrippa's blockade. The battle of Actium, although reported at the time and to this day as a complete defeat for Antony and Cleopatra, in fact gave them a qualified tactical success, although it required a division of their naval force and the abandonment of legions on the ground. A local battle continued with the remaining ships, but they were defeated by the end of the day, and the impact on the land army was dreadful. Nonetheless, the Egyptian fleet remained a considerable military resource.

What Antony lost most of all at Actium was not lives or ground or strategic position but his reputation. The sight of his ships trailing after Cleopatra's, in addition to his insufficient provision for the leadership of the remaining ships and his ground troops in his absence, made his maneuver seem a hasty and abject defeat. Whether Herod, had he been on the ground at Actium rather than on his fruitless campaign against Nabataea, could have helped consolidate Antony's forces in his absence remains an imponderable factor. At the least, he might have provided leadership among the troops left behind.

Most decisively, however, Octavian had prepared the political ground for the battle with consummate care. He had cast his entire effort as a Roman campaign against the foreign rule of Cleopatra as if Antony were simply her pawn. As Antony sailed back to Egypt, the huge armies he had amassed began to leave their posts. They saw his return to Cleopatra's realm as a desertion, and they answered in kind. The awareness of his soldiers' desertion broke Antony's resolve to fight. The great general, at last aware that Octavian had successfully poisoned his own troops against him and wrongly informed that Cleopatra had killed herself, took his own life. He was defeated politically rather than militarily, not so much at Actium as in the esteem of his troops. After a brief flirtation with the gambit of seducing Octavian as she had Julius Caesar and Antony before him,[26] Cleopatra also committed suicide. Octavian, the new Caesar, alone ruled Rome and made his way east to claim what now was his.

The events that followed Actium compounded Herod's urgency to reverse the Nabataeans' advance and vindicate his honor after his defeat at their hands. In this, the earthquake had ironically provided him with a tactical advantage. His army, camped in the field, had not suffered major damage, while the Nabataeans were emboldened by the mistaken belief that Herod was less ready for battle. The king made a famous speech to his newly rallied troops in which he called them to defend the godliness and justice of their nation—and excoriated Cleopatra.[27] He even claimed that the lack of casualties during the earthquake proved that God saw the war against the Nabataeans as just; Herod led his army to victory yet again, inflicting bloody retribution on his enemies.

Compared to his loss of Antony, his principal protector, even Herod's travails with the Nabataeans were merely a skirmish. The absolute imperative was to propitiate Octavian, the new ruler of Rome. Herod had mastered the military threat that he faced as a consequence of Cleopatra's trap, neutralizing Nabataea as a potential enemy so that the border with Rome's Parthian adversaries was secure. Now he needed to assure Octavian that he was the best possible agent of Rome's power in

Judea. Everything depended on his making a successful political pilgrimage to appease the new Roman ruler, who was then staying in Rhodes.

Before departing Jerusalem, however, Herod finally dispatched Hyrcanus. The former high priest, in his indecisive and oversubtle way, had been corresponding with the Nabataeans during the recent war and angling for their possible alliance with the Maccabees, so betraying both Rome and Herod. By order of Herod's handpicked Sanhedrin, the old man was found guilty of treason, and Herod had him executed by strangulation.[28] Octavian therefore had one less option apart from Herod for maintaining the interests of Rome in the Near East.

Octavian and the Imperial Transition

BEFORE HE EVEN met the conquering Octavian, Herod prepared a succession for his own dynasty in case he himself was executed or exiled under Roman custody. Pheroras, his single surviving brother after years of war, acted under Herod's orders to take charge of Herod's mother, his sister Salomé, and the two young sons of Herod and Mariamme, Alexander and Aristobulus. He brought them to the fortress at Masada, a Maccabean redoubt that Herod had reinforced and extended on a palatial scale. Even if the worst happened and Octavian turned against Herod, they could hold out against a siege and hope for a moderation of the new Caesar's attitude.

In the aftermath of his execution of Hyrcanus, however, Herod did not plan for the survival of Mariamme or her mother, Alexandra, in the case of his own death or exile. They did not join the dynastic succession in Masada. Instead, Herod had them escorted to another fortress in Judea at Alexandreion, where they were confined to the care of two officers. Their orders provided for the execution of both women should Herod be removed from power. On this occasion, secrecy was not an issue: the segregation of Mariamme and Alexandra from the rest of Herod's family signaled his intention clearly. By his design, the only Maccabean alternative to power in the event of his removal would be that of his sons by Mariamme under the regency of his brother Pheroras.[29] No chance of angling for power should remain for his mother-in-law or wife, according to his plan, and only their deaths could ensure that result.

Herod traveled to the island of Rhodes for his interview with the new Caesar.[30] For this conversation, he removed the diadem that sealed his status as a king under the aegis of Rome. During the audience, he freely acknowledged his friendship with Antony, whose only folly, he said, had been Cleopatra, and he promised the same kind of loyalty to Octavian. Herod had already dedicated to his friend and savior Mark Antony a huge new fortress adjacent to the temple. The Antonia fortress kept its name even after Herod swore fealty to Antony's rival, Octavian. Firm friendship, he argued, had been proven in his conduct toward Antony and was of such a character as would serve Caesar well. Caesar should ask himself, "What sort of friend, not whose, I have been."[31]

Octavian was won over, and he confirmed Herod's power and status; he told him to restore his diadem and accepted Herod's escort along the seacoast on his way to Egypt along with lavish gifts that Herod conveyed to the new conqueror on behalf of Judea. Octavian was prepared to invade Egypt, but Cleopatra's suicide had obviated that operation and put Herod in an enviable position. The lands she had taken were quickly restored to him, with interest, because Octavian knew an able leader when he saw one. Cleopatra's plotting at the end of her life had inadvertently kept Herod from attacking Octavian directly; her decision to commit suicide enriched her Idumean competitor with the land she had long coveted. She had even served Herod as the scapegoat for Antony's folly, a rhetorical gambit he deployed with his new master that echoed Octavian's own propaganda in Rome.[32]

The extraordinary success Herod enjoyed with Octavian, however, did not prepare him for his reception back home. In his absence, Mariamme and Alexandra had fantasized that Herod's power would be circumscribed, if not dissolved, by Rome's new leader. The formerly loyal wife complained of her husband's arrogance to members of his own court, and she expressed the old Maccabean sense of superiority to the Idumean interloper. When Herod returned, she did not moderate her complaints and refused to accompany Herod during his customary afternoon naps. Herod, who normally bore Mariamme's superior air with equanimity, did not abide her attitude as he assumed the enhanced status he enjoyed after his interview with Octavian. He came to resent the raucous notes her voice took more frequently as she treated him without the regard given him by the new Caesar and even the now deceased queen of Egypt.

More fundamentally, however, Herod's new attitude toward governance made for the disastrous turn in his relationship with Mariamme. He no longer needed her as a connection to the Maccabean dynasty because the sons she had borne him embodied just the hybrid of Idumean and Maccabean nobility he had long pursued. He ruled increasingly as a Roman, even submitting the old Hyrcanus to death by strangulation, a Roman rather than Judaic means of execution.[33] Although Herod governed by reflex and instinct rather than by theory, he emerged as an instrument of Rome with largely Judaic subjects rather than a Judaic leader who accommodated to Roman rule. Octavian's approval now represented the sole determinative foundation of Herodian rule.

While Herod's public image became dominant in the eyes of his subjects,[34] his private life unraveled in constant drama. After Mariamme, he would go on to marry eight more women—mostly for political reasons—but his enduring desire for his second wife was real and sometimes unhinged, marked by wild fights, prolific sex, accusations of adultery, and bizarre romantic gestures. The palaces, gardens, and parks he built for her pleasure are monuments to his profligate passion, most notably and ostentatiously the royal tower named after her in Jerusalem.[35] An unfriendly observer might say that this relationship—between a woman of royal pedigree and the intriguer who killed most of her family—was cursed from the start, but even with that in mind, their conflicts appear remarkably intense.

Roaring disputes between Mariamme and Herod were hardly a novelty, but by this point, her principal enemy in the court was prepared to put household strife to political opportunity. Salomé, Herod's sister, had long resented what she saw as the posturing of the Maccabean princess, and she planted the story among the serving staff that Mariamme had been asking servants to secure and prepare potions. The initial tale involved a love charm, as if Mariamme had taken a paramour, but in the hothouse gossip of the court, there emerged the suspicion of an attempt to poison Herod, an accusation that often features in conspiracy theories.[36] In his black mood, Herod ordered members of his staff to be tortured under interrogation, and he found evidence for just the conspiracy that he most feared between his wife and his courtiers.

Summary execution awaited any courtier who fell under Herod's suspicion. Mariamme herself endured a trial, a parade of concocted testimony from a long list of accusers, and—Herod having finally decided against clemency—she was executed by strangulation in 29 BCE. As she walked to the gallows, Alexandra joined in the abuse of her daughter, hoping to avoid Herod's wrath. The king had acquired additional personnel from Cleopatra's court, including a historian, the former tutor to the children of Antony and Cleopatra, named Nicholas of Damascus. He witnessed the macabre death of Mariamme and remarked on her calm nobility to the end.[37] Royal by blood and in her demise, although deprived of power despite her considerable efforts, Mariamme was strangled as a noblewoman and purportedly remained composed as she died, dispatched by means of the *laqueus*, a garrote Herod liked to use when he killed aristocrats, no doubt dyed an appropriate purple.[38]

Nicholas also recounted Herod's apparent madness after Mariamme's death. The king called out to her in the halls of his palace in Jerusalem and asked servants to summon her. A later legend in the Babylonian Talmud claims that Herod preserved Mariamme's body in honey; opinions divide on whether he did or did not have intercourse with the corpse.[39] Huge banquets and heavy drinking did nothing to distract him, and the outbreak of an epidemic convinced many in the country, including Herod himself, that God was punishing him for the execution of his beloved wife. The king sought solace in the countryside of Samaria, taking long excursions in order to hunt, even as he battled terrible pain in his head, from which physicians could offer him no relief. The death of Mariamme left Herod bereft not only of his hope of appropriating the status of the Maccabees for himself but also of his favorite sexual companion; moreover, he had violated his residual Idumean sense of loyalty to family. When he returned from Samaria to Jerusalem, he sought out and killed members of his court, including some who had been friends, for any suspicion of conspiracy. Herod vented his violence against Alexandra, whom he ordered to be executed for plotting against him, as well as Costobar, the new husband of his sister Salomé, who had offered protection to some of the Pharisees who had long resisted Herod.[40] His dragnet included the guilty as well as the innocent. His sons represented his only remaining Maccabean connection; Herod himself ruled Judea as an Idumean client king of Rome, as a tyrant, and more and more as a madman.

A Time to Build and a Time to Tear Down

HAVING BEEN THE victim of intrigue within his court, Herod turned himself all the more into a Roman potentate. In terms of public spectacle, he ruled increasingly as a Roman and introduced quinquennial games in honor of Caesar.[41] He built in Jerusalem a hippodrome, an amphitheater, and elaborate halls—all for the sake of games, contests with animals and gladiators, chariot races, gymnastics, wrestling matches, and musical entertainment.

The violation of ancestral practice throughout these and other cultural projects was blatant, but in regard to one issue in particular, Herod could hardly justify his policy.[42] To honor Caesar's conquests as well as his own, Herod had set up within the amphitheater south of Jerusalem trophies that commemorated victories and were decorated with military insignia lavishly covered in gold and silver and precious stones and draped with rare fabrics. Pious opinion rumored that these trophies included images of men whose forms were hidden by the drapery, making them a crude violation of the Torah's prohibition of idolatry. This anxiety surmised that the fabrics surrounding the trophies served the same purpose as in many pagan processions: to be clothing for the gods or goddesses of the city, making Herod's decorations an instance of idolatry.

Herod summoned religious leaders to the amphitheater. He demanded to know their complaint, and when they answered that no human image could be permitted in Jerusalem or its vicinity, he ordered the wrappings taken off the trophies. The leaders shuddered in anticipation, but he demonstrated—and explained at considerable length—that what was concealed beneath the fabric was the wooden staff of whatever military unit was honored, topped with its metallic emblem.

The complainants had mistaken a stick of wood for a human image, although he did not address the principle of their complaint. Instead, he reduced the audience to laughter with the thought that religious experts could suffer such a pathetic confusion.

Triumphant though Herod appeared to prove in argument, this meeting with religious leaders led to a conspiracy to assassinate him. His instant recourse to violence and torture was met in kind by the conspirators' vengeful treatment of informants; on one occasion, they threw their dismembered bodies to the dogs of Jerusalem.[43] Herod responded periodically with the carrot of relief from taxes and the stick of a sophisticated network of spies, but the Pharisees remained particular antagonists, and over time, some of them used the increasingly prevalent divisions within Herod's family against him. His own loyalties increasingly lay with Rome.

Julius Caesar's grandnephew and adoptive son Octavian had become Rome's first emperor on January 16, 27 BCE, taking the title *Imperator Caesar Divi Filius Augustus*: "Conqueror Caesar, God's Son, Revered." The affinity between Caesar and the divine was not only titular: the new building of temples in Rome set his status literally in stone.[44] Herod celebrated his new patron's renown, and his commitment to the new order was deep and vigorous.[45] With Octavian having been named Augustus, Herod built an entire city over the ruins of ancient Samaria for the emperor, which he called Sebasté—the Greek equivalent of the new imperial name (but in the feminine form, agreeing with a city's designation). Here, unconstrained by the scruples of religious experts in Jerusalem, he built a temple to Augustus on the acropolis of the new city, and Sebasté became a host of Mediterranean cults, in some of which Herod took a personal interest.[46] He also married a Samaritan woman, Malthaké, who mothered both Archelaus and Antipas, who inherited parts of Herod's realm.

Even after the shipwreck of his attempted alliance with the Maccabees, then, Herod pursued his dynastic ambition, albeit in a new key. He was determined that Rome and Jerusalem could be reconciled within his and his family's rule, and his policy to bring about that reconciliation changed the architectural face of his realm.

Building projects of this kind became Herod's trademark, and their leverage within the hitherto underdeveloped economy of Judea was great. Every major project involved employment on a wide scale, expert as well as menial, together with the development of water and sewage facilities, the provision of roads and shops, and greater access to the trade that came from the cities Augustus had granted to Herod. His realm was larger and wealthier than King Solomon's.

Agriculture nonetheless remained fundamental to the economic life of the nation, and a series of droughts and epidemics during 25 BCE and 24 BCE jeopardized everything.[47] Herod intervened with the new wealth and contacts at his disposal. He melted down the gold and silver plates and ornaments of his court into ingots and made that massive currency the basis of a special relationship with Petronius, Augustus's prefect in Egypt. Even when rainfall failed, the Nile did not, and its wheat was a mainstay of the entire Roman Empire. For that reason, export permits were difficult to come by for any purpose apart from feeding Rome its bread, and Herod needed to use both his money and his prestige to acquire grain and seed for his people. He prevailed with Petronius, and his generosity to his subjects did not end there. In cities where people were too old to prepare their own food, he even provided bakers.

Agricultural and economic revival brought increased tax revenue, and Herod's fortunes rebounded. So did his taste for marriage: he expanded his consorts with the addition of Cleopatra of Jerusalem in 25 BCE and another woman named Mariamme—routinely known as Mariamme II—in 24 BCE, the daughter of a priest named Simon.[48] (Confusingly, Cleopatra and Mariamme II each produced a son today called Philip.) To elevate the new Mariamme's status, he made her father high priest, an act that increased both Simon's and the new Mariamme's prestige. Herod was free of Maccabean insistence; of interlopers from outside his borders, such as what Cleopatra had once been; and even of effective priestly resistance from the elite of Jerusalem; he ruled increasingly as the Hellenistic monarch in Judaic dress that he longed to be. He built a new palace in Jerusalem and a brilliantly conceived fortress on the hill where he had bested the forces of Antigonus and Pacorus, calling it Herodium.[49] To advance his position within the empire, Herod sent his sons by the first Mariamme to finish their education in Rome, where they were accepted into Caesar's household.

Not content with having built a city in honor of Augustus, Herod embarked on an ambitious project in terms of engineering and aesthetics—construction of the artificial harbor and magnificent city of Caesarea Maritima.[50] The city and the port and yet another temple honored the emperor but also vastly improved the mercantile position of Herod's realm. Caesarea Maritima eclipsed Joppa as a harbor because it could accommodate the largest vessels engaged in trade and offered superb facilities for Roman visitors, military and commercial. In his building projects as well as in his cultural enterprises, Herod imitated his new master in Rome.[51] The king and his dynasty had been secured from the point of view of the Roman support that was their sine qua non, and Caesarea Maritima was fittingly Herod's most splendid achievement in the genre of political architecture.

A visit by Augustus to Syria enabled Herod to meet with him personally, and Caesar heard out a deputation of subjects from Herod's new lands that wished to object to Herod's cruelty.[52] They found little sympathy from the emperor, who had ceded extra territory to Herod, adding a region northeast of the Sea of Galilee (including what is today called the Golan Heights) to Herod's realm, and granted him the right to determine his own succession in power.[53] Augustus wished not only to favor a successful client king but also to break the old pattern of banditry that plagued the region. When it came to brigands, Herod was ruthless and effective. Once in power in a territory, he treated crimes against property with a particular vengeance. Housebreakers could be sold into slavery and deported, and simple theft might be punished with an assessment of quadruple recompense for the victim.[54]

The Torah was understood to forbid that one Israelite should make another the slave of a foreigner, and some objections to Herod's rule were made on that basis.[55] Augustus, however, had no patience with any such argument; in his client king, he saw only evidence of effective governance. But what was most notable about this meeting in Antioch is that Herod himself was entirely at ease, confident, and at the height of his form. He asked for the right to make Pheroras, his last surviving brother, a tetrarch over part of his territory east of the Jordan.[56] Augustus agreed. At the time, that was a triumph for Herod, but his later dispute with Pheroras would make him regret the victory.

The imperial favor is easy to understand because Herod was proving to be as successful a king as he had been resourceful a commander. His domain both buffered Rome from the Parthians and opened the East to trade, and Augustus's prestige directly benefited from Herod's building programs. Herod even built a temple of white stone for Augustus in Paneion (later known as Caesarea Philippi and ruled by one of Herod's sons).[57] For much of his reign, Herod had more men engaged in construction than he had ready on the field of battle.

Herod's continuing problem was the restive response of a large segment of his subjects; he tried at first the gambit of reducing taxes and then attempted to repress public meetings and gather information from a network of spies. He was not above disguising himself in an effort to learn of conspiracy. Finally, he even imposed an oath of loyalty. Those who resisted were met with all the means at Herod's disposal, although among the Pharisees, he did exempt Shemaiah, whom he favored on his accession.[58] Eager for support from any quarter, he also did not impose the oath on the Essenes; according to the propaganda of his court, Menahem the Essene had predicted Herod's rise. If that truly was Menahem's prophecy, however, in all likelihood, it had more to do with Essene fatalism than with a genuine endorsement of Herod.[59] Herod's contention with the Pharisees reached into his own family when the wife of his brother Pheroras tried to protect those Pharisees who were willing to prophesy that Pheroras would succeed Herod. In exchange, she would pay fines Herod imposed for refusing the oath of loyalty to himself and Augustus.[60] Herod found them out, tried to compel Pheroras to divorce his wife, and when that failed, he banned his brother from his court.

With strategic brilliance, Herod found a new approach to the task of solidifying the basis of his power in religious terms. From halfway into his reign (during the years 20–19 BCE), Herod began expanding, renovating, and effectively reconceiving the Temple in Jerusalem, a structure that had been built by King Solomon, destroyed by the Babylonians in

586 BCE, and then rebuilt in a piecemeal fashion by successive generations. While Herod's work on the temple enhanced his standing as a Judean king,[61] it also demonstrated his commitment to Greco-Roman architecture by featuring a golden eagle above the entrance[62]—symbolic of his divided loyalties, an unresolved but productive tension throughout his life. While Caesarea Maritima was his most magnificent building achievement from the point of view of Roman politics, the temple, designed to crown his dynasty, came to completion decades after Herod's death and has proven to be the most enduring emblem of his legacy.

The mammoth platform, covering some thirty-five acres, exists to this day; he also undertook the construction of the sanctuary and courts that were destroyed centuries ago, in 70 CE. Ten thousand masons were hired for this project, among whom one thousand priests were trained for work in stone; the temple was to bring glory to God as well as to Caesar's client king, and it did so while enriching Jerusalem beyond all expectation, with added commerce, donations from abroad, and the patronage of Herod's Roman friends.

Herod's extension of the temple was an act of statecraft. He established his own position as patron of Judaic sacrifice as well as the agent of Roman might. Augustus, meanwhile, had extended the recognition of Judaism as a legal religion, which allowed donations for the temple to be collected by Jews throughout the Roman Empire and ensured that Jews would not be required to worship pagan gods. Out of this consensus, Augustus and Herod crafted a ritual alliance, according to which the emperor would arrange for sacrifices in the temple, morning and evening;[63] Jews could not worship the emperor, but they would pray for him by means of these sacrifices. By this settlement, made concrete in Herod's project, Rome and Jerusalem were reconciled, and that reconciliation would last as long as the temple stood.

Herod made a state visit to Rome as his program of building consolidated his rule and reputation (in 17 BCE), and Augustus received him in splendor. One of his children by Mariamme had died of an illness in Rome, but Caesar returned the two surviving sons—Alexander and Aristobulus—to Herod's care with the implicit understanding that Mariamme's children were to be Herod's heirs.[64] Herod's old ambition of a combined Maccabean-Idumean succession looked feasible, after all, even if he could not harness his own standing to the status of the wife he had killed.

Roman support extended far beyond the state visit. Agrippa, Caesar's closest friend and adviser, came to Judea in 14 BCE and toured with Herod both there and into Asia Minor and Greece in a remarkable circuit of diplomacy, punctuated by the inauguration of building projects financed by Herod.[65] Architecture projected his powerful pretensions far beyond Judea. Agrippa cemented the sense of the special relationship between the house of Herod and the imperial court by joining in the dedication of these structures and linking himself to Herod in the public imagination. Agrippa confirmed the rights of Jews outside of Herod's territory, and Herod undertook building works by way of benefaction to cities and communities there.

As he reached the age of sixty, Herod was physically robust and politically triumphant. Riding still came easily to him, and on hunts, he excelled in his accuracy with bow and spear. He had long since desisted from wrestling, although he still enjoyed watching the sport. His lifelong enjoyment of banqueting showed up in his weight; nonetheless, he remained strong.[66] Although he fell short many times of Solomon's reported seven hundred wives (1 Kgs 11:1–3), notwithstanding, he put the precedent for royal polygamy to good use. Afternoon naps, as well as nights, were never spent alone. In addition to his first wife, Doris, and Mariamme I, he had eight other wives, most of whom gave him children. No matter what the palace or fortress he resided in, in Samaria, Caesarea, Jericho, Masada, or Herodium, Herod had a consort at hand.

With so much in his favor, the stirrings of old family jealousies at this time must have seemed to be more an annoyance than a serious problem. Alexander and Aristobulus, Herod's sons by Mariamme, had been groomed to reign, and yet their behavior seemed discordant with their father's esteem. They were distant with him, criticized his accent when he spoke Greek, and regretted his inability to speak anything but the most basic Latin. His practical language skills were prodigious, but compared to the tutored elegance of his sons' Greek and

Latin—the product of the Roman education he had arranged—Herod made the impression of a rustic. They saw themselves as wiser than he in the ways of the Roman court, and they would never understand—much less accept—the execution of their mother.[67] Worse, they articulated these attitudes with little regard for who might be listening.

Whenever they spoke unwisely, complained, or compared Herod's Palestine invidiously with Augustus's Rome, word came back to Salomé. Herod, suspicious to the point of paranoia concerning his reputation, had developed the habit of going into Jerusalem in disguise to listen to what people said about him[68] and ruthlessly dispatched any relative or friend who proved disloyal. But Herod had never stopped trusting Salomé. She was the last person in his court who remained in the circle of Idumean trust that came naturally to him. He never realized that she had poisoned his attitude against Mariamme I and did not see that his sons by the Maccabean princess, although foppish and self-indulgent, could not do Herod any harm.

Mariamme's sons touched Herod's most sensitive nerve: his character demanded unconditioned loyalty, the trait that kept Idumean clans together no matter what pressures they endured—the same trait that had endeared Herod's family to the Romans since the time of Antipater. Pursuit of that virtue became disproportionate in the case of Herod the Great, making him as unwise in his resentment of his children as he was in his unreserved trust in Salomé. Piqued by his feeling that his relatives should appreciate him and that his sons by Mariamme fell short of the standard of loyalty required, Herod summoned his first son, Antipater, back from his exile away from the court. Even Doris returned, as if the legacy of Herod might be defined entirely by their Idumean inheritance after all.[69] Salomé felt encouraged by this turn of events, and even Pheroras became embroiled—and entangled, as a result of his wife's alliance with the Pharisees—in the desperate struggle for succession between Idumean and Maccabean partisans in Herod's court.

Although Herod came to realize that he was receiving no wisdom from his confidantes, neither did he have any to offer himself. He intended his new favor toward Antipater more to caution Alexander and Aristobulus than to result in the actual appointment of Antipater as king. As his firstborn son realized that, his bitterness after years of exile from the court became deep and inexorable.

In genuine confusion, Herod sought the counsel of the emperor himself, meeting with Augustus together with Antipater, Alexander, and Aristobulus in Aquileia (between Venice and Trieste) in 12 BCE.[70] Herod put in the only rambling performance he ever gave before a Caesar. He recited a loose catalog of complaints and half-remembered, half-fabricated slights from Mariamme's sons, lamented the abuse of his family when he had been nothing but generous and beneficent, and cursed the fate that had made him a hero in the world and a victim of deceit at home.

Augustus was for a moment speechless. Yet it was evident to him, and to all concerned, that Herod used Antipater only as a pawn to address the perceived treachery of Mariamme's sons. Alexander took up the defense for himself and his brother, insisting on their innocence through his tears and with all the rhetorical skill with which his Roman education had equipped him and blaming the court politicians in Jerusalem for the soured relationship with their father. Caesar was visibly moved and admonished the young men to show greater respect to their father and much more caution in their speech. As Herod embraced his sons, also in tears, he announced himself prepared to arrange the succession of the kingdom right then and to hand over his powers forthwith. Caesar, in a rare moment of indulgence, said he did not wish the king to deprive himself of his own authority.

As Herod made his way home, he might well have believed that, with Caesar as an intermediary, his family's war against itself was at an end. But Antipater seethed in resentment, the loyal son, the first son, who had been used as little more than a cat's-paw in Herod's fraught relationship with the sons of Mariamme. Even when his father seemed to favor him, he did not feel secure.[71] In addition, Herod did not reckon with faults in his children by Mariamme that had escaped even his suspicion. Alexander and Aristobulus, in addition to all their other lapses, could not pass up sexual temptation, some of them distinctly unusual by the standards of Judaism at that time.

Herod, in his luxuriant lifestyle, kept eunuchs in his court. They drew his baths, saw that his bed was made as many times as necessary during the day, and rubbed down sore muscles. Eunuchs were a symbol of status in the Near East and had become fashionable among Romans.[72] Herod's favorite three, who sometimes traveled with him, were especially attractive, with the androgynous beauty that sometimes comes from castration in early adolescence. For an old man who, despite his remarkable vigor, felt the weight of six decades on the earth and the crawling of age on his skin, the young men were a comfort.

Alexander found them accommodating as well as comforting and paid them bribes for sexual favors. Word spread through the court of Alexander's sexual predilections and disloyalty; accusations of many liaisons, involving several members of the court, filled the air. Herod might have dealt with the stirring of this scandal at an earlier stage in his life, but his emotions got the better of him. His self-isolation made him more and more suspicious,[73] both with reason and without. The eunuchs testified under torture that Alexander became so free and foolish in his liaisons, as well as intimate, that he blathered about Herod being ill—and that he had his hair dyed to avoid the impression that he was aging.[74] Only the king of Cappadocia, who was the father of Alexander's wife, could reason with Herod, and he convinced him to go to Rome and make a good account of himself to Augustus, since word of the relapse into calumny in Herod's household had reached the imperial court.

The trip to Rome proved productive, but vigorous or not (and with or without hair dye), a king over the age of sixty might be thought to be in ill health, and when Herod left for Rome, the rumor spread among the uneducated that he had died. In Trachonitis, a part of the region Augustus had recently given him, the old pattern of brigandage had erupted again, to the point of looking like an insurgency. On returning from Rome, Herod reacted as he had as a young ruler in Galilee and took to the field with his men. Sixty-three years old, he routed the enemy in Trachonitis and pursued them to the south.[75] When he arrived at the border of Nabataea, he was outraged to find that the minister Syllaeus had given protection to the outlaws. He ignored the border and gave chase to his enemies, imposing his rule so thoroughly in territory that was not his that he settled three thousand Idumeans in the area to occupy the region.

Herod's boldness had won him another military triumph but also contributed to what was nearly a diplomatic debacle.[76] Syllaeus made his way to Rome and produced a tall tale in which Herod undertook an unprovoked attack on the Nabataean nation. Augustus might have been skeptical, but he was also well aware of Herod's intemperate state of mind since the meeting with him and his sons. He wanted the answer to one question: Had Herod crossed into Nabataea without imperial orders to do so? Acting outside one's territory without leave from the emperor made a client king look like a usurper.

Herod was, for the first time in his reign, in danger of putting himself at cross-purposes with the controlling authority of Rome. The last thing Augustus needed was to have a surrogate freelancing on the sensitive eastern edge of his empire. Augustus was so angry that he wrote his client king and said that while he once treated him as a friend, now he was only a servant.[77] Wounded though Herod was by this stinging rebuke, he fortunately had Nicholas of Damascus at his disposal; Nicholas traveled to Rome and set out all the conditions of the incursion into Nabataea. By the end of this explanation, Augustus was so impressed with Nicholas's exposition and so disgusted by Syllaeus's lies that he considered ceding even Nabataea to Herod.

That would have represented a crowning achievement in Herod's extraordinary reign. But Augustus hesitated. The behavior of the king and his sons made him doubt the wisdom of expanding Herod's realm, and the affair of Herod's sons and the eunuchs in Jerusalem had come to his attention. This time, Caesar did not wish to mediate at all when Herod asked for help again. The limits of imperial patience with family intrigue in Judea had been pressed too hard.

Instead, Alexander and Aristobulus would be tried in a Syrian court under Roman aegis, without the intervention of Augustus.[78] The emperor left arrangements to Herod, and the result was a sham trial. One hundred and fifty notables were impaneled in Beirut (*Bêrutos*), but the accused did not even appear before the court. Herod did not want their rhetorical gifts and shameless tears to sway the jury as they had earlier swayed Caesar. He alone spoke, and the flimsy incoherence of his speech struck the audience. An indeterminate result left the adjudication

of guilt or innocence to the king alone along with the pronounce-
ment of a sentence. He ruthlessly punished many of those who had
sought to intervene and mitigate his anger, convinced they were traitors.
In Samaria, where he had married their mother, Herod had his sons by
Mariamme strangled on the charge of treachery.

Herod's evident incoherence seems at least partially to have been the
result of progressive circulatory failure. Incoherence and mental lapses
became frequent, his rages became less and less explicable, and fatigue
overwhelmed him sporadically. When he responded to the demands of
his office and the intrigue of his family, he overreacted wildly.

By 4 BCE, symptoms of gangrene spread through his legs and
reached his groin.[79] Fluid built up through his lower body, and the
stench of his breath indicated his internal organs were affected. He had
himself taken to a spa near the Dead Sea so that he could bathe in oils
and mineral water. He fainted when immersed in the hot bath.

Premature rumors of his death were inevitable. As they circulated,
two rabbis of the Pharisees urged their followers to strike a blow against
Herod's idolatry. The matter of the trophies had not died but festered.
When Herod built a splendid portico on the south side of the temple,
so high he could survey building operations as well as the sacrificial
worship of Israel, he had decorated it with an eagle, an emblem dear to
Rome and its culture.[80] In a nighttime raid, the rabbis' disciples scaled
the portico and cut down the offending eagle; the fall smashed the idol
on the stone floor below.

By now Herod was unable to walk; any movement had become
excruciating. But he had the two rabbis, Judah and Mattathias, brought
with their followers to his splendid, constantly renovated palace in Jericho, one of his most sumptuous installations. He heard the case himself
in the amphitheater, recounting all his efforts for the nation and its religion. He found the conspirators guilty of sacrilege, not merely of lèse-
majesté. The two rabbis were burned to death, and their forty followers
were both shot with arrows and beheaded.

It was as if Herod was forming up an entourage of victims to escort
him into the shades of death. From this period comes the story in Matthew's Gospel that Herod killed the young children of Bethlehem for

fear of the birth of the messiah there. That would be in keeping with his paranoid cruelty, but his remorseless anger now focused much closer to home. So many villages had been razed during Herod's campaigns that it is easy to see how the legend in Matthew might have emerged. The historical record, however, Roman as well as Jewish, shows that Herod did not pursue predictions of future messiahs but hunted down competitors whom he saw as living, known, and present dangers.[81] The story about what happened in Bethlehem is more accurately associated with events after the death of Herod the Great, at the time of his son Archelaus.

Meanwhile, Antipater was also charged with a plot to kill the king and appeared before the new governor of Syria, Varus. Proof that the substance with which Antipater had provided his servants was poison was incontrovertible: the servants were compelled by the court to drink from the vial Antipater gave them and died within minutes. The active agent was apparently cyanide, a fashionable poison in Rome.[82]

With Nicholas of Damascus as prosecutor, Antipater was condemned to death and languished in the dungeon in Jericho, awaiting his father's pleasure. Herod delayed execution, sparing the son who was named after his father; perhaps, on some days, he considered showing mercy. But he was unpredictable to the point of frenzy. One day, sensing death and in despair, Herod tried to kill himself—pathetically, with a dinner knife.[83]

Pandemonium broke out in the palace as servants ran through its corridors with premature news of the king's death. Antipater, just over forty years old, felt that vindication was near. His father had already made out a will naming other children, from lesser-known wives, his heirs. But Archelaus and Antipas, whose mother was the Samaritan Malthaké, and Philip, whose mother was of local Jerusalem lineage, were not of the purer Idumean pedigree of Antipater, at least in his mind, and they were not prepared for office. The provisions of the last will also divided Herod's kingdom into parcels, an act of strategic folly.

Antipater roared out for the guards to release him, banging his shackles to make as much noise as possible. He would claim power, then seek Rome's blessing later, all for the good of the country that only he could unify. It was as if the whole Idumean family was crying out for due regard at long last and for recognition of the benefits of its ascendancy.

One last time, however, Herod recovered. The wound of the knife was nowhere near fatal, although he had fainted when he thrust it into his body. As he came to consciousness again, he heard the screams of Antipater, although muffled by the masonry of his palace so that he could not understand a word of what he said. When Antipater's demands were explained to him, Herod ordered his guards to kill him. Five days later, the king himself died, his legacy in chaos.

5

ARCHELAUS

CONFUSION OVER SUCCESSION: REBELLION AND VIOLENCE

Archelaus, Herod's first son by his Samaritan wife, Malthaké, was to inherit the royal title by the terms of the dying king's last will. He pressed the dynastic claim to monarchy by organizing a magnificent funeral for his father, flaunting his personal status as Herod's rightful heir at the same time. But his own brother, Antipas, contested the will, and this challenge came to Rome with the support of Herod's sister Salomé and even Malthaké, mother of both Archelaus and Antipas. Worse, factions among the Pharisees and Sadducees hardened in their opposition until militant resistance emerged to both Archelaus and Rome. Archelaus responded by means of the generalized use of force, often unleashing disproportionate devastation against opponents, whether real or imagined. Augustus, who had supported Archelaus out of loyalty to the memory of Herod, finally exiled Archelaus and ordered the direct Roman rule of Judea by means of a prefect.
The ethnarch: *Vain, beleaguered, capricious, brutal*

Introduction

HEROD'S ARRANGEMENTS TO assure what he saw as appropriate mourning for his demise were commensurate with his state of mind at the end
of his life. He ordered that hundreds of Judean notables, whom he had
summoned to Jericho, be conducted into the hippodrome there; they
were to be killed at the news of his death so that Herod could be sure
that his passing would bring grief.[1] Come what may, he would guarantee
mourning at the time of his death, if not for his death.

This final decree captures the pathology as well as the tyrannical
confidence in his singularity that animated Herod's view of government.
For him, the Judean kingdom was the creature of its king. Herod gave his
orders to his sister Salomé in the last days of his life; in the same breath,
he commanded the execution of his son Antipater. Although Antipater
was killed, Salomé abandoned the bizarre scheme for ceremonial assassination and released the notables when her brother finally expired.[2]
At the same time, together with Herod's son Archelaus, she assured a
massive funeral of state for her brother, because she understood that the
future of the dynasty was in question.[3] Salomé had succeeded in eliminating competition from the Maccabean side of the family and seemed
at ease working with the sons of Herod's Samaritan wife, Malthaké. Yet
for all the energy behind his dynastic enterprise, Herod's final instability left the prospects for his realm uncertain. His successors recovered
from his deliberate devastation only by deploying the same remorseless
opportunism that had made him a success. For the dynasty to be sustained, his heirs would need to be as ruthless, energetic, and talented as
he. And they would need some of his unsurpassed luck, as well.

By the end of his life, Herod saw the future of his dynasty, not
as a combined inheritance of Idumean and Maccabean rule, but in
terms of loyalty to Roman hegemony. His execution of Mariamme's
sons Alexander and Aristobulus, as well as of Mariamme herself, had
removed viable candidates to succeed Herod. A final will left by Herod
divided up his kingdom. It favored his two sons from Malthaké, Archelaus and his younger brother, Antipas, and—very much in third place—
Philip, the son of a woman of aristocratic descent from Jerusalem named

Cleopatra. All these three had been raised in Rome,[4] but Archelaus enjoyed the preeminent position: he was put in charge of Judea, and his father's will had bestowed the title of king upon him. His treatment of Philip as compared to his preference for Archelaus and Antipas—both children of a Samaritan mother—might even be seen as a deliberate provocation of Judean nationalists. Herod experimented with a base of power in his preferred hunting grounds in Samaria. Doing so, however, ran up against the deep prejudice within Judaism against what once had been a kingdom separate from Judea and then, after 722 BCE, a zone of occupation and the settlement of gentiles on the part of the Assyrians.

Archelaus understood the delicacy of his position and at first attempted to accommodate public opinion in Jerusalem and through-out his new realm: King Herod's funeral amounted to propaganda for his own succession, and Archelaus spared no expense in mounting a spectacular display of Herod's royal regalia in a military parade, which began in Jericho with a reading of the will in Archelaus's favor and ended in Herodium for the interment.[5] He understood the politics of Rome intimately and applied himself to Judean politics with a vigor commensurate with his father's while suppressing coordinated dissent whenever it emerged. More than any other single figure, Archelaus proved pivotal in the events that unfolded between 4 BCE and 6 CE.

Archelaus's Play for Power

"BETTER TO BE Herod's pig (*hus*) than his son (*huios*)":[6] Augustus Caesar, not generally known for his sense of humor, permitted himself what passed for a quip.

A degree of nervous bemusement underlies the commonplace anti-Semitism of the remark. After all, before he took his imperial title, Augustus was simply Octavian, *adopted* son of Julius Caesar. He had less genealogical claim on power in Rome than Herod's sons did on rule in Jerusalem. Yet Mariamme's children, Alexander and Aristobulus, and Doris's son Antipater, groomed as heirs and duly named as inheritors in a dizzying sequence of wills, had all been executed at their father's command. All the while, swine did not feature on the menu of Herod's feasts. Augustus's joke not only unfavorably compares Herod's treatment of his sons with respect to his reserve in regard to pigs but also implicitly contrasts Caesar's adoption of Octavian with Herod's insistence on blood relatives as inheritors of power.

Sons did survive Herod, however; they remained in waiting despite the policy of the old, suspicious king to dispose of those whom he suspected of sedition against him. His death at last put an end to his hunt for treason among his own progeny. The sons favored with inheritance were more like survivors than carefully groomed heirs, and each understood that success was vitally dependent upon the favor of Rome, a city they knew well from their upbringing. The sons of Malthaké could expect some resistance to their Samaritan pedigree, and even Philip, although his mother was of Jerusalem lineage,[7] had to rule the most Hellenistic region of Herod's old domain and so would confront demands for accommodation with non-Judaic cultures. The final will bequeathed the kingdom of Judea to Archelaus; Philip inherited the northeastern territories on the other side of the Sea of Galilee (Gaulanitis and adjacent regions, comparable to the Golan Heights today); and Antipas took over his father's old appointment as tetrarch of Galilee (with Perea as well).[8]

That arrangement, put in place by Herod just before his death, invited contention. A slightly earlier will had put Antipas in the lead position, as heir of Herod's kingdom, although this arrangement was inherently unstable: in 4 BCE, Antipas and Philip were teenagers, while Archelaus was just coming to the age of twenty. The reversal in priority between the two sons of Malthaké resulted from the intrigue of Herod's last years, when accusations of conspiracy thrived as hardily as the conspiracy itself, and Antipater mounted a campaign of defamation against Archelaus and Philip.[9] Once Antipater was imprisoned and sentenced to death, Archelaus and Philip were back in the will with Antipas, and Archelaus took first place as the royal inheritor of Judea. The youth and inexperience of all three heirs played into the hands of intrigue, and it is the mark of Augustus's regard for Herod the Great that he worked out arrangements for governance along the lines of the will.

Archelaus's character lacked nothing of Herod's audacity, and he was also capable of decisive action. At the same time, his love of spectacle—another trait he shared with his father—sometimes verged on narcissism. Perhaps Herod understood this when he wrote the will that had advanced his younger son Antipas to the position of Judean kingship. Yet Archelaus's failings were no more pronounced than his father's, and Herod himself had proven that tyrannical self-indulgence could accompany a finely tuned strategic cunning. Knowing his son's faults as well as his strengths, Herod had at the end endorsed him to rule Judea.

In any case, Archelaus's youth made his amour propre appear more charming than it would have seemed in an older person. He also developed a sense of strategy in short order, which showed promise for the survival of the dynasty. Yet he also proved changeable in the execution of policy, a characteristic his father showed in an exaggerated fashion at the end of his life. Herod's capriciousness manifested itself increasingly with age; in his early years, Antipater, Phasael, and Sextus Caesar were tempering influences. Archelaus enjoyed no such benefit, and then he had the example of his father's increasing volatility before his eyes in the last years of Herod's life, and it was a trait that seemed effective in its own way. Governing Jerusalem involved a multivariable computation of interests during the entire period of Archelaus's rule; the introduction of some degree of unpredictability on the part of the ruler, as Herod the Great had shown, might simplify the interests in play as subjects tried as best they could to adjust to new and unexpected policy changes. Chaos at the top can serve to rationalize the interests of those subject to incoherence.

At the outset of his rule, Archelaus faced opposition from relatives who coveted his power, Antipas in their lead. In addition, Judean supporters of the Pharisaic rabbis whom Herod the Great had executed at the end of his life were emboldened by his death. The rabbis' martyrdom, as Archelaus quickly came to see, had only enhanced their reputation. At first, he tried to win their supporters' sympathy by dismissing those of his father's advisers who had recommended their execution. With that gesture, performed with spectacular aplomb as he appeared personally in the temple prior to Passover in order to meet with those who demanded the change,[10] Archelaus signaled that he wanted to take a break from his father's policies.

Much as Herod had once appeared as a young man before the Sanhedrin, Archelaus appareled himself in finery and postured before the crowd of pilgrims in Jerusalem: Judeans, Pharisees, and rabbis, all eager to see a new ruler who promised to show greater respect for their ancestral ways than his father had displayed. Although Archelaus had no pretension to priesthood—and could have none, as the son of a Samaritan mother and an Idumean father—he came into the temple clad not in kingly purple as his father had before the Sanhedrin but in white garments as though an undefiled Israelite and assumed his position on an elevated throne that he had commanded should be installed for the occasion. His position on a throne signaled that Archelaus was the king in waiting, although he said he would await Augustus's confirmation before actually taking that title.

His white garments had perhaps been intended to signal the humility of a king who had not yet been confirmed as such by Rome, but in symbolizing purity, they could be taken as a claim to exercise priestly authority in the temple. Layers of self-contradiction undermined his credibility. Archelaus appeared in the temple in quasi-priestly regalia and ostentatiously arranged for the offering of sacrifice,[11] but he addressed the crowd in the temple as a Roman politician might operate, by compromising among competing interests. Indeed, he declared that he wanted to be kinder to his subjects than his father had been. Predictably, this offer provoked calls from the crowd for what many people might want from a new ruler: a reduction of general taxes, a removal of specific duties on goods, and the release of prisoners who had been arbitrarily detained. He heard these requests with an agreeable demeanor, as if prepared to accept them, but as evening approached and Archelaus retired to a feast, the crowd in the temple made a new demand. They took up the rites of mourning to grieve the execution of Mattathias and Judah, the rabbis who had engineered the demolition of the golden eagle that Herod had set up in the temple, and insisted that Archelaus physically punish the councilors who had advised Herod and dismiss the current high priest.[12]

Archelaus abhorred this petition because it amounted to instructing him on how to govern. Nonetheless, he took two actions designed to defuse the crowd's restive fervor. First, without granting the demands, he indicated his general sympathy and said he would consult with the crowd again after his return from having seen Augustus, who was to confirm his royal title as specified by Herod's will. That position, from the point of view of Rome, was quite reasonable, since Archelaus could only overrule a previous royal order if he were a king himself. He explained that his powers remained restricted until such time as he was actually named by Augustus as king of Judea (including Idumea and Samaria, the full territory that his father's will set out for him). Second, recognizing that the crowd pressed for immediate action, he deployed a senior officer with a small contingent to mitigate with persuasion the zeal of those gathered in the temple and convince them to await a just resolution of their grievance.

Each of these actions was reasonable and measured, yet in combination with one another, they made a tense situation much worse. By refusing to act more fully before he had imperial confirmation, Archelaus bought time, but at the expense of deepening the impression of his utter dependence upon Rome and of his tendency to give way under pressure. Though he had entered the temple boldly and grandly, his attempt to finesse a difficult situation by conceding on the one hand and refusing on the other served to undermine his credibility.

Prevarication wrong-footed him as he attempted to find his political balance. Archelaus's low esteem in the eyes of the crowd in the temple became all too obvious when the officers sent in to persuade needed to resort to argument, and then the crowd's temper shifted to the point that they beat the contingent back with stones. Jerusalem stood at the edge of rebellion, just the situation, as he well knew, that could bring Archelaus down in Roman esteem and see him out of the power he had not yet fully inherited.

The approach of Passover began to look increasingly like the prelude to a full-scale revolt, with raucous processions in and around the temple, replete with chants calling for a new high priest and the punishment of the discredited councilors. Demonstrations grew as the population of Jerusalem swelled, which it always did at the time of the major feasts, in spring (Passover), summer (Weeks or Pentecost), and autumn (Sukkot). The holy calendar promised a disruptive year.

Archelaus responded to the growing challenge from the Pharisees to his decision (or as perceived by many at the time, his indecision) by changing his approach again. Without any of the reticence he had claimed to have about utilizing legal and military force prior to imperial confirmation of his title, he deployed a detail of troops inside the temple to gain control of events on holy ground. Proving that his own kingly entrance there had been much more than symbolic, he ordered his soldiers to break up and put an end to the demonstrations. After all, the temple throughout the Herodian settlement projected loyalty both to the Torah and to the emperor, whose sacrificial offerings there were accepted twice every day. From Rome's point of view, those sacrifices were much more than a formality; rather, they represented an acceptance of the legitimacy of imperial rule within the most important institution in Judaism. A breach of that understanding would amount to a Judaic declaration of independence. Decades later, that breach actually came to pass, with the catastrophic consequences in 70 CE that the war with Rome entailed. Long before that disaster, however, intelligent observers and political players had appreciated how vital it was to preserve the good order of sacrificial worship as the seal of God's supremacy and Rome's dominion. To Herod's son and newly named heir, it was more important to restore order in the temple in accordance with the arrangement with Rome than it was to placate the phalanx of Pharisees, priests, and opportunistic rebels that opposed him.

The cohort of soldiers led by a tribune entered the temple under orders from Archelaus to act as a police force.[13] They were to arrest those who used the religious occasion to promote revolt and bring them to appear before the new ruler. The decision to use military force to intervene on holy ground predictably outraged many Israelites who had gathered for worship as well as the initial demonstrators who demanded retributive justice against Herod's councilors. The crowd and all opposed to Archelaus's seemingly fickle policies turned on the soldiers, some of whom died under a hail of stones and other projectiles that were near at hand.[14] Even the pelting of Alexander Jannaeus by the Pharisees during the previous century,[15] which resulted in deadly violence, was mild compared to the violence of the demonstrators against

Archelaus. Still, when the tribune and his force retired from the temple, sacrifice—rather than protest or preparation for armed conflict—became the order of the day once more. The tenor of public resistance to Archelaus's policies had not yet deepened into a dedicated revolt against the Romans. The problem was more one of disorder than of insurrection.

Archelaus's limited operation so far had been hardly a success, but neither was it a complete failure. His earlier appearance in the temple had produced mixed attitudes at best; his standing in the light of the military intervention he ordered seemed defensible if tenuous. Taking himself away from Jerusalem at this moment was hardly propitious, yet preparations were well advanced for his voyage to Rome and the all-important confirmation of Herod's will. Departure while leaving an uneasy peace behind him must have seemed hazardous, but Archelaus hoped that after appearing before the emperor, he could return to Jerusalem in a much stronger position. Under these circumstances, however, he decided on one more display of power prior to his departure.

For the major feasts, pilgrims streamed into Jerusalem not only from the traditional land of Israel but from all over the known world.[16] The population of Jerusalem could easily double at those times. The massive work of temple renovation and extension undertaken by Herod the Great proceeded on its way to completion (which still lay decades ahead), but even gentile travelers came to visit the increasingly impressive sanctuary complex, the largest edifice for public worship in antiquity. Herod had deliberately designed a great outer court so that non-Jews could enjoy his magnificent edifice in all its splendor. The eyes of Rome were on the site through wealthy sightseers as well as through the Roman officers on the scene, all of whom had good reason to wonder whether Archelaus could preserve Roman interests as his father had done. Neither they nor Archelaus could know how many of the pilgrims who had arrived at the temple were minded more for revolution than for worship. Disorder can conceal a multitude of threats.

Archelaus sensed the need for decisive action, and he commanded the entire army at his disposal, not a mere cohort, to fall upon the Israelites camped in the open in proximity to the temple, a class of people that would not normally include wealthier pilgrims (whether Israelites or not), who could afford accommodation in the city of Jerusalem. People inclined to insurrection were more likely to be found in the encampment. Deploying both infantry and cavalry, Archelaus ordered the camp to be broken up, the pilgrims there to be scattered, and their access to the temple to be prohibited. Their blood was not to be spared, any more than their counterparts inside the temple had spared the blood of the cohort Archelaus had ordered in earlier. Both his vengeance and his honor would be satisfied. Faults in character might be evident in his actions and attitudes, but inexperience perhaps played a greater role in the failure to master the kind of situation his father had confronted more than once. In any case, the scale of opposition he faced would have daunted any leader, and to that extent, his resort to violence is understandable. Yet he no doubt undermined his own position by using force belatedly, in order to appear decisive, after having assumed an accommodating position. An action that was intended to convey an impression of strength could all too easily be seen as querulous and reactive, a problematic reputation that increasingly sapped Archelaus's political position.

His new order brought about the deaths of some *three thousand* of the Passover pilgrims outside the temple.[17] Archelaus followed up the slaughter with an edict that all those who had been in the encampment were to return to their homes. That year there would be no Passover in Jerusalem for them.

By this point, Archelaus's opponents could portray him both as weak in trying to accede to popular sentiment and also as violent in reacting disproportionately and unpredictably to disorder. Although the child of a Samaritan mother and an Idumean father, his assertion of authority concerning the temple implied a priestly pretension that stirred his opposition into organized revolt. His intervention in and around the temple goaded the pilgrims he had ruthlessly repressed into rebellion. Finally, his prevention of access for sacrifice at a major feast of the year demanded a priestly response. He had antagonized both the elite and the multitude encamped in Jerusalem by his actions. Rebellion across the whole of Judea became increasingly probable.

Archelaus damaged his position further still by timing. He departed for Rome, where he hoped to have Emperor Augustus endorse Herod's will, just after he ordered the breakup of the encampment, and the Holy City had become the scene not merely of unrest but of slaughter at his hands. Neither the Romans nor the Judeans could endorse his precipitous resort to violence, and Archelaus's absence from Judea sapped what credibility he continued to enjoy. Yet the trip to Rome was necessary, and he sailed with Herod the Great's sister Salomé, who agreed to strengthen his case for the confirmation of Herod's last will, just as she had supported him during the arrangement of Herod's funeral. Meanwhile, the shambles he had left behind him offered opportunities for maneuvers at his expense, and not only from the Judean quarter.

At the time of Herod the Great's death, Augustus had designated the imperial procurator Sabinus to provide an inventory of the royal estate. His accounting—and particularly his zeal for acquisition—undermined Archelaus's position. Sabinus acted within the jurisdiction of Varus, the Syrian legate, one of the most famous Roman generals of his time. Varus had long understood that the transition of power from Herod to Archelaus would be delicate, and he urged Sabinus to assure Archelaus's continuing custody of the property until Augustus could confirm arrangements.[18] But the emperor's procurator acted on the behalf of Augustus rather than Judea and with tactics that assured his own profit.

With Varus in Antioch and Archelaus on his way to Rome, Sabinus seized the royal palace in Jerusalem and took charge of its treasury.[19] Rebellion, mounted especially by Galileans and Idumeans in protest of what seemed to many to be a seizure of Israelite property, followed swiftly, and Sabinus, in order to confiscate wealth from the holy treasury, took advantage of the precedent of Archelaus's incursion into the temple by mounting his own. He launched an operation to seize both royal and sacred wealth, and the violence of the response to him was commensurate with his transgressions. Jerusalem proper descended into street fighting in which Sabinus and the rebels alternated in seizing buildings. Violence peaked during the Festival of Weeks (or Pentecost, seven weeks after Passover), maximizing the numbers of people killed and injured and symbolizing the rupture of the peaceable settlement between Judea and Rome. Recently constructed porticoes in the temple went up in flames, and the Romans used the opportunity to occupy favorable positions for combat, to loot treasure, and to kill as many of the opposition as possible.

Sabinus's self-dealing and its violent aftermath could have been ruinous for Archelaus because at the same time, his position weakened unexpectedly in Rome. A threat from within his family complicated his claim to be the next king of Judea. Herod's younger son by Malthaké, Antipas, had also traveled with an entourage to Rome to make a vigorous defense of the earlier will that would have made *him* the new Judean king. Even more damning for Archelaus, his aunt Salomé switched sides and joined Antipas's supporters. Her aims were more opportunistic than anything else, since the younger Antipas might prove more pliable than his self-regarding brother where Salomé's interests were concerned. But her position for public consumption was that she had lost confidence in Archelaus's capacity to govern. She joined those who mounted prolonged public attacks on Archelaus's alleged arrogance, hypocrisy, and now—according to a letter from Sabinus—anti-Roman motivation.[20] Those arguments, ably represented by a professional spokesman, might well have carried the day had another letter to the emperor not arrived from the legate Varus exposing Sabinus's incompetent venality and proposing that Varus himself should restore order to Jerusalem and Judea. From this point, with the emperor's leave, Varus took control of Herod the Great's former realm, leaving Archelaus and Antipas to dispute over who should rule after Varus's presumed victory. Neither of the sons of Herod claimed to rival Varus in the ability to restore order.

As Varus prepared for what ultimately proved to be a massive campaign, in Rome, Augustus gave audience to the opposing candidates for the kingship of Judea. Herod the Great's cunning and vindictiveness, distributed among his progeny, were on full display from all quarters, but Archelaus profited to the same degree that Sabinus was discredited. He also benefited from the advocacy of his father's trusted advisor and longtime friend of Rome, Nicholas of Damascus. Nicholas offered just the intimate link with Herod the Great that the professional representatives that Antipas relied upon did not enjoy. As this diplomatic courtier made the case for his client, Archelaus availed himself of his theatrical skills and fell at the feet of Caesar. These tactics bought Archelaus both time and advantage but, in the end, not full vindication. Augustus came to the decision not to choose between the two claimants to the royal throne but to await the outcome of Varus's campaign. The emperor knew better than to attempt a definitive resolution while the Roman situation on the ground appeared vulnerable and victory in battle remained a prospect rather than a certainty.

One of the most successful and experienced generals of his time, Varus set out for Judea and Jerusalem with what he thought to be an adequate force. He believed he had restored order with the arrival of a full legion, but even though he seemed to have full command on the ground for several months, he learned that his efforts at pacification were still being undermined. His problem was not limited to rebels in Judea. Sabinus, whose taste for plunder in Caesar's name had not yet abated, engaged in freelance pillaging with his own forces and mercenaries.[21] That brought the inevitable response of the members of the populace that were abused, and they saw the enemy as Rome, not one personality among the many agents of Roman power. Varus had not been defeated, but the return of hostilities and the insubordination of Sabinus gave the impression of defeat, and local movements of insurrection emerged in several parts of Herod the Great's former territories. Taken together, these factors combined to make Judea seem ungovernable.

Remnants of Herod's army banded together and attempted to exert power in the name not of Archelaus or Antipas or Philip but of still other claimants.[22] Thousands gathered from Idumea, the ancestral stronghold of Herodian power; their predations could not be contained by one of Herod the Great's cousins, named Achiab. Judas, the son of Hezekiah (the brigand chief whom Herod had executed), captured Sepphoris in Galilee. Even one of Herod's former slaves, named Simon, claimed the kingship and tried to set up a court of his own. He conducted a campaign of plunder and arson against Herod's palaces, starting with the magnificent complex at Jericho. He went to the point of wearing the diadem, which had been Herod's right alone to wear. Simon's absurd pretension and disastrous defeat assumed dimensions that attracted the notice of the Roman historian Tacitus long after, in the second century.[23] The breakdown of order in Judea at this time became a scandal throughout the Roman Empire.

A man named Athronges also claimed to be king.[24] As a shepherd, he implicitly compared himself to both King David and the prophet Amos, but his immediate authority rested on the gangs he headed, which harried both Roman and Herodian troops. His four brothers, all of them physically imposing men, joined in the movement. In addition to the Davidic and prophetic symbolism he invoked, Athronges's claims were akin to those of the famed brothers of Judas Maccabeus in the second century BCE, who made the Maccabean movement a success in spite of overwhelming odds by means of the heroic efforts of their kinsmen in battle. Other guerilla fighters during this time also achieved prominence, but Athronges posed a particular challenge to Archelaus and an implicit threat to the Roman regime in Judea as such. The assertion of a kingship other than Archelaus's and Caesar's on the premise of being God's "anointed," his messiah, challenged the Roman and Herodian hegemony at its base. When Athronges even overwhelmed a superior Roman force at Emmaus near Jerusalem, Judea reeled on the brink of a catastrophic civil war.

Varus responded with the overwhelming force of two additional legions, some fifteen thousand personnel altogether, who marched south to join the legion already in Jerusalem.[25] Dividing his force at Ptolemais on the coast, he ordered his son, who was also a seasoned commander, to head an army to recapture Sepphoris: the city was besieged, burned, and destroyed, its inhabitants sold into slavery. Varus himself showed more mercy on his campaign through Samaria, where resistance to his advance proved nominal and the revolt had been far less severe from the outset.

But when Varus arrived in Judea, he burned Emmaus to the ground. No token of Athronges's victory could be permitted to stand. Decades later, two of Jesus's disciples shared a meal with their master after his death while they were traveling to Emmaus; against their expectation, he had been raised from the dead (Luke 24:13–35).[26] Their account resonates with the knowledge that their destination was remembered as a place of defeat and despair. Just as crucifixion by the

Roman authorities appeared to put an end to the movement of Jesus, so Varus's destruction of Emmaus seemed the final word in regard to rebellion against the Romans. Emmaus symbolized the broken hope of expectations of Judaic redemption and independence from Rome, which made the appearance of the risen Jesus to his disciples near there all the more poignant. In this and other cases, Archelaus left his mark, indirectly but indelibly, within the texts of the Gospels.

From Jerusalem itself, Varus rounded up those identified as instigators of revolt in the region and inflicted Rome's exemplary punishment. After *two thousand* men were crucified, the Holy City, Judea, Idumea, and Galilee were pacified. Sabinus fled to Rome, frightened to face Varus in person. Varus's victory was crucial, and the necessity of his campaign showed that Archelaus did not have an effective grasp on his realm. Antipas had given little sign of anything like mastery over Galilee, and the de facto headquarters of his tetrarchy under Rome hegemony, Sepphoris, lay in ruins. Meanwhile, Herod's son Philip, who ruled over Gaulanitis and the adjacent territory and had once been favored by Herod,[27] had escaped injury to his standing, largely because the majority of his population was gentile; he contented himself with minting coins that flattered the emperor and avoided the conflict that radiated from Jerusalem. In short, no Herodian ruler had shown himself equal to the chaos that had overtaken Judea and Galilee. Between the dynasty and the end of its power stood only Augustus's judgment in respect to Herod the Great's last will.

Imperial Intervention

A DELEGATION OF fifty representatives from Judea claimed in a vociferous plea before Caesar in Rome that Judeans would prefer to be ruled directly by Roman authority through the greater province of Syria than see Archelaus confirmed as king.[28] Before he had even secured imperial support for his royal title, then, Archelaus's unpopularity threatened the existence of the Herodian kingdom under Roman aegis. The delegation included Pharisees, for whom opposition to anyone in Herod's line had become a reflex since the time that Herod the Great appeared before the Sanhedrin for his extrajudicial execution of Hezekiah and especially after his savage punishment of the rabbis and their followers who had dismantled his eagle in the temple.[29] More fatefully, Archelaus faced resistance from a non-Pharisaic faction of priests who had served on the Sanhedrin for generations. Archelaus's incursions into the temple, his disruption of the sacred calendar of offerings, and his vicious decimation of pilgrims in Jerusalem constituted a threat to the regimen of well-ordered and pure sacrifice that, according to the priestly perspective, was the very purpose of Israel. When this group of Sadducees[30] joined the front against Archelaus, it did so with a viable plan for continuing and legitimating Roman power over Judea without a client king. If the Romans governed Judea by means of their legate, they might rely on the Sadducees to administer the temple without provoking further revolutionary activity.

By pressing the argument for direct Roman rule, the delegation inadvertently strengthened the case for Archelaus. The Herodians (now including the sensible Philip, who had made his way to Rome) were horrified at the prospect that their quarrel over which of them should rule might bring down their dynasty altogether. More importantly, Archelaus had one factor in his favor that proved decisive despite every consideration against him, including his tendency to incite opposition to himself—namely, the emperor. The delegation unwisely complained not only about Archelaus but also about Herod the Great. Nicholas of Damascus, representing Archelaus with all his skill, deftly pointed out the convenience of attacking a man after his death and played on Augustus's long friendship with the dead king, a perhaps surprising but remarkably durable element in Caesar's decision. Augustus wanted to continue Herodian rule in order to remain loyal to Herod the Great even after his death, notwithstanding the fact that his sons evidently needed to be brought to order.

So Augustus, sitting in state in the temple of Apollo he had recently constructed, confirmed Herod's last will in its substance.[31] Yet he also made an implicit concession to the criticism that had plagued Archelaus by appointing him not as king (the title stipulated in the will) but as ethnarch (or the "ruler of the people"). Still, the emperor did not wish to assert Rome's direct military control in Herod's former kingdom. He pronounced Archelaus most worthy among all the claimants to rule and even indicated that he might eventually inherit the royal title. After all, the title ethnarch had been granted to Hyrcanus by the Romans, and the Maccabees were a royal lineage. Augustus did not find Antipas a plausible candidate for his father's throne, partly on account of his age (he was then well shy of twenty years old) and perhaps more importantly because the emperor held the would-be usurper and his duplicitous aunt Salomé in some contempt.[32] Coming to Rome as she did in support of Archelaus and then switching her partisanship to support Antipas, she opened herself to the charge of falling under the influence of bribery. Naming Antipas king instead of Archelaus would in any case have diminished Herod in the memory of Rome. Philip, on the other hand, did not join in any challenge to Archelaus, and although earlier he had been favored by Herod the Great, now he lacked support to supplant his brother and had no wish to do so.

Philip was the second son by Cleopatra of Jerusalem[33] and had received his education in Rome. He chose prudently not to put himself forward but supported Archelaus; he was better off contenting himself with the rule of Gaulanitis and avoiding the contention for the throne of Judea. His character during a long tenure was marked by accommodation, a taste for governance, and a certain appreciation of the arts in his building projects. In any case, Augustus came to the judgment that client rule was preferable to direct rule and that Archelaus was the son of Herod most suited to assume the lead position. Considering himself fortunate to have been named in the last will at all after Antipater defamed him and the youngest of the three Herodians in the running to rule their father's realms, Philip was satisfied with his domains in Gaulanitis.

By maintaining in power three of Herod's sons—Archelaus, Antipas, and Philip—Augustus allowed different experiments in government to unfold, even as he showed himself loyal to the memory of his friend Herod. Each of the sons showed signs of inherited attitudes, policies, strengths, and weaknesses of Herod the Great but with distinctive approaches. Archelaus took up his father's program of consolidating Herodian power by exerting an authority over the temple reminiscent of the Maccabees; Antipas, whose region of control did not include Jerusalem, decided to govern with a claim to legitimacy that permitted the temple relative autonomy while insisting on Antipas's own Herodian pedigree; and Philip pioneered a syncretistic amalgam of Hellenistic religion and Israelite nostalgia. Augustus showed himself at his manipulative and innovative best in engineering a competition among the three regimes.

Archelaus's experiment disposed of by far the best resources of the three, drawing in an annual income double that of his brothers combined.[34] Augustus solved Archelaus's potential problem with Salomé, who had sought to undermine him in favor of Antipas, by allocating her a palace in Ascalon together with other territories and emphasizing that on her death, all her inheritance would fall within Archelaus's jurisdiction. The arrangement gave her every reason to avoid the impression of contending against Archelaus, since to do so might cause her property to be assigned to him *before* her death. She never gave the ethnarch trouble after his appointment by Augustus; the emperor's guile and virtually unlimited power overrode Salomé's long-standing passion for intrigue, and in any case, she had won herself a significant degree of wealth, independence, and power.

Yet trouble overtook Archelaus from other quarters. Antipas had challenged Herod's last will, and as revolutionary tendencies gained strength in Judea, the Sadducees had coalesced into a priestly movement for closer collaboration with Rome. They contributed to the storm of conflicting claims in which Archelaus had been undermined on too many fronts for his claim to inherit his father's throne to go unopposed. Together, these multiple precedents invited further challenges to Archelaus's legitimacy; one of them made its way to the imperial court.

A man from the coastal city of Sidon put himself out as Alexander, one of Mariamme I's sons whom Herod had executed and therefore in the genealogical line of the Maccabees through his mother as well as a son of Herod who stood senior to Archelaus, Antipas, *and* Philip.[35] Enthusiastic crowds celebrated his royalty as the false Alexander made his way to Rome itself, where he hoped to be crowned gloriously in succession to Herod the Great. Augustus, however, uncovered the ruse.

He realized that the man before him was too calloused and well muscled to be Herod's effete son; by means of cross-examining the claimant and then offering him clemency in exchange for a confession, he winkled the truth out. The public acclaim for the false Alexander had demonstrated unmistakably that Archelaus was far from having won over the hearts of his subjects. Only an unloved ruler could provide the occasion for so transparent an imposter, and the turmoil that the false Alexander caused in Rome and the need for Augustus's involvement were signs that the situation in Judea was untenable.

Archelaus nonetheless devised a strategy of survival that utilized his capital as Herod's principal heir. Augustus had made him head of the nation (although not king, a position that would have given him wider scope for action), and Archelaus made the most of this appointment by projecting his status on newly minted coins, which he produced in greater numbers than either of his brothers did. The coinage illustrates how he wished to address himself to his subjects. Otherwise, his reputation comes through the usually negative interpretations of others. Whatever the challenges he faced on the ground in the form of competing claims to the legitimate rule of Judea, his sea power—owing to his father's construction of Caesarea Maritima— could not be denied. His coins sometimes flaunt an anchor and even a war galley as symbols of maritime preeminence, with a double cornucopia or wreath on the other side, advertisements of fertility. In this way, Archelaus promised prosperity, identifying himself as "ethnarch" and "Herod Archelaus" rather than by his own name alone. Both Archelaus and Antipas cloaked themselves with their father's name on their coinage, arrogating to themselves both the legitimacy that Herod the Great had established and the fear that he inspired, besides bequeathing to generations after them an invitation to confuse the father with one son or another.[36] Archelaus's intention was to shroud himself securely in Herod's shadow until he could emerge from it as Judea's new king. Toward the end of a decade in power, he minted new coins, and they reflect the final element of his stratagem to hold onto and even extend his power. In allusions to coins of his father and even Maccabean symbols, he advertises himself as "ethnarch" in association with a helmet and depicts a grape cluster, symbolizing one of the doors of the temple in Jerusalem.[37]

By announcing himself as protector of the temple, Archelaus also assumed the role of appointing the high priest. He turned that appointment into a source of revenue for his increasingly expensive program of retaining power and thereby alienated many of the priests and temple loyalists whose favor he sought to gain. Just as Archelaus took his father's name, he adopted many of his tactics, including the use of marriage as a means of legitimation. His bride was Glaphyra, a princess from Cappadocia and the widow of his brother Alexander, the son of Mariamme—murdered by Herod—who the imposter had claimed to be. As long as they lived, Alexander and his brother Aristobulus represented Herod's effort to produce a Maccabean line within his dynasty, so that by this marriage, Archelaus associated himself with Hellenistic aristocracy as well as the memory of his nation's priestly glory. By marrying the widow of the actual Alexander, Archelaus also further discredited the campaign of the false Alexander. At the same time, however, he broke the law of Moses by marrying the widow of his brother so that the marriage became another occasion for pious opinion to object to Archelaus.[38] He would not be the last Herodian to breach the Torah in an imitation of Hellenistic mores of marriage, but he did so with uniquely bad timing in respect to antagonizing Sadducees who already preferred direct rule from Rome and Pharisees who had opposed the family from the time of Herod the Great.

Fragile though Archelaus's hold on power proved, his taste for the projection of power never waned. From the perspective of his subjects, Archelaus's return from Rome was a magnificent—if brutal—triumph. He even built a city named after him to mark his achievement. Nearly thirty years later, Jesus passed by this city—Archelaïs—as he made his way to Jerusalem and told the parable of a nobleman who went away to receive a kingdom and on his return dealt harshly with rebellious subjects, who had even sent a delegation of protest after him (Luke 19:11–27), an echo of the controversy that Archelaus faced in Rome.[39] Until the time of Jesus, the violence of Herod's son was legendary, and this parable (which is Luke's equivalent of the parable of the talents in Matthew's

Gospel, a later version of the story; see Matt 25:14–30) evokes remembrance of Archelaus's brutality. The entire period of transition, from Herod the Great's last maniacal years to Archelaus's determined projection of power, was a mine for images and metaphors of misspent sovereignty. Jesus and teachers in Jesus's movement were all too aware of the costs that Herodian arrogance inflicted on its subjects. By their time, the actual name of the ruler no longer mattered (and is not mentioned in this parable), but the pattern of a ruler consolidating his power abroad and then wielding it without pity at home was vividly remembered.

Even Augustus, who wielded power in multiple forms, whether military or diplomatic, without remorse wearied of Archelaus's profligate recourse to violence and expenditure in his campaign of self-aggrandizement. The emperor began to avoid direct communication and instead sent messages from Rome to the ethnarch by means of an emissary. Archelaus's profession to be the ruler of his people (his *ethnos*) rang increasingly hollow as formal complaints came to Rome from both Judean and Samaritan leaders.[40] Even after their experience of Varus's authorized barbarism, sealed by the mass crucifixions that characterized Rome's policy of state terror, they appealed to Caesar against what they called the savage tyranny of Archelaus. Whereas Varus had been cruel but selective, Archelaus was indiscriminate in the cruelty of his attempt to project power. In what amounted to a local program of outright genocide, Archelaus used his authority to seize ancestral sources of water near Jericho in order to expand his palace and his plantation of date palms, exposing displaced peoples to homelessness and starvation.[41] Entire villages were destroyed in a broad-spectrum campaign of violent repression of any royal or messianic pretension. Archelaus could brook no further pretenders to the throne he coveted. This is the brutality, detested in both Rome and Judea, that has marked the Gospel according to Matthew.

Uniquely among the Gospels, Matthew describes the destruction of the village of Bethlehem in Judea and the killing of its children (Matt 2:16–18). Although Matthew attributes this crime to Herod the Great,[42] it instances the tendency to random violence, insecurity, and the concern with messianic pretenders in particular that are characteristic more of Archelaus than of his father. Herod was cruel and often paranoid (especially concerning his own family), but he had a supreme confidence about his royal title that Archelaus could only envy. And unlike his father, the would-be king never showed the care for his people that should have been central to his purpose within his imperial charge as ethnarch. Archelaus's recourse to violence was more reflexive than it was a calculated reaction to particular persons or groups. He was less vindictive than Herod the Great but attempted to assert strength by means of force whether or not the occasion called for that response.[43] Where most of the Herodian family were politicians possessed of keen social intelligence, Archelaus was a limited ruler who never grew beyond imitating Herod the Great's behavior at the end of his life.

The Gospel according to Matthew unequivocally places Jesus's birth in the time before Herod the Great's death (Matt 2:13–23) and prior to the accession of Archelaus (Matt 2:22). Luke's Gospel disagrees, placing the event a decade later. Luke makes Jesus's birth coincide with the Roman intervention that ended Archelaus's tenure in a census under the Roman governor Quirinius that provoked a rebellion (see Luke 2:1–7 with Josephus, *Antiquities* 18 §§ 1–10). Both Matthew and Luke cannot be correct in their chronologies, and Luke's is far more plausible. The difference between Matthew and Luke in regard to the time of Jesus's birth typifies inconsistencies that often appear in biblical accounts. The hypothesis or presupposition that the Gospels are directly historical writings is disconfirmed by such cases. Matthew and Luke cannot both be accurate in their timing of Jesus's birth. Luke seems correct in placing it prior to 6 CE rather than prior to 4 BCE, as does Matthew.

The leading concern of Matthew's narrative at this point is not to locate events historically or chronologically but to correlate the narrative with citations of the prophets. As in the case of all the Gospels, Matthew is not the product of a single author; rather, an editor combines several sources. One of them, which streams through the Gospel, cites formulaic quotations of Scripture, which it says have been fulfilled by the events concerning Jesus. The purpose of this source is to explain Jesus's significance in terms of the treasury of the Bible of Israel.[44]

In the case of Jesus's birth, which is not reported in Mark or John, events are deduced from Scripture in Matthew rather than from historical memory. As a result, implausible claims are sometimes made. For example, Matthew has Jesus and his parents receive lavish gifts from eastern magi (2:1–12), amounting to a value that would have sustained a family in a prosperous lifestyle for several decades. This portrayal presents the imagery of Isaiah 60:1, 5–6 as fulfilled during the nativity, but it contradicts the fact that the family was well known to have been far from wealthy. Within the story of the magi, it is interesting that the perspective from which the "star" is described lies east of the Jordan River, a likely allusion to the geographical origin of the literary source within Matthew.[45]

The family of Jesus also travels back and forth to Egypt (Matt 2:13–23), as if that were a readily effected journey. That voyage is said to fulfill Hosea 11:1, where the term "son" is used, but that is actually a reference to the people of Israel coming out of Egypt. Plausibility is strained so much that it is doubtful whether the references are made to narrate actual happenings at all; connection with Scripture is the real motive. Nonetheless, Matthew cites the news that Archelaus ruled over Judea as the reason that Joseph settled with his family in Galilee.

Similarly, Matthew complemented the bare memory of a slaughter with a citation of Scripture; by the time this part of Matthew was composed, it was more important to relate events to the book of Jeremiah (31:15) than to detail the events themselves (Matt 2:16b–18): "He delegated, and murdered all the boy children in Bethlehem and in all its regions, from two years old and under, according to the period that he had established from the magi. Then what was said through the prophet Jeremiah was fulfilled, 'A voice is heard in Ramah, weeping and great lamentation: Rachel weeping for her children, and she will not be comforted, because they are not.'" The traditions of Jesus's birth during the census in Luke and Matthew's story of the slaughter of the holy innocents authentically reflect the turmoil of the period between 4 BCE and 6 CE, but they also articulate particular theological themes that can be understood only in the context of the time and circumstances when the narratives emerged decades after the events they relate.

Archelaus's predations were wide ranging, egregious, and ultimately contrary to the interests of Rome. Precise connections between
his actions and the narrative of the slaughter of the innocents in Matthew
cannot be drawn, both because Matthew is more scripturally reflexive
than it is historical[46] and because Archelaus's excesses by the end of his
reign were disproportionate to the point that their full breadth surpassed
even Josephus's delight in recounting them.

The End of Archelaus and
the Sadducees' Opportunity

FROM HIS BEGINNINGS as a willing, ambitious, but equivocal prince,
Archelaus emerged as a petty tyrant whose behavior brought Roman
rule into disrepute among the peoples of Judea. A limited capacity to
adapt to new circumstances sapped his effectiveness and made him turn
to brutality as a policy of the state, but he also confronted powerful
forces of resistance, not only among his people, but also within his family. Yet political misfortune and incompetence of this scale, even coupled
with tyrannical excesses, might not have been enough to see the ethnarch out of power; Archelaus was neither the first example of ineptitude
nor the worst that came to Augustus's notice. But Archelaus stirred the
rising tide of rebellion in a way that suggested Rome needed to govern
Judea directly. This need seemed all the more pressing within the wider
strategy of imperial rule.

Augustus faced military exigencies on several fronts; in concert
with an increasingly influential general named Tiberius (who would
eventually rule as emperor), he determined that Varus needed to be
redeployed far to the north of the empire, to Germania. Tiberius himself could then see to another rebellion nearer to Rome, in Illyricum.
But Varus had been key to restoring Roman preeminence within the
chaos that Archelaus had produced in Judea, so now it was not clear that
Augustus could afford to move him from the scene in Syria, the Roman
base of operations in the Middle East. As long as Judea was in question,
Varus was the obvious choice of commander to intervene rapidly and
decisively in the event of further turmoil. Judea needed pacification if
Varus was to be redeployed to Germania.

Events in Germania and Illyricum, then, pressed Augustus to impose a military solution on Judea. The territory would be ruled directly from Rome. If matters could be settled there, Varus would be available for deployment elsewhere. "Judea" at this stage included Samaria and Idumea; by intervening there, Augustus would still leave Galilee (with Perea) in Antipas's hands and Gaulanitis under Philip's control. Some remnant of loyalty to Herod the Great would be preserved. Dividing Herod's old kingdom should also divide any opposition there, leaving the most violent rebels for the Roman army to deal with in Judea while Antipas and Philip kept their respective regions in order.

Archelaus was summoned to appear before the emperor, and—although Augustus gave him the courtesy of a hearing[47]—his removal from power was a foregone conclusion. He was banished to Gaul in the west, and the wealth he had pillaged was seized along with the estates he had inherited from his father. Rome put all Judea under the control of an administrative officer, a "prefect" (later called a procurator) directly responsible to the legate in Syria. The heartland of Herodian power was now in effect a Roman military colony.

The first prefect was named Coponius; he acted under the new legate of Syria, Quirinius. As Augustus had anticipated when he confirmed Herod's will, by taking direct control, Rome became the focus of opposition in Judea. When plans for a census were put in place by Quirinius, the consequence was a tax revolt. During this period, a census did not require a household-by-household accounting, but assessments were made by professional publicans contracted by Rome to collect the tax. Together with local officials, publicans assessed the global payments of towns and regions and collected a commission.[48] In addition to the perennial objections to paying taxes, resistance in Judea appropriated the biblical imperative against census taking as a motivation[49] and forwarded the ideology that only God could be regarded as the true ruler of Israel.[50]

While Rome ruled through a surrogate such as Herod the Great (Idumean by descent but nonetheless a Jew), the brutal reality of its intervention from across the sea was somewhat blunted. And in any case, Rome in the person of Pompey had first marched into Jerusalem after two Maccabean brothers, Hyrcanus and Aristobulus, had bribed him to resolve their dispute with one another. Census arrangements from that time had been a semihostile takeover, but one that the Judean leadership had prompted. In 6 CE, however, the overt hostility of the takeover and of the resulting census had become patent with the elimination of client kingship in Judea.

Rome was firmly ensconced in power, but now a fresh and recalcitrant variant of Judaism had emerged, which Josephus attributed to a new kind of revolutionary: Judas the Galilean[51] and his Pharisaic supporter, Zadok. Had Augustus foreseen the reaction that direct rule would produce, he would perhaps have relented in his attitude toward Antipas after he had deposed Archelaus so as to grant the younger brother his father's territory and even his title.

Josephus divides all of Judaism into four schools or philosophies. The first three (the Essenes, the Pharisees, and the Sadducees) had long existed; the fourth philosophy responded to direct Roman rule over Judea and became a revolutionary movement that would twice take the whole region into war with Rome over the next century and a half (in 66 CE and once again in 132 CE).

Josephus calls those associated with the high priestly aristocrats Sadducees; they were named after the legitimate line of succession from Zadok designated by the prophet Ezekiel. Their priority was the correct functioning of the temple, whose sacrificial system enabled Israel to live in covenant with God. The Pharisees, on the other hand, believed that the purity that made each Israelite fit to enter the temple should be practiced by the people as a whole, and their teaching of how to maintain the pure state God desired radiated from Jerusalem as far as to many parts of the Diaspora. The Essenes, some of whom lived near the Dead Sea at Qumran, insisted by means of their interpretation of the Bible and their claim of fellowship with angels that apocalyptic change in the temple and its personnel was required for God to join his people and defeat the "children of darkness" who opposed the "children of light."

With Judas the Galilean and Zadok the Pharisee, a new school appeared, according to Josephus: the "Fourth Philosophy." This new school wanted to supplant the kingdom of Caesar with the kingdom of

God. With the strategic help of the Sadducees, who sought to reinforce the status quo in the temple, Rome had succeeded in imposing direct rule and would collect its tax, but the ideology of God's kingdom, once articulated, sustained a more successful resistance than the revolutionary leaders—such as Judas (the son of Hezekiah), the false Alexander, Simon, and Anthronges—whose claims to power were royal and personal rather than national and divine.

The ideological resonance of this resistance best accounts for why the census is well remembered in the New Testament. Luke's Gospel coordinates that event in 6 CE with the year of Jesus's birth (Luke 2:1–5), although Jesus seems to have been born four years before that. Acts also echoes a memory of the revolt under Judas the Galilean (Acts 5:37). The New Testament in this way endorses the view that Rome's decision to exert direct rule from Syria in the governance of Judea, Samaria, and Idumea produced a profound dislocation. The heart of the Herodian kingdom had been removed.

Augustus's removal of Archelaus could easily have complemented a decision to displace Antipas and Philip as well. But the other sons of Herod fared much better than Archelaus, to some extent because Augustus was dealing with imperial border issues on three continents (Europe, Africa, and Asia) and was in no position to stretch his forces any further than necessary in the province of Syria.

Later events confirmed Augustus's concern about his overextended forces. A decade after his victory for Rome in Judea, Varus—though one of the most talented generals of his time—walked his legions into an ambush in the Teutoburg Forest and committed suicide as he watched his three entire legions routed and slaughtered by the allied Germanic forces. Tacitus claims that soldiers who were taken captive were sacrificed and cooked for ritual purposes.[52] Augustus had every reason not to thin his military lines by expanding the front of direct rule as long as Philip and Antipas proved competent and cooperative. Fortunately for him, they did so for several decades.

Philip remains a shadowy figure, although he struck contemporaries as a responsible and diligent ruler.[53] A meticulous magistrate, he was willing to travel through his territory in order to dispense justice with

Solomonic attention, but he also embraced his Roman identity. Unlike his brothers, Philip minted coins in a way that took no account of the Judaic aversion to reproducing the human image. His own head featured on the reverse of his coins, identifying him as Philip the Tetrarch. Archelaus and Antipas took the name Herod as a proud title, but Philip dealt cautiously with the association. His self-confident and personal assertion of authority came along with public association with the emperor, who appears on the face of the coin, complete with his image and the legend in Greek, "Caesar Augustus."[54] The prudent praise of the emperor on whom he was dependent eventually prompted Philip to replace his own image with that of a temple dedicated to Augustus in his principal city. He curated that shrine personally, which was an obvious case of idolatry from the perspective of the Torah, indeed to the point that Philip's Judaism was little more than an ethnic reminiscence.

Philip's unusual policy, compared to that of his brothers, corresponded to the demographics of his territory, to the north of historic Israel and predominantly gentile. But Philip played his imperial politics with abandon, although the goal of his posture was conservative in a classic sense: the consolidation of power. The temple to the emperor, known as an Augusteum, became the center of Philip's realm. Built by Herod the Great on a site traditionally known as Paneion (after the god Pan), the temple was near the source of the waters flowing into the Sea of Galilee and the Jordan River. In the course of extending the city, Philip conducted surveys to specify the source of the fertility of the region, pursued a program of building, and styled himself as the founder of "Caesarea Philippi."[55] At the same time, the prosperity and security he maintained kept Parthian incursions, open or covert, to such a low level that Philip vindicated the imperial preference for client rulers at this stage of Rome's confrontation with its eastern rival.

Philip's methodical competence in governing, combined with his shameless flattery of Augustus, made him a formidable competitor for Antipas. While Archelaus's dismissal encouraged Antipas's ambition and even offered him the prospect that he might one day take the diadem of kingship, immediately Antipas needed to consolidate his position in relation to Philip and above all as concerned the "Fourth

Philosophy" militants who had gained a foothold in his territory under Judas the Galilean. Antipas's parlous situation, together with his ambition, typified the Herodians' difficulties in the wake of Archelaus's failure. The Sadducees, on the other hand, had at last entered into league with the Romans so as to assume control of the temple, complete with their own police, who kept order during the course of sacrifice. From a Herodian point of view, they had emerged as potential competitors—priestly but non-Maccabean—who pursued the prospect of dominance among the factions of Judaism that vied with one another to reach a modus vivendi within the Roman Empire.

ANTIPAS, HERODIAS, AND PHILIP

JOHN THE BAPTIST AND JESUS
UNDER HERODIAN AMBITION

*No Herodian pursued advancement toward the dynastic end
more persistently than Antipas. Disappointed in his attempt
to be named king of Judea in a hearing before Augustus to
adjudicate Herod the Great's will and again after Archelaus
was deposed, Antipas contented himself with shoring up
his position as tetrarch of Galilee and Perea. With stolid
effectiveness, he rebuilt Sepphoris after the rebel occupation
by Judas the Galilean and made a marriage alliance with the
king of Nabataea. After Augustus's death and the accession
of Tiberius, Antipas's ambition burned anew. He married
Herodias, daughter of Herod's son Aristobulus and therefore a
Maccabean heiress. She was already married to Antipas's brother
Philip, and the union was criticized by John the Baptist. Just
as Antipas eliminated John in Machaerus, he sought to dispose
of John's disciple Jesus in Galilee. He only achieved that aim in
Jerusalem, however, with a strategic alliance with the prefect
of Jerusalem, Pontius Pilate. With John and Jesus dealt with
and his brother Philip dead, Antipas seemed secure in his reach
for the royal title, provided the aging Tiberius would reward
decades of loyal service yoked with smoldering ambition.*
Antipas: *Ambitious, cautious, focused in his violence*

Salvaging the Dynasty: Antipas and Philip

ANTIPAS WAS LEFT with the wreckage of Galilee and Perea when he assumed power again as tetrarch. His own aspirations to assume the royal status of his father had been crushed, first by the appointment of Archelaus in his stead and then—after Archelaus's rule came to grief—by Rome's assumption of direct rule over Judea. In addition, the revolt of Judas the Galilean, followed by his taking Sepphoris, brought the destruction of that Herodian garrison by a contingent commanded by the son of the Roman general Varus.[1] Antipas began his tenure in a weakened position militarily.

The rebuilding of Sepphoris was Antipas's first priority, so it might serve as his administrative center. He erected a three-thousand-seat theater, a colonnaded street that imitated the downtown of a Greco-Roman city in miniature, and a comfortable palace. He turned the town into a fortress—with adequate provision for brothels, baths, and circuses to entertain soldiers—and gave it the imposing new name of Autocratoris to honor the Romans with the Greek equivalent of the Latin word for "emperor."[2] It was no Caesarea Maritima (nor even a Caesarea Philippi, which emerged as the ornament of Philip's rule), but it was a sign of fealty to Rome and command over Galilean territory—the two conditions sine qua non of ruling as an imperial client over Roman lands. Antipas also fortified a city in Perea and renamed it "Livias" in honor of Augustus's wife, Livia,[3] but the result was unimpressive. In any case, Augustus never looked with complete favor on Antipas, perhaps under the influence of a comparison with Herod the Great and the memory of Antipas's subversion of Archelaus's standing in Rome during the dispute in regard to Herod's will. The death of Augustus in 14 CE cannot have come as any blow to the morale of Antipas; his actions show that his royal ambition had not been extinguished, and it flourished under Augustus's successor.

Antipas pursued a pragmatic strategy of political survival and military readiness, but in the field of public building, he suffered in comparison to Philip. His brother's heterogeneous subjects appreciated his willingness to build in honor not only of the emperor and his family but also of non-Israelite gods, most prominently in the city Panias. Traditionally named in honor of the god Pan, Philip dubbed it "Caesarea Philippi," and the site served a host of cults for centuries to come.[4] Given the Judaic demographic in Galilee and the concomitant imperative not to inflame militant nationalism, Antipas was, in contrast, constrained to use imagery even on his coins that paid homage to Judaism without transgressing the Torah.

While Philip was willing to mint his own profile on coins, palms appear on Antipas's coins instead of human images, sometimes with seven branches in order to evoke the menorah in the Jerusalem Temple without actually picturing it.[5] Antipas billed himself as "Herod," like Archelaus and unlike Philip, although he wisely qualified the claim by calling himself "Tetrarch Herod" to avoid even an implicit assertion of kingship. In the early years of his rule, Antipas issued relatively few coins, and it is notable that the Herodian dynasty as a whole relied on older currency, some of it in circulation since the time of the Maccabees, for large transactions and minted only coins of lower value. Galilee remained an agricultural region for the whole of Antipas's tenure; urbanization did not yet demand routine exchanges in currency within many farming enclaves.

Over the course of their tenures, Antipas and Philip used their coins to acknowledge the emperor. The inscriptions deployed by both Philip and Antipas underscore a political reality that the Herodians generally had to reckon with when it came to ruling Galilee and (when they could) Judea. Their power depended on the emperor, and their ability to remain as rulers depended on their capacity to reconcile the Judaism of their heritage (contentious though that was by virtue of their Idumean background and their absorption of Roman culture), the pressure exerted by their subjects' various demands, and the imperial appetite for obeisance. Between them, Antipas and Philip had inherited the divided house of Herod but without any assurance that they would offer their descendants any lasting legacy besides political extinction.

Philip played to the advantage of not having to please a Judaic majority among his subjects. He branded himself successfully in the trappings of Hellenistic culture by associating himself closely with the emperor (whose image as well as his own he minted on coins)[6] and by relying on trade to finance his signature urban projects. Despite Philip's lower tax revenue (one hundred talents a year to Antipas's two hundred talents),[7] he could build more extravagantly because domestic levies were applied to the use of buildings once they were constructed; increased infrastructure generated commercial activity and increased levies, which could finance more infrastructure.

Leveraging of this kind had been part of the secret of the success of Herod the Great and allowed Philip's cities to exert an influence far beyond what a garrison town such as Antipas's Sepphoris could produce. Bethsaida on the Sea of Galilee, also called the Sea of Tiberias in the New Testament,[8] became a major center of fishing that largely dominated local trade; Philip cleverly renamed it Bethsaida Julia in honor of Augustus's wife and Tiberius's mother.[9] Its mixed population included Jews, a few of whom became followers of Jesus: Philip and two brothers named Simon (later called "Rock" by his rabbi, *Kêpha'* in Aramaic or *Petros* in Greek) and Andrew (John 1:44). Life in Bethsaida brought exposure to the Greek language (unlike, say, Aramaic-speaking Nazareth); the disciple Philip is identified as a Greek speaker later in John's Gospel (12:20, 21). The presence of natives of Bethsaida in Jesus's entourage attests to their mobility as a result of the fishing trade as well as the influence that they could consequently exert beyond their local setting. They also sowed the seeds of a transition from Aramaic to Greek in Jesus's movement, although decades would be required to make that change definitive.

Trade brought Hellenistic language and culture as well as profit and extended the tetrarch Philip's prestige to an extent that can only have galled the ambitious Antipas. Philip's policy from the outset—of foregrounding what Jewish sensibilities condemned as idolatry in order to align himself with Rome—made him an unlikely candidate to rule Judea and Jerusalem. The demographics of Gaulanitis, a predominantly gentile region, would have made it difficult for any Jewish ruler to govern in a manner consistent with the Torah. This problem had, after all, bedeviled Herod the Great as well, and the lower proportion of Jews among Philip's subjects reduced the likelihood of his being seen as a plausible Jewish king. Beyond the gentile influence of the constituency he administered, Philip himself took a Roman pride in his rule, calling himself the founder of cities he had really only renovated and announcing himself by his own name, Philip (itself an echo of the father of Alexander the Great), rather than as a Herod. He seemed determined to set himself up as a Hellenistic client of Rome whose Judaism was incidental. His pride in the use of his own name also intimates that he thought of himself as incidentally Herodian as well. His education in Rome seems to have shaped his character and values. Ambition for ruling Judea proper did not animate Philip's actions, but it did obsess Antipas.

Although quite successful as a modest client of Rome, Philip did not share the Maccabean aspiration to control Judea from its center in Jerusalem. His appeal for Rome's imperial jurisdiction was strictly as a competent client ruler and a residual practitioner of Judaism. His association with the temple of Augustus in Caesarea Philippi (as he proudly called the city of Panias), together with his minting of coinage that displayed imperial images and his own name, made him less appropriate than Antipas to accede to power in Judea proper, even though Antipas himself pushed at the boundaries of what could be accepted at that time by Jewish public opinion.

Antipas, however, utilized to his own advantage the fact that he had greater military responsibilities than his brother did. His territory included both Galilee and Perea (formerly the tetrarchy of Pheroras[10]), the latter of which served as a buffer between Philip's territory and Nabataea. Although that protected Philip, giving him scope for his development of the regional economy, Antipas used his position to develop relations with Nabataea. He already had possession of Machaerus, Herod the Great's fortress east of the Dead Sea, so that a vigorous defense of Perea was already provided with infrastructure, without the destruction caused to Sepphoris by the onslaughts of Varus and Judas the Galilean in Galilee. Strategically, this gave Antipas a distinct advantage.

In addition to forces on the ground, when it came to Perea, Antipas also enjoyed new politics that were in the air following Rome's fresh assertion of control in the area. When the Roman general Varus marched his armies into Judea against the outbreaks of revolt that followed Herod's death, he had found an unlikely ally in Aretas IV, the Nabataean king. Previously, Aretas had been at odds with Herod the Great, and he saw in cooperation with the Romans an opportunity both to ingratiate himself with the growing power that was making the lands bordering on the Mediterranean its own and to vitiate whatever Herodian succession might emerge. Accordingly, Aretas put both infantry and cavalry at Varus's disposal.[11]

Once confirmed as tetrarch of Galilee and Perea, then, Antipas had to deal with Nabataea, not as a hostile power, but as a common friend of the Romans. Especially since he had lost in his bid to succeed his father in Judea both at the time Herod's will was confirmed and after Archelaus was removed, he needed to shore up the inheritance that he was able to claim. The tried and true method of sealing alliance was by marriage, and Antipas married Aretas's daughter.[12] With the marital link with the Nabataeans, his command of the military fortress of Machaerus in Perea, and his rebuilding of Sepphoris in Galilee, Antipas made himself tactically useful to the Romans. Augustus never apparently liked him, but his utility was undeniable.

Until the death of Augustus in 14 CE, Antipas pursued his policy of military readiness, efficiency in administration, and alliance with Nabataea. Relative to the recent chaos produced by Archelaus, his achievement of stability was impressive, and Rome had no reason to remove him. One reason for his success was that he was able to assuage his subjects, predominantly practitioners of Judaism, with an appearance of continuity with the more philo-Judaic policies of Herod the Great. In the matter of coinage, he continued to use species issued by his father, and when he eventually struck new coins, he privileged well-worn motifs, chiefly palm fronds and wreaths, that were not considered idolatrous.

Antipas's Tiberian Breakout

THE ACCESSION OF Tiberius, however, who had been adopted by Augustus and yet developed a fraught relationship with the dying emperor that made his rise a sweet success, opened new possibilities for Antipas. His aim since he came into adulthood had been to succeed his father as king of the unified lands of Judea, including Idumea, Samaria, Galilee, Perea, and Gaulanitis. Appeasing his subjects was a necessary but not sufficient condition to achieve that aim. He also cultivated contacts and friendships with members of the imperial court and undertook the support of shrines outside Israel that, from the point of view of Judaism, were idolatrous. An inscription from the Greek island of Delos shows that Antipas became a benefactor of the temple to Apollo there, far away from his Judaic territory.[13] Although he had founded a city in honor of Tiberius's mother, his leading project was the establishment of the city of Tiberias, in honor of the emperor himself.[14] The foundation represented a challenge to Judaic sensibilities and marks Antipas's entry into a new and blatant campaign for imperial favor and inheritance of his father's title and realm.

Clearly, Augustus had not been prepared to accept Antipas as a replacement for his father. Antipas had tried and failed after Herod's death to dispute the claim of Archelaus, take the title of "king," and rule Judea. He had also failed to co-opt that prize after Archelaus had proven a disaster. But Antipas now angled, as he approached the fifth decade of his life, to receive from Tiberius what Augustus refused to grant him. He had maintained a public face that was consistent with Judaism, even as that policy frayed with his growing flattery of Tiberius. His political equation traded local criticism by his subjects for imperial pleasure in Rome. If balanced, calculated striving was ever to be rewarded, it should have been in his case.

Antipas set about building Tiberias soon after Tiberius's accession and was minting coins from the site, his new capital, by 19 CE. By putting the name Tiberias on this coinage, Antipas honored the emperor and extolled his own creation. In addition to a new palace, the city offered a forum, a theater, an agora, and baths within an already prosperous area by the Sea of Galilee. Magdala, a center for catching and preserving fish with salt, lay a convenient walk nearby, and the surrounding land was fertile, which allowed for the development of a strong commercial infrastructure. More serviceable than splendid, Tiberias was nonetheless a seal of Antipas's competence. The new capital, once finished, was readily protected by the Sea of Galilee on the east; the fortress cities of Machaerus to the southeast and Sepphoris to the northwest completed a ring of protection. The military acumen of the choice of location was as striking as its homage to the new emperor.

A significant obstacle to the success of the city remained, however. The footprint of Tiberias included an old, disused cemetery, which made the area unclean according to the Torah (see Num 19:11–22). Galilee and Judea evidence an intensified concern with purity during this period, shown especially in stone vessels designed for cleansing with water and bathing pools (*miqvaoth*).[15] Antipas pushed through the problem by paying Galileans to come and settle there, offering furnished houses and parcels of land. Eventually, his approach was effective, but it required decades for Tiberias to be considered clean.[16] During the interim, the issue of how to deal with the resulting impurity that emanated from the new city was a matter of controversy, giving occasion to confrontations over the issue of purity, a central category within early Judaism.

Mary from Magdala, for example, is described as suffering from seven demons (Luke 8:2): when seen from a contemporary perspective in Galilee, the statement is as much about the proximity of Magdala to Tiberias and Antipas's willingness to release impurities as it is about Mary's condition.[17] Mary departed northward from her native Magdala and the vicinity of Tiberias to seek exorcism from Jesus in Capernaum and eventually would become one of his disciples. In the cultural wars concerning purity and impurity, Capernaum and the new city of Tiberias emerged as headquarters of opposing forces.

The tetrarch had still other ways to advance his course to the royal title of a reunited Judea. His father's dream had once been to join the Idumean family to the Maccabean dynasty by means of Mariamme I; when he executed her and then her sons, this ambition seemed to be destroyed. But Antipas, an assiduous strategist who kept his eye on his aim, found a thread of hope that the combination of Idumean acumen and Maccabean prestige might yet become possible.

Although Herod the Great had killed both his sons by Mariamme I, their progeny survived.[18] Herod even showed his favor to one such descendant, a granddaughter named Herodias (whose father was Aristobulus), by proposing to marry her off to one of his sons. His reasoning was that the son (also named Herod) was of priestly lineage, being descended from Mariamme II. For a time this son, Herod II, was named as Antipater's successor when Antipater was to inherit the throne. But Mariamme II admitted to a plot to poison Herod the Great, and so Herod II was expunged from the will.[19] In the midst of the intrigues of the court, the course of that marriage can only be inferred, but even when Herod II saw his prospects dashed, Herodias's genealogy, as a Maccabean descendant, remained. So, it turns out, did her ambition.

Near the time of the erection of Tiberias, she and Antipas conceived a plan to revive Herod the Great's project of a combined Idumean and Maccabean dynasty by marrying one another. From the point of view of the Torah, the audacity of their project is evident. Such marriages were within the degrees of relationship prohibited by the Torah,[20] although Herod the Great and his family had already set the precedent for acting more like Romans than like Israelites in that regard. In addition, Herodias was already married, and as a practical matter, Antipas had not only his current wife but also his father-in-law, Aretas IV, the king of Nabataea, to bear in mind. All these tensions could not be resolved positively: Antipas was in the process of breaking some relationships in order to favor others.

Antipas had clearly committed to a change of ideological policy by the time he founded Tiberias. He pursued the erection of his new city in honor of the emperor despite opposition from many of his Jewish subjects; inside the palace, he built for himself, he even installed stone representations of animals, which were widely considered idolatrous.[21] He wanted to honor Tiberius by taking on Roman ways yet also incorporate Maccabean legitimacy within his claim to take the throne of Judea. In coordination with friends in the court in Rome, he made his way to see Tiberius, formally proposing marriage to Herodias on the way there before setting sail.[22] She readily agreed, although she also insisted that Antipas dispense with his current wife, the daughter of Aretas. Herodias knew all too well how much trouble disfavored wives had caused within the court of Herod the Great; she wanted Antipas for herself as much as she wanted him to succeed to the throne of Judea. He would have to spurn a Nabataean princess in order to make a Maccabean his queen.

The timing of the agreement of marriage with his visit to Rome shows that Antipas wished to mimic the Roman practice of marrying a patron's relative. Tiberius himself, as part of Augustus's decision to designate him as his imperial heir, had divorced his wife in order to marry Augustus's sister. In this case, Antipas's new marriage was a signal of his intention to gain the kingship of Judea, which he had long sought, and of his deference to the emperor, who could alone fulfill his desire. While Antipas ingratiated himself with Tiberius as best he could, Herodias curried her contacts within the imperial court, where her brother Agrippa was an on-and-off favorite with Tiberius.[23]

Antipas's decision was a bold move that would inevitably involve him breaking off his relationship with Aretas, and it ran the risk of inflaming popular opinion in Galilee *and* turning Judea against him. There was no mystery about a likely Jewish reaction against the marriage; after all, Archelaus had run afoul of criticism when he married Glaphyra, the wife of a *dead* brother.[24] Antipas is usually credited with more sensitivity to the demands of the Torah than he showed in this case, and it is doubtful he acted out of simple passion. This was a period that demanded political shrewdness to negotiate Rome's attitude toward its Jewish subjects. In addition to the possible advantage in marrying Herodias, Antipas also dealt in Rome with a uniquely sensitive situation in regard to the practice of Judaism. In 19 CE, Tiberius and the Senate, by a *Senatus consultum*, attempted to forbid practices deemed "foreign" under the threat of banishment from Rome, and Jewish practices were evidently in view.[25] In the setting of such cultural bias against Judaism, the arrangement between Antipas and Herodias advertised Antipas's philo-Roman credentials, burnishing his long-standing claim to be his father's worthy successor. So although the marriage involved risks, it was tactically ingenious.

Executing John the Baptist

ALTHOUGH THE AUDACIOUS plan of marriage was brilliant, it suffered from a bungled execution. Before it could be finalized, court intrigue did its work so that Antipas's first wife was alerted. The Nabataean princess had no intention of being sent away in humiliation by her Idumean husband. With Antipas's permission, she made her way as if for pleasure to Machaerus, the elegant fortress in Perea near the border of Nabataea. By arrangement with her father, Aretas, full preparations were made for her to be provided with a cavalcade of transport back to her homeland. Rather than be put away ignominiously, she publicly deserted Antipas, the tetrarch and would-be king. The message was clear: Herod was a poor husband and an inept ruler, lacking both scruples and control over his own wife. Aretas, in any case, needed no convincing that he and Antipas were now at enmity.[26] Nabataean goodwill, like the marriage to Aretas's daughter that sealed the alliance with Nabataea, was collateral damage resulting from the tetrarch's new policies under Tiberius.

In the aftermath of his wife's preemptive departure from Antipas's court and her marriage, the tetrarch also had to face the criticism of John the Baptist. John had emerged as a famous and popular figure, whose practice of immersing people in water in natural sources provided by God—rather than in artificial bathing pools—offered pious Israelites the prospect of being pure and knowing they were pure when they arrived for worship in the temple. John championed a direct application of the Torah without following the particular customs of the priests, the Pharisees, or the Essenes, all of whom pursued different views of the kind of bathing pool that God preferred. John believed that his practice of immersion in the water God provided naturally, together with repentance, would pave the way for a new and transforming advent of God's Spirit.[27]

John the Baptist's intervention came at a moment of extreme sensitivity. The Gospels are clear that Antipas seized John for criticizing his marriage to his brother's wife (Mark 6:18–29; Matt 14:3–12; Luke 3:19–20).[28] An assertion that his marriage was illegitimate amounted to delegitimating Antipas's rule in terms of Judaism, and he did not shrink from striking back against John. Perea was near enough to Judaea (John's usual place of activity) for Antipas to send in troops in order to seize John, and he enjoyed a good working relationship with the Roman prefect of Judea at the time, Valerius Gratus.

Gratus had good reason to give Antipas scope to act within Judea. The prefect himself had taken an active hand in pacifying Judea on behalf of Tiberius;[29] any destabilizing movements against Antipas in Galilee would not serve Rome. And John the Baptist's attack on Antipas was very public and involved the observation that one tetrarch had taken the wife of another tetrarch, Philip.[30] Although in an arranged marriage with Herod II, Herodias had preferred Philip and then Antipas. In the report of Josephus, Antipas acts decisively, conducting John to Machaerus and beheading him there.[31] The location would be entirely suitable given the use to which his Nabataean wife had put the fortress for her successful escape from the humiliation of being divorced. Antipas covered his political tracks by insisting that he acted to prevent an insurrection against Rome, although his real motivation is stated in the Gospels and is evident in any case: he wanted to silence critics definitively and in a way that would frighten those who might join in the criticism.

The Gospels present an unusual account in which a dance by Herodias's daughter[32] during a birthday celebration for Antipas pleases him to the extent that he promises her whatever she might wish. She asks for John's head on a platter (Mark 6:14–29; Matt 14:1–12), and her request is carried out. Given the threat to Antipas's legitimacy represented by John as well as the account in Josephus, it seems unnecessary to suppose that the performance was really necessary. In its telling, the account characterizes Antipas as weak and the women of his household as corrupt in the style of Jezebel.[33] Yet a result of this stylized telling is to suggest a certain hesitancy on Antipas's part; although he is not portrayed as sympathetic, he appears ambivalent. His key fear, that Jesus might be John the Baptist raised from the dead (Mark 6:14; Matt 14:2; Luke 9:7–9), is the occasion of the narrative and reflects a degree of irresolution on his part.

Although the account is stylized, it reflects a conflicted reaction within Antipas's court to the events concerning John. A comparable attitude is also reflected in a later vignette concerning Jesus (Luke 23:6–12, discussed later). A woman who followed Jesus, named Joanna, was the wife of Chuza, one of Antipas's officials (Luke 8:3);[34] later still (well after Jesus's death), someone from Antipas's circle of friends appears among

the "prophets and teachers" of Jesus's followers in Antioch (Acts 13:1–
3). Although Antipas had John killed and later attempted to inflict the
same fate on Jesus, the eclecticism of his court gave an opportunity for
diverse groups within Judaism to find some degree of support there. The
story about Herodias and a daughter who came to be identified with
Salomé provides a window into the ferment within Antipas's regime as
it struggled for royal power and at the same time attempted to find its
way among the varying strains of Judaism represented within its region.

The teacher behind the source of the story of Herodias's daughter
(Joseph Barnabas, a wealthy Levite from Cyprus; see Acts 4:32–37)[35]
argued for an accommodation of Jesus's movement with the house of
Herod (under the much more benign form of Agrippa II, discussed in
chapter 8), and so the story depicts Antipas as a nearly innocent victim
of intrigue within his own court. A trope had emerged by that time
in the literature of Judaism in which gentile rulers, to whom Antipas
was comparable, were especially swayed by women.[36] The source even
refers to Antipas as "king" (Mark 6:14), which was the case only in
his dreams but became a fact for later Herodians. Barnabas's source
incorporated the influences of teachers who were related to courtiers,
such as Joanna, and took sides within Antipas's entourage, in this case
vigorously against Herodias.

No matter how conflicted Antipas might actually have been in
the course of adjusting his conduct to accommodate the teachings of
Judaism, he acted decisively where it concerned the foundation of Tiberias, his marriage to Herodias, and his execution of John. He also acted
with increasing confidence in relation to the imperial court in Rome.
His wife's brother Agrippa had grown up in the city; with his mother's
encouragement, he became friends with Tiberius's son and heir, Drusus,
and shared a tutor with Claudius, the future emperor. With Agrippa's
sister Herodias now married to Antipas, the tetrarch from Galilee could
profit from a further line of connection with the court. In fact, the connection was multiple, because the Herodian proclivity for intermarriage
made Antipas Agrippa's uncle as well as his brother-in-law.

With Drusus as his friend, Agrippa had little to fear, and neither he
nor Drusus was reluctant to show off his position of privilege.[37] Tiberius

had permitted an advisor, named Sejanus, to become too powerful to suit Drusus, and on one occasion, the emperor's son made his displeasure known by punching Sejanus in the face.[38] Agrippa, his natural arrogance buttressed by his imperial friendship, abused his status by running up debts that he could not discharge. Drusus's death in 23 CE[39] changed everything. Disconsolate, the emperor no longer wanted to see his son's friends, an attitude that left Agrippa at the mercy of aggrieved creditors.

Agrippa's vulnerable position presented Antipas and Herodias with an opportunity to prove themselves friends of the imperial court, and they seized on it. His sister Herodias was the point of contact for Agrippa (although he characteristically used his wife as an intermediary), but Antipas was his lifeline.[40] Both to resolve a financial embarrassment that could reflect on the Herodians generally and to perform a service to the imperial court, Antipas gave him an allowance and the position as the market officer in the new agora of Tiberias, a lucrative sinecure, albeit in so relatively insignificant a setting that Agrippa was never satisfied with the appointment.

Keeping Agrippa away from the imperial court in Rome served Antipas's interests well. While Antipas had married into the Maccabean lineage of the family, Agrippa had that lineage in his veins. The grandson of both Herod the Great and Mariamme through Aristobulus, he personally embodied the genealogical ambition of the dynasty, putting him at inevitable odds with Antipas. The tetrarch had cleverly and quietly neutralized a potential rival.

Pontius Pilate, Jesus, and Antipas's Ambitions

ACCESS TO TIBERIUS would in any case have been difficult for Agrippa, even had he remained in Rome, because the emperor began to withdraw from active governance in the city. Always reserved and in some ways insecure except on the field of battle, the emperor relied increasingly on Sejanus, a man of equestrian rank rather than noble birth, who headed up the Praetorian Guard in the city of Rome as its prefect. Indeed, Sejanus made the guard into an instrument of government, not just a security force. Tiberius referred to Sejanus as his "fellow in labors," and Romans began to see statues erected to the honor of the Praetorian prefect; at the height of his power, Sejanus had his name struck on coins to associate himself with Tiberius.[41]

Drusus's death played into Sejanus's hands. In mourning, Tiberius increasingly preferred to live outside of Rome, and the emperor departed for Capri in 26 CE. The historian Suetonius depicts the purpose of this departure as the pursuit of sexual experiments of epic proportions;[42] whatever the motivation, the impact on Judea was immediate, because in the same year, Pontius Pilate became the prefect of Judea. Antipas suffered the consequences, but they were nothing as compared to those borne by the city of Jerusalem.

Pilate was Sejanus's man, and he understood his task as involving the visible assertion of Rome's prerogatives in Jerusalem. Roman anti-Semitism, despite the legality of Judaism, was fashionable; from the time of Cicero, Jews had been attacked for their alleged laziness (in refusing to work on the last day of the week), strange diet, and refusal to acknowledge the gods of Rome.[43] Pilate, however, took prejudice beyond routine Roman convention. Once ensconced in his palace at Caesarea Maritima, the Roman headquarters, he ordered the garrison stationed at the Antonia fortress in Jerusalem to set up their shields in sight of the temple and the Herodian palace adjacent to it, complete with Caesar's emblem.

Pilate's gesture implicitly interrupted the long-standing agreement between Rome and the Maccabees for mutual recognition and support and openly violated the arrangement in the temple established under Herod the Great and Augustus that gave Israel's sanctuary autonomy under the emperor's aegis with acceptance of the sacrifices that his financial cooperation provided. Pilate's installation of the shields announced Roman subjugation, rather than protection, of the temple.[44] Popular opposition was immediate, and Pilate faced a large gathering of leaders who protested the move at Pilate's headquarters in Caesarea. They welcomed death at the hands of the Roman soldiers who guarded the meeting rather than accede to the presence of anything idolatrous within the environs of the temple.

But the most effective opposition to Pilate's outrage came from the descendants of Herod the Great, Antipas at their head, who objected on the grounds of both the settlement in the temple and the integrity of their ancestral palace in Jerusalem. They argued with Pilate himself in Caesarea and then wrote directly to Tiberius in Rome. They insisted that the action would provoke revolution, and to no purpose, since "dishonor of ancient laws is not an honor for the emperor," as a contemporary, Philo of Alexandria, explained the argument.[45]

Despite the formidable influence of Sejanus, this intervention succeeded, and a letter from Tiberius—who in any case was more reserved about receiving divine honors than some other emperors—ordered Pilate to remove the standards from Jerusalem and to mount them in the shrine to Augustus in Caesarea Maritima. The imperial command represented a sensible compromise that maintained Rome's agreement concerning the temple and its alliance with Judea while allowing for an imperial flourish in a location where it would be welcomed. Despite the emperor's reversal of Pilate's order, Sejanus was able to maintain his protégé in his role, and the prefect of Judea needed only to bide his time before undertaking a similar act in the future. He proved as persistent in antagonizing Jews as his protector in Rome and was the first prefect of Judea to introduce coinage with ritual objects of Roman worship.[46]

Antipas, however, had marked a coup and could reasonably hope that at the close of Pilate's tenure, he might after all accede to control of his father's principal territory. But he also appreciated that he needed to keep his Herodian relatives as well as his Roman colleagues under watch. His brother Philip, a placid ruler as far as Judea was concerned, posed no particular threat, even though he had good incentive to seek revenge, but Agrippa was unscrupulous and needed to be watched. Pilate remained, and Sejanus had by no means been dislodged, so Antipas had to content himself with demonstrating mastery of his own domain against the day when Tiberius would recognize his fitness to reign as his father before him had.

By the time Antipas had returned to Galilee after the incident of the shields, Jesus of Nazareth resided in Capernaum with a growing number of disciples and an established reputation as a rabbi. As he came into his own as a teacher in his own right, he also developed a sardonic way of referring to Antipas and his pretensions to power. Like Antipas's nephew Agrippa, Jesus was not impressed by the new city Tiberias or by much else that the ambitious tetrarch did.

Rabbi Jesus never forgot his mentor, John the Baptist, and loved to contrast him with Antipas, John's executioner. Recalling what had brought people to seek out John's purity, Jesus asked rhetorically (Luke 7:24–28),

> *What did you go out into the wilderness to observe? Reed*
> *shaken by wind? But what did you go out to see? A man*
> *attired in soft garments? Look: those among the royals subsist in*
> *splendid apparel and luxury! But what did you go out to see? A*
> *prophet? Yes, I say to you, and more than a prophet. This is he*
> *concerning whom it is written, Look: I delegate my messenger*
> *before your face, who will prepare your way before you. I say to*
> *you, no one among those born of women is greater than John!*
> *But the least in the kingdom of God is greater than he!*

At every turn, this concentrated antiphony of praise and insult targets Antipas.

The tetrarch was proud to associate his new city of Tiberias with the image on his coins of what appears to be a reed.[47] To this day, experts in the field of numismatics identify the image as such, although it is also possible that the intent was to represent a palm. The whole Herodian family minted many different designs of coins during their century and half of power, but they were of lower amounts than Roman and Maccabean currency that also circulated, and the quality of work was inferior. Whether Antipas's coin represented a reed or a reed trying to look like a palm, the opportunity for caustic humor at its expense was latent.

For Jesus, all Antipas's affectations could be blown away as a reed; all it would take was a decent wind. The architecture of Tiberias was as pretentious as Antipas's clothing, and all those trappings of power would be swept away with the coming of God's kingdom. During his period in Capernaum, Rabbi Jesus flourished, and his willingness to call out what he saw as the illegitimacy of Antipas's regime sears through the desire of later tendencies in the Gospels to portray Jesus as an otherworldly teacher, unconcerned with the politics of his time. The "reed shaken by wind," the reference to the pretension of royal apparel, and the comparison with John the Baptist disclose Antipas as the target of Jesus's criticism. The saying itself comes from one of the earliest sources within the Gospels, a collection of sayings amounting to Jesus's Mishnah (conventionally known as "Q,"[48] after the German word for "source," *Quelle*, while the term *Mishnah* means "repetition") and compiled after Jesus's death around the year 35 CE.

This saying is by no means the only instance of Rabbi Jesus directly making reference to Antipas the tetrarch in order to criticize him. Together with Jesus's sayings, another early source (reflecting Barnabas's interest in issues of purity) provides Jesus's prophetic explanation of his own deeds. In it, Jesus provides the meaning of his giving bread to crowds in the wilderness by saying, "Watch out for the yeast of the Pharisees and the yeast of Herod" (Mark 8:15).[49] To Jesus, Antipas and the Pharisees are alike in their false direction of God's people; in his analysis, the tetrarch was a vehicle of impurity, while the Pharisees' attempt to maintain cleanness excluded too many Israelites. Like yeast permeates bread, both distortions could only corrupt the whole people with their false character.

Like his teacher John the Baptist, Rabbi Jesus believed that Israel, the people of God, could only fulfill their destiny if they understood how to maintain a stable, pure relationship with their God. Where John's preferred method involved immersion in water with repentance, Jesus practiced meals of fellowship, in which forgiveness was offered and accepted and God's presence celebrated. Because he extended these meals to those whom the Pharisees considered impure, including tax agents and others deemed to be sinners, he had a long and well-known contention with them. But Jesus also insisted that this celebration of purity was under the growing power of God's kingdom, so he constitutionally opposed Antipas's agency of Rome.

Jesus's awareness of Antipas's desire to fulfill the Herodian ambition of a combined Roman and Judean state came through contact with people within the tetrarch's court. Joanna was married to an officer named Chuza (Luke 8:3), and Manaen had actually been a companion of Antipas in his youth (Acts 13:1). The details of the roles performed by Joanna and Manaen are not known; they left little more than their names in the evidence that remains from their time. But they account for indirect yet two-way communication so that Jesus could be aware of Antipas's policies and Antipas could understand that, as he said, Jesus posed a threat to him akin to John the Baptist's criticism (Mark 6:14). To his mind, it was as if John had been raised up from the dead, and this fear fed into the popular sentiment, of which Antipas was aware, that Jesus taught with the authority of a prophet (Mark 6:15–16). That sense was one of the few matters that Jesus and Antipas could agree upon. The consensus that Jesus was a prophet made a collision between him and Antipas imminent.

Some Pharisees were sympathetic to Rabbi Jesus; after all, his aim was purity, even though the means of attaining purity were open to dispute. A few Pharisees even warned him that Antipas had ordered Jesus's execution (Luke 13:31), just as he had ordered John's years before. Jesus's reaction was as dismissive of Antipas as ever, but what he said also illustrates Jesus's own sense of prophetic identity: "Depart, tell that fox, Look: I cast out demons and will send healings today and tomorrow, and on the third day I am finished. Except it is necessary for me today and tomorrow and the next to depart, because it is not acceptable for a prophet to perish outside Jerusalem" (Luke 13:32–33). Jesus followed a pattern of evading Antipas for as long as he remained in Galilee with a view to making his way to Jerusalem for the decisive moment of his prophetic aim. To evade Antipas, he both skirted the territory of Galilee, crossing back and forth between east and west, and also sent out a few of his disciples as his delegates to undertake the same activity that he did himself: announcing God's kingdom, healing, and expelling unclean spirits.[50] They both extended his activity as surrogates and provided camouflage.

In any case, Antipas exerted himself less in tracking down Jesus than he did in the case of John. Jesus did not yet have John's stature in public opinion and had no influence as yet on opinion in Judea proper.[51] Josephus makes it plain that John was a more famous teacher than Jesus, and Judea, rather than Galilee, was the more authoritative source of the kind of criticism on the basis of the laws of Judaism that Antipas had to monitor and control. Given Antipas's relatively modest effort to eliminate Jesus, it is nonetheless striking that when Jesus acknowledges that he is God's "Anointed" (Messiah or Christ), he does so outside Galilee in the territory of Philip, near Caesarea Philippi, and even then he swears his disciples (represented by Peter) to silence (Mark 8:29–30).

Jesus believed he could evade Antipas by making his way to Jerusalem, where the tetrarch of Galilee and Perea lacked political authority. Yet he already had taught against the administration of the temple, so he had every reason to suspect that Jerusalem would be a place of danger to him, as it had been to other prophets.[52] He urged resistance against paying the regular tax to the temple, which was exacted in addition to the tithes for the temple and priests. The "double drachma" was the name of the annual donation of a half shekel (two drachmas) per Israelite male throughout the world,[53] and Jesus refused to pay it. When you add the 10 percent of a person's earnings in a tithe (Num 18:21–32) and what is traditionally called the "second tithe" (produce to be consumed during sacrifice in Jerusalem; Deut 14:22–29) to the taxes of Rome and the temple, the result was a considerable sap on one's income.[54] No wonder Jesus lashed out against the whole system of collecting levies, even for the temple:

> *Yet as they came into Capernaum, the collectors of the double drachma came to Peter, and said, "Your teacher does not pay the double drachma?" He says, "Yes." And when he came into the home, Jesus anticipated him, "How does it seem to you, Simon? Who do the kings of the earth take customs or tax from? From their sons or from foreigners?" Yet as he was saying, "From the foreigners"—Jesus stated to him, "Therefore the sons are indeed free! But so that we will not cause them to falter, proceed to a sea, throw a fishhook, and take the first fish that comes up. Open its mouth, and you will find a stater [that is, a coin sufficient to pay the tax for two]: take that, give to them for me and you!" (Matt 17:24–27)*

Later Christian tradition made this *halakhah* (the Mishnaic word for ethical teaching) of Jesus into a miracle story, but the original sense of

Jesus's words points in a different direction.[55] He is telling his preeminent disciple that all Israelites, as sons of a king, should be free of taxes for the temple and that those who collect such taxes can, in effect, go fish for them. While that is not quite a categorical refusal to pay the tax, neither is it anything like an obedient agreement to support the temple with money. The temple for him was to be supported not with currency but by the offerings of one's hands. He was speaking the language of Galilean revolution, centered on the act of sacrifice. But apart from his systematic antipathy to practices of the religious authorities in Jerusalem, there was also a factor that made Antipas an even greater threat to him there than he was in Galilee. Jesus proved ill informed in that regard.

Prior to what proved to be his final departure to Jerusalem, Rabbi Jesus was given grisly news of some "Galileans, whose blood Pilate had mingled with their sacrifices" (Luke 13:1). Although Luke does not explain the reference, Josephus provides full details.[56] Pilate wanted to build an aqueduct in Jerusalem, a practical measure and also an iconic gesture of Roman power. Financing the project was difficult, so Pilate seized funds from the treasury of the temple. Protest was inevitable, and on this occasion, Pilate was prepared for it in a way he had not been in the case of his bringing Roman shields into the proximity of the temple. In the cruelest, most cynical maneuver of his tenure, he agreed to meet with a large group of protesters within the great court of the temple itself and had a podium built so he could speak to them. When he mounted the podium, however, it was not to explain his policy or his behavior but to signal to his soldiers—dispersed out of uniform throughout the crowd—to begin clubbing the people who were gathered. Hundreds of them died under the blows and in the stampede of frightened demonstrators. Their blood had indeed been mixed with their sacrifices, and all this on holy ground.

Any Galilean prophet would find Jerusalem a particularly dangerous place at that moment. But Jesus probably did not know that Pilate was emboldened to act as he did because Sejanus had tightened his grip on Rome. The prefect of the Praetorian Guard had reached the point where he actively planned to usurp Tiberius. Sejanus's success was sufficiently assured to the extent that Pilate went much further than he had in the affair of the shields and stepped away from Tiberius by aligning himself with Sejanus. That was what emboldened him to act with the violence he did toward the demonstrators in the temple.

When Jesus entered Jerusalem in the autumn of 31 CE, tension roiled the city. Nonetheless, the Galilean rabbi proceeded to his prophetic act of clearing the outer court of the temple of merchants, their animals, and all that was required for commerce there (Mark 11:15–17). The high priest of the time, named Caiaphas, had introduced the trade there in order to control it (in the Babylonian Talmud, see Shabbat 15a; Sanhedrin 41a; Abodah Zara 8b);[57] Jesus objected not only on the grounds of tradition but also to fulfill his own prophetic purpose. His ideal was what had been forecast in the book of Zechariah (14:21), a temple open to all nations and peoples, who might join in sacrifice freely—without any trade. That would be the supreme sign that at least in that place, God's kingdom and no other power ruled. Jesus entered Jerusalem and the temple as a prophet and enacted a prophet's program, taking his agenda from the Scripture of Israel.

Jesus's incursion into the temple was bold, prophetic, and necessarily violent because the outer court of the temple was vast, amounting to some twenty acres, and clearing it of merchants devoted to trade, their animals, and their associated equipment required several hundred sympathetic, able-bodied, and motivated followers. One of them, Barabbas, even killed someone during the melee (according to Mark 15:7). Under any circumstances, Jesus had to have known that he was courting a response not only from the high priestly authorities who administered the temple but also from the Romans, for whom the temple was a symbol of their pacification of the territory of Judea and associated regions.

Events in the imperial court made the Roman response more lethal than anyone might have anticipated. A judicial assassination in Rome on October 18, 31 CE, turned a military reaction by Pilate against Jesus from a possibility into a certainty. On that day, the Senate took action on Tiberius's complaint against Sejanus, whose program of conspiracy the emperor had at long last understood.[58] A purge was undertaken, with Sejanus himself garroted, his body dismembered by a crowd; subsequently his family was killed and his allies executed. He was not even spared the postmortem indignity of having his name effaced from coins in a procedure known as *damnatio memoriae.*[59]

With his mentor dead and dishonored, Pilate needed radically to change his position and to enter into a working agreement with the Judaic leadership. He did so deftly and quickly and sealed his new alliance with Caiaphas by crucifying Jesus. The same events in the imperial court that blindsided Pilate strengthened the hand of the high priest Caiaphas and sealed Jesus's fate.

Caiaphas had long become accustomed to routine humiliation by Pilate,[60] but he seized the opportunity to make common cause with him. Pilate could restore order in the temple and deflect any blame for the unrest that might fall on Caiaphas by executing Jesus as a threat to public order. It was Caiaphas who had approved an innovative arrangement of making merchants and their wares available in the temple, so it would have been possible—had circumstances been different—to make him responsible for the disturbance that had taken place. But by scapegoating the relatively obscure Galilean prophet, Pilate could make a friend of the high priest and also cover his earlier action against the Galileans by associating them with organized insurrection in the temple.

Even more crucially from the point of view of his position in Rome over the longer term, Pilate also ingratiated himself with Antipas. The actual arrest of Jesus occurred near the time of Passover in 32 CE, and Antipas had taken up residence in the palace that his father had built on the western edge of the city. As he prepared for the feast there, Pilate sent him Jesus as a prisoner to seek Antipas's advice, as tetrarch of Galilee, regarding what should be done (Luke 23:1–12).[61] In an unmistakable sign, Antipas had Jesus costumed in a magnificent garment and then sent him back to Pilate. The gesture accused Jesus of assuming royal pretensions, and Pilate did not delay his judgment, beyond toying with the crowd assembled around him with an offer to release Barabbas. Luke observes that Antipas and Pilate became friends from that moment, having been at odds before (Luke 23:12). Together, they faced the new reality of Rome without Sejanus.

Although Jesus had already expressed himself in cynical terms in regard to Antipas as well as the temple administration and had directly confronted the latter on its own territory, his position in regard to the Romans was subtle. A clever questioner posed the issue of the imperial power clearly: Should the taxes owed Caesar be paid or not? The Gospels portray this question as a trap, an attempt to induce Jesus to side with a call to arms, because a refusal to pay tax was tantamount to a revolt against Rome. Had they succeeded, he could have been denounced to the prefect as a rebel, not merely an apolitical cultic upstart (Mark 12:13–17; Matt 22:15–22; Luke 20:20–26). No doubt, as Mark indicates, there were some Pharisees present who sympathized with Herod Antipas as a relatively benign government official who let them worship as they pleased; even the Romans could be accommodated if they would honor their permission of the practice of Judaism. But Pharisaism itself was riven by the dilemma of whether to take up arms against foreign rule (and Jewish officials such as Herod Antipas who disregarded the Torah). This was at its base a genuine, heartfelt question: Did relying on God necessarily involve revolution and the certain prospect of Roman countermeasures?

Jesus's response is acute and not merely a truism (Mark 12:17; Matt 22:21; Luke 20:25): "Caesar's repay to Caesar, and God's to God!" Rome's coin, Rome's economy, Rome's goods could indeed be traded and all its duties and taxes paid. But this teaching had nothing to do with submitting to Rome as an end in itself. Instead, Jesus urged his followers to enter into commercial transactions for the instrumental purpose of acquiring for God what could be used for God's purposes. People were in God's image; Rome was owed only coins. In that sense, Rome could be recognized without being accorded full loyalty, which belonged to God alone. Yet even as he crafted this calibrated teaching, an alliance among Caiaphas, Pilate, and Antipas was forming against him. Jesus's death in 32 CE was the predictable result of their strange coalition.

Comparatively speaking, Antipas was in a better position than Pilate. With newfound confidence, he indulged himself in matching insults with his profligate brother-in-law Agrippa in the course of a drinking session. He accused Agrippa, with ample justification, of being a freeloader,[62] and his wounded ward deserted him and sought refuge with Flaccus, then the legate in Syria. Having Agrippa away from the scene suited Antipas, because Philip was approaching the end of his life, and Agrippa both coveted Gaulanitis and wished to avert any competition from Agrippa. Since Antipas had not in any sense been within Sejanus's orbit and he had attempted—inconsistently but with more dedication than Philip had ever approached—to improve his position among his own Jewish subjects, he might reasonably hope to inherit Philip's territory. Philip died in 34 CE; immediately speaking, the Syrian legate assumed control of Gaulanitis by Tiberius's order,[63] but Tiberius also ordered the revenue of the tetrarchy to be set aside for future use. During the same period, Antipas began to strike coins in his mint in Tiberias with a star above the name; although not explicitly idolatrous, the symbolism could be read from a Roman point of view as an acknowledgment of imperial divinity.[64] Antipas, still not yet sixty years old, could still realistically maneuver for the fulfillment of his ambition.

Antipas's principal aim, in any case, had always been his father's throne—the kingship of Judea. Events moved swiftly, putting him in range of possessing his heart's desire. Although Pilate had managed to ingratiate himself with Caiaphas and Antipas, he showed unnecessary cruelty in dealing with a group of Samaritans.[65] They had met on Mount Gerizim, as the Samaritans called their holy mountain, the counterpart of the Judean Zion, to renew their tie with Moses and his promise that they would inherit control of the land of promise; one of their prophets even claimed he knew where Moses had hidden sacrificial vessels there. With those in hand and proper sacrifice restored, he insisted, they would be invincible. The Samaritan gathering was not a spontaneous act but a response to being harried by Pilate's forces. When he ordered wholesale slaughter, the survivors complained to the legate in Syria at the time, Vitellius, who removed Pilate from power and ordered him back to Rome.[66] The unfortunate prefect had exhausted all Roman goodwill; Vitellius, in an act rich with symbolism, ordered that the priestly vestments held in the prefect's custody should revert to the care of the high priest, so that priestly authority in the matter of sacrifice was advanced over that of the Roman administrator. Pilate followed Sejanus in a definitive fall; although he was not executed, he proved unable to cling to his post.

Vitellius, crisp and effective as a general and a diplomat, had acted quickly in dealing with Pilate because a pressing priority intruded. He had to meet with the Parthian king, Artabanus, in order to secure an agreement concerning spheres of influence. Achieving such a settlement had become the pivot of Roman policy in the area, including all the lands that Herod the Great had once ruled. The meeting, which took place on the Euphrates, was a success, promising stability for the fortunes of the Roman Empire in the Near East. Hospitality for the negotiation was provided by none other than Antipas, who also took it on himself to write a dispatch directly to Tiberius.[67] Vitellius did not appreciate Antipas's assumption of a role that should have been his as Rome's legate to the entire region, but that was a less important consideration for Antipas than the favor his gesture might win from the emperor. At long last, he seemed on the threshold of success. His momentary reversal in Vitellius's estimation seemed a small price to pay for the chance to play a formative part in the politics of the imperial court and the empire itself.

Agrippa, who had found a tortuous way back to Rome, nonetheless sought to oppose Antipas in that court. Ever adept at finding resourceful solutions to his problems and then betraying those who helped him, he also had a habit of leaving creditors, including Antipas and Flaccus, on bad terms. Denounced for accepting a bribe to influence Flaccus,[68] he returned to Rome by way of Alexandria, trailed by still more bad debts but hoping yet to find financial backing in the imperial city.

By this stage, Agrippa's finances were in a ruinous condition, and it seems that despite the memory of Agrippa's friendship with Drusus, Tiberius treated him with disdain. In particular, he did not wish to hear about Agrippa's complaints in regard to Antipas.[69] The key figure in restoring Agrippa to favor was Antonia, Tiberius's sister-in-law. Her friendship with Agrippa's mother, Bereniké, meant he had her lifelong support.[70] She undertook a massive loan to Agrippa, providing an advance through Alexander the Alabarch (the chief collector of customs) in Alexandria. The families of Antonia, Agrippa, and Alexander all became tightly linked from this moment.

As he approached the end of his life, Tiberias groomed two possible heirs, one of whom was his grandson, Tiberius Gemellus. Although

Agrippa did not yet control any of the ancestral lands of the Herods, the emperor brought him into his advance planning. He asked Agrippa to accompany his grandson on travels and look out for his interests.[71] With the consequences of his exorbitant debt behind him for the moment, Antipas's nephew had worked his way back into imperial favor.

Agrippa also befriended Caligula, Tiberius's adoptive son, another possible heir (and the grandson of Antonia). Indeed, by pursuing that friendship with his inveterate taste for intrigue, Agrippa inadvertently enhanced Antipas's position and ruined his own. Within earshot of a servant, Agrippa expressed the hope to Caligula that Tiberius's death would be hastened so that Caligula might quickly accede to power.[72] Tiberius, for all his nearly eighty years, had lost none of his punitive instinct: when he verified the report, he imprisoned Agrippa and put him in chains.

On any reasonable reading of the ever-chaotic politics of the imperial court, Antipas—although far from Rome due to his governing duties—had triumphed over any potential threat from Agrippa. Even at this moment of vindication, however, Antipas had to address a potentially mortal challenge to his entire enterprise. The king of Nabataea invaded his territory in Perea. Aretas had long sought vengeance for the humiliation of his daughter, whom Antipas put aside in order to marry Herodias,[73] and it is notable that one reason for Antipas's defeat was that soldiers previously loyal to Philip refused to defend Antipas when ordered to advance against the Nabataeans.

Aretas acted when he did for a strategic reason: to increase his hold on trading cities east of the Jordan River and as far north as Damascus. His efforts to extend his influence on these centers of commerce had been consistent, and now he calculated that he could pry Perea itself from Antipas's hands. At a different moment, Tiberius might have viewed Antipas's defeat as a sign of unacceptable weakness. But in the wake of Agrippa's unreliable behavior, Tiberius ordered the Syrian legate Vitellius to undertake a punitive expedition against Aretas on Antipas's behalf.[74] Antipas now operated with the direct support of Roman military power, making up for his own palpable lack of prowess in the battle with Aretas and the disloyalty of Philip's troops.

Antipas had maneuvered himself and had been placed by events outside his control into the position of being the most obvious heir of his father, Herod the Great. Relegated by Augustus and only gradually favored by Tiberius, he achieved an enviable position largely because his own nephew and brother-in-law had envied him too openly and had acted too brazenly. Strategic ambition seemed at last to have found its reward, bolstered by the fecklessness of the relative who had sought Antipas's harm.

⟨ 7 ⟩

AGRIPPA I

AN IMPROBABLE OPPORTUNIST
MASTERS ROMAN POLITICS

Agrippa I, grandson of Herod the Great and son of Aristobulus, formed an intimate friendship with Caligula, Tiberius's heir by adoption. When Tiberius died, Agrippa suddenly became the Herodians' golden boy. Caligula appointed his friend to Philip's former tetrarchy but as king. *When Antipas petitioned Caligula to be named a king of his own tetrarchy, false charges by Agrippa instead ensured that the emperor banished Antipas altogether. With that, Agrippa I became king of Galilee and Perea as well. The new king used his influence on behalf of Judaism and was a key figure in convincing Caligula to rethink and delay the order to set up a statue of himself in the temple. Only Caligula's assassination, however, spared Jerusalem this "abomination of desolation." In the transition to Claudius as emperor, Agrippa proved himself useful and was rewarded with the inheritance of the whole realm of Herod the Great, again as king. Lavish spending, skillful diplomacy, and (like Claudius) selective persecution of minorities such as Jesus's followers earned him admiration and broad success. His one misfortune was his health, however, and his premature death threw Judea into confusion. Amid a rising tide of rebellion, Claudius resorted to the appointment of procurators (rather than prefects), whose increased authority was nonetheless inadequate to the rising tide of revolt.*
Judea's last king: *Lucky except in health, wily, unscrupulous, faithful to Judaism and his immediate family*

Agrippa's Revenge

ANTIPAS HAD CAREFULLY paved the way for realizing Herodian ambition by means of his own career. His steady increase in the estimation of Tiberius had been remarkable and proved durable even with the set-back of Aretas's invasion, but imperial change in Rome would alter the political landscape throughout Herod the Great's former realm. Tiberius died in 37 CE; prior to his death, he arranged through torturous deliberations for Caligula to succeed him.[1] Caligula took care of his friend Agrippa and reversed Antipas's carefully developed fortunes. The tetrarch's personal aspirations would be left in ruins. All Antipas's efforts seemed to turn to his profligate brother-in-law's benefit.

Caligula had Agrippa released from custody and gave him a golden chain that was equal in weight to the iron shackles to which Tiberius had consigned him. Caligula's favor did not end there; he handed over to Agrippa the tetrarchy formerly governed by Philip, together with the revenues that had been held in reserve, and supplemented the realm with additional territories.[2] This moment probably represented the first time in Agrippa's adult life when he was fully (however temporarily) solvent. Most galling to Antipas, however, Caligula also placed a diadem on Agrippa's head and named him as *king* of the territory—the first Herodian since Herod the Great to accede to that title. During his youth, Agrippa's mother, Bereniké, curated a friendship with Antonia, grandmother of Caligula. She wanted to provide a sound foundation for her son's advancement. Agrippa himself had built on the foundation by borrowing funds in order to offer Caligula lavish hospitality and entertainment.[3]

Antipas's unenviable military position compounded his frustration. The general Vitellius had been ordered to engage with Aretas, but Tiberius's death was announced while he and his troops bivouacked in and around Jerusalem. To spite Antipas, he decided to use the emperor's death as a pretext not to complete his mission and claimed he needed renewed orders in order to proceed. In addition, while in Jerusalem—and with Antipas present—Vitellius named a new high priest to the temple,[4] demonstrating who did and who did not govern Jerusalem with Rome's authority and also that the accession of Caligula meant a reduction of the imperial favor accorded to Antipas.

While Antipas's advancement languished in Vitellius's shadow, Agrippa delayed his departure from Rome, ostensibly to please Caligula but more vitally to shore up his own position in the imperial capital. He had just been named king of Gaulanitis and its adjacent territories, and events would quickly reveal his ambition for a broader kingship. But this adopted child of Rome never forgot the source of the power that he wielded. The diadem bestowed on him justified his purchase and display of royal garments, even in Rome. From there he set out with his royal accoutrements on a journey designed to advertise himself as a benefactor of Diaspora Judaism as well as the ruler of the sector of Herod the Great's old territories that was assigned to him. He made his way to Alexandria, second largest city in the Roman Empire and home to a large but sometimes beleaguered community of Jews. When Agrippa arrived, his royal entry was celebrated by the Jews of the city and deplored by the "Egyptians," as Philo of Alexandria—a contemporary of the events, noted philosopher, and soon-to-be delegate representing the Jewish community in an embassy to Rome—calls the gentile enemies of the Jews. Through it all, the new king vaunted his status. He paraded himself in his new royal apparel; even his armed guards sported armor decked with gold and silver.[5] Philo's own description belies his rhetorical claim of Agrippa's modest discretion.

Philo had every reason to praise Agrippa and to attribute humility to him, however unconvincingly. By exculpating him of blame in riling the "Egyptians," he pursued his theme of Jewish innocence in civic unrest. After Agrippa's departure, deadly pogroms against "the nation [or people, *ethnos*] of the Judeans" broke out, in which the Roman Prefect of Egypt Flaccus took a guiding role, according to Philo.[6] Crowds in Alexandria protested Agrippa's coming as a "king" of the Judean population, as if their city were to fall under the jurisdiction of the Herodian dynasty. The reaction reveals one source of ancient anti-Semitism. Because Roman law recognized "the nation of the Judeans" as legitimate, Judaism was legal.[7] But that raised the issue of the extent to which practitioners of Judaism *outside Judea* (a group to which the English term

"Jews" is typically applied) in fact owed loyalty to Judean governors or rulers of lands that had once been part of Judea. The title of *ethnarkhês tôn Ioudaiôn* as borne by Hyrcanus (and later by Archelaus) had already raised this question, but Agrippa pressed the matter in Alexandria with visual splendor.

The crowds in Egypt were reacting against what might be called Judeanism as much as against Judaism because the nation and the religion shared a common designation and were conceptually linked so closely as to be indistinguishable in the minds of many people. But Agrippa, like Herod the Great before him, was more than happy to accept the adulation that came his way as a benefactor of Judaism wherever it might be found; cultural and political tensions were inevitably the result.

Philo believed that Flaccus's ignominious end—first exiled and then order to be killed by Caligula—was proof of providence and of Agrippa's special place within it.[8] It comes as a relief to Philo that even Caligula rejected the deliberate, Sejanus-like anti-Semitism of Flaccus.[9] Caligula had recommended to Agrippa a route through Alexandria to his new royal domain, and it seems clear the emperor was after information on Flaccus and wanted to weaken his position.[10] The opening of the new imperial regime could be read in hopeful terms by supporters of Judaism.

Yet the whole dreadful episode in Alexandria seeded a malignant possibility in Caligula's mind. As part of their anti-Semitic measures, rioters and officials desecrated synagogues,[11] burning them down in many cases and in others setting up images of Caligula within them.[12] Flaccus, aware of his precarious position within the emperor's entourage, had encouraged the latter tactic. It did him little good but opened a prospect that pleased the infamously narcissistic Caligula. Flaccus was summoned back to Rome, while Philo of Alexandria joined a delegation to protest the prefect's behavior. Suetonius called Caligula insane;[13] whatever the clinical judgment, his compulsion to harm and to exalt himself made for mad acts of statecraft. Flaccus's desperate act of flattery, in erecting within a synagogue a bronze statue of the emperor mounted in a chariot, would survive the prefect himself.

Although Caligula has become known as the most pretentious of all Roman emperors, even by comparison, his friend Agrippa never appeared to suffer from modesty, false or not. By flaunting his new royal status, he had carelessly played a role in inflaming local sentiment. An early indication of anti-Semitic aggression in Alexandria was that those who protested Agrippa's visit equipped a local eccentric as if he were a king, paraded him into the gymnasium, and hailed him as *"Marana,"* the Aramaic word for Lord.[14] The demonstration was transparently designed to ridicule Agrippa, most of whose subjects in Judea spoke Aramaic and who flaunted his royal status during this visit.

Agrippa also took the opportunity of his visit to secure his own financial position, arranging the marriage of his young daughter (named Bereniké after his mother) to Philo's nephew, Marcus Julius Alexander.[15] He was one of the wealthiest men in Alexandria, and by promising the ten-year-old Bereniké to him, Agrippa secured access to deep financial resources, political influence, and an enduring alliance of families. At this point, Bereniké, owing to her age, was not quite a sexual pawn, but she showed the promise of becoming one; with time she would wield power with talents that included—but were by no means limited to— the deft use of her sexuality.

Agrippa had indulged himself in the benefits of Egypt, and his obvious lack of concern for the impact of his visit on the Jewish community in Alexandria was nicely camouflaged by the ruin of Flaccus's career and the eloquent propaganda of Philo (a prominent intellectual who disseminated his works orally prior to their eventual release in writing). Now he proceeded to Jerusalem, a city under Vitellius's new and capable governance. But as Rome's protégé within a territory under military administration, Agrippa wisely did not continue to flaunt his royal airs and his wealth as he had in Alexandria. Instead, he used the occasion to ingratiate himself with the people and the hierarchy of the temple. He presented as a gift to the temple the splendid golden chain that Caligula bestowed on him, in effect devoting his monarchy to God and at the same offering his protection to the holy sanctuary. In a spectacle of lavish piety, he also underwrote the expenses of devout Israelites who had taken the Nazirite vow.[16] This costly ritual involved a practitioner in keeping scrupulous purity for a period of a month or more, stipulated at the time of commencing the vow, and refraining from cutting or shaving any hair for that time. At the close of the period promised for this sanctity, the person who made the vow had become consecrated: one's very hair was holy. At this point, before any impurity could arise, the hair was shorn and offered on the altar in the temple together with several animal sacrifices. Many people could only afford to keep the vow with the support of a benefactor, and Agrippa—despite his background in Rome's imperial court—emerged as a champion of Israelite purity. Chronically challenged when it came to raising money and therefore constantly in quest of funds, he was as gifted as his grandfather when spending was involved.

Despite the uncertain circumstances in Alexandria and elsewhere in the initial phase of Caligula's rule and his own lack of experience in governance, Agrippa moved decisively to consolidate power from his base at Caesarea Philippi. Immediately on his accession,[17] he ordered up coins that honored the new emperor, with a portrait of him and his three sisters as well. Agrippa's own portrait features on another coin, in the manner of what Philip had struck, though naming himself as king, which Philip could not do. The image pictured him with the royal diadem,[18] along with images of his son, Agrippa II, and his wife, Cypros. By title and in the depiction of his family, King Agrippa set himself up as the dynastic fulfillment of all Herod the Great had wished to accomplish.

Antipas was left to consolidate his own position in Perea in order to deal with Aretas's incursion and to develop a strategy to accede to power in Judea and Jerusalem.[19] If, despite his lack of experience, Agrippa could be named as king in Philip's former domain, why could Antipas not claim the same title? And if he could rule as king in Galilee and Perea, the greater prizes of Judea, Samaria, and Idumea would be ripe for consolidation into his realm.

While Antipas and Herodias planned to appeal to the emperor for this arrangement, Agrippa had completed his lavish display of loyalty to Caligula by means of the coins he struck. The new emperor was suspicious of conspiracy, and not without reason. It had been rumored that his own father, the famed warrior Germanicus, had been poisoned in order to benefit Tiberius;[20] defamation and lethal intrigue had dogged the family precisely because Germanicus was famous. Caligula's survival was due to a significant extent to his own duplicity; he could be as obsequious as necessary with Tiberius in the period when the aging emperor sought a replacement for the arrogant Praetorian prefect Sejanus and—more crucially—an heir. Suetonius passed on the aphorism that "no one had ever been a better slave or a worse master" than Caligula.[21] Now on his own with imperial power, he wanted to assure himself of loyal supporters throughout the Roman Empire. Agrippa appeared to be a model of what Caligula wanted.

Seemingly oblivious to how outclassed he was in the struggle for favor in the imperial court and how vicious Caligula could become, Antipas thought the moment propitious to ask that he, like Agrippa, be granted the title of king. Even as applied solely to his current domains of Galilee and Perea, this would bring him partway to inheriting his father's principal lands.[22] He and Herodias journeyed to Rome in order to make their appeal.

The tetrarch and his wife had not reckoned with the influence and the cunning of Agrippa or with the cruelty of Caligula. Agrippa concocted a spurious tale, set out in a letter he sent by a servant to the emperor. He claimed that Antipas had conspired against the interests of Rome with both Sejanus and Artabanus of Parthia. In fact, Antipas had resisted Sejanus's protégé, Pontius Pilate, and had supported Vitellius in bringing Artabanus to accept Roman hegemony in the Near East. But Caligula was disposed to think ill of Antipas for the same reason he had been willing to depose Flaccus and then see to his execution: loyalty to Tiberius, who had allegedly had Caligula's father poisoned, had become a crime in Caligula's mind. On each occasion that he punished that crime, he punished it with greater vehemence, and Antipas had long curried the favor of Tiberius. Agrippa knew the emperor's character intimately and used it to destroy his sister's prospects as well as his brother-in-law's (and uncle's), although they had once protected him.

And so on a single day in 39 CE, Antipas lost the realm and position that he had taken decades to secure. Caligula pronounced an exile to Lyons in Gaul. When he remembered that Herodias was Agrippa's sister, the emperor offered her the possibility of keeping her own property, provided she accepted the protection of her brother. In form, this was an expression of regard for a family connection; in substance, it was a gratuitous effort to inflict more harm on the hapless Antipas by disaffecting his wife from him. To her credit, she refused the offer out of loyalty to her husband; characteristically, Caligula became annoyed and assigned all the couple's property to Agrippa. He now ruled as king over a large domain on both sides of the Sea of Galilee and the Jordan River, leapfrogging over Antipas without showing any sign of martial prowess or capacity for governance. He was a new kind of Herodian, whose fortunes derived from friendship, deception, and intrigue within the imperial court, all consummately practiced. By means of the brilliant opportunism that was the trademark of his family and the core of his own strange genius but without his grandfather's military acumen or physical courage, Agrippa had won a kingdom.

Careful once again to venerate his mentor, Agrippa had coins struck in honor of Caligula; his wife, Caesonia; and his daughter Drusilla, along with images of himself with his own wife and son.[23] He also shifted his capital to Tiberias, the more central location within his new realm. At this stage, if not before, he had inherited his uncle Antipas's ambition to acquire the entire realm of Herod the Great; the city of Tiberias was geographically and culturally an auspicious headquarters for the political conquest of Samaria, Judea, and Idumea—the final aim of his spectacular rise to power.[24] After all, Herod the Great had made Galilee his base of power. Agrippa would follow suit, making the city Antipas had founded the pivot of his operation. All his uncle had achieved seemed to provide for Agrippa's rise to the pinnacle of Herodian power.

That ultimate extension of his realm required Agrippa to rule both as a Judean as well as a Roman king. His long residence in Rome and his evident success within the imperial court should, one might think, have made his appeal to Judean sensibilities problematic. But a series of events unfolded that made him the unlikely hero of people and leaders alike in Jerusalem and throughout the Diaspora. Caligula furthered Agrippa's project not only by his generosity and trust but also by his wildest miscalculation.

The Edict of Caligula

THE FACT THAT people called the emperor Caligula—"little boots," replacing his official designation as "Gaius" in common usage—signaled the root of the issue. As a very small child, he accompanied his father, Germanicus, on a military campaign, and the proud father kitted him out in uniform from head to foot, complete with the little military sandals that gave him his nickname. The death of Germanicus put him under Tiberius's protection and watchful eye, and Caligula himself survived, even while living with Tiberius in Capri, by his studiously obsequious attitude. Beneath that facade, a very different personality developed, in which self-regard superseded other concerns. His apparently compliant temperament caused an astrologer to remark once to Tiberius that Caligula had as much chance of becoming emperor as he had of riding across the gulf of Baiae on a horse. Caligula took the comment to heart.

After accession to power upon Tiberius's death, Caligula commandeered enough ships to make a bridge on which he did just what the astrologer hypothesized, traversing the gulf mounted on horseback and clothed in a golden robe. In fact, he did so several times, changing costumes in between passes.[25] That was not the most expensive of his ostentatious projects, several of which were designed to give him the stature of a god within his own lifetime, complete with a temple and clothed statue.[26]

Agrippa knew how to entertain Caligula and shared extravagant tastes with him. The new king of his uncles' former tetrarchies also did not scruple to break the commandment against idolatry when it came to the use of the imperial image (and his own) on the coins of his new realm. But beyond that routine, bureaucratic impiety, Caligula's aspiration for divine honors increasingly contradicted Judaism's primal tenet: that God is one and there is no other. Anyone of the time, whether from the people of Israel or among the "worshippers of God" (gentiles who admired the monotheism of Israel's faith), knew that weekly worship reminded everyone in the synagogue of God's oneness and difference from any other power, human or otherwise.[27] No reasonable ruler could have expected that the Judaic community would accord Caligula divine honors.

But Caligula was not reasonable, and some of his subjects knew how to inflame his thirst for reverence and his taste for retribution. Alexandria remained in turmoil. Among the competing petitioners who sought the emperor's favor in Rome was an orator, Homeric scholar, and public intellectual named Apion. He opposed a Jewish delegation (including Philo) that insisted that the Jews of Alexandria were innocent of inciting violence and disloyalty to Caligula. The quarrel had survived the exile and execution of Flaccus; the persistence of the delegations colluded with the emperor's enjoyment of practicing revenge, and the combination assured a long contention. Apion skillfully complained that Jews alone among all Roman subjects refused to erect altars, temples, or statues in Caligula's honor[28] and that they disavowed the multiple gods of the empire as a whole.

All of this was, of course, the simple truth, but Apion folded that undeniable characteristic of Judaism into one of the most comprehensive attacks on the religion and its people known in antiquity. His anti-Semitic tour de force, which he went on to publish, became so well known that Josephus produced an entire book to refute the tract at the end of his life.[29] Some of the charges against the Jews—worshipping the head of an ass, cannibalism, hatred of anyone but their own, to name a few tropes with a very long afterlife—entered the common stock of crazed accusations that persisted into the Middle Ages. Apion's attack included pseudohistorical assertions clustered around claims that the Jews picked up various crude practices in Egypt that they took with them when they were expelled for impurity and later deformed into their own religion.

Caligula's attention by this stage of his life (still in his twenties and fiercely making up for his subjugated status while Tiberius was alive) focused on the devotion that he believed he deserved. Apion's onslaught could claim support from a report that had come in from Jamnia (also known as Yavneh), a town on the coastal plain west of Jerusalem, that a local mob had destroyed an altar that the gentiles of the city had erected in honor of the emperor.[30] Philo of Alexandria contested Apion's charges, and by all the evidence, he was a clearer thinker than Apion and might well have been a more effective speaker. But he used no fewer words than his opponent, and Caligula lost patience with the back and forth arguments and at last cut off the discussion. Taken by Apion's accusation that the Jews denied him the honor he was due, he devised a stratagem to resolve all disputes of the sort that had erupted in Alexandria. It appeared simple, direct, and straightforward. Confronted with verbose complexity and disputes that in principle might break out anywhere in the Roman Empire, the emperor's narcissism had uncovered a bold solution.[31]

Caligula ordered a new legate into Syria, named Petronius, to replace Vitellius—who had been Tiberius's man in any case. He commanded Petronius to take his forces into Jerusalem to execute his stratagem: setting up a statue to the emperor in the temple. The response to the threatened sacrilege, a public policy that was clearly announced, was instantaneous. Even Tacitus acknowledged that Caligula had made open war inevitable.[32] Petronius was met by thousands of protestors in his march to Jerusalem. The climax of the confrontation transpired at Tiberias, now the center of Agrippa's realm, where thousands of people anticipated Petronius's arrival.

Demonstrations lasted over a month while Agrippa's younger brother, Aristobulus, and other leaders of the city pleaded with Petronius to stay the order he had received. Public opposition, they insisted, would be to the death, because the imperial order violated the recognition of the temple and worship in Judea that had been honored since the time of the republic and fixed by the arrangement of Augustus and Herod the Great. Erecting the statue would bring on a revolution that would devastate and weaken the land as a bulwark against Parthia; the people would die rather than violate their laws, and their protest was interfering with their tending to the land. Any failure of the crops could only mean distress, desperation, rising criminality, and violence aimed at Rome.

Petronius, at great personal risk, allowed himself to be persuaded and wrote to Rome with a request that the order be rescinded. King Agrippa, at this time, was in Rome, and his skill as a courtier enabled him to discharge his greatest service to Judaism—and perhaps the greatest single service of any Herodian. Agrippa was an extraordinary host, and because Caligula regularly spent beyond his means, he recognized and admired the same trait in Agrippa. The king decided to put on a sumptuous feast beyond even the extravagance of the emperor's imperial fare, and of course Caligula was the guest of honor. Josephus depicts a well-fed and intoxicated emperor asking Agrippa for any favor he would like. Agrippa took what he knew very well was a risk[33] and asked him to abandon the order already given to Petronius.

Given Caligula's frame of mind and his usual pride in refusing to rescind resolutions he had already made, his reaction was startling. He replied that he would send another message to Petronius, this time commending him for the rapid deployment of his soldiers. Taking that preparation as fulfilling the intent of the original order, Caligula allowed that if the statue had already been erected, it was to remain in the temple, but if it was not in place, the army should be dismissed and the ordinary demands of governance taken up.

For all the doubts that have plagued Agrippa's claim to practice Judaism (from his own time until the most recent historians), his courage in making his request to Caligula remains. The emperor's cruelty was legendary and his self-esteem famously fragile, and after all, an imperial order had already been given. The request could easily have started what seemed an impending bloodbath with the shedding of Agrippa's own blood.

How close Agrippa had come to disaster was demonstrated when Petronius's message, also asking Caligula to rescind the order, arrived belatedly in the imperial court. Caligula, enraged that a subordinate had questioned his command and reactive to any intimation that Judea might revolt, wrote to Petronius again. He accused him of accepting bribes and directed him to take his own life, implicitly an offer to avoid a more grisly form of execution and the confiscation of any legacy that might go to his heirs.[34] Petronius, prompted by Aristobulus, had ruined his career and apparently forfeited his life, while Agrippa had just managed to prevail on the emperor's goodwill and desire to be seen doing good for a loyal friend, only to see his design threatened by Caligula's rage against the same request made by another man.

Both in Tiberias and in Rome, Agrippa's court had stood behind the nearly successful effort to change Roman policy. Yet Caligula's anger at Petronius spilled over into his high regard for Agrippa, and he began to make arrangements to revoke his grant to Agrippa so that the plan for the statue's installation could continue under Petronius's replacement. His order was now for the statue to be made in Rome and then set up with a dedication to himself in Jerusalem as "the New Epiphany of Zeus."[35] By this stage, Caligula planned to take a tour through Alexandria as part of a program of self-deification, so stirring within the Senate and even the imperial court the old Roman fears of Egyptian intrigue that had helped bring down Antony and his lover Cleopatra.[36] Applauded at his accession by many as a charming rogue, the sociopathic depths of Caligula's narcissism had become apparent to Rome's ruling class.

The crisis exerted a profound influence at the time and reverberated in literary sources for decades after the edict of Caligula. Within Jerusalem and throughout the Mediterranean world, Jewish opinion showed new concern for the temple, prompted by accounts of the episode of Caligula's arrogance such as Philo's *Embassy to Gaius*. Caligula's endorsement of popular efforts to set up worship sites for himself and his family invited direct and sometimes violent Jewish resistance.[37] Some intellectuals, including Philo, aligned themselves closely with the Herodians and increasingly saw Agrippa's role as providential because it defended the temple's integrity while avoiding violence.

Others took up the most accessible form of sacrifice to Israelites as a whole, the Nazirite vow, in order to declare and assure the inviolability of the temple. A legendary rabbi named Simeon, as recorded in rabbinic literature, had taught that maintaining the pattern of worship commanded in the Torah would assure that God would annul Caligula's decree. He assured those in Jerusalem, on the authority of word (*davar*) that came from the holy of holies, that the edict would not stand.[38] Simeon is also associated with a famous Haggadah concerning the Nazirite vow. In it, he remarks that he had very rarely met a Nazirite who had to interrupt the period of his vow owing to uncleanness.[39] Those who undertook the vow committed themselves to purity, and the temple was to be the guarantee of purity.

James, the brother of Jesus, was a famous Nazirite surrounded by a loyal community in Jerusalem (see Acts 21:18–26; and Hegesippus's account[40]). His standing in the city and within Jesus's movement was such that he became the leading figure in discussions of ritual, most importantly the decision in 46 CE that those of the gentiles who sought baptism in Jesus's name should not be required to keep the covenant of circumcision (Acts 15:1–19). By that time, he had been well established in Jerusalem and in a position to join the increased Nazirite devotion during the period that includes Caligula's edict. James's capacity to win the reverence of many Jews in Jerusalem (not only his brother's followers) derives from this practice and his encouragement of others in the practice.

The fact is frequently overlooked but needs to be emphasized: the Mishnah envisages Nazirite practice as including Israelites as a whole, both males and females (see Nazir 9:1).[41] James's focus was purity in the temple under the aegis of his risen brother, the Son of Man, but there is no trace of his requiring the circumcision of gentiles. It needs to be kept in mind that Jesus had expelled traders from the temple not as some indiscriminate protest about commercialism but as part of Zechariah's prophecy (see Zech 14): that all the peoples of the earth would be able to offer sacrifice to the Lord without the intervention of middlemen.[42] James's practice of the vow realized that prophecy in his brother's name, by creating a core of faithful Nazirites dedicated to Jesus who were supported by gentiles who sustained the community (see Acts 15:12–21).

A title attributed to James, "Oblias," has caused understandable puzzlement (especially when Hegesippus's rendering of the term as "bulwark" is accepted[43]), but it is easily related to the Aramaic term *'abal*, which means "to mourn." Recent finds in the vicinity of the Dead Sea (not only near Qumran) have greatly enhanced our understanding of Aramaic as spoken in the time of Jesus and his followers. The use of the term is attested there.[44] James was probably known as "mourner." A minor tractate of the Babylonian Talmud lays down the rule that a mourner (*'abal*) "is under the prohibition to bathe, anoint [the body], put on sandals and cohabit" (Semachoth 4:1). This largely corresponds to the requirements of a Nazirite vow and to Hegesippus's description of

James's practice; for Jesus himself to have called his brother "mourner" would fit in with his giving his followers nicknames (such as calling Simon "Rock" and the Zebedee brothers "Sons of Tumult"; Mark 3:16–17).

Persistence was central to James's Nazirite practice. As long as the temple functioned according to its purpose, the key was to remain there. That imperative is ambient within a discourse in the New Testament that centers on the threat to the temple,[45] first under Caligula in 40 CE and later under Vespasian and Titus, who destroyed Jerusalem thirty years later. But if Caligula's edict had been executed, that would be the "abomination of desolation" that signaled it was time to flee from Jerusalem to the Judean mountains (Mark 13:14). That phrase had been used in the book of Daniel (9:27; 11:31; 12:11) to refer to the altar to Zeus that Antiochus Epiphanes had set up, but now apocalyptic interpreters saw Caligula as the fulfillment of the prophecy. More commonsense concerns for safety seem to have provoked teachers such as Mary Magdalene to retreat to the relative safety of Galilee and remain there. Yet the options for opposition to Caligula were not limited to the persistence of worship in the temple and the withdrawal from Jerusalem. Some teachers, whom Agrippa I would have to deal with, harnessed the power of apocalyptic thinking to promote direct action against the Roman occupation.[46]

The Claudian Settlement and Agrippa's Glory

LED BY A tribune of the Praetorian Guard named Chaera, a conspiracy succeeded in cutting Caligula down as he made his way to observe the Palatine games.[47] According to Suetonius, his corpse bore more than thirty wounds. Caligula's death was hailed as providential at the time and long thereafter. By a combination of Petronius's daring, Chaera's fortitude, and Agrippa's diplomacy, the tyrant had been stopped, and the temple had been saved. The assassination threw Roman politics into chaos, but the definitive annulment of Caligula's plans produced a realignment in Judean politics, reprieved Petronius, and produced a stunning opportunity for Agrippa by means of the enhancement of his prestige.

For Agrippa to master the new alignment of power in relation to Judea and his region, he needed to involve himself in the deadly politics of Rome; the clash of interests was now so fraught that the Principate itself, the legal instrument that gave the emperor his power, looked to be collapsing. Factions of the Senate took advantage of the situation, some exhorting their colleagues to seize the moment as an occasion to secure freedom against the tyranny that had taken control of Rome since the time of Julius Caesar and return to a republican model of governance.[48] Others advocated the extermination of Caligula's wider family and supporters; his wife and daughter had already been summarily put to the sword.[49] The dead emperor's uncle, named Claudius, hid away in the palace, only to be taken into custody by soldiers.

Ill with a neurological condition since his birth, frustrated in repeated quests for office that he ventured, Claudius had long submerged himself in study, becoming a noted scholar of Greek. He was not up to the occasion that confronted him. The soldiers had seized him, Claudius feared, in order to kill him. But an officer of the palace guard, Gratus, used the military custody of Claudius as a form of safekeeping to assert that Claudius should be named as emperor.[50] The Senate and the army seemed to be at odds.

In the past, standoffs between the senators of the Republic, endowed with the supreme authority of Rome, and the generals of the soldiery, possessed of spectacular force, allowed the will of emperors to prevail over divisions that also pitted faction against faction, army against army. Now the sudden killing of Caligula left the army confused; the Senate for its part was also far from united. Claudius's vacillation only compounded political confusion.[51] Into this turbulence King Agrippa stepped with the astonishing assurance that marked the best of the Herodians at their peak. Caligula's murder might easily have meant that Agrippa's whole house of cards would tumble down. But far from his own assigned territory yet well connected at Rome, this luckiest and wiliest of all the Herodians proved a friend of Claudius as much as he had been to Caligula, and he helped the new emperor secure power.

Agrippa showed such attention to mourning Caligula as was expected but then forced his way in to see Claudius when he learned that he had been taken into custody.[52] He pleaded with Claudius, with whom he had shared a Roman upbringing, to pursue his claim to governance with the support of that section of the army that he could count on. The Praetorian Guard in Rome had the enormous advantage of armed force on the site of decision-making, and by their support of Claudius, they assured their future in power, provided he did become emperor. Having secured at least a tentative agreement, Agrippa then proceeded to the Senate. There he argued with dexterous duplicity that although he would die for the honor of the Senate, the arms behind Claudius made him an unstoppable force. He concluded by offering to act as an ambassador between the Senate and Claudius. Agrippa continued his shuttle diplomacy between the two, even as factions and violence multiplied, until Claudius was in fact proclaimed emperor. The bloodshed that followed was, by Roman standards, moderate, to some extent because Agrippa had convinced Claudius to temper his actions. When Claudius secured imperial power, he was a greater Greek scholar than Agrippa would be, yet Dio Cassius reports that both Agrippa and his brother Herod (soon to be known as Herod of Chalcis) gave welcoming speeches to the new emperor before the Senate in the Greek language.[53] Their presence was the seal of a brief but decisive diplomatic campaign to reconcile the emperor with the Senate, while the emperor, with Praetorian backing, retained a controlling position.

In Rome proper, no Herodian had ever been in a more powerful position than Agrippa I now was. Claudius rewarded his crucially effective loyalty by conveying to him the lands of his grandfather and under the title of king. He now had secured without going to battle not only all the territory that Herod the Great had ruled but also all the lands Herod ever desired. At the same time, Claudius allocated to Agrippa's brother Herod, with the title of king, the much smaller region of Chalcis in the Lebanon valley, north of the greater Judea that Agrippa now ruled.[54] Agrippa endorsed this arrangement for his brother warmly and in a characteristically Roman manner. His daughter Bereniké had become a widow on the death of Marcus Julius Alexander. He then offered her to his brother in marriage; Bereniké went on to bear two sons with Herod of Chalcis, Berenikianus and Hyrcanus,[55] and was referred to with the title of "queen" for the rest of her life.

Agrippa's masterful agreement with Rome was sealed in public ceremony and recognized throughout the Roman Empire. Agrippa celebrated the occasion, having coins struck to celebrate himself as "the great king," under his own name (without the prefix Herod), swearing his friendship to Caesar, the Senate, and the people of Rome. One coin shows both "King Agrippa" and "King Herod" together holding wreaths over Claudius, who is styled "Augustus Caesar." In the image, each king wears a diadem yet is equipped as if for military readiness in cuirass over subarmalis and tunic, while Claudius is in a toga and pours out a ritual libation.[56] Although designed to praise Agrippa and Herod, these coins represent Herodian fealty to imperial power and symbolism.

Claudius followed Agrippa's counsel to placate Jewish insurgencies, particularly in Alexandria, in the wake of Caligula's edict. Balance became a hallmark of Claudian policy in this regard, and Agrippa enabled the new emperor to distinguish among Jewish factions between those whose ancestral rights could be confirmed and those who should be repressed.[57]

Rome itself had seen rioting in protest of Caligula's edict, and Suetonius remarked that disturbances broke out periodically "under the impulse of Christ" during the time of Claudius.[58] The phrase may seem mysterious and has puzzled historians. But when Claudius rose to power in 41 CE, not even ten years had elapsed since the time of the crucifixion, and Christianity had no profile independent of Judaism. There were still disciples who believed in direct action to secure the temple; their resources fell short of a professional military, but the precedent of physical intervention had been set. Jesus had been willing to confront Caiaphas, who had introduced commerce into the temple, and some of Jesus's disciples felt compelled to resist Caligula, who planned for blatant idolatry in the temple. Claudius acted, likely on Agrippa's advice, to put down the disturbance among Jesus's Jewish followers in Rome by means of exile because they were part of an apocalyptic tendency of growing importance within the movement. These disciples saw Roman threats to the temple as signs that God would intervene in human events because his dwelling place in Jerusalem was eternal.

By the time Agrippa entered Jerusalem as king of Judea, he had consolidated his power base in Rome and had acted decisively to master his new, united kingdom of Judea, which now included Samaria, Idumea, Perea, Galilee, Gaulanitis, Trachonitis, adjacent territories, and (through his brother Herod) Chalcis. But he knew he needed desperately to win the loyalty of those who passionately defended the integrity of the temple. He wisely centered his concern on Jerusalem, the focus of all the disruption that Caligula had caused. Although his coins outside Judea proper continued to display images that broke the injunction against idolatry, in and around Jerusalem, he avoided minting coins with a human image. He fully deployed the priestly status that his descent from Mariamme had bestowed on him. He entered the temple to offer sacrifices of thanksgiving and paid for the vow of thousands of Nazirites.[59]

Agrippa had also learned from Claudius's recent experience that a wise ruler could turn the wider Judaic population against apocalyptists within the circle of Jesus. They developed an eschatological reading of the threat to the temple under Caligula (see Mark 13:14–23) as a sign that God was about to unleash war, earthquake, and famine in order to vindicate the place of his dwelling (Mark 13:3–8) and insisted that even persecution of the kind Claudius had directed against them was only a passing part of the inevitable events of the end times (Mark 13:9–13). By taking on the policy of Claudius and treating Christianity as a *superstitio* (rather than a recognized religion, a *religio licita*) that should be persecuted, Agrippa could both coordinate his actions with the emperor's and ingratiate himself with Jewish opinion that was either opposed to Jesus's movement (as in the case of much of the high priestly caste[60]) or skeptical of it. He beheaded James, the son of Zebedee, as part of that policy and also had Peter put into custody (Acts 12:1–19).

His role as protector of the temple also accounts for the New Testament's memory of him as an enemy of Jesus's followers. The book of Acts attributes enmity against Jesus's movement as a whole to Agrippa, but his actions demonstrate a calibrated initiative on behalf of public order. While he had James, the son of Zebedee, put to death, Peter was merely imprisoned. Peter was a relatively pacific teacher, while James had a more literal view of the kingdom of God replacing Roman hegemony and of Jesus's followers exerting control over the temple. James and his brother John had even asked Jesus to let them reign with him in his kingdom (Mark 10:35–40), and in Luke's Gospel, they propose that fire should be called down from heaven against Samaritans who did not accommodate Jesus and his disciples (Luke 9:52–54). When Jesus nicknamed the two sons of Zebedee as "sons of tumult," he showed that he knew the kind of enthusiasts he was dealing with (Mark 3:17[61]).

The Gospels according to Matthew and Luke share a considerable run of material—for the most part sayings of Jesus (amounting to some two hundred verses)—that appears to derive from an earlier source. Much of the early work to identify the source was conducted by German scholars, with the result that the source came to be known by the first letter of the German word for "source," *Quelle*—hence, "Q." The source can only be identified by a comparison of Matthew and Luke rather than by an actual ancient document.

Recent discussion of the source known as "Q" has brought about a remarkable consensus that at least some of the sayings within it were circulated a few years after the crucifixion, around the year 35 CE, and that—with modification—Luke's Gospel is probably the best guide to its order.[62] The earliest version of "Q" probably included a charge to Jesus's disciples (Luke 10:3–6, 9–11, 16), a strategy to cope with resistance to their message (Luke 6:27–35), examples of how to speak of the kingdom (Luke 6:20–21; 11:2–4, 14–20; 13:18–21), curses to lay on those who reject those sent in the name of the kingdom (Luke 11:39–48, 52), and a section relating John the Baptist and Jesus as principal emissaries of the kingdom (Luke 7:24–26, 28, 33–34).

Jesus's teaching was arranged in the form of a memorized message (a Mishnah) by his disciples after his death. They took up activity in Jesus's name to Israel at large after the resurrection. "Q" was preserved orally in Aramaic and explained how the twelve apostles were to discharge their purpose.

One of the themes in the "Q" tradition concerns the definition of the community of Jesus's followers during his lifetime, in the near future (from the perspective of his followers), and in the new age that God was about to establish. His followers are portrayed as those who in the present age are deprived and scorned: they are the poor, the hungry, the sorrowful, the hated, the excluded, and the reviled (Luke 6:20–22). They are promised a reversal of their condition "in that day"—that is, the moment when God's purpose is achieved through the Son of Man. Their reward is already stored up in heaven in anticipation of that deliverance and vindication. Meanwhile, however, they are to love those who oppose them, to pray for their abusers, to respond generously to those who do them injustices, and to do so in the confidence that God will reward their gracious actions in the new day that is coming (Luke 6:27–36). By refusing to judge others and extending forgiveness to them, disciples will be amply rewarded by God in the future (Luke 6:37–42). Since their lives are founded on the compassion of God, they will be able to withstand the difficulties and storms that await them in the future (Luke 6:43–49), because divine compassion will be all in all.

Disciples must be prepared, however, for radical conflict with their loved ones, and they must be ready to give up traditional obligations toward the family in view of the higher demands involved in proclaiming the advent of God's kingdom in the near future (Luke 9:57–62). Their commitment to the work of the kingdom will cause violent disruptions in their domestic lives (Luke 12:51–53). What is called for in the cause of discipleship is described as hatred toward one's own family and even a willingness to abandon one's own life, as Jesus did in his fidelity to what he believed was God's will for him (Luke 14:26–27). There can be no wavering as to where one's ultimate obligations and values are directed: followers must be devoted to God and his work in the world (Luke 16:13).

Jesus's followers are to carry forward the work he launched: they must heal the sick and announce the coming of God's rule. To carry out this activity, they must move from town to town, indifferent to any conventional system of support, relying only upon the generosity of their hearers but ready to move on if their message is rejected. Their responsibilities are discharged when they proclaim by word and act the triumphant message of what God is doing through Jesus. God will bring judgment in his own way on those who refuse to heed the message (Luke 10:2–16). The members of the community of Jesus rejoice in the special wisdom about God's purpose that has been disclosed to them through Jesus (Luke 10:21–23). As time went on, the degree of opposition to teachers such as James, the son of Zebedee, caused opponents to be compared with the ancient antagonists of Israel, Tyre and Sidon (Luke 10:13–15). This attitude of confrontation and threat brought about predictable persecution.

By triaging the various threats inherent in Jesus's movement and other movements, Agrippa was able to pacify his kingdom. His uncle's policy toward John the Baptist and Jesus had allowed for less nuance. Although as ruthless as any ruler thought he had to be, Agrippa was also skillful and effective. Peter in the end went free, albeit as a result of angelic intervention according to Acts (12:6–11). Yet Agrippa did not have Peter pursued, despite his involvement with James, the son of Zebedee. Nonetheless, Peter would increasingly take his activities outside Jerusalem. The principal follower of Jesus there was James, the brother of Jesus, who integrated his brother's movement within the practice of Nazirite vows. That gave those around him cover from persecution for decades. James's Nazirite practice and Agrippa's were oddly complementary. It is even conceivable that James and those associated with him benefited from Agrippa's sponsorship of Nazirites.

The book of Acts does not explain the process by which James emerged as the leader of the community of Jesus's followers in Jerusalem. But it portrays him as the senior figure in a meeting that included Peter, Barnabas, and Paul and took place in 46 CE. In that consultation, James took the lead in finding that non-Jewish followers could be immersed (that is, baptized) in Jesus's name without the requirement of circumcision being imposed. Yet James also came at a later time to insist that gentile believers needed to keep basic rules of purity in regard to the foods they ate and their sexual ethics (Acts 15:1–29).[63] His practice of the Nazirite vow made him not only acceptable but also reputable within the practice of the temple, and his reputation was only enhanced with time and even survived his death. That would not have been possible without Agrippa's differentiated policy in regard to followers of Jesus.

For the book of Acts, however, Agrippa was just another "Herod," and that is what it calls him in the passage about James, the son of Zebedee, and the following narrative, which relates the miraculous escape of Peter from prison (Acts 12:1–19) in a way that recapitulates Israel's exodus from Egypt.[64] In the image of his grandfather, he orders people executed without reason, much as Herod the Great allegedly slew all the children of Bethlehem in order to avoid the threat posed by Jesus's birth (Matt 2:16–18). One Herodian is merged into another as mythological figures of the repression of God's word. Herodians as a whole are understood to be at odds with the fledgling movement.

Agrippa's splendid display of piety in underwriting Nazirite vows paved the way for his thorough coordination of worship in the temple.[65] Now fully in charge of the hierarchy, he proceeded to dismiss and name tenants of the high priesthood, although he kept up friendly relations with the families that had long exercised control and did not accede to the highest priestly office himself. He also used his Roman base of power to please those who adhered to Judaism by remitting taxes in Jerusalem. In a city outside his jurisdiction, Dora in Phoenicia, some local sycophants had sought to please the new emperor by setting up his image in a synagogue. Agrippa protested to Petronius, who was only too happy under his authority as Claudius's legate in Syria to discipline those involved and have the image removed and set up in an imperial temple instead.[66] The sensitivity of Agrippa and Petronius as compared to the harsh blasphemy of Caligula's edict was palpable throughout the world of Judaism. For the benefit of his own subjects as well as for Jews living in the Diaspora, Agrippa had established himself as just the figure that his coins now proclaimed: "Great King Agrippa, friend of Caesar."[67] His propaganda for his own success as his grandfather's true heir found a ready audience.

Naturally, voices of doubt made themselves heard. A teacher from Jerusalem named Simon argued that Agrippa's background in Rome and constant contact with gentiles made him ritually impure and therefore unqualified to enter into the temple. Agrippa appeared with him in public and, according to Josephus, gently refuted the charges.[68] Although Josephus's account (or rather his source) is more than tinged with hero worship, Agrippa did display consummate skill in defending himself from challenges along these lines.

The Mishnah (Sotah 7:8), although written long after these events, is not in any sense a Herodian document and yet sets out a moving scene. Agrippa reads from the Torah in the temple and comes upon the words "You shall not place a foreigner over you" (Deut 17:15); he begins to weep. This passage identified the key point of resistance to him, as he well understood; his Idumean background, his education in Rome, and his advancement in the imperial court all counted against him. His involvement in idolatrous festivals while in Rome and his hosting of feasts in the Roman manner were also probably well known, and his decision to give his daughter Berenikė in marriage to his brother Herod must have been scandalous to at least the well-informed public in Jerusalem. But the crowd shouted in Sotah 7:8, "Fear not, Agrippa: you are our brother, you are our brother, you are our brother!" As far as his standing in the temple was concerned, he had surpassed Herod the Great.

The principal advantages he had over his grandfather were his descent from Mariamme and—crucially—his status as the hero who had saved the temple from Caligula's "abomination of desolation." This made him the brother of all who cared for worship in accordance with the Torah.[69]

Agrippa's strategy to ingratiate himself with public opinion in Jerusalem caused him to make one known misstep with respect to the imperial court. He decided to reinforce and increase the city walls, but this was thwarted by Petronius's replacement in Syria, Marsus (who treated Agrippa with deep suspicion).[70] He reported back to Claudius that the move could facilitate campaigns of rebellion, and Agrippa wisely desisted. But Agrippa's only military aim was to consolidate his own and Rome's hegemony on the ground. For this purpose, he pursued operations against all those suspected of insurrectional activities at the time of Caligula's edict and thereafter. While Petronius was in Syria, cooperation was straightforward; Marsus's accession meant that Agrippa had to act on his own.

For a politician of Agrippa's skill, however, Marsus seemed a relatively minor annoyance. Agrippa and his supporters understood the story of his ascent to be an example that "God raises what has fallen," in the words of Josephus.[71] Agrippa pressed on in his continuing effort to develop fully the power implicit in his royal title. In the manner of his grandfather, he built expensive structures outside his territory, endowing a theater in Beirut, which he dedicated with spectacles that included gladiatorial combat. For the pleasure of that sport, he had 1,400 criminals fight each other to the death.[72] Moving back to his palace in Tiberias, he convened a meeting of client kings on his own initiative, an act of independent sovereignty that thoroughly annoyed Marsus. The governor could say nothing, however, of Agrippa's trip to Caesarea Maritima in order to celebrate the games there in honor of Caesar that Herod the Great had instituted. Here he received delegations and appeared in public in a garment of silver, so resplendent in the sun that it lit up and dazzled spectators.[73] He had achieved the apex of power.

What happened next threw those same spectators, and many others, into panic and mourning.[74] They had hailed Agrippa I as a god in public, and shortly after, he experienced immense pain that remained with him through his last illness and to an excruciating death. Josephus at the time (44 CE) was seven years old and was scarcely an actual witness of what happened. His distance from the events is signaled by his observation, passing on the account from a source, that Agrippa had seen an owl that prefigured his death after he accepted the flattery of the crowd that he was more than mortal. But the symptoms Josephus describes are consistent with the much briefer notice in Acts 12:23 and center on Agrippa's worm-eaten intestines. The similarity of the description of his symptoms to those of Herod the Great, who lingered much longer, may point to a common disease. In 1883, a condition known as Fournier's gangrene,[75] affecting the genitals and abdomen, became a medical diagnosis. Dreadful pain, dead tissue, and accompanying infestation would have been the distressing signs of the lethal end of the disease. Five days after his splendid appearance in public, Agrippa was dead at the age of fifty-four.

The book of Acts abbreviates notice of Agrippa's illness and death but generally agrees with Josephus's account. A crowd cries out in their enthusiasm for Agrippa, resplendent in his royal robes and accompanied by representatives from Tyre and Sidon, "God's voice, and not man's." The source continues, "Immediately, the Lord's angel struck him in that he did not give glory to God, and he became worm-eaten and expired" (Acts 12:22–23). By contrast with Agrippa's sudden collapse (v. 24), "The Lord's word grew and prospered." Both Tyre and Sidon had become stock references in the kind of apocalypticism within Jesus's movement[76] that Agrippa had opposed to the point of having James, the son of Zebedee, killed; thus the brief reference in Acts is a tale of revenge. Agrippa shows no signs of repentance for accepting divine honors as he does in Josephus's account. From the point of view of both Acts and Josephus, however, his death provided a lesson of what a hasty ascent might mean to a mere mortal.

From the point of view of Rome itself, however, the pressing issue was not theological but political and strategic. How were the former realms of Herod the Great to be governed after the death of his most gifted heir?

After Agrippa

CLAUDIUS REMAINED LOYAL to Agrippa even after his death. He resolved, for example, to replace Marsus as the legate to Syria.[77] Moreover, his initial instinct inclined him immediately to name Agrippa's son, Agrippa II, as king of Judea.[78] At the time, the younger Agrippa was in Rome, following the custom that often put the heirs of client kings within imperial orbit from an early age. But events in Judea made Claudius hesitate and then move in another direction.

At both Caesarea Maritima, Agrippa I's capital, and Sebasté in Samaria, gentile demonstrations broke out against the dead king and especially his daughters. Their father had left a hostage to fortune by setting up statues in their honor. The images were brought to brothels for public humiliation in effigy, while banquets were held to honor Charon, the divine ferryman of death, for escorting Agrippa I out of this life.[79] The defamation of Bereniké was grotesque. Having been married off twice in order to further Agrippa's connections, the sixteen-year-old was a ready target for the crowds' outlandish attacks. She was dismissed as a whore and her father as a pimp in obscene pantomimes with the statues posed in various sexual positions in displays of violation.

Claudius knew that the challenges to Agrippa's former territory were more formidable than crass displays and he perhaps recalled the barely containable sequence of bloody incidents and revolts that Archelaus's youth at the time of his appointment had engendered. Military operations were clearly in the offing, and Agrippa II boasted no experience in that regard. Moreover, Jewish rebels in Perea commenced warfare with the neighboring city of Philadelphia over a boundary dispute,[80] reminiscent of the campaigns that pitted the Nabataeans against Antipas. With Agrippa II only seventeen years old, it seemed wise to keep him in Rome and to keep Judea under close Roman control. Cuspus Fadus was sent as procurator, with more direct authority (fiscal and military) than the former prefects had, yet his short tenure (44–46 CE) faced constant outbursts of violence. The Perean rebels were well organized—albeit highly factional—and militant: Fadus pursued a policy of capture followed by exile or execution. Sometimes, gruesome methods were employed.[81] A prophetic revolutionary named Theudas gathered followers at the River Jordan with the promise that, as in the case of Joshua, the waters would part for them and they would all inherit the land of promise. Fadus's squadron of soldiers ended their quest, and the decapitated corpse of Theudas was put on display in Jerusalem.

Fadus showed no want of capacity in deploying military force, but interference that came his way from Rome inhibited his attempt to reorganize his troops, as he rightly wanted to do. He had been charged to see to public discipline in Caesarea and Sebasté over the disrespectful and rebellious behavior in the wake of Agrippa's death. Part of his strategy involved the transfer out of the region of those soldiers whom he evidently believed had inflamed local opinion.[82] Claudius, however, received representatives from the troops who appealed for stability in their deployment, and he allowed them to remain.[83] Even worse for Fadus, when he determined that he would keep the high priest's vestments in the Antonia fortress as a security measure, as had been the case under Pilate, Claudius again thwarted him. A delegation arrived from Jerusalem to appeal to Claudius, and their arguments against Fadus were reinforced by Agrippa II. The younger Agrippa was able to undermine Fadus and enhance his own position by supporting the authority of the high priesthood. He also supported his uncle Herod of Chalcis in his successful request to assume authority over the temple proper so that the procurator would find his power limited there by a new assertion of Herodian authority.[84] Fadus was soon replaced altogether, and these reversals made that predictable.

The replacement enhanced Agrippa II's standing further still. The incoming procurator, Tiberius Alexander, was the brother of Berenikeʹs first husband. Although he was a careerist within the Roman Empire, his background in Judaism must have made him an appealing candidate to Claudius, and he proved a resilient ally of Agrippa II. Yet Tiberius's tenure in Judea did not proceed smoothly. He crucified the two sons of Judas the Galilean, who had led the revolt against the census under Quirinius,[85] but the tide of violence continued to rise. Famine in Judea, Josephus believed, only encouraged revolutionary activity.[86] Whatever the explanation for events, however, a change in policy appeared the only answer to mounting violence in Judea and the surrounding region.

Yet that famine, which broke out in 46 CE, also brought to expression quite a different dynamic, one that offered the prospect of the peaceful integration of Judea within the Roman settlement. Queen Helena of Adiabene, a convert to Judaism, bought Egyptian grain and figs from Cyprus in order to feed the hungry of Jerusalem, where amid years of lavish donations, she established residence in order to fulfill her frequent Nazirite vows.[87] She did so at the time another Nazirite, James, the brother of Jesus, had come to such prominence that he had determined policy within Jesus's movement in regard to circumcision.

Within the circle of Nazirite practice in Jerusalem, this issue had already been addressed for Judaism more generally. Queen Helena's son, King Izates, was also a convert. His initial teacher, named Ananias, had cautioned him not to accept circumcision on the grounds that it would promote outrage among his subjects, but later a teacher named Eleazar from Galilee encouraged him to change his mind.[88] The ethos in which James thrived and rose to prominence involved making calls of judgment of that kind, representing a Nazirite focus in which Judaism was ritually exact and yet also accommodating of cultural realities in such a way that integration and even prominence within the broader world of Hellenism were reasonable hopes.

Claudius also attempted, in his own way, to appeal to the unifying force of the temple as a religious institution while also strengthening the Roman military response to outbreaks of violence. So he brought in Ventidius Cumanus in 48 CE to replace Tiberius Alexander and the following year appointed Agrippa II to have some power on the ground. With Cumanus, a more aggressive military stance was ensconced. Agrippa II was brought to bear experimentally to replace Herod, king of Chalcis, who died in the same year as Cumanus's appointment.[89] Agrippa assumed power with his widowed sister, Bereniké, as an active associate. Together, brother and sister forged a formidable alliance and took the Herodian dynasty into its most fraught phase since Herod the Great was made king by Octavian and Antony.

As the two great-grandchildren of Herod the Great searched for the means to restore all the lands of the region of Judea under their rule, Cumanus proved inept and needlessly provocative in antagonizing his Jewish subjects. He set up an extra force around the parapets of the temple one Passover, anticipating trouble. That anticipation, naturally enough, brought about the trouble that he feared. Guards on the inner walls of the temple and worshippers began to taunt one another until one of the soldiers exposed himself to those below and gave vent to his flatulence.[90] Rather than simply discipline his force, Cumanus brought in reinforcements, and thousands died in the confused panic and rioting that followed.

Bad feelings rose further when some of those involved in the riot robbed a Roman slave outside Jerusalem. Cumanus ordered a punitive raid on surrounding villages, and in the course of that, a soldier desecrated a copy of the Torah publicly. A crowd of such size converged on Cumanus's headquarters in protest that he ordered that soldier beheaded,[91] showing himself as vacillating as well as cruel.

Cumanus's final flaw—and his undoing—was venality. A group of pilgrims from Galilee passed through Samaria on the way to the temple, and they were attacked and some killed.[92] Although he promised to take punitive action in response, Cumanus in fact accepted a bribe from the Samaritans and did nothing. The scale of the consequent violence unleashed was so widespread as to be without precedent. Galileans entered into an alliance with brigand chiefs, with the result that Josephus—a contemporary historian then in his teens—observed that "Judea in its entirety was filled with brigandage," and even Tacitus described the situation as bordering on the collapse of Roman rule.[93]

By this stage, Cumanus's career was over, and a series of appeals that went all the way back to Claudius saw him off in exile. The Syrian legate, Quadratus, had been forced to intervene on the ground; he meted out sentences of crucifixion and also ordered Judean and Samaritan leaders, as well as Cumanus, back to Rome for the matter to be adjudicated by the emperor. If the procurator had no real hope of a career, the question remained whether the Galileans or the Samaritans would be favored in regard to the initial dispute and the violence that came from it. Agrippa II, again present in Rome, interceded with both Claudius and Claudius's wife, Agrippina. She was the granddaughter of Antonia, a protector of Agrippa I; in court intrigue, Agrippa II could be as effective as his father. Claudius so favored the Galileans that he ordered one of the Roman officers who opposed them dragged through the city of Jerusalem and then put to death by beheading.[94]

Cumanus's ruin offered new hope to Agrippa II and Bereniké. A new procurator, named Felix, took over Judea (including Samaria, Galilee, and Perea). He was the brother of Pallas, Claudius's trusted secretary, and therefore closer imperial attention to Judea could be anticipated. In addition, just a year before his death, Claudius appointed Agrippa II to the former tetrarchy of Philip in 53 CE.[95] This had been precisely the starting point of Agrippa I's ascent to power, and Agrippa II came into his realm with the title of king and with a wider allocation of lands than his father initially had. Although the times were deeply troubled and complicated for all the lands Agrippa II and Bereniké hoped to inherit, Herodian fortunes appeared to be on the rise again.

BERENIKÉ AND AGRIPPA II

INSTABILITY AND
INEVITABLE WAR WITH ROME

*The turbulence of the period after Agrippa I as well as a concern
over his son's inexperience prevented Claudius from appointing
Agrippa II in his stead. The reticence was shown to be justified,
because when Agrippa II did finally come into power over parts of
Herod and Agrippa I's old realm, he administered it tentatively, as
a Roman client. In stark contrast, there was nothing tentative about
his sister, Bereniké. Twice married by the time of Agrippa I's death,
she and her sister, Drusilla, continued to forge marriages
to advance the dynastic cause. But no spouse was as interesting to
Bereniké as her brother. Despite rumors of incest, she even left
a third husband to join Agrippa II's court. In that setting, she
and her brother attempted to moderate legal action against
the apostle Paul, but neither that prosecution nor the extralegal
execution of James, the brother of Jesus, could be prevented.
The temple occupied a position at the center of controversy and
increasingly saw violence. The last procurator before open war with
Rome broke out, Gessius Florus, overreacted while Agrippa was
in Egypt on a diplomatic mission at the crucial moment, when
revolt might have been averted. But Bereniké was in Jerusalem
undertaking a Nazirite vow, and she attempted to mitigate the
procurator's tactics. Even with Agrippa II's belated arrival and
support of his sister's approach, the revolt came. When it did, sister
and brother supported the general Vespasian and his son Titus, both
of whom would accede to the position of emperor as their Flavian
dynasty came to power. Bereniké began an affair with Titus that*

*was no passing liaison and became the basis of speculation from
Jerusalem to Rome that the Herodian dynasty would join with
the Flavians to shape a new settlement for the empire as a whole.
Bereniké, the most prominent figure in her generation of the
Herodians, brought their ambition to its most extensive aspiration.*
Bereniké: *Poised, devoted, and relentless*

The Queen

THE HERODIAN DYNASTY came to power, held on to its acquisitions
with both military and diplomatic tenacity, suffered setbacks, and arose
from apparent defeat, all with the help of its women. They acted, until
this juncture, not independently on the whole but within their family
structure, yet their influence was often decisive. It is difficult to con-
ceive of Herod the Great's rise to power apart from his mother, Cypros;
of his dynastic strategy without Mariamme; or of the court intrigue
that both anchored and undermined his success without his sister
Salomé. Although Antipas's rise had long been his ambition, without
his marriage to Herodias and the involvement of her brother Agrippa I,
the transition to the remarkable reestablishment of the united Herodian kingdom (albeit at the expense of Antipas) would not have been
conceivable.

Yet the one female of the dynasty whose name echoes most in
current culture was not a mature woman, may or may not be correctly
named, and almost certainly did not act in the way that is described.
That is Salomé, of course, not Herod's sister but Herodias's daughter—or
at least she could have been named Salomé. At the time of her famous
dance in two Gospels (Mark 6:17–29; Matt 14:3–12), she is described
as a "girl" (*korasion*) rather than a woman, and calling her "Salomé"
relies on a brief and passing notice in Josephus.[1] The necessity of her
dance is a matter of debate, and Luke's Gospel omits reference to it
(Luke 3:19–20); its celebrated "seven veils" relies on Oscar Wilde's
imagination in the play *Salomé*, which debuted at the end of the nineteenth century.

Such is the force of cultural memory, however much it is a matter of synthesis, that *Salomé* the dramatic artifact has obstructed the historical memory of the person who was unarguably the most powerful woman in the Herodian dynasty: Bereniké. Her intelligence, passion, devotion to Judaism, and human loyalty made her into much more than a supporting figure; she brought Herodian fortunes to an apex of which not even Herod the Great was likely to have dreamed.

At only sixteen years old when Agrippa I died, she was prominent, the subject of abuse, and a political figure. Her father, by marrying her off to the son of one of his most important Egyptian financiers and after his death to his brother, Herod of Chalcis,[2] had given her the reputation of prostitute. Because Agrippa I successfully asked Claudius for a diadem for his brother, Bereniké was a queen and known as such thereafter. She bore two sons, Berenikianus and Hyrcanus, whose names convey her ambition. "Berenikianus," the masculine form of Bereniké, means "bearer of victory," and "Hyrcanus," of course, continued an ancestral name from her Maccabean lineage. The modesty of the region she ruled with Herod of Chalcis dampened neither her aspirations nor his pretensions. The platform of governance at the service of Rome had, after all, served as the basis of Agrippa I's appointment to his grandfather's throne. With a royal title and a reputation for sexual license, Bereniké always drew criticism and made herself an easy target for critics who used her reputation in the service of self-interested motives. When her father, Agrippa I, died, crowds in Caesarea and Samaria raped and sodomized her effigy.

The death of her second husband, Herod of Chalcis, in 48 CE prompted Claudius to appoint Agrippa II (Bereniké's brother) in his uncle's place as ruler of Chalcis;[3] Bereniké continued with her title as queen. Because Herod of Chalcis had also petitioned the emperor successfully to administer the temple, with the authority to appoint high priests,[4] the inheritance of his little realm came with considerable influence in Jerusalem. When five years later Claudius transferred and promoted Agrippa II to what had been the tetrarchy of Philip, his unmarried sisters came to live with him in Caesarea Philippi. Drusilla complained of hard treatment from Bereniké, only justified, Drusilla alleged, because she was more beautiful than her older sister. Agrippa resolved the issue when he married off Drusilla to the king of the Syrian city Emesa, who converted to Judaism in order to contract the marriage. But Felix, the new procurator of Judea, was much better placed in terms of influence. The family had every interest in tolerating Drusilla's liaison with him, despite its contradiction of the Torah, and she left her husband to marry Felix in 54 CE.[5] Both sides of the marriage gained prestige and authority, as Felix showed he understood when he incorporated a well-known symbol deployed by Herod the Great, a pair of crossed palm branches, on his coins.[6]

From a promising base of territorial power and marital alliance, together with the established claim of Herodian and Maccabean bloodlines, Agrippa II and his sister Bereniké seemed poised—if they could elude the mounting tide of violence throughout Judea—to inherit the united kingdom of Herod the Great that their father, Agrippa I, had managed to restore within the contested politics of Rome. Theirs was the most fraught campaign ever mounted by the Herodian dynasty, and in the end, it was Bereniké's alone to carry out.

Ensconced with her brother at Caesarea Philippi, Bereniké reigned over the palace like the queen that she was. Having already acquired her title from her marriage to her deceased uncle Herod, king of Chalcis, she behaved as if she were Agrippa II's consort. Rumors inevitably emerged, especially because Agrippa II remained unmarried. Even the Roman satirist Juvenal, writing at the beginning of the second century, refers to the incestuous scandal as if it were common knowledge.

The gossip was too promising for Juvenal to resist alluding to when he came to write his sixth *Satire*, which warns against marriage generally. He describes the departure of a wife from her husband. She takes valuables along with her, including a ring that once belonged to Bereniké. Juvenal wrote with his anti-Semitism and misogyny on full display: "She will carry off large crystal vases, the most enormous pieces of agate, plus a legendary diamond, made more precious by Bereniké's finger. The barbarian Agrippa gave it to his incestuous sister to wear, where barefoot kings observe sabbaths as feasts, and custom grants clemency to old pigs."[7] Juvenal's questionable humor, of course, does not prove that the incest occurred, although he eloquently demonstrates his own bias and the fact that rumors about Agrippa and Bereniké circulated in the Roman Empire even in the first quarter of the second century, when he composed his witticism.

Josephus reports that Bereniké tried to shed her reputation for incestuous relations by marrying the king of Cilicia, Polemo. But the marriage did not last, despite the king's willingness to accept circumcision and convert to Judaism, because Bereniké was unfaithful. That, at least, is Josephus's version of events; at this point, according to him, Bereniké was simply a libidinous beauty,[8] a "little Cleopatra" as later historians, poets, and playwrights called her.[9] Her case is somewhat like that of Mary Magdalene, a woman whose influence on history has been hopelessly confused with her sexual history.[10]

From the time just after the death of her father, Agrippa I, however, Bereniké's influence grew, despite the chaotic environment of increasingly violent politics in which she lived for most of her life. That accumulating power involved her sexual opportunism, but always at the service of her political acumen and ambition, her fierce loyalty to her family and its legacy, and a dedication to Judaism that proved at times nothing less than heroic.

Her departure from her brother's court to marry the king of Cilicia had largely been for reasons of state: to broaden Herodian influence in accordance with Agrippa II's strategy of marrying off his sisters to important actors in the Roman Empire as well as to launder her own reputation. The rumors that Josephus and Juvenal reproduce were no doubt current and played their part in her decision, but they were not the single decisive factor. After all, Bereniké's fear for her own reputation did not long keep her from the prospects of Herodian power. She left the new marriage and Cilicia in order to rejoin Agrippa II in Caesarea Philippi. She ignored criticism for leaving a husband and accompanying her brother again because, with Caesarea Philippi as a base, she understood that a shift in power had occurred that needed to be exploited. Her timing proved impeccable.

The Neronian Opportunity, Confrontations in Jerusalem

CLAUDIUS DIED BY poisoning in 54 CE, probably at the hands of his wife, Agrippina, who wanted to promote her son Nero at the expense of other aspirants to the Principate of Rome before Claudius could change his mind about who should come to power after him.[11] In many ways, Nero continued to be loyal to the house of Herod, and his early reign (which began when he was only seventeen) was widely considered successful, to some extent owing to the influence of his tutor, the Stoic philosopher Seneca. Agrippa II profited from Nero's reign with the imperial grant of control over Tiberias and other cities in Galilee and Perea, steadily accumulating territory in the manner of his father.[12] Increasing wealth, which they cleverly brought to bear in several small-scale but strategic building projects, enabled Agrippa II and Bereniké to pursue their aspirations to rule in the manner of their great-grandfather, Herod the Great.

Bereniké and Agrippa II managed Roman politics well, but even as compared to the years immediately after Caligula's edict, violence in Judea grew to the point of becoming unmanageable. Part of the problem lay in a growing rift between Felix, the procurator, and the high priests, who attempted to curry favor with popular opinion by criticizing Felix. Felix, in turn, fatefully enlisted petty criminals as his enforcers; called the *sicarii*, or "dagger men;" they hid their weapons in their clothing so as to execute their victims in public, even by daylight.[13] By means of their knives, Felix dispatched an annoying high priest, but he thereby set Roman power on a footing with gang violence in the estimation of much of the population of Jerusalem.

Gangs of assassins prowled the temple, and Josephus wrote that God in response "brought the Romans upon us, and to the city purifying fire."[14] That, of course, was a judgment in the hindsight of events much later, which culminated in the conflagration that destroyed the temple in 70 CE. Yet even during the 50s, the situation seemed untenable. Agrippa II and Bereniké nonetheless remained committed to their alliance with Rome, even as acts of insurrection became baffling and bizarre and the Roman response to them appeared cruel beyond measure, especially in its resort to criminal enforcers.

A self-designated prophet—one of many imposters, as Josephus styles them—came from Egypt and claimed the walls of Jerusalem would collapse at his command, as Jericho had fallen for Joshua. Felix killed four hundred of his followers, capturing another two hundred, but the Egyptian escaped, and rebels sprang up around Jerusalem, setting fire to villages that did not support them.[15] Even within Jerusalem, not only Romans but also different Jewish factions, quite apart from the Romans, used the *sicarii* and other thugs to seek advantages.[16]

This was the cauldron that Paul entered on his last visit to Jerusalem in 57 CE. His mission was desperate from the point of view of his conception of himself as an apostle. He made the city of Ephesus his base of power, and Ephesus was where rioting took place against him and other followers of Jesus for their resistance to the worship of local gods. Looking elsewhere for a base among the gentiles, whom he believed Christ had commissioned him to save, Paul devised a plan. He would first travel to Jerusalem in order to complete in the temple what he called "the offering of the gentiles" and then make his way to Rome and even to Spain (Rom 15:16, 23–25).[17] As an Israelite, he had the right to enter the temple and to offer sacrifice on behalf of others; he called that his priestly service and his very purpose as an apostle.

In order to fulfill that purpose, Paul needed the help of James, the brother of Jesus. In the midst of rising tensions in and around the temple, James's reputation had only grown. Over time, he insisted all the more emphatically and devotedly on the practice of the Nazirite vow, sealing the centrality of the temple for Jesus's movement.[18] Never was this identity more important to James; this discipline embraced his identity as an Israelite *and* as the leader (the *mebaqqer* in the language of Qumran, or first bishop, *episkopos* in Greek) of his brother's community. Paul acceded to James's program and readily agreed to his proposal to enter publicly into the temple in order to complete the Nazirite vow with some of James's disciples (Acts 21:17–19, 22–26).

James hoped this visible association with the worship of Israel would launder Paul's reputation in Jerusalem so people would stop saying he encouraged Jews not to keep the Torah. The rumor that Paul told Israelites not to circumcise their children was patently untrue: it was circumcision among *gentile* believers only that Paul opposed with his characteristic intensity (see, e.g., Gal 3:1–18; 5:2–12). Yet his claim was so intense that it was easily exaggerated and made to appear to be a global refusal of the ritual practices of Judaism generally; that claim made the rounds in Jerusalem, even among Jews who believed in Jesus (Acts 21:20–21). James needed to distance his brother's movement from all such rumors of blasphemy for his Nazirite community in Jerusalem to continue and thrive.

Paul's motivation was all his own. He wanted to walk into the temple as a representative of baptized gentiles, whether they had been worshippers of God or simply pagans prior to baptism, accomplishing his offering for the gentiles as their apostolic priest. He had actually arrived in Jerusalem with non-Jews in his entourage, so it was all too easy for ordinary worshipers in the temple, seeing Paul with a large group of Nazirites and their supporters, to suppose that the leading apostle of the non-Jews had finally consummated his blasphemy by attempting to introduce gentiles into the inner sanctuary that was prohibited to non-Israelites (Acts 21:27–29).

Bringing gentiles into the interior temple reserved for Israel was a sacrilege punishable by death. Josephus refers to inscriptions in stone around the sanctuary, authorized by the Romans, that prescribed capital punishment for doing that; remains of those plaques have been discovered.[19] So instead of welcoming Paul's display of public piety, a mob in the temple rioted against him (Acts 21:27–32), ready with the cooperation of the police of the high priest to execute him. But Paul himself also enjoyed support in the city, and a series of running street battles ensued among his followers, temple police, and zealots for the purity of the sanctuary. The Romans could not permit street fights in Jerusalem, and soldiers under a commander named Claudius Lysias attempted to restore order by arresting Paul (Acts 21:33–40).[20] Acts portrays the commander as permitting Paul to make a lengthy public speech at this point (21:39–22:22),[21] an unlikely way to restore order; later events show it is more likely that Claudius Lysias wished to deal with the fracas quietly. The fly in the ointment was that Paul was a Roman citizen (Acts 22:22–30): the otherwise expedient means of interrogating a renegade prophet by flogging could not be deployed.

Claudius Lysias, acting rationally and within the law, found a way to resolve the dispute: get the Sanhedrin to see that the charge was moot because Paul really had no gentiles with him when he went into the temple. But in front of the Sanhedrin, Paul resorted to his characteristic rhetoric and undermined Claudius Lysias's stratagem. He insulted the high priest, calling him a whitewashed wall, and claimed that the real reason behind the charge against him was his belief in the resurrection of the dead. That was patently untrue but clever: Paul intended by this feint to stir up controversy among the Pharisees and Sadducees present because they had profound differences over the issue of the resurrection (Acts 22:30–23:1–10).[22] Paul had been a Pharisee in Jerusalem prior to his conversion at the time of his commission by the risen Christ, and he was thoroughly familiar with the fault lines of theological dispute in Judaism and in the Holy City. He also judged correctly that Pharisees were an increasing influence within the Sanhedrin. The session even turned violent, and Claudius Lysias had to bring Paul back into custody.

Not even Roman protection could assure his safety. Paul's nephew informed the officer in charge of the Antonia fortress where the apostle was held that there was a conspiracy in Jerusalem to kill Paul. Claudius Lysias had no choice but to get Paul out of harm's way, with or without the consent of the Sanhedrin; he dispatched him to appear before Felix in Caesarea Maritima (Acts 23:12–35). Felix reacted by keeping Paul in custody, acting in accord with Claudius Lysias's attempt at a resolution with the high priest Ananias, who came to Caesarea with a lawyer named Tertullus. Tertullus understood that the charge of bringing gentiles into the sanctuary, the only premise on which Paul could be put to death within the statute of protection for the temple's sanctity, could not be sustained. So he shifted the ground of accusation to focus on sedition (Acts 24:1–9),[23] a crime against the Roman Empire that he imputed to "the Nazoreans"[24] generally (Acts 24:5). After he heard the accusations against Paul afresh and Paul's insistence that he was practicing his ancestral religion in good faith, Felix in consultation with Drusilla ordered Paul to pay for his own accommodation and remain in Caesarean custody (Acts 24:10–27). Felix may have been slightly frustrated by the legal impasse, but any such feeling was compensated for by the hope that Paul's supporters could be a source of profit. There the matter languished.

Whatever hope Felix might have cherished of securing a new source of income from Paul's backers, rioting that had broken out between Jews and Syrians within Caesarea Maritima put an end to his career. Troops under his command, levied from Syria, crushed the Jewish side without mercy and looted the homes of so many people[25] that protest reached Rome. The end of his eight-year tenure as procurator might have been described as leaving a civil war behind, except that there were too many factions to use even that phrase. As they increased in number, they did not diminish in violence, and many of them hired the same killers to effect their will.

The *sicarii* were the first order of threat confronted by the new procurator, Porcius Festus,[26] who confronted the consequences of Felix's erroneous belief that he could bend them to his own purposes. Festus approached this as a straightforward military operation, but he also knew that since he was less well connected than his predecessor, the cooperation of Agrippa II and Bereniké would be immensely valuable, and they increased their influence over Jerusalem in the role of useful advisors. The book of Acts describes them meeting with Festus in order to determine the fate of the apostle Paul; their advice put Paul on his way to Rome and eventual martyrdom.

Agrippa II and Bereniké had a complex attitude toward Paul. He was devoted to Jesus, the same man that their uncle Antipas had denounced to Pilate as a royal pretender by wrapping him in splendid apparel when he dispatched him to the prefect (Luke 23:11) after Jesus's occupation of the temple. But that was nearly thirty years earlier, and in any case, neither Agrippa II nor Bereniké had much residual family affection for their father's rival, who had unsuccessfully attempted to keep Agrippa I in check.[27] Their sister, Drusilla, had married Felix and so was associated with the decision to keep Paul in custody (Acts 24:24–27). The matter was left unresolved by the time Felix made his trip back to Rome after his troops had abused the Jewish population of Caesarea Maritima. He wisely did not wish to raise the issue of Paul and make another request for imperial adjudication in response to unrest in Judea, because that would only advertise his lack of control of the overall situation.

Agrippa II, Bereniké, and Festus were also reluctant to dispatch Paul to Rome for judgment, and for much the same reason. Festus, however, had inadvertently complicated the situation. Newly arrived in Caesarea Maritima, he proposed to have Paul travel to Jerusalem for judgment. Paul wished to avoid another chaotic session involving the Sanhedrin and another possible plot of assassination, and so he formally appealed to Caesar (Acts 25:1–12), which would require a trial in Rome. Despite the risks of the maneuver, it seemed the best way to extricate himself from machinations in Judea. Such was the complex background when Agrippa II and Bereniké visited Caesarea in order to welcome Festus in his new office; all three of them gave Paul a hearing (Acts 25:13–26:1).

Throughout the episode, Agrippa II is portrayed in sympathetic terms: he expresses interest in the case (Acts 25:22), sits in state with Bereniké to hear Festus's public account of the matter (Acts 25:23–27), and is learned in the intricacies of Judaism (Acts 26:2–3, 26) and dedicated to the prophetic books in particular (Acts 26:27).[28] Agrippa even responds to Paul's speech with a combination of humor, irony, and admiration that he is on the point of making him a Christian (Acts 26:28). While Festus exclaims that Paul's learning has turned him delirious (Acts 26:24), Agrippa is sympathetic, and he advises Festus in agreement with Bereniké that, apart from the appeal to Caesar, Paul should have been released, since he committed no crime deserving death or imprisonment (Acts 26:30–32).

Although the portrayal of Agrippa II is so favorable as to appear unlikely, it seems clear that Agrippa and Bereniké joined Festus in the view that no overt act against Rome was involved in the internecine battle of Paul and his contemporaries in Judaism. That was the best outcome Paul could have expected, since it delivered him from local threats to his life while sending him to Rome without a major accusation lodged against him.

Yet the case engaged the interests of Agrippa II and Bereniké from another angle; within that perspective, Paul's fate was an incidental matter. Agrippa chose this moment to increase his stature in Jerusalem by extending the Herodian palace in the city, and that extension featured a dining room that overlooked the temple. Josephus said that Agrippa enjoyed reclining at meals times there to look at the ritual events within the sacred precincts.[29] In addition, he had in 59 CE appointed a new high priest,[30] so the priestly complainants against Paul, including Ananias, were sidelined within the structure of power. By dispatching Paul to Rome for trial without supporting the priestly interests that had accused Paul in the first place, Agrippa, Bereniké, and Festus exercised an autonomy in relation to Ananias that did not go unnoticed. Agrippa II wished not only to overlook the temple but also to oversee it within an overall plan of Roman pacification. It therefore suited his purposes to see Ananias's accusations against Paul discarded.

Festus had the authority to send Paul or any prisoner on to Rome as he saw fit with or without a recommendation that accorded with Ananias's wishes. But Festus, Agrippa II, and Bereniké would pay dearly for overruling the priests of Jerusalem. Even Ishmael, the high priest whom Agrippa II had appointed to take the place Ananias once held, either could not or would not protect his onetime sponsor.

Priestly objection to the alliance formed by Festus, Agrippa II, and Bereniké took shape in a dispute in regard to Agrippa II's extension of the Herodian palace. The view that he enjoyed of ritual life within the temple aroused the complaint, shared by much of the aristocracy of Jerusalem, against anyone reconnoitering the sacred proceedings of Israelite sacrifice.[31]

An obvious and practical measure against the perceived intrusion was to build up the wall around the holy enclosure, between the palace and the temple, so as to cut off Agrippa's view. In accomplishing that aim, the builders working under the direction of the priests who managed the temple also blocked the view of Roman guards who were posted on a portico on that same side at the time of major feasts. A single building project, conducted in the name of piety, directly confronted Agrippa II, Bereniké, and Festus, so Festus responded by ordering the wall demolished.

Although Festus, Agrippa II, and Bereniké saw the new wall as an affront and wanted it demolished, they were also bound by the tradition of Rome's deference to the high priesthood in Jerusalem. When High Priest Ishmael asked for permission to send an embassy to Nero himself to *reverse* the order to demolish the new wall, Festus therefore acceded to the request. Neither he, Agrippa II, nor Bereniké had reckoned adequately with the priestly faction led by Ananias when they offered this accommodation. Even Agrippa's appointee Ishmael had been suborned, as events would prove.

Ishmael and his entourage appeared before Nero and won their case: the wall that impeded Agrippa's view would stand. The key to their success, according to Josephus, was that Nero's wife, Poppaea, who was keenly interested in Judaism, supported the high priest and his group. Faced with a choice between high priests and the procurator with his Herodian supporters, Poppaea preferred what seemed to be the more authentic spokesmen of Judaism. Nero agreed that the temple authorities should be favored over Festus and Herod's great-grandchildren. For the first time in his career, Agrippa II had been outplayed at the imperial court. His extension of the Herodian palace came to a halt, and the wall remained. His defeat proved costly for everyone involved over the long term, even Rome. Agrippa's only consolation was that Poppaea decided to keep Ishmael with her in Rome so that Agrippa could appoint another high priest (named Joseph Cabi).

This episode is an example of the procurator acting in what was intended to be a judicious manner by preventing a construction that impeded Roman control, but his decision played into the hands of growing violence. Events had shown that anyone who had borne the title of high priest could galvanize the high priestly faction as a whole; Ananias remained a leading figure. The faction was in a position not only to change physical arrangements in the temple but also to hire in gang members—the notorious *sicarii* among them—to see that worshippers conducted themselves as they wished. The high priests made it clear they wanted the temple to function independently of anyone's control but their own. At one time a crucial support for accommodation with the Romans in the status quo regularized by Herod the Great and Augustus, the Sadducees of Ananias's persuasion began a disastrous drift toward an alliance with the *sicarii* and other rebellious groups. They had recourse to forty such men in their plot to kill Paul (Acts 23:12–15), and connections of that kind, although initiated for practical reasons, pulled them into a new ideological fervor whose only possible outcome was a disaster.

So it was that the dispute concerning the extension of the palace and the wall that blocked its view of the temple, in the context of the general increase of violence, marked the appearance of priestly nationalism, the ideology that saw control of the sanctuary, the city, and Judea with its surrounding lands as a uniquely priestly prerogative. That ideology would consolidate the fragmented forces of rebellion and propel greater Judea (i.e., the Herodian realm) into direct war with Rome.

Agrippa II and Bereniké had to face the consequences of the reversal on their own because Festus died so suddenly that there was a brief interregnum before his successor came to power. Agrippa appointed a new high priest, named Ananus, who took the opportunity of the absence of a procurator to have the Sanhedrin order the execution of James, the brother of Jesus, by stoning.[32] Ananus's family had been involved in the execution of Jesus; Caiaphas was the son-in-law of its patriarch (also called Ananus, or Annas in the New Testament); the dispatch of James can be considered as the intended resolution of a long-standing feud and the elimination of a prominent Nazirite who had been associated with Paul.[33] But the move only inflamed the internecine violence that plagued Jerusalem.

Because he was a well-known Nazirite, James was a venerated figure in Jerusalem, and not just among the followers of Jesus. At a time when armed groups attempted to impose their will on others, when Roman soldiers might intervene at any time in Jerusalem, and when the new Herodian power couple attempted to reassert the power of their family, the quiet devotion of Nazirites reminded all who saw them of the temple's intended purpose. Every Nazirite leader in Jerusalem stood out as a calm center of holiness in the violent storm that threatened to engulf the worship of Israel. A second-century Christian writer named Hegesippus exaggerates when he claims that the war with Rome broke out soon after James's execution,[34] yet he captures the tenor of a seemingly inevitable rush to destruction that eliminated any moderating tendency in its path.

Open War

JAMES'S BARELY JUDICIAL murder in 62 CE was greeted by a protest that was heard by Festus's replacement, whose name was Albinus, and Agrippa II duly deposed Ananus from the high priesthood.[35] As in the case of Caiaphas and Jesus, a high priest paid the price for a convenient execution with a weakening of his own base of power. Agrippa II and Bereniké managed to begin a cooperative arrangement with Albinus by coordinating their efforts in finding a better high priest. Agrippa II also attempted to repair his now damaged standing in the imperial court by enlarging Caesarea Philippi, which he now called Neronias, and constructing a theater in Beirut.[36] Such actions only made Agrippa II appear less a generous Jewish king, however, than a fawning Roman subaltern.

In any case, the symbolic politics of pleasing Rome paled in contrast to the roiling conflicts in Jerusalem, tipped into permanent violence by recourse to contract killing and kidnapping by *sicarii*. High priestly families used them in recourse to violence against local opponents, and Albinus fell into a disastrous policy of catching and releasing violent offenders, a precedent he left to his successors. By this stage, there was probably no turning back from the revolt that was about to break out.

Work on the temple—the crowning architectural project put in motion by Herod the Great—came to an end; massive unemployment was the predictable consequence. Agrippa II exacerbated this destabilizing factor by failing to initiate a new large-scale project in Jerusalem, but he funded work in the newly named Neronias and lavished gifts on the city of Beirut outside of Judaea. His odd sense of priorities was not lost on the population of Jerusalem, and his attempt to play one priestly faction against another provoked more internecine violence.[37] Just when a renewed commitment to the purpose of the temple might have been effective, Agrippa refused a proposal from the city authorities to renew building work to fortify the edifice and ceded to the immediate interests of currying Roman favor. Still, the speed of the decay of the situation into open revolt against Rome could not have been anticipated.

Two players in the unfolding action badly misjudged the situation, misplayed their roles, and contributed to the disaster. Gessius Florus, who succeeded Albinus in 64 CE, not only resorted to pacts with violent offenders but also seized property and flaunted the wealth he expropriated. He owed his position to his wife's friendship with Poppaea and may have been emboldened in his predatory practices by the example of what Nero did to Christians in Rome at the time of the great fire. The ruthless pogrom Nero unleashed—which took the lives of Paul and Peter—was designed to cover his own use of the occasion to build on the ruins left by the fire and his possible role in igniting it.[38] Although the procurator Gessius Florus did not imitate Nero's cynical cunning in scapegoating Christians within the population as a vulnerable minority, Josephus expressed the view that he forced war upon his Judean subjects.[39]

For Josephus to make that statement is especially telling. After all, he would soon join the revolt himself and accept a commission to lead Jewish forces in Galilee, although after the war, he consistently criticized the mentality and tactics of the rebels, and before the war was even over, he had become a propagandist for Rome. That trajectory is not merely one of opportunism, although the whole pattern of his behavior includes that. Josephus attempted to uphold the interests of the priestly aristocracy[40] of which he was part and was willing to tack to one side or the other—the revolutionaries or the Romans—in the absence of a stable, coherent partner. In his view, Gessius Florus represented the Roman inconsistency that made war inevitable.

After a series of disputes with the Jewish community in Caesarea Maritima, still embroiled in controversy since the time of Felix, Florus accepted a bribe from a Jewish community that wished to extend its synagogue but then did not intervene when vandals desecrated the site with a bird sacrifice. By imprisoning moderate leaders who organized protests, Florus encouraged those who wished to respond violently because he demonstrated that temperance was ineffective where he was concerned; violence only grew when he commandeered seventeen talents from the treasury of the temple in Jerusalem.[41]

Earlier there had not been systematic coordination between the priests in Jerusalem and those ready for rebellion in the rest of the country—but that is just what Florus now faced as a result of his actions. Whether or not he knew of the similar action of Pilate nearly thirty years earlier in confiscating sacred funds, he produced a similar but greatly magnified result in the form of public opposition. Florus answered challenges to him with crucifixions and military pogroms that took the lives of 3,500 men, women, and children in Jerusalem under his direction. While Nero had acted with clever cruelty in fixing guilt on a small minority, Gessius Florus proved cruel and feckless in turning a majority of his Jewish subjects against Rome.

The second player to misjudge the situation and misplay his role was Agrippa II. While Gessius Florus deployed marauding troops in Jerusalem, Agrippa was in Alexandria visiting Tiberius Alexander, the former procurator of Judea and the brother of Bereniké's first husband. Tiberius Alexander had come to take up the office of prefect of Egypt, and Agrippa wanted to celebrate with him.[42] When tension had reached a pitch never before seen in Jerusalem, he had decided to play the Roman courtier rather than the advocate of the temple. His absence from events in the Holy City at this critical juncture revealed his casual attitude toward his own people and undercut his claim for a place in the succession of Herod the Great and Agrippa I as king of Judea.

But Queen Bereniké *did* take up a position in Jerusalem and attempted to defend the temple and the integrity of Judea. She undertook a Nazirite vow that she completed in the temple, and during the period of her abstinence, she sent in commanders of her personal guard to Florus in order to deplore outrages against civilians—including women and children—by Roman soldiers.[43] The soldiers responded by torturing victims in her sight and threatening her own life; Gessius Florus did nothing. Violence appeared uncontainable, and one night, Bereniké herself was besieged in the Herodian palace on the west of the city. She appeared before Gessius Florus the day after she had completed her Nazirite vow, head shaved and barefoot, to intercede personally for the people. He remained unmoved.

Many priests and much of the Jerusalem aristocracy, even in the midst of the prevailing Roman carnage, feared the complete devastation that revolt against Rome might bring; they appeared in public mourning to urge caution on the populace, but Gessius Florus took every opportunity and made opportunities for slaughter.[44] The faction in the city that wanted revolution pursued military preparations and building work to make the temple a fortress. Revolutionary leaders broke down the portico between the main structure and the Antonia fortress, denying the Romans access to the temple for operations with their still relatively small residential garrison.[45] Building a wall between the temple and the Herodian palace during the time of Festus had been the high priestly equivalent of declaring autonomy; breaching the link between their temple and the garrison housed in the Antonia fortress announced an intended resort to military force. Faced with the choice between mounting a siege and withdrawal, Gessius Florus withdrew to Caesarea Maritima, leaving in Jerusalem only a small force in an agreement with the rebels that marked a temporary truce.

Gessius Florus's maneuver was strictly provisional: his broader intent was to appeal to the governor of Syria to have him deploy an overwhelming force. He was disappointed in that aim, however, because Bereniké and other leaders in Jerusalem made a written appeal to the governor, Cestius. Rather than send his army, he dispatched an officer to investigate the situation.[46] The officer, Neapolitanus, met at Jamnia (also known as Yavneh) with a delegation from Jerusalem. Unfortunately, Bereniké was not a member of that delegation. Agrippa II, back from Alexandria, also took part in the investigation, and he might have shifted the balance in favor of the complaints against Florus. Instead, Agrippa again played the role of imperial courtier. In the most disastrous decision of his life—and perhaps of the Herodian dynasty altogether—Agrippa sided with Florus.

Josephus offers a complicated explanation of this behavior. He argues that by appearing to criticize the rebels, Agrippa II hoped to dissuade them from violent action. But from the beginning, Agrippa was Rome's agent more than he was his people's defender, and he did not deviate from that trajectory. He even resisted the request to send an embassy to Nero, instead appearing in Jerusalem to make a speech—in Josephus's account—of Thucydidean dimensions.[47] As in the case of Thucydides, the narrator is speaking as much as the alleged speaker is. The nub of Agrippa's position is precisely the view that Josephus himself espoused, after the war he waged was lost and he acknowledged defeat on the field of battle: so great an empire as the Romans commanded could only have emerged with God to sustain it, and therefore resistance amounted to a form of impiety that would only be exacerbated by the necessities of war.[48]

Agrippa II's position came as no surprise; his personal loyalties were well known throughout Jerusalem. But as he made the speech, he set Bereniké up in clear view, high in the Herodian palace.[49] She represented, better than he, deep devotion to the temple; brother and sister burst into tears at the end of the address and for a time appeared to stem the tide of revolution. But this attempt to convince the rebels to restore the connection between the temple and the Antonia fortress and to pay tribute in loyalty to Rome came to an end when Agrippa urged continued obedience to the hated Florus until a successor was named from Rome. At the threat of physical violence, with Bereniké, he retreated from Jerusalem to Caesarea Philippi, now called Neronias.[50]

The rebels seized the Herodian fortress at Masada as a strategic redoubt, and the priestly administrator (*sagan*) of the temple, named Eleazar (the son of Ananias), declared in 66 CE that no gift from a foreigner was to be accepted for sacrifice. The emperor's agreed provision of an offering twice a day, a condition sine qua non of the settlement with Rome, was thereby rejected.[51] Priestly nationalism had coordinated the revolutionaries into a coherent force. Their fulcrum was the temple, the most magnificent institution of Judaism that had ever existed, and from there the equivalent of war was declared on Rome.

Eleazar entered into dispute and sometimes deadly combat with other factions, but his priestly contingent prevailed in Jerusalem.[52] Agrippa even sent in two thousand cavalry to buttress resistance against Eleazar by some leading citizens who opposed revolt, but they were no match for fighting in close quarters with the *sicarii* and many thousands of rebels who answered Agrippa's intervention by burning down his palace, together with debt records in the city. Jerusalem was lost to Agrippa II and the Romans. The force that was garrisoned in the Antonia surrendered, only to be butchered by Eleazar's partisans.

Gentiles in surrounding cities, beginning with Caesarea Maritima, began pogroms against Jews, provoking Jewish counterattacks in the surrounding region; throughout Syria, massacres broke out between communities whose relations had been reasonably good until that time.[53] Rioting also erupted in Alexandria, where Tiberius Alexander intervened *against* the Jewish population despite his connection to the Herodians, leaving thousands of dead at the hands of his soldiers.[54] Agrippa II's domain was by no means spared. He departed his capital to consult with the Roman governor in Antioch and unwisely left a counselor in charge who devised a scheme to round up, denounce for rebellion, and slaughter leading Jews in the region in order to benefit his own position afterward. Agrippa managed to intervene before the elaborate conspiracy could be put into action.[55]

As he dealt with that internal threat, Agrippa II also organized a force of some five thousand to march with the larger numbers of Roman soldiers under the governor, Cestius.[56] With that contingent in place, Agrippa stood as a junior officer to Cestius and a creature of Rome; any vestigial pretense to governing in the interests of his Jewish subjects was thoroughly discredited. Although the force achieved quick victories on the way to Jerusalem, the city itself had benefited by an influx of zeal with the Feast of Tabernacles—the largest sacrificial gathering of the year—and the rebels fought the Romans to a standstill outside the city. Agrippa sent two negotiators into the city to offer truce and amnesty: one was killed, the other was wounded and fled. By this stage, Josephus reports that Cestius was in the superior position and could have pressed his advantage to take the city. Instead, he retreated out of caution and consigned Judea to years of war and his own forces to losses of men and matériel at the hands of fighters who plagued his withdrawal. The withdrawal of Cestius was a Roman disaster.

Riots against Jews raged in Damascus in response, but in Jerusalem, the rebellion had consolidated in accordance with the policies of Ananias and his faction. A revolutionary council in Jerusalem assigned generals to various regions, including Idumea; Jericho; Perea; cities such as Lydda, Joppa, and Emmaus; and Galilee. Josephus, later to become Rome's agent, was assigned to a command in Galilee.[57] He reports in loving detail his own preparation to meet the invading force of Romans. But tales of his energy, even if true, cannot conceal the chaos that threatened to hollow out the rebellion from within.

Men from a village named Dabaritha, for example, waylaid one of the officers of Agrippa II and Bereniké, confiscating the considerable wealth in the convoy and delivering it to Josephus in Tarichaea. Josephus faced mob violence when it appeared he would return the booty but saved his skin by saying it had been his intention all along to use it to pay for fortifying Tarichaea, then in a parlous defensive position.[58] Josephus mounted a defense both against the Romans and on behalf of his own interests by unbridled means, belying his later claims of moderation; in a macabre scene, he ordered one of those who resisted his authority to cut off his own left hand.

Agrippa II, on the other side of the war, failed to take action, even when offered the opportunity to aid the city of Tiberias in defecting from the ranks of the rebels.[59] Instead of intervening in force, he delayed in favor of the arrival of Roman cavalry. Agrippa in his way and Josephus in his were now concerned only with the greater game: the approach of Rome's armies in overwhelming force.

Nero was convinced that a failure of leadership had cost him possession of Judea, and he assigned Vespasian, an experienced general nearing sixty years old, to take command. From the outset, he coordinated with his son Titus, who commandeered the fifteenth legion from Alexandria; Agrippa joined with Vespasian in Antioch with all the forces he could muster.[60] From there, in 67 CE, Vespasian undertook a massive invasion, backed by his own full legions (the fifth and tenth), as well as ancillary forces from Agrippa and other dependent rulers. He took Sepphoris without a fight. After meeting up in Ptolemais with Titus's legion from Alexandria, he crushed his way through Galilee, making decent terms with villages, towns, and cities that capitulated; he razed those that did not, selling entire populations into slavery.

Josephus, with his command of Galilee as ordered by Jerusalem, found himself in the path of a fearsome military machine, although he claimed that when his instructions were followed, the fortifications he had built and the deployments he ordered held up well against the Roman onslaught.[61] Yet already he doubted that victory would be the outcome for his side, as he fell back from engaging the Romans to Sepphoris, to Tiberias, and then to Jotapata, an old Maccabean fortress north of Sepphoris that he had reinforced. Hidden in a nearby cave after the city fell around him under Vespasian's brutal forty-seven-day siege, Josephus later recounted that he had a dream that, by his priestly powers of interpretation, he knew to signify that "all fortune had passed to the Romans."[62] His companions were not at all ready to surrender, so Josephus put his trust in a system for drawing lots to determine the order in which the soldiers would heroically slay one another rather than fall into Roman hands. The lots left only Josephus and one of his soldiers standing, and they both surrendered.

By this time in Josephus's narrative, God has entered into action on both Josephus's side and the Romans'. When he was brought before Vespasian, he claims Titus interceded with his father in the name of compassion. Josephus, in audience with Vespasian and Titus, predicts (correctly, it eventually proved) that Vespasian and Titus would become Caesars.[63] This prediction came on the eve of the removal of Nero and the stirring of ambitions in Vespasian himself on the basis of oracles associated with his campaign in Judea.[64] Josephus was spared definitive sentencing and gradually made his way into the Flavian entourage as a propagandist on behalf of Rome. His apologetic defense of Vespasian's rule was remarkably akin to Tacitus's claim that a Judean prophecy had pointed the way forward to the accession of the Flavian dynasty.[65] As the military confrontation between Rome and the Judean revolutionaries reached its bloody climax, a remarkable confluence emerged between a Judaic and a Hellenistic construction of providence as the guiding principle in human affairs.

Striking as this story of prophecy is, all the more remarkable is its virtual repetition—though attributed to a completely different person—in the Babylonian Talmud and related literature. From a period slightly later during the siege of Jerusalem, the rabbinic story relates the escape of Yochanan ben Zakkai,[66] who is credited with founding Rabbinic Judaism itself in the midst of the collapse of the Pharisaic movement, which was predicated on the existence of the temple. In the story, Yochanan makes a daring escape from Jerusalem when his disciples carry him out of the city in a coffin, as if he were dead, and he greets Vespasian as a king. When Vespasian denies that honorific, Yochanan replies that only royalty could destroy the temple (citing Isa 10:34).

A messenger quickly arrives, bringing the news of Vespasian's acclamation as emperor. The new emperor acknowledges Yochanan's wisdom by granting him the town of Yavneh (also known as Jamnia) as a settlement, together with its sages, the family group of Rabbi Gamaliel, and physicians to care for Rabbi Zadok.

If Josephus's tale of his prophetic acclamation of Vespasian is self-serving and improbable, the Talmudic version, as it is told, is simply impossible. At the close of the siege of Jerusalem, Vespasian was no longer in Judea: his son Titus had taken over the operation. And whoever was in command was scarcely concerned with the details of accommodating rabbinic personnel and providing them with medical care. This is a case in which, over time, the sages of the Talmud incorporated a story harvested from a neighbor's terrain, in this instance the memoirs of Josephus. Historically inaccurate though it is in regard to events, however, the Haggadah of Yochanan ben Zakkai and Vespasian reflects the historical ethos of the rabbinic movement as it emerged over time. The practitioners of Rabbinic Judaism accepted the governance of the Romans and adjusted to the loss of the temple through their dedication to the Torah as given to Moses, both in writing and in their own oral tradition, and by the fulfillment of faithful love on that basis, taken as the equivalent atoning sacrifice.[67]

Another reaction to the events unfolding around the temple took a very different course within the early Christian movement. "In those days there will be suffering, such as has not been from the beginning of the creation that God created until now" is the prediction in Mark 13:19, the discourse known as the "little apocalypse" and assigned to this period in its present form by most scholars.[68] This apocalypse, contemporaneous with the final assault on the temple, sums up the devastation of the entire region. Internecine strife, destruction, Roman genocide, and famine had become the order of the day. For the early movement centered on Jesus, the catastrophe was deep. The sanctuary that had been their focus was in its death throes; James, the brother of Jesus, who had been their leader in Jerusalem, was dead. Paul and Peter had been executed during Nero's pogrom in Rome; Mary Magdalene had been killed in 67 CE as the Romans slaughtered the resistant population of Galilee. In Mark 13, as in many passages of the Gospels, a quest for meaning in the midst of despair comes to expression. This source, associated with the apocalyptic thinker Silas (an associate of James),[69] framed events of the past and present as well as the future within an understanding that Scripture, rather than the guidance of memory or tradition, provided the best understanding of the chaotic circumstances that surrounded believers. In this source, scriptural passages are the reliable sign of truth, so whether the matter was how the world would end (Mark 13, with its corresponding passages in Matthew and Luke) or how Herod the Great had persecuted Jesus's family and the magi who visited his crèche (Matt 2:1–23), all was a matter of Scripture's fulfillment. No source of this kind had existed before, and none like it would appear again, because the times were appallingly unique.

As compared to the emerging Rabbinic principle that the study of the Torah took the place of sacrifice in the temple and the apocalyptic conviction that the destruction of the temple signaled the end of the world, both of which vied with other responses to the Roman siege of Jerusalem within Judaism and Christianity over several centuries, another interpretative option remained. Even as Josephus relates events leading up to the destruction of the temple in 70 CE, he lays the groundwork of his persistent hope that sacrificial worship in Jerusalem will be restored. Only the Romans could make that possible, and for just this reason, Josephus is determined in his flattering attention to Titus. He claims that Titus was sympathetic to him from the time of his capture and even describes the commander's magnificent rallying of his troops when he urged them to victory at Tarichaea as divinely inspiring.[70]

Titus's own inspiration, however, by now had another source. While Agrippa II offered the Roman forces lavish hospitality in his capital in their deployment to occupy Galilee,[71] Bereniké began an affair with Titus. Her impact on Roman conduct of the war saved many lives; at the insistence of Bereniké and Agrippa II, Vespasian treated the leader of the rebellious contingent in Tiberias mercifully after an attempted revolt.[72] Josephus does not give full weight to the affair, speaking rather of Vespasian's and Titus's regard for Agrippa, but Roman sources make it plain that Bereniké became an influential actor at the heart of military force and was making a final attempt to make Herodian power permanent.

The mountain-ensconced town of Gamla held out persistently, and Agrippa II was wounded during an attempt to negotiate terms.[73] Ultimately, the Romans pressed their siege until five thousand men, women, and children threw themselves to their deaths, and the Romans killed another four thousand. The revolt had entered into its suicidal, vengeful, and painfully protracted denouement. At this stage, the nobility of suicide rather than surrender was an ambient sentiment among those who opposed Rome, including those who had escaped to Jerusalem after the conquest of Galilee. Josephus referred to the "Zealots," the epitome of extremism, now taking power in the Holy City.[74] They turned against even the priestly nationalists, with the high priest Ananias at their head, whom they and their allies slew and even denied burial. The butchery, Josephus claims, was God's reason for giving the city over to the Romans; he claimed that Vespasian saw the matter this way as well.[75]

Vespasian's careful preparations for the siege were interrupted by news of Nero's death by suicide in the face of revolt within his own entourage on June 9, 68 CE. Warfare abetted, although internecine strife still raged in Jerusalem. The Roman general Galba was acclaimed emperor by his troops in Spain; Titus and Agrippa II both made their way to Rome for new orders, but Galba was killed, as were two other generals in succession, Otho and Vitellius, who also rose to imperial power and died within that same year. Vespasian bided his time, and while Agrippa also remained in Rome, Titus returned to Caesarea Maritima, Josephus said by "divine impulse."[76]

However divine his impulse, Titus's political instincts were perfectly suited to the chaotic time. His quick return to Judea put him back into Bereniké's company and assured him of her contacts. If he and his father were to succeed where Galba, Otho, and Vitellius had failed, they needed to be acclaimed, not by an army or two, but by a phalanx of military power that would brook no debate and permit no assassination. Titus had already supplemented his father's troops with a legion from Egypt. In addition, Vespasian wrote to Tiberius Alexander for assurance of his backing, and Bereniké's former brother-in-law promptly had Egyptian officials and populace alike take an oath of allegiance to Vespasian, who made his way to Alexandria. She was central to that pivotal endorsement, which set in motion widespread acclamation of Vespasian as emperor in the Roman east.[77] Vespasian left for Rome from Alexandria, leaving Titus to resume the siege of Jerusalem in earnest.[78] It needed to be completed for Vespasian to maintain a profile of imperial invincibility.

Defeat and the Last Herodian Meteorite

TITUS NOW COMMANDED more than four legions; he put Tiberius Alexander in charge of additional forces[79] and used Josephus as a go-between with the rebels and to deliver Roman propaganda, which he shouted from outside the walls of Jerusalem.[80] Titus shrewdly alternated a policy of apparent conciliation with cruel displays of vengeful and irresistible power. He crucified rebels within sight of the city to drain the morale of those within and in some cases amputated the limbs of enemy soldiers by way of spectacle.[81] During the campaign, Titus rode around the city with a companion who was struck with an arrow; he replied by unleashing destruction in the environs of Jerusalem.[82] On one occasion, Josephus also approached too close to the city's wall, and a stone knocked him out. He would have been dragged into the city and dispatched but for the rescue ordered by Titus, whom Josephus calls "Caesar" by this stage of his narrative.[83] Within the walls, some people were reduced to cannibalism, and internecine assassination and riot continued; clearly, taking time to make Vespasian emperor and Titus his heir had done nothing to reduce the prospects of the success of the Roman siege or of the suffering inside the city.

Josephus has Titus declare that God is on the side of the Romans, the preamble to his claim that Vespasian's son also wished the temple to be preserved, despite what happened.[84] Josephus's apologetic argument reaches the point that he describes rebels as setting fire to the sanctuary, with the Romans only following suit for tactical reasons.[85] Titus allegedly remained reluctant to continue those tactics and even attempted to stop the final conflagration.[86] It was only against his wishes, Josephus implausibly insists, that the temple was lost, and the fire consumed all. Whatever the mitigating motivations in play, brutal facts were plain: Jerusalem was Roman, public sacrifice ceased in the temple, and Judea had been captured. A policy clearly enunciated by Vespasian to overthrow the Jewish insurgents wherever they arose[87] had been pursued to its logical outcome.

To Josephus, all this was deserved, allegedly "predicted" in Scriptures that no one, however, has ever identified categorically.[88] He loved repeating that Titus appreciated God's support,[89] yet there is no denying that Titus's celebrations were thoroughly Roman. His troops brought their military emblems into the old temple court and offered sacrifices before them in celebration of Titus's victory.[90] The Roman dance of victory was not restricted to that act—an abomination by all the principles of Judaism—or to Jerusalem. Agrippa and Berenikė offered Titus and his troops hospitality again in Caesarea Philippi (the name Neronias now quickly dropping out of fashion). Titus offered public games, during which his Judean prisoners numbering in the thousands were killed by wild animals, forced to enter into mortal combat with one another, or simply burned to death.[91]

Titus's dreadful sports and celebrations, the seal of his victory, were intended as preparatory for this ceremonial triumph in Rome, yet Titus did decline to expel the Jewish population of Antioch on his way.[92] Josephus would have the reader believe that this was all part of Titus's quasi-pious concern for Judaism and its temple, but Roman historians reveal the motivating factor that Josephus elected to ignore. That is where Berenikė features again.

Josephus's silence about Berenikė's role in Vespasian's accession was diplomatic for reasons that emerged fully only after the destruction of the temple in 70 CE. But Tacitus, writing thirty-five years later, openly acknowledged Vespasian's appreciation of her efforts to rally support for him as the *princeps*-to-be and Titus's sexual infatuation with her.[93] When Titus returned to Rome for his triumph in 71 CE, he brought plunder and prisoners (some of whom he had executed as part of the celebration) but not his mistress. Public opinion was against Berenikė, whose beauty and power reminded too many people of Cleopatra and whose Judaism made her suspect. Titus had no ambition to become Rome's new Antony.

Yet in 75 CE, both Agrippa II and Bereniké came again to Rome; the former was made a praetor, a ceremonial position of magistracy perfectly suited to a successful courtier, and the queen openly moved into the imperial palace with Titus. She demanded her royal right in Rome as she had done in Chalcis and Caesarea Philippi, and whatever scandal her liaison with Titus provoked, she had no need to answer charges of incest. Dio Cassius complains that she behaved "in every respect as if she were his wife,"[94] venturing into the adjudication of suits as if it were her right. Titus at first tolerated no criticism of his union; public speakers who denounced the arrangement were known to be flogged and even beheaded. But Bereniké left Rome for Caesarea Philippi as doubts began to be raised over whether Titus would be able to succeed the aging Vespasian after all. Attempts to kill the putative heir made Titus fearful that the rising disapproval of the impending marriage could ruin his chances of becoming emperor.

Hope did not die with that visit, and in any case, Agrippa II had extended his territorial grip. Jerusalem's disaster had brought him great benefit, and he could hope that a final extension of his regional power might bring him the full Judean kingdom of his great-grandfather and his father. When Vespasian finally died in 79 CE, a last and perhaps definitive Herodian victory seemed within reach. Bereniké returned to Rome, apparently anticipating marriage with the emperor. Her brother celebrated by minting a coin with a veiled female bust on one side and an anchor on the other, evidently a jubilant reference to Bereniké's journey.[95]

The expectations she had raised were not only for the house of Herod. In his *Judean War*, published in 75 CE, within a description of the temple as it was about to be destroyed, Josephus addresses Jerusalem as the victim of the rebels' violence: "What comparable injury had you suffered from the Romans, most miserable city? They entered to cleanse your internecine defilement with fire, because you were no longer God's place, neither could you continue, after becoming a tomb of kinspeople's bodies, and making the Sanctuary a mass grave of internecine war! Yet it might become better again, if ever you appeased the God who laid waste."[96] That "if" was the theological condition in Josephus's mind, but there was also a political condition: that Rome would permit the temple to function again. Josephus believed that possible, and he acted wisely by not mentioning anything about Bereniké as the possible but controversial instrument of Jerusalem's redemption. She was now the hope not only of the Herodians but also of former priestly nationalists like Josephus and all who wanted to see the temple of the *religio Iudaeorum* restored. Josephus's silence about her and his relentless propaganda for the view that Titus really had wanted to "save the city for himself and the Temple for the city"[97] were designed to nurture hope and see to the restoration of the temple that had, after all, been rebuilt before.

Titus was active and able, completing the Colosseum that his father had started, engaging in many new projects, and ending the trials for treason that had plagued the aristocracy. He also had to deal with the eruption of Vesuvius (which killed Bereniké's sister Drusilla and her son[98]), yet another fire in Rome, an outbreak of plague, and rebellion in Britain. As his reputation in the empire rose, so did the chances that Bereniké would at long last, after an affair of well over a decade, become his wife. The consequences—not only for Jerusalem and the temple but for Judaism in every part of the world—promised to be incalculable.

Just after the dedication of the Colosseum's new facilities, however, Titus fell ill with fever on a journey. He died in 81 CE at the age of forty-two, far short of his father's life span. His death, as sudden as that of Agrippa I, was also as harmful in its consequences for Judaism, Jerusalem, and the temple. Bereft, Bereniké returned to Caesarea Philippi; she and her brother finished out their days in their technical monarchy, but their royal patch of land was now little more than a courtesy. Rome had come to prefer direct rule; Titus's brother Domitian had no time or patience for foreign cults. Herodian ambition and Josephus's hopes for the restoration of the temple had breathed their last.

By the time Josephus wrote his *Antiquities* in 93–94 CE, Agrippa and Bereniké were spent political forces. Josephus backed away from his support of Bereniké. Earlier, after the destruction of the temple in

70 CE, she had given him hope for the revival of the fortunes of all adherents to Judaism in the Roman Empire, but by the end of the first century, little remained of the legacy of Bereniké and Agrippa II apart from disappointed expectations and salacious rumors.[99] Agrippa had taken to issuing coins actually minted in Rome, no longer of his own manufacture.[100] The Herodian dynasty disappeared into the Roman Empire, its progeny largely lost to historical memory.

EPILOGUE

THE HERODIAN CAESURA WITHIN
THE POLITICS OF EMPIRE

CLAIMS OF THEOCRACY, ancient and modern, have been articulated across a spectrum running from simplistic brutality to exquisite sophistication. Political assertions of divine mandate as played out by the Herodians and their contemporaries epitomize that rich diversity and also reveal models of how God is involved in governance that continue to be part of the contemporary political scene. The principal actors on the whole did not engage in theoretical reflection or set out to implement preconceived political ideologies. That helps explain how differing and sometimes self-contradictory ideologies could be embraced in short succession or concurrently, on occasion by a single ruler. Conceptual engagement for these rulers was not a prerequisite of governance and might even get in the way of success. Over time, those who reacted to the pressure of Herodian governance from Judaic or Christian perspectives, at best at the margins of power and frequently excluded from it altogether, have through a literature that ranges from endorsement to dissent exerted greater influence than the Herodians themselves. Eventually, the least of these perspectives—that of Jesus in the period that concluded with his crucifixion—became associated with power to a degree unimaginable to observers during his time.

From the point of view of Judaism, Herod the Great and his house were unique; some observers then and now would say aberrant. He and his grandson, Agrippa I, the last kings of Judea, achieved their royal stature not by virtue of prophetic promise or obedience to the Torah but as a direct function of Roman hegemony in the region and their extraordinary facility in political manipulation. Within that perspective, Herodian rule can be seen as disruptive,[1] a breach in the tradition of the legitimate governance of Israel.

Rome's perspective was quite different and offers a way of seeing Herod and his dynasty within a larger and generally consistent pattern of governance. Distinctive in cultural terms, the Herodians were part of a political equation they shared with others. Comparison with Archelaus of Cappadocia[2] shows that features of Herod's rule that might be imagined as anomalous were rather consequences of his status in relation to Rome.

Archelaus of Cappadocia, like Herod, owed his royal title initially to Antony; once appointed in 36 BCE (four years after Antony and Octavian presented Herod to the Senate), he more than compensated Rome for investing in his kingship, as Herod did also. Archelaus's mother, Glaphyra, had been a courtesan (*heitera*) who became one of Antony's mistresses, and her son's appointment was a mark of his gratitude. But Archelaus also belonged to a noble Cappadocian house that boasted priestly connections as well. So Archelaus could claim from the beginning what Herod had to attempt to construct: a combined royal and priestly legitimacy. Both Archelaus and Herod survived the transition to the Principate; in fact, each saw his realm expand, with enhanced status and reputation, as Octavian became Augustus.

Augustus promoted friendships among his clients, and in the case of Archelaus and Herod, their amicable alliance was sealed with marriage. Herod's son by Mariamme, Alexander, married Archelaus's daughter, who was named Glaphyra after his mother.[3] This union with a royal and priestly house from Cappadocia was natural for Herod, mirroring his ambition for an heir descended from the Maccabees, while Archelaus cherished the pairing of his noble line with Idumean/Maccabean nobility. In time, Archelaus himself would contract a marriage to extend his own influence to the Black Sea; he occupied crucial territory to the north of the Roman province of Syria, much as Herod had secured a vital territory on its south. The combination of the house of Archelaus and the house of Herod was therefore a significant strategic reality within Rome's confrontation with Parthia.

When Alexander fell out of his father's favor, Archelaus of Cappadocia interceded for strategic, political, and personal reasons. He did so successfully when Herod and his sons by Mariamme appeared before

Augustus in 12 BCE.[4] Archelaus had skillfully prepared the ground for the interview by means of his relationship with Herod personally as well as with the imperial court. At the time of Alexander's trial five years later, however, Herod did not impanel Archelaus as a judge, although that had been Augustus's expectation.[5] The king's absence was a sign that the result of the proceeding was a foregone conclusion, and Alexander was put to death together with his brother Aristobulus. Despite a period of delusional suspicion of Archelaus and his daughter, Herod finally did not hold Glaphyra responsible for her husband's alleged misdeeds. Indeed, he arranged her marriage to another of Herod's sons, also (and interestingly) named Archelaus. Although that marriage was successful, the younger Archelaus's reign was not. Designated as king by the terms of Herod's will, Augustus made him only an ethnarch and then deposed him altogether, and Glaphyra went with her husband into exile.[6]

King Archelaus of Cappadocia survived because neither Alexander's nor the ethnarch Archelaus's behavior reflected badly on him within the imperial court—or even, at the end of the day, in Herod's estimation. He long survived Herod's death in 4 BCE as well as the transition from Augustus to Tiberius in 14 CE. By then Archelaus was elderly and by several accounts infirm, and he had in any case many years before he treated Tiberius with less deference than the *princeps*-to-be would have liked—and indeed in the apparent expectation that Tiberius would not be the *princeps* at all. Denounced before the emperor for a lack of loyalty, King Archelaus was in Rome for a hearing when he died in 17 CE. Perhaps with the example of Augustus's recourse to direct rule after he removed the ethnarch Archelaus from Judea in mind, Tiberius installed a procurator in Cappadocia. Emperors encouraged client kingship as a utilitarian convenience, but only as long as it was in fact utilitarian. There might be a greater or lesser degree of friendship among the kings and between individual kings and the emperor, but the emperor alone ruled.

Imperial rule was explicitly based on divine sanction. The theological dimensions of the Roman settlement are sometimes not recognized because *theokrateia* is the Greek term used by the first-century historian and apologist Josephus as if it were sui generis within Judaism in its insistence upon "attributing all power and might to God."[7] But imperial theocracy, in which the *princeps* was viewed within a divine lineage that gave his rule deified authority, was a ritual fact throughout the extent of Roman rule, when the emperor's genius, his inhabiting spirit, was accorded devotion in sacrifice.[8] The degree to which that personally made him a god can be now, and was then, a matter of dispute, and Stoic conceptions were deployed to give the assertion of imperial divinity (variously defined) a philosophical basis. But however asserted, the link between religion and politics, might and devotion, was embedded within the Roman panoply of power. Although Seneca was a famous apologist for Nero, philosophers were repressed and expelled from Rome by Flavian emperors,[9] so it is clear that the divine identity of the emperor did not depend on any single intellectual apology or the support of public intellectuals. It was a ritual and political fact long before a coherent justification emerged in philosophical terms.

Theocracy had in any case become part of the governing furniture of the Near Eastern world for millennia and was well established before Israel as a people or a nation saw the light of day. With the founding of the first cities eight thousand years before Herod came to power, the conception that a god protected their people by means of a specially anointed king became widespread. The king, sometimes styled as the "son" of the deity, embodied divine power.[10] The Judaism of Herod's time later hosted a ferment of different conceptions of how and by whom God ruled his people; disputed definitions of the term *messiah*, both in current scholarship and in the ancient sources, are only one index of contention among conflicting models of theocracy. The Herodians appropriated elements from some theocratic models, resisted others, and unleashed genocidal violence against opponents who invoked a divine warrant for their own revolutionary programs.

At the beginning of the Herodian saga, however, Antipater and his father served another theocratic regime, that of the Maccabees. At their height, the Maccabean dynasty of priest kings ruled a realm more extensive than even David or Solomon ever commanded, but in its diminished state by the time of Hyrcanus II, Idumean mercenaries had become crucial to its survival. Without compromising his commitment to his Maccabean patron Hyrcanus, Antipater collaborated with the Romans in order to preserve a delicate balance in favor of survival in the face of the growth of Parthian power.

When Antipater defended himself before Julius Caesar in opposition to Hyrcanus's nephew Antigonus, he stood for a style of rule that *separated* his application of force from theocratic power, while Antigonus represented an attempted restoration of Maccabean glory.[11] Neither Antigonus nor Antipater could fully have appreciated that alongside their personal animosity, they represented profoundly different options of government. Many cultures and countries have been riven between the alternative claims of rule by a single authority, religious and political, and the insistence that the two realms should be kept separate to a greater or lesser degree. The appeal of the first option is that the concentration of power makes the polity stronger and that of the second is that, in the end, separation makes both religion and politics healthier.

Neither of the two claims has ever been entirely excluded by any culture, although in times of civil peace, one of them usually occupies the upper hand. Equally resourced and armed, however, both sides are willing to resort to strife to gain their ends. Europe's historic wars of religion display the violence underlying the debate over how religion should relate to power.[12] Catholic kings invaded Protestant lands during the Thirty Years' War; Puritans decapitated their Catholic king in England. Following the lead of thinkers of the radical Reformation, William Penn founded a colony in America that made life safe for Quakers by tolerating all religions. The American Revolution followed that precedent at the federal level (although the individual states maintained religious preferences at the time the Constitution was ratified). Since then every modern nation—including the United States—has seen reference to religion incorporated within the ideology of governance, even when political separation from religious norms has been enunciated as a principle.

Violence is not the inevitable result of a recourse to religion within governance, but it is always a possible result. Once force is deployed in the confrontation between secular and religious authority, finding peace again has never been easy. In the case of Judea two millennia ago, it would require much more than a generation to resolve the conflict between integrating religion and government and allowing them an interval of separation. Both Antigonus and Antipater gave their lives in ways that could not have been predicted before the combat over governance was finished. Even then, it only ended because Judea itself was engulfed by the Roman Empire, which went on to replicate the struggle to demarcate the distinction between religion and state on its own terms.

Antipater's son Herod enriched the Romans while appropriating wealth for himself and his heirs. He could do both because, together with the advantage he gave the Roman Empire, he knew how to play the politics of God, asserting a theocracy of his own. While Antipater finessed his loyalty to the Maccabees to be compatible with fealty to the Roman invaders, Herod elevated his father's opportunism to a political art. So it was the Romans who rewarded Herod with the title of "king" for the military service that he had already rendered and for what they hoped would be the key function he would fulfill in their contention with Parthia,[13] but he wove an assertion of theocratic Judaism into his own royal claim by marrying the Maccabean princess named Mariamme.[14] He deliberately crafted a dynastic claim grounded in both Roman might and an Israelite version of *theokrateia*, although at the end of his life, he threatened his own project by assassinating much of the Maccabean line within his family. His jealousy for power was finally stronger than his ambition for his progeny.

The competitors and victims of the Herodian project were often as compelling as the Herodians themselves in their political claims; many of them contributed to models of governance that exercise influence to this day. As Rome developed a theocratic rationale for its empire, eventually complete with a philosophical justification, the Herodians—all of them accomplished in the Greek language and knowledgeable in classical learning—understood how to express their Judaism and their authority in terms compatible with imperial Rome. As they entered into their sustained dynastic advocacy over the course of several generations, the Herodians contended with theocratic competitors, including Maccabeans, Essenes, gangs of marauders who claimed religious motivation, Pharisees, Sadducees, Christians, and rabbis. Some of these groups first came into existence while Herod and his progeny ruled, and all of them had to adapt to the Herodian reality on the ground. Christianity, for example, did not even have a name of its own or an identity separate from Judaism when Antipas, the son of Herod the Great, decided to have Jesus killed (Luke 13:31). Each of these groups took pride in a theology of divine rule so rigorous that they proved capable of disputing Herodian theocracy, sometimes violently, all too often to the death, but with a dynamic impact that has been exerted in some cases for two millennia.

The Maccabean project that brought Antipater and his progeny into power confronted resistance from practitioners of Judaism who understood the legitimate rule of Israel in terms of the house of David and who believed that authentic priesthood derived only from the family and the tradition of Zadok. As compared to the Maccabees, Herod came as something of a relief to this group, which included the Essenes,[15] precisely because he personally had no claim of priestly or royal lineage. One Essene prophet, it was claimed, even predicted Herod's kingship, so that a benign détente became possible in which Essenes were excused from the requirement of taking an oath of loyalty.[16] Fatalism could make them an implicit ally (as events would prove only implicit and eschatologically tentative) of a regime that offered no real competition to the Essene vision of how the promises of God to Israel would eventuate.

The Pharisees were quite another matter. From the time of the Maccabees, they had entered into conflict with the high priest, and their physical interference when Alexander Jannaeus officiated as high priest had brought in response a gruesome degree of violence. After his death, Salomé Alexandra famously repaired relations, to the point that Josephus would declare that she was under some sort of spell of Pharisaic influence.[17] No doubt that is an exaggeration from someone who, as events proved, pursued another view altogether of the appropriate influences on and factors within governance. In any case, Herod ran afoul repeatedly of Pharisees—in the cases of his execution of the rebel leader Hezekiah,[18] his introduction into Jerusalem of trophies that could be and were construed as idols,[19] and his erection of a giant eagle within the temple complex proper.[20]

Pharisaic reaction to Herodian rule bifurcated: some Pharisees moved in the direction of revolt, while others espoused accommodation, and that division survived long after the time of Herod the Great himself. Although resistance was a common response among the Pharisees, some (notably Shemaiah) portrayed his growing power as an inevitability that had to be accommodated,[21] whereas the famous two rabbis, Judah and Matthias, whom Herod so horribly had executed for urging the destruction of his eagle in the temple, stood for the option of open resistance against an intolerable tyrant who flouted the Torah.[22]

During the tenure of Herod's son Archelaus the ethnarch, the degree of open revolt became intolerable in the Roman estimation. The revolutionary tendency that had emerged during Herod's time became stronger, to the point that it was by no means limited to Pharisaic opposition. Rather, Pharisees were co-opted within rebellions that they could no longer control. Archelaus, whose mother was the Samaritan Malthaké, exacerbated the problem with his volatile changes of approach between accommodation and intransigence and his assertion of control over the temple. Yet it is notable that his marriage to Glaphyra, the widow of Archelaus's half brother, Alexander, became a particular occasion for controversy.[23] Marriages within the prohibited degrees of affinity set out in Leviticus (18:16; 20:21) were elevated to a virtue within the Roman imperial court, and Archelaus's union with Glaphyra had been an act of Herod's statecraft. A fault line between the appeal to Israelite tradition and the satisfaction of Rome's expectations had opened up very plainly under Archelaus's feet and contributed to his downfall.

Key within the collapse of Rome's backing of Archelaus were the Sadducees, some of whom articulated the position that it would be preferable not to have any Herodian at all in control of Judea. They favored direct rule from Rome, with themselves in charge of the temple.[24] This represented a version of separating worship from governance but along quite different lines from what Antipater had represented when he appeared before Julius Caesar. In the Gospel according to John, it is the attitude fatefully attributed to Caiaphas (11:47–53).

The line of criticism against Archelaus developed by the Pharisees was continued by John the Baptist against Antipas, again over the issue of marriage, when Antipas married the wife of his brother Philip (Mark 6:18)—with Philip still living. When Antipas responded by having John executed, he represented not only his own vehemence and continuing ambition for Roman preferment but also his expectation that he could use force to extinguish such attempts to delegitimate him within his realm and even within Judea (which he did not then control and, despite his best efforts, never would).[25] Pursuing his policy further, he also sought to eliminate Jesus in Galilee. Jesus's critique of Antipas, however, went beyond that of his teacher. His dismissal of the tetrarch's attempt to have him killed made him a "fox" in Jesus's estimation, a nuisance rather than a force to be reckoned with (see Luke 13:32; Song 2:15). Jesus even went out of his way to scoff at the scruffy reedlike images on coins that Antipas produced from Tiberias (Luke 7:24), the city he founded and in which he took great pride.

Although Jesus's response to Antipas is represented episodically in the Gospels, it articulates a rejection of Herodian legitimacy as such. One of his followers was married to Antipas's officer Chuza (Luke 8:3), so his stance appears to be both deliberate and seditious. Jesus's departure from Antipas's territory in order to escape execution and make what proved to be his last pilgrimage to Jerusalem was therefore sensible in political terms. The perfect storm of politics that awaited him there—combining Pilate's febrility in the wake of the assassination of Sejanus in Rome, Caiaphas's desire to insist on his own authority in the temple against Jesus's prophetic protest against Caiaphas's relocation of vendors and their animals, and Antipas's ability to make himself useful to both the high priest and the prefect[26]—resulted in the crucifixion.

Within the precincts of the temple that he entered in order to realize Zechariah's prophecy of sacrifice without commerce, Jesus declared opposition to the high priest; his contempt for Antipas had already been expressed and was well known. He also articulated a policy toward Rome when he contrasted Roman coins and the artificial image of Caesar on them, which could be taxed by Caesar as the owner who minted them, with what was owed to God as the source of humanity itself (Mark 12:17). Rome could make coins, while the human image derives uniquely from God. The least powerful teacher, in political terms, of all those who contributed to the New Testament, Jesus nonetheless set out an influential attitude toward government that is better described as skeptical tolerance rather than acceptance or endorsement.

Jesus's reaction to Antipas, the local client of Rome, may have influenced what he had to say in regard to Caesar near the time of the crucifixion in 32 CE, but his position is unlike that of the rebel leaders in his past or those who were to come after his death. Caligula's edict for his statue to be erected in the temple in 40 CE, however, radicalized an opposition in Galilee as well as Judea that included Jesus's followers. One reason for the development of the assertion of deified emperors, taken much further by Caligula than by his predecessors, was that the theocratic claims of the ancient Near East, assumed reflexively by rulers such as Cleopatra of Egypt and grandiosely by Antiochus Epiphanes, prompted an imperial response from Rome. Ritualized in devotion to the sitting emperor as *divi filius*, or "a god's son," and over the long term conceptualized by means of Stoic teaching, Roman ideology came centuries later to serve the Christian theology it once persecuted by making the emperor the earthly counterpart of Christ.[27] Largely because devotion to the emperor had itself been, all along, a theological claim as well as a policy of state, this development had been richly precedented—however ironically—by imperial devotion.

Within the time of Caligula, however, Roman as well as Jewish opinion considered his imperial pretension a grotesque exaggeration, and the legate Petronius played a role equal to that of Agrippa I in assuring it never went into effect. But Caligula's attempt to establish a new "abomination of desolation" left its mark within the New Testament (Mark 13:14; cf. Dan 9:27), and the source of teaching associated with Silas, a follower of James, the brother of Jesus, became a major vehicle of apocalyptic teaching pointed against Rome within earliest Christianity by the time the temple was actually destroyed in 70 CE.[28] Although James himself was neither an Essene nor an apocalyptist, he shared several traits with the Essenes—for example, the avoidance of oil—as a result of his particular concern with purity and his practice of the Nazirite vow and took on the role of leader of Jesus's followers in Jerusalem under the title translated into Greek as *episkopos* ("bishop"), which corresponds to the *mebaqqer* of Qumran.[29]

In the deteriorating political conditions of the decades after Jesus's death, the Essene prospect of apocalypse gained credibility, and apocalyptic thought gathered traction among Jesus's followers, particularly under the influence of Silas. Agrippa I, when he came to power, had to deal with widespread apocalyptic resistance to Rome, and it suited his interests to target followers of Jesus in particular (notably James, the son of Zebedee; Acts 12:1–2) in order to warn away those tempted by confrontation with the Roman rulers.[30] In this regard, Agrippa followed Claudius's example in seeing that this tiny subgroup of the Jewish populace, when subjected to exemplary punishment, could be made to serve as a warning to the whole.

Yet the drift among Jesus's followers in a direction away from Rome was by no means universal. Another stream of tradition within the New Testament attests not only connections with the court of Antipas (Acts 13:1;[31] Luke 8:3) but also a favorable assessment of Agrippa II and Bereniké in their interactions with Paul (Acts 25:13–26:32). By the time of this revised attitude toward the Herodians, leading teachers of Christianity who originated in the Diaspora, including Barnabas and Paul, had emerged for whom Roman rule, however fraught with danger, should be taken to be a fact of life. Barnabas's position is represented only indirectly in a source within the Gospels and Acts that represents his teaching, but Paul speaks in his own voice within the New Testament.

Paul, a Roman citizen by virtue of his birth in Tarsus, provided a qualified endorsement of Roman power, which he could describe as a force legitimated by its reward of good behavior and its punishment of crime (Rom 13:1–7). This was not identical with Seneca's Stoic claim that the emperor (and Nero, at that) conducted human affairs in accordance with divine justice.[32] Yet Paul's apologetic thought and that of an emerging veneration of the *princeps* were similar enough that it is not altogether surprising that, in the following century, some readers of Paul and the Gospels would be willing to offer sacrifice to the emperor's image rather than accept martyrdom.[33] By that time, an emphatic inflection of Stoicism, crafted by first-century philosophers such as Seneca and at last stamped by the imperial stylus (if not the imperial seal) by Marcus Aurelius, increasingly animated Roman political thought. When Constantine legalized Christianity and accorded it such preference that it eventually became Rome's official religion, his fourth-century apologist Eusebius by no means rejected the Stoic ideology of imperial rule; rather, Eusebius modified it. Instead of the emperor being portrayed as the soul in the body of the empire, which is how Seneca depicted Nero,[34] Eusebius lauded Constantine as framing government on earth in accordance with God's kingdom, so that the emperor bears the image of supreme rule.[35] That was centuries after Paul, of course, and the apostle himself, under arrest three years after he wrote his Letter to the Romans, had in any case amended his stance to observe that for the believer, "citizens' status is in heaven" (Phil 3:20).

A stunning development saw the appropriation of Stoicism within Christianity to the extent that pre-Christian philosophers such as Cicero were embraced as preparing the realization of who Jesus was.[36] But this could only occur because of another, more subtle shift in the apologetics of power during the first century that was also associated with the Herodians. Providence had emerged within the first century as a central theme of two writers in the Diaspora, Philo and Josephus. Both in their different ways used the concept to explain how and why God had preserved his people from harm. For Philo, only providence could account for how various individuals could act in unknowing coordination to thwart the edict of Caligula and therefore avert what would have been the outbreak of warfare throughout the known world.[37] Josephus, however, is even more specific in his pursuit of the theme.

In dealing with the reign and, on any account, the extraordinary good fortune and unfortunate death of Agrippa I, Josephus details omens of an owl.[38] An owl appears when Agrippa was arrested at Tiberius's order for expressing the hope that the old emperor would soon die, so as to prepare the way for Caligula, and again at the end of his life when Agrippa received the adulation of admirers in Caesarea, who addressed him as a god. Even the significance of *both* omens is explained at the first occurrence by a German prisoner who is present—who cites the workings of "the providence of the divine" (*tou theiou hê pro-noia*). The prisoner explains that the first appearance of an owl augurs Agrippa's release and vindication, while the second will augur his death within five days. At the second appearance, Agrippa himself acknowledges that his impending death is a part of his fate as allotted by God. The similarity with Roman augurs—for example, the omens associated with Julius Caesar, Augustus, and Vespasian[39]—is striking, especially since Josephus claims personally to have foreseen Vespasian's accession to power.[40] But providence is a more powerful matter when an augur represents not simply the preference of one god or another but the will and purpose of the single God. Conceived in monotheistic terms, biblical providence is a more powerful apology of governance than augury in the classical period generally.

Josephus's embrace of providence enabled him to assimilate Agrippa I's remarkable rise but also his sudden and painful death. Portrayed in this light, Agrippa becomes the hero of a future that might have been, a kind of first-century Camelot.[41] Josephus even has Agrippa himself reflect on a tendency to arrogance that precipitated his end. The book of Acts partially agrees with Josephus's account of Agrippa's death but accords the king no such redeeming virtue. Acts has him struck down immediately after the crowd in Caesarea says of him, "The voice of a god, not a man" (12:21–23). This portrays Agrippa I, who died in 44 CE, in a way reminiscent of Nero, who died in 68 CE, stabbed to death after years of being fawned over at various concerts he staged with paid audiences for having "a divine voice."[42] In contrast, by keeping his focus on Agrippa I, Josephus is able to portray the king as essentially humble, despite his lapse, and as attesting the irresistible power of providence.

From Josephus's point of view, Agrippa I's tragedy permits the greater catastrophe of the temple's destruction to be explained and offers the prospect of hope after disaster.[43] Josephus is at pains to claim that Titus did not want the temple to perish in flames and had even ordered its preservation, to the point that he blamed those besieged for defiling their own sanctuary.[44] In this regard, Josephus shares a theodicy with the Targum of Isaiah, whose earliest framework was developed near the time of the destruction of the temple.[45] Unlike the Targum, however, Josephus was such an apologist for the Flavian dynasty (in the cases of Vespasian and Titus) that he merited the designation "Flavius Josephus," which has long been his. But at a deeper level, the apology is more on behalf of God than on behalf of Titus, whom Josephus says profited because "turns of war and dangers to kings matter to God."[46] Josephus imagines a new era in which the temple can again thrive while the Romans rule directly.

Josephus's passionate dedication to this possibility helps explain two respects in which his attitudes have seemed perplexing. First, when referring to the temple, he addressed himself to its prospects directly and rhapsodized over a conceivable future in which sacrifice according to the Torah would continue under Roman protection. The paradigm for such an arrangement was established by the Sadducees, who complained before Augustus of Herodian rule, whether especially in the person of Archelaus. Yet when Josephus speaks of the Sadducees, he calls them brutal in social relations, whether with outsiders or among themselves.[47] Second, Bereniké, the one member of the Herodian dynasty in its whole history who might have realized the vision that closes Josephus's account of the war, with a temple rebuilt, thriving, and protected under Roman aegis, is sexualized as the incestuous object of Agrippa II,[48] undermining any tendency to see her relationship with Titus as promising.

In both cases, Josephus's apparently anomalous response is controlled by his political rationality. He never saw the temple as definitively destroyed and embraced the approach that he describes as emerging among priests during the tenure of Archelaus the ethnarch.[49] Priestly control of the temple under Roman hegemony is just what he positioned himself to participate in. Until near the time of his death, his sacerdotal identity was prominent in his presentation of himself, and his assertion of aristocratic standing within the priesthood is notable.[50] But while the temple stood, he never joined the circle of those who were in control of the Sadducean faction, and the most prominent position he ever achieved was in Galilee, not at the center of power in the temple. By the time he arrived in Judea, it was to circle the walls of Jerusalem as a propagandist on behalf of Rome.

Although Josephus is perhaps the first century's most famous turncoat, he describes his change of heart on the basis of his priestly identity, which he said gave him the stature to understand prophecy and so acknowledge the providential role of the Romans. At the same time, he claimed that the priests (or at least those priests he associated with) went to war not so much in order to throw off Roman rule but rather to achieve a position of authority among the revolutionaries in order to regain control and restore order.[51] Although that claim may seem only marginally plausible, in times of armed revolution, the famous insight of Carl von Clausewitz is often reversed:[52] war is not an extension of politics by other means, but politics becomes an extension of war, because armed violence is the universal language during revolutionary conflict. During this period, any continuation of Essene quietism was evidently abandoned, for example, and they became known for their nobility under torture.[53] Josephus saw the priests as rightly in charge from the point of view of Judaism and did everything he could to achieve that end. His apparent dismissal of the Sadducees with the laconic remark about their antisocial ways reveals his own bitterness at never advancing within the faction whose interests he served and whose ideology he enthusiastically embraced.

When he came to the moment of disseminating his *The Jewish War* in 75 CE, Bereniké and Agrippa II were in Rome, and Josephus expressed pride—even years later, writing in *Life*—that Agrippa endorsed his project.[54] At the time of writing *The Jewish War*, he expressed his hope that the temple would see its purpose fulfilled again, and Bereniké's relationship with Titus was the most prominent vehicle of that hope. After Titus died and Josephus came to compose his *Antiquities*, his disappointment finds expression in his seemingly routine reference to Bereniké's incest with Agrippa II; still, he refers approvingly to Agrippa II himself. Josephus's dedication to the temple survived its destruction. He endorsed the imperial ideology, going so far as to bolster it by means of his own claim to be a priestly prophet who foresaw the Flavian ascendancy. For him, Roman theocracy and divine providence were compatible insofar as the prospect of a restored temple could be maintained.[55]

This dedication was by no means limited to priests, as the Bar Kokhba revolt during the second century unmistakably showed. Rabbi

Aqiba's support of that effort, whose failure put territorial Israel definitively under Roman control, demonstrates that the Pharisees' successors continued the political bifurcation produced during the reign of
Herod the Great. "Aqiba, grass will grow out from between your cheeks
before the messiah, ben David comes":[56] with these words, the rabbis
signaled that events on the ground had proven that the mandate of
heaven did not endorse attempts at rebellion against the Romans. Israel
was to maintain its distinction from the empire,[57] even while acknowl-
edging its rule, until the messianic age. With the definitive destruction
of the Essene movement as a consequence of either the first-century
revolt or the revolt of Bar Kokhba and the sustained privation of the
priesthood's natural base in the temple, the rabbis' inheritance of
the Pharisaic position in regard to governance and relationship with the
Roman Empire predominated.[58]

Christianity, however, resisted a synthesis between God and mam-
mon, at least in its first centuries. Differing attitudes toward governance
are evident within the movement. They included Jesus's highly qualified toleration but not his endorsement;[59] Paul's qualified endorsement,
which was recalibrated after his arrest;[60] Barnabas's association with the
Herodian court itself;[61] and Silas's committed apocalypticism, a hybrid
of the approach of James, the brother of Jesus, with its comparability to
some Essene teaching, and of the zeal of James, the son of Zebedee.[62]
One reason for the fractious quality of these perspectives is the absence
of any access to power, even on the margins of the prevailing hegemony,
which would have encouraged greater cohesion.

The transition to a Stoic point of view began not with increasingly
Christian influence but in the context of persecution. Justin Martyr's
dedication to a theology of the "word" (*logos*) during the second century,
as a line of connection between Christ and philosophy,[63] was part of an
apology rather than an assertion of power. The paradoxical contrast with
the direct claim upon all forms of political authority that came with the
embrace of Christianity as a religion of state after Constantine shows
how protean theocratic models could be. Although the influence of this
Constantinian model can seem irreversible,[64] it was in fact subjected
to the same sort of radical transformation that had seen its emergence.

Eusebius's claim that the emperor bears the divine image of God shifts, in the argument of John Milton in the seventeenth century, to an insistence that the image of God resides within every single human being.[65]

Milton's insistent shift of the location of the image of God came with violence: his tract was a defense of the execution of Charles I in 1649. At many points, theocracies come into conflict, and each naturally invokes its particular view of the divine to sustain it in war. But warfare among theocracies was by no means a continuous state under the Herodians. Their capacity to manage an extraordinary array of assertions of divine governance that could and did come into conflict—forwarded by Romans, Maccabees, Idumeans, Samaritans, Essenes, Pharisees, and Sadducees, as well as prophetic groups within Judaism such as the earliest Christians and a series of rebellious factions under the name of one revolutionary leader or another—was a major accomplishment; they served their imperial masters extremely well and, for all their violence, generally exerted a benign influence on their subjects.

But that achievement depended on those ruled as well as on their rulers. When Petronius faced demonstrations against the imperial edict to set up Caligula's image in the temple, the legate heard an argument that convinced him. The same Jews who offered sacrifice for Caesar twice a day would be willing themselves to be sacrificed in opposition, should the statue be set up.[66]

Were it true, as a modern orthodoxy would have it,[67] that theocracies are inherently violent, intolerant, and prone to war, accommodations such as what Petronius and Agrippa I engineered would not have been possible. In their adaptability and exploitation of new opportunities, the Herodians' subjects mirrored the Herodians' resourcefulness. Dealing with those who desire religious legitimacy for governmental authority by demanding that they relinquish their religion has never been likely to succeed, nor to reduce recourse to violence. Attention to God's politics as a fulcrum of governance made Herod the Great's legacy, both direct and especially indirect, more formidable in its influence than in the power he achieved in his own time or even dreamed of achieving.

CHRONOLOGY

722 BCE: Destruction of the kingdom of Israel under the Assyrian Empire with forced deportation, leaving only Judea in the south as the inheritance of the people of Israel

586 BCE: Destruction of the First Temple in Jerusalem under the Babylonian Empire, followed by a deportation known as the Exile

539 BCE: Cyrus the Persian's edict permitting a return to Jerusalem by Judeans so that the Second Temple could be dedicated before the end of the century, encouraged by prophets such as Zechariah and Haggai and under the aegis of Zerubbabel, the last known Davidic king of Judea

333 BCE: Conquests by Alexander the Great bringing the region under his control and, after his death in 323, the control of his successors

198 BCE: The victory of the Seleucid Antiochus III at Panium, with the Ptolemies of Egypt ceding control of Judea to the Near Eastern Seleucids

175 BCE: The accession of Antiochus IV Epiphanes, the Seleucid king who wished to make Jerusalem a Hellenistic city

167 BCE: The beginning of the Maccabean revolt in response to Antiochus IV's attempt to convert the temple to the worship of Zeus

164 BCE: The Maccabean recapture of the temple

134 BCE: The accession of John Hyrcanus (who died in 104 BCE) as high priest, who extended Maccabean hegemony to territory larger than the holdings of David and Solomon

74 BCE: The birth of Herod

66 BCE: Aristobulus II deposes his brother Hyrcanus II as king and high priest

63 BCE: The entry of Pompey into the temple as part of his assertion of Roman hegemony, backing Hyrcanus II as the high priest and supported by the Idumean Antipater

60 BCE: Formation of the First Triumvirate of Pompey, Julius Caesar, and Crassus

57 BCE: Establishment of a system of five Sanhedrins to govern Judea under Gabinius, the proconsul of Syria

53 BCE: The defeat of Crassus at Carrhae by the Parthians, by now the principal adversaries of Rome

49 BCE: Caesar's crossing of the Rubicon with the Thirteenth Legion, pitting himself against Pompey in a civil war

48 BCE: Caesar's victory at Pharsalus over Pompey, who dies by assassination in Egypt

47 BCE: Caesar's installation of Cleopatra as queen of Egypt, Antipater as procurator of Judea, Hyrcanus as ethnarch, and Sextus Caesar as governor of Syria

45 BCE: Julius Caesar's victory, aided by Phasael and Herod, at Apamea over Caecilius Bassus

44 BCE: Caesar's assassination on the Ides of March

43 BCE: Formation of the Second Triumvirate of Antony, Octavian, and Lepidus and the assassination of Antipater by Malichus, a member of Hyrcanus's entourage

42 BCE: Defeat of Brutus and Cassius at Philippi by Antony and Octavian; arrangement of marriage of Herod to Mariamme, the granddaughter of Hyrcanus

40 BCE: In response to the united front of Antigonus and the Parthians, naming of Herod as king of Judea by the Senate in Rome under the sponsorship of Antony and Octavian, after the death of Phasael and the disfigurement of Hyrcanus

37 BCE: The execution of Antigonus by Antony in Antioch; the effective beginning of Herod's reign and of his marriage

to Mariamme I, producing his sons Alexander and Aristobulus

35 BCE: The drowning of the high priest Aristobulus, Mariamme's brother, at Herod's instigation

32 BCE: Herod's disastrous campaign against Nabataea, followed by an earthquake the following year

31 BCE: The battle of Actium, with Octavian's emergence as victor, followed by the suicides of Antony and Cleopatra

29 BCE: The execution of Mariamme I

28 BCE: Herod's inauguration of games in honor of Caesar in Jerusalem, drawing on himself a Pharisaic conspiracy to assassinate him

27 BCE: Octavian named "Imperator Caesar Augustus"; Herod's marriage to the Samaritan Malthaké (the mother of Archelaus and Antipas) and his founding of Sebasté

25 BCE: Herod's marriage to Cleopatra of Jerusalem, who bears a son named Philip

24 BCE: Herod's marriage to Mariamme II amid drought, famine, and disease, which produces another son today called Philip

23 BCE: Alexander and Aristobulus's departure for Rome; Herod's founding of Herodium

22 BCE: Start of construction on Caesarea Maritima

20 BCE: Herod's initiation of the generational project of "restoring" the temple, after the dedication of a temple to Augustus in Paneion and the imposition of a loyalty oath, from which Essenes were exempt

17 BCE: The return of Alexander and Aristobulus from Rome

12 BCE: Augustus's meeting with Herod, Antipater, Alexander, and Aristobulus in order to resolve the contentious issue of succession

7 BCE: The execution of Alexander and Aristobulus

4 BCE: The executions of Judas and Mattathias and the death of Herod the Great, followed by the revolt of Judas, son of

Hezekiah, as Archelaus takes office in Judea, Antipas in Galilee and Perea, and Philip in Gaulanitis

2 CE: The birth of Jesus

6 CE: The removal of Archelaus from office in the midst of a tax revolt led by Judas the Galilean; accepting the view of the Sadducees, Augustus's appointment of a Roman prefect to administer Judea in the midst of a census under Quirinius, the legate to Syria

14 CE: The death of Augustus and the accession of Tiberius

19 CE: Antipas's dedication of the new city of Tiberias

21 CE: The beheading of John the Baptist at Antipas's order

23 CE: The death of Tiberius's son Drusus, leaving Herod's grandson, Agrippa I, bereft of his most important imperial friend

26 CE: Pontius Pilate's appointment as prefect of Judea; Tiberius's retirement to Capri, leaving Rome to Sejanus; Jesus's recognition as a rabbi in Capernaum

27 CE: Antipas's first efforts to have Jesus killed

31 CE: The death of Sejanus in Rome

32 CE: Jesus's arrest and execution in Jerusalem with Antipas's involvement

34 CE: The death of Philip the tetrarch

35 CE: The earliest sources of the Gospels, which are a collection of sayings of Jesus (often called "Q" today) and the narrative of Peter, available at the time of a meeting in Jerusalem among Paul, Peter, and James, the brother of Jesus, in Jerusalem (Gal 1:18–20)

36 CE: The removal of Pontius Pilate from power

37 CE: The death of Tiberius, the accession of Caligula, and the promotion of Agrippa I to become king of Gaulanitis

39 CE: Removal of Antipas from power

40 CE: Caligula's order that his statue be erected in the temple; teaching authorized by James is promulgated in Jerusalem

41 CE: The assassination of Caligula and Claudius's accession; Agrippa I's elevation to become king of Herod the Great's territories

44 CE: The death of Agrippa I, with Cuspus Fadus named as procurator

45 CE: The insurrection of Theudas; in Antioch, invention of the name "Christians"

46 CE: Famine in Judea and the apostolic meeting in Jerusalem, headed by James, that determined that keeping the covenant of circumcision was not to be a requirement for gentiles who were baptized in Jesus's name

46–48 CE: Tiberius Alexander, related by marriage to Agrippa II and Bereniké, named procurator; Agrippa II appointed to the former realm of Herod of Chalcis

52–59 CE: The tenure of Felix, procurator of Judea, who arrested the apostle Paul; Paul's major letters (to the Galatians, the Corinthians, and the Romans); Agrippa II's appointment to the former tetrarchy of Philip

54 CE: The death of Claudius and the accession of Nero

57 CE: Paul's arrest in Jerusalem

59–62 CE: Felix replaced by Festus, who sends Paul on to Rome in consultation with Agrippa II and Bereniké

62 CE: The death by stoning of James in Jerusalem

64 CE: The fire in Rome, followed by Nero's pogrom against Christians; probable time of the executions of Peter and of Paul

66 CE: Refusal of the *sagan* in the temple to accept the imperial offerings; Cestius's retreat after attempting to secure Jerusalem

68 CE: The death of Nero

69 CE: The accession of Vespasian, after Galba, Otho, and Vitellius

70 CE: The destruction of Jerusalem and the temple

71 CE: The triumph of Vespasian and Titus celebrated in Rome; the composition of Mark's Gospel

73–74 CE: The fall of Masada

75 CE: Dissemination of Josephus's *The Jewish War*; Agrippa II and Bereniké visit Rome

79 CE: Vespasian's death and the accession of Titus

80 CE: The composition of Matthew's Gospel in Damascus

81 CE: The death of Titus; his brother Domitian's accession to power

90 CE: The composition of Luke's Gospel in Antioch

93 CE: Josephus publishes his *Antiquities of the Jews*

100 CE: The composition of John's Gospel (in Ephesus) and of Josephus's *Life*

DRAMATIS PERSONAE

OWING TO THE large number of Herod's marriages and children, along with the proclivity of his progeny to co-opt the name Herod, it can be confusing to sort out the dramatis personae of the period. (The New Testament often conflates differing rulers under the name Herod.) Those who feature here are on the whole referred to only by their distinctive name (so Archelaus, Antipas, and Agrippa) without calling them "Herod," even when they appropriated that name on their coins and for purposes of propaganda and official discourse.

AGRIPPA: Octavian's admiral at Actium, close adviser, and friend of Herod the Great

AGRIPPA I: Herod the Great's grandson, whose connections in Rome and persistent bankruptcy made him a nuisance to his uncle Antipas, but as Caligula's protégé and Claudius's adviser, king of the realm of Herod the Great in 41 CE

AGRIPPA II: Son of Agrippa I, who inherited a crown, though not that of Judea, and ruled increasingly as a Roman functionary

ALBINUS: Procurator of Judea, 62 CE–64 CE

ALEXANDER: Herod the Great and Mariamme's first son, who with his brother Aristobulus was intended as Herod's heir but was put to death at Herod's order in 7 BCE

ALEXANDER YANNAI (ALEXANDER JANNAEUS): Maccabean ruler who died in 76 BCE, a scourge of the Pharisees until he advised his wife to make peace with them

ALEXANDRA: Mariamme's mother and instigator with Cleopatra of divisions within Herod the Great's family

ANANEL: The high priest named by Herod to replace the mutilated Hyrcanus

ANTIGONUS: The Maccabean nemesis of Herod the Great, who allied himself in a deadly campaign with the Parthians against Rome, Antipater's sons, and Hyrcanus

ANTIOCHUS IV: Seleucid king between 175 BCE and his death in 164 BCE, who converted the temple in Jerusalem to the worship of Zeus

ANTIPAS: Herod the Great's son by his Samaritan wife, Malthaké, who ruled Galilee and associated regions between 4 BCE and 39 CE

ANTIPATER: The father of Herod the Great, an Idumean clan chief who established the basis of cooperation between his family and both the Maccabees and the Romans

ANTIPATER: Herod the Great's eldest son by his first wife, Doris, whom he called back from exile as the issue of succession became critical but was executed at Herod's order in 4 BCE

ANTONY: The general who became Herod's protector, sponsoring his position in Rome as king of Judea

APION: An anti-Semitic public intellectual who goaded Caligula into setting up a statue of himself in the temple in Jerusalem

APOLLONIUS: The principal general of Antiochus IV, who implemented the policy of forced Hellenization in Seleucid Jerusalem

ARCHELAUS: Antipas's brother and Ethnarch of Judea between 4 BCE and 6 CE, the son most favored in Herod the Great's last will

ARETAS III: King of Nabataea, who offered Antipater crucial help in his battle against Aristobulus on behalf of Hyrcanus

ARETAS IV: King of Nabataea whose daughter Antipas divorced in order to marry Herodias

ARISTOBULUS (ALSO KNOWN AS ARISTOBULUS II): Son of Salomé Alexandra, who went to war against his brother Hyrcanus in order to succeed her

ARISTOBULUS: Mariamme's brother, named high priest to replace Ananel but drowned at Herod the Great's order

ARISTOBULUS: Herod the Great and Mariamme's second son, younger brother of Alexander

ATHENION: Cleopatra's general, who attacked Herod's forces by stealth during his Nabataean campaign

ATHRONGES: A messianic pretender who challenged the legitimacy of the Herodians after Herod the Great's death

AUGUSTUS (FORMERLY OCTAVIAN): Emperor, 27 BCE–14 CE

BERENIKÉ: Agrippa I's daughter, whom the general Titus, the Roman emperor-to-be, brought to Rome as an empress in waiting

CAECILIUS BASSUS: Leader of a mutiny against Sextus Caesar in Syria in 46 BCE, who attempted an alliance with Parthia in opposition to Julius Caesar

CALIGULA (GAIUS): Emperor, 37–41 CE; adoptive son of Tiberius and friend of Agrippa I

CASSIUS: One of the conspirators against Julius Caesar; replaced Sextus Caesar in Syria until his defeat by Antony near Philippi in 42 BCE

CESTIUS: Legate to Syria, whose forces suffered an unexpected defeat in 66 CE at the hands of the rebels against Roman rule in Jerusalem

CLAUDIUS: Emperor, 41–54 CE

CLAUDIUS LYSIAS: The apostle Paul's arresting officer in Jerusalem in 57 CE

CLEOPATRA: Antony's lover and Egypt's queen (47–30 BCE), who attempted repeatedly to undermine Herod the Great's governance and to acquire his territories

CLEOPATRA OF JERUSALEM: Herod's wife from 25 BCE, who bore Philip, the eventual tetrarch

COPONIUS: The first prefect of Judea, appointed by Augustus, 6–9 CE

CUMANUS: A notably aggressive procurator of Judea, 48–52 CE

CUSPUS FADUS: Procurator of Judea, 44–46 CE

CYPROS: Wife of Antipater and mother of Herod, whose Nabataean background made her a diplomatic asset

DIO CASSIUS: Produced *Roman History*, written in Greek, during the third century CE

DOMITIAN: Emperor, 81–96 CE

DRUSUS: Tiberius's son and friend of Agrippa I

ELEAZAR: An elder and scribe who refused under torture and eventual execution during the regime of Antiochus IV to betray the laws of Judaism by eating pork (2 Macc 6:18–31)

ELEAZAR AVARAN: An early Maccabean warrior and martyr who died in combat with the Seleucids (1 Macc 6:43–46)

THE FALSE ALEXANDER: An impersonator of the son of Herod the Great and Mariamme, unmasked by Augustus

FELIX: Procurator of Judea, 52–58 CE, and husband of Agrippa II's sister Drusilla

FESTUS: Procurator of Judea, 59–62 CE

FLACCUS: Prefect of Egypt, appointed by Tiberius; recalled by Caligula in 38 CE in disgrace after rioting in Alexandria; ordered to be executed the following year

GESSIUS FLORUS: The last procurator of Judea (64–66 CE) prior to the great revolt

GLAPHYRA: Princess from Cappadocia married first to Herod the Great's son Alexander and then to his son Archelaus

HEROD II (SOMETIMES CALLED HEROD PHILIP): Herod the Great's son by Mariamme II, designated as heir to the throne after Antipater but then struck out of the will when Mariamme II was accused of plotting against Herod

HEROD OF CHALCIS: Brother of Agrippa I, who married his niece Bereniké and became the king of Chalcis

HEROD THE GREAT: King of Judea by virtue of his military prowess and benefactor of Jews in the Roman Empire (74–4 BCE)

HERODIAS: Daughter of Aristobulus and therefore granddaughter of Herod the Great and Mariamme, a born player within the combined Maccabean and Idumean succession

HEZEKIAH: A warlord in Galilee, executed by Herod

HYRCANUS (ALSO KNOWN AS HYRCANUS II): High priest, Herod the Great's relative by marriage, and heir to Maccabean power in opposition to his brother Aristobulus

JAMES AND JOHN, THE SONS OF ZEBEDEE: Disciples of Jesus, the first of whom was executed under Agrippa I

JESUS: The teacher from Nazareth whom the Romans crucified in 32 CE

JOHN HYRCANUS: The most powerful of the Maccabean rulers, who brought the territorial extent of the hegemony to its greatest extent by the time of his death in 104 BCE

JOHN THE BAPTIST: A teacher of purity who opposed Antipas's marriage to Herodias and was executed for his stance in 21 CE

JOSEPH: Herod the Great's brother, beheaded by Pappus

JOSEPH: Herod's brother-in-law, killed summarily by the king on Salomé's charge that he had a liaison with Mariamme I

JOSEPHUS: The priestly general appointed to oppose the Romans in Galilee, who betrayed the cause to support the siege of Titus and went on to compose histories while living in Rome after the destruction of the temple

JUDAH AND MATTATHIAS: Two rabbis who conducted a campaign against the golden eagle Herod the Great had installed in the temple, only to be burnt to death at his order

JUDAS, THE SON OF HEZEKIAH: Leader of a credible military threat to Roman hegemony in the wake of Herod's death in 4 BCE

JUDAS THE GALILEAN: A revolutionary who led the tax revolt in 6 CE and framed an understanding of Judaism with the Pharisee Zadok that committed practitioners to resistance to Rome

JULIUS CAESAR: Rome's effective but deliberately nonroyal dictator, whose relationship with Antipater established the precedent for the Herodian dynasty

JUVENAL: Rome satirist who reflected the scandal of Bereniké's reputation during the first quarter of the second century

LIVY: Roman historian who likely lived until 17 CE or shortly before

THE MACCABEES: A priestly family that led a revolt against the Seleucids under Judas, called the "Hammer" (*Maqôbah* in Aramaic, typically Anglicized as "Maccabeus"), forming a dominant high priestly and royal dynasty

MALICHUS: A principal councilor of Hyrcanus, who urged an alliance with Parthia and arranged for the death of Herod's father, Antipater, by poisoning

MALTHAKÉ: Herod's wife from 27 BCE, who bore Archelaus and Antipas

MARCUS JULIUS ALEXANDER: Bereniké's first husband, a wealthy relative of Philo of Alexandria

MARIAMME (ALSO KNOWN AS MARIAMME I): The Maccabean princess, granddaughter of both Aristobulus II and Hyrcanus II, who became Herod the Great's wife, only to be executed at his order in 29 BCE

MARIAMME II: The daughter of a priest whom Herod the Great married after the death of Mariamme I

MARSUS: The Syrian legate who chastised Agrippa I for his meeting with other kings in Tiberias

NERO: Emperor, 54–68 CE

NICHOLAS OF DAMASCUS: Diplomat and historian in the service of Herod the Great whose writings, simultaneously historical and propagandistic, were a source plumbed by Josephus

PACORUS: The name of both the Parthian crown prince and his commander, who allied with Antigonus in an attempt to wrest Judea from Roman control

PAPPUS: General in the service of Antigonus, who pressed scorched-earth tactics of conquest, including the beheading of Herod the Great's brother Joseph

PETRONIUS: The legate to Syria, charged with executing Caligula's edict, whose delay was an act of heroism

PHASAEL: Herod the Great's older brother, who administered Jerusalem on behalf of his father, Antipater

PHERORAS: Last surviving brother of Herod, who was appointed tetrarch by Augustus in 20 BCE but then involved in court intrigue against Herod (especially with Antipater) until his death in 5 BCE

PHILIP: Son of Herod the Great and Cleopatra of Jerusalem, tetrarch of Gaulanitis

PHILO: A Jewish philosopher and statesman present in Rome at the time of Caligula's edict

PILATE: Prefect of Judea, 26–36 CE

POLEMO: King of Cilicia, who agreed to be circumcised in order to marry Bereniké only to see her return to her brother, Agrippa II

POMPEY: The Roman general who occupied Jerusalem in 63 BCE and later formed the First Triumvirate with Julius Caesar and Crassus

QUIRINIUS: Roman legate to Syria, under whom the census of 6 CE was conducted

SABINUS: Augustus's emissary to Judea, charged with an inventory of Herod's estate

SALOMÉ: Sister of Herod, always a force to be reckoned with inside the royal court

SALOMÉ ALEXANDRA: Wife of Alexander Yannai (and previously of his brother), who ruled from 76 BCE until her death in 67 BCE; mother of Hyrcanus II and Aristobulus II

SEJANUS: Prefect of the Praetorian Guard, executed as a usurper by Tiberius in 31 CE

SEXTUS CAESAR: A cousin of Julius Caesar and an early ally of Antipater, Phasael, and especially Herod, who was assassinated in 46 BCE by his own troops at the instigation of Caecilius Bassus

SHEMAIAH: A Pharisee who warned the Sanhedrin against Herod yet found his life spared on Herod's accession when the Sanhedrin was purged

SILO: A Roman commander under Ventidius, who probably took more benefit from Herod than he gave

SIMON: A slave a Herod the Great, who claimed the royal diadem after Herod's death

SOSSIUS: The Roman general who worked effectively in tandem with Herod during the Parthian campaign, but with increasing cruelty

STRABO: A philosopher historian who traveled extensively and produced his *Geography* early in the first century CE

SUETONIUS: Historian, in his *De Vita Caesarum*, of the first Roman emperors through Domitian, published during the period 119–121 CE

SYLLAEUS: The powerful Nabataean minister who resisted Herod's incursion in pursuit of bandits and then complained to Rome of his behavior

TACITUS: A contemporary of Suetonius, whose *Histories* (composed between 105 and 110 CE) and his subsequent *Annals* are a rich and brilliantly written resource for the period after Tiberius

THEUDAS: A prophet who in 45 BCE claimed the waters of the Jordan would part for him and his followers as they had for Joshua

TIBERIUS: Emperor between 14 CE and 37 CE, Augustus's successor, whose skill as a general did not translate smoothly into imperial rule

TIBERIUS ALEXANDER: Brother of Bereniké's first husband and procurator of Judea between 46 and 48 CE

TITUS: Emperor between 79 CE and 81 CE; the son of Vespasian, Roman emperor; and Bereniké's lover

VALERIUS GRATUS: Roman prefect of Judea, who coordinated a plan of pacification that included cooperation with Antipas in the execution of John the Baptist in 21 CE

VARUS: Famed Roman general and legate to Syria at the time of Herod's death

VENTIDIUS: Roman general allied with Herod in combat against Antigonus and Pacorus

VESPASIAN: Nero's general of preference to reconquer Judea; subsequently becaming emperor (from 69 CE until his death in 79 CE) with the support of Agrippa II and Bereniké

VITELLIUS: The legate to Syria, to whom it was left to manage the indiscipline of Pilate

ZADOK: Pharisaic supporter of Judas the Galilean and a champion of religious resistance to Roman rule

NOTES

Preface

1 Bruce Chilton, *Resurrection Logic: How Jesus' First Followers Believed God Raised Him from the Dead* (Waco: Baylor University Press, 2019).

2 A procedure I also followed in Bruce Chilton, "Joseph Bar Matthias's Vision of the Temple," in *The Temple of Jesus: His Sacrificial Program within a Cultural History of Sacrifice* (University Park: Pennsylvania State University Press, 1992), 69–87. Readers of that earlier work will notice its approach applied across a broader field in this book. A perspective on Josephus commensurate with mine, together with a presentation of many sources cited here, is available in Julia Wilker, *Für Rom und Jerusalem: Die herodianische Dynastie im 1. Jahrhundert n. Chr*, Studien zur Alten Geschichte 5 (Frankfurt am Main: Verlag Antike, 2007), 36–48.

Introduction

1 The preliminary descriptions of principal Herodians within the introduction are repeated in slightly different form at the head of each chapter. The intent is to provide the reader with an overview at the outset and then with reminders along the way of the stage that has been reached in a sometimes complex series of events.

Chapter 1: Antipater

1 In the legendary etymology of the story, he bears a name derived from the term "heel" (from the root *'aqeyv*) in Genesis because as he left the womb, he clenched on to his brother Esau's heel in an attempt to supersede him (Gen 25:26). The later name, Israel, refers to Jacob's struggle with God (Gen 32:24–32). See Yair Zakovitch, "'For You Have Striven with God and with Men and Have Prevailed': Jacob's Homebound Encounters," in *Jacob: Unexpected Patriarch*, Jewish Lives, trans. Valerie Zakovitch (New Haven: Yale University Press, 2012), 93–115.

2 See James F. Downs, "The Origin and Spread of Riding in the Near East and Central Asia," *American Anthropologist* 63, no. 6 (1961): 1193–203; Philip Mayerson, "P.Oxy.3574: 'Eleutheropolis of the New Arabia,'"

Zeitschrift für Papyrologie und Epigraphik 53 (1983): 251–58; Philip Mayer-
son, "Nea Arabia (P.Oxy. 3574): An Addendum to ZPE 53," *Zeitschrift für
Papyrologie und Epigraphik* 64 (1986): 139–40; Daniel Vainstub and Peter
Fabian, "An Idumean Ostracon from Ḥorvat Naḥal Yatir," *Israel Exploration
Journal* 65, no. 2 (2015): 205–13.

3   The Samaritans continued to make a case for their descent from Abraham,
Isaac, and Jacob and even for the superiority of their tradition of the law
of Moses as compared to the Judeans'. Their paschal sacrifice on Gerizim is
conducted to this day. See Ingrid Hjelm, *Samaritans and Early Judaism:
A Literary Analysis*, Journal for the Study of the Old Testament Supplement
Series 303 (Sheffield, UK: Sheffield Academic Press, 2000).

4   As a nation, it appears that Edom had been submerged during the course
of these imperial onslaughts until the reorganization of the region following the conquest of Alexander the Great; see Yigal Levin, "The Southern
Frontier of *Yehud* and the Creation of Idumea," in *A Time of Change: Judah
and Its Neighbours in the Persian and Early Hellenistic Period*, ed. Yigal Levin
(London: T&T Clark, 2007), 239–52. In his analysis, Idumea came back
into existence—but as a regional entity rather than a kingdom—with the
withdrawal of Qedarite hegemony. Even so, Persian dominance had already
regionalized Idumea; see Alexander Fantalkin and Oren Tal, "Judah and Its
Neighbors in the Fourth Century BCE: A Time of Major Transformations,"
in *From Judah to Judea: Socio-economic Structures and Processes in the Persian
Period*, Hebrew Bible Monographs 43, ed. Johannes Un-Sok Ro (Sheffield,
UK: Sheffield Phoenix Press, 2012), 134–97.

5   See Livy, *History of Rome* 35.19. For the military and strategic position of
the Seleucids, see Nick Sekunda, *The Seleucid Army under Antiochus IV
Epiphanes: Seleucid and Ptolemaic Reformed Armies 168–145 BC* (Stockport,
UK: Montvert, 1994); and Bezalel Bar-Kochva, *The Seleucid Army: Orga-
nization and Tactics in the Great Campaigns*, Cambridge Classical Studies
(Cambridge: Cambridge University Press, 2001).

6   Nabataea, east of Edom and south of Judea, was a more considerable,
centralized power, but it had made its peace with the Seleucids, concen-
trating on commercial relations as a kind of Near Eastern Switzerland that
kept itself out of the fray, if not above it altogether. Both Judea and Idumea
adjusted to Nabataea more by accommodation than confrontation and with
varying degrees of success. Mordechai Gihon, "Idumea and the Herodian
Limes," *Israel Exploration Journal* 17, no. 1 (1967): 27–42, has shown that
Herod exercised care in guarding his border with Nabataea and discusses his
policies within the strategic position overall.

7   The immediate aim does not seem to have been religious but was part of
the attempt to enforce Seleucid domination. Indeed, Victor Tcherikover
came to the conclusion, "It was not the revolt which came as a response to

the persecution, but the persecution which came in response to the revolt"; Tcherikover, *Hellenistic Civilization and the Jews* (Philadelphia: Jewish Publication Society of America, 1959), 191. His perspective is renovated to brilliant effect by Sylvie Honigman in *Tales of High Priests and Taxes: The Books of the Maccabees and the Judean Rebellion against Antiochos IV*, S. Mark Taper Foundation Imprint in Jewish Studies (Oakland: University of California Press, 2014). She argues, "Once we accept normalizing the ancient Judean cultic system, it may be easier to accept the proposition that as with all other peoples in antiquity, the Judean rebellion against Antiochos IV was in essence caused by economic distress and political destabilization" (Honigman, 567). Part of understanding the "normal" in antiquity, however, involves an appreciation of the interpenetrating demands of today's separated authorities of politics and religion. That consideration may explain why, when Honigman argues for "what may be called a minimalist view of the 'religious persecution'" (Honigman, 566), it is not always clear whether she wishes to minimize the violence of persecution or the specifically religious purpose of the violence. The Maccabees' propaganda for martyrdom evidently maximized both dimensions, but from their perspective, they responded to an evident program of Seleucid domination. If we go back to Tcherikover's aphorism, we might say that revolt and persecution were the idioms in which Seleucid culture and Maccabean culture interacted. In neither case was the culture reducible to or extricable from religion. For this reason, Boris Chrubasik rightly highlights the importance of Honigman's view, developed in chapter 3, that 2 Maccabees was designed "to create the social world of *Hellênismos* as a counter world to that of *Ioudaïsmos*," in which the latter is not a religious term of reference but an ideal social order; see Chrubasik's review of *Tales of High Priests and Taxes*, by Sylvie Honigman, *Journal of Hellenic Studies* 135 (2015): 237–39. The reality of the persecution seems manifest; see Bezalel Bar-Kochva, "The Religious Persecutions of Antiochus Epiphanes as a Historical Reality," *Tarbitz* 84, no. 3 (2016): 295–344, although by way of reaction to Honigman, he reverts to an ideological perspective that is determined by religion.

8 See Michael J. Taylor, "Sacred Plunder and the Seleucid Near East," *Greece and Rome* 61, no. 2 (2014): 222–41.

9 The name has its own resonance, since a son of the biblical Eleazar, named Phinehas, earned a "covenant of peace" for his violent zeal for purity (Num 25:1–13); see Lauren A. S. Monroe, "Phinehas' Zeal and the Death of Cozbi: Unearthing a Human Scapegoat Tradition in Numbers 25:1–18," *Vetus Testamentum* 62, no. 2 (2012): 211–31. The name was evidently current in the period, since the martyred scribe also bore it; the Maccabean brother was distinguished from other Eleazars by his surname ("Avaran," of uncertain meaning). Josephus's version of the martyrdom of the Maccabean

Eleazar belittles the tactical value of the death, in telling contrast to the account in 1 Maccabees (although he acknowledges the value of the act in terms of morale). It is also of interest for the description of the elephant's equipment (a "tower" on its back and ornamented armor) and for the proportion of infantry (fifty thousand), cavalry (five thousand), and elephants (eighty). See Josephus, *Jewish War* 1 §§ 41–46. It is notable that at the end of the passage, Josephus attributes Antiochus's withdrawal of the bulk of his army at this stage not to the resistance of the Maccabees but to a shortage of supplies. For further overlaps between Maccabean literature and Josephus, see Joseph Sievers, *Synopsis of the Greek Sources for the Hasmonean Period: 1–2 Maccabees and Josephus, War 1 and Antiquities 12–14*, Subsidia Biblica 20 (Rome: Pontifical Biblical Institute, 2001).

10 The legend has it that, because the high priest's seal remained on the vial, the Maccabees knew it had not been polluted by the Seleucids. The prophetic resonance of the story (compare the account of Elisha and the miraculous jar of oil in 2 Kgs 4:1–7) is apparent. See Solomon Zeitlin, "Hanukkah: Its Origin and Its Significance," *Jewish Quarterly Review* 29, no. 1 (1938): 1–36.

11 The dynasty Judas founded is also known as the Hasmoneans, after the ancestor of Judas's father; see Josephus, *Antiquities* 12 §§ 265–66 (cf. Josephus, *Jewish War* 1 § 36); and Kenneth Atkinson, *A History of the Hasmonean State: Josephus and Beyond*, T&T Clark Jewish and Christian Texts Series (London: Bloomsbury, 2016). On my reading the term *Hasmonean* featured as part of a skillful campaign of propaganda, designed to emphasize the priestly descent of the family, see Alison Schofield and James C. VanderKam, "Were the Hasmoneans Zadokites?," *Journal of Biblical Literature* 124, no. 1 (2005): 73–87. For that reason and for the sake of simplicity and clarity, I prefer to speak of both the movement and the dynasty in terms of the Maccabees.

12 The shifting boundaries of Idumea are nicely summarized with reference to archaeological evidence and recent literature by Bruce R. Crew in "Did Edom's Original Territories Extend West of 'Wadi Arabah?," *Bible and Spade* 15 (2002): 3–10. The conversion at the time of Maccabean expansion is well explained in Michal Marciak, "Idumea and the Idumeans in Josephus' Story of Hellenistic-Early Roman Palestine (*Ant. XII–XX*)," *Aevum* 91, no. 1 (2017): 171–93. He offers a slalom course between the claim of forced conversion (Ptolemy, *Historia Herodis*, cited in *De Adfinium Vocabulorum Differentia* 243; see Menahem Stern, ed., *Greek and Latin Authors on Jews and Judaism*, vol. 1, *From Herodotus to Plutarch* [Jerusalem: Israel Academy of Sciences and Humanities, 1974], 355–56) and previous commonality of customs (see Strabo, *Geography* 16.2.3). Josephus concurs with the former view, but Marciak shows how he can be read as supporting a "political agreement between the Hasmoneans and the Idumean elites"

(Marciak, "Idumea," 188). He also importantly stresses that conversion in this setting was "a cultural development rather than a strictly religious phenomenon." The view of Geza Vermes that "voluntary Judaization" followed the Maccabees' military conquest is as unique as it is unlikely; see Geza Vermes, *The True Herod* (London: Bloomsbury, 2014), 29. His approach involves an evaluation of the Maccabees that makes them the last truly Jewish regime in Jerusalem "until 1948, when the new independent Jewish state of Israel was created" (Vermes, 35).

13 The Seleucids themselves inadvertently offered opportunities for further expansion. Long before the Maccabees' victory, disintegration threatened the Seleucid Empire. In the heart of Persia, a tribal chief named Arsaces consolidated power among the Parthians and challenged the Seleucids within their own territory, while the Roman Republic pressed against Seleucid claims in Asia Minor (present-day Turkey). Antiochus IV himself died in a campaign against the Parthians, and after his death, dynastic squabbles caused local rulers to make their peace with regional forces such as the Maccabees. See Kyle Erickson and Gillian Ramsey, ed., *Seleucid Dissolution: The Sinking of the Anchor*, Philippika 50 (Wiesbaden: Harrassowitz, 2011).

14 Chilton, *Resurrection Logic*, 29–64, traces the Maccabean conception among other Judaic views of resurrection.

15 See Jonathan Bourgel, "The Destruction of the Samaritan Temple by John Hyrcanus: A Reconsideration," *Journal of Biblical Literature* 135, no. 3 (2016): 505–23.

16 The implications of turning circumcision into a policy of domination are thoughtfully developed in Steven Weitzman, "Forced Circumcision and the Shifting Role of Gentiles in Hasmonean Ideology," *Harvard Theological Review* 92, no. 1 (1999): 37–59. As he shows, the fact that circumcision was practiced among some Idumeans already did not make it the sign of the covenant with Abraham, its meaning within the practice that the Maccabees championed. He also refutes several attempts to dismiss the description of the policy of compulsory circumcision as anti-Maccabean propaganda; compare Aryeh Kasher, *Jews, Idumeans, and Ancient Arabs: Relations of the Jews in Eretz-Israel with the Nations of the Frontier and the Desert during the Hellenistic and Roman Era (332 BCE–70 CE)*, Texte und Studien zum antiken Judentum 18 (Tübingen: Mohr, 1988), 46–78. Straightforward evidence for the policy is given by a historian named Ptolemy, cited by Menahem Stern, *Greek and Latin Authors on Jews and Judaism*, 146; and Josephus, *Antiquities* 13 §§ 257–58, 15 § 254. This, of course, does not mean that all Idumeans were *not* Jews; Herod's grandfather served in the court of Alexander Jannaeus according to *Antiquities* 14 § 10.

17 Well laid out in Tessa Rajak, "The Jews under Hasmonean Rule," in *The Cambridge Ancient History, IX: The Last Age of the Roman Republic,*

146–43 B.C., ed. John Anthony Crook, Andrew Lintott, and Elizabeth Rawson (Cambridge: Cambridge University Press, 1994), 274–309. Rajak's explanation of the relationship with the Essenes of Qumran is particularly lucid, and her treatment of the Pharisees is also very helpful. In the case of the Sadducees, however, in my opinion, she dates the movement too early. Each of these groups will be introduced as the narrative proceeds.

18   This decisive shift in hopes of resurrection is detailed in Chilton, *Resurrection Logic*, which treats the tradition of Dionysus, among others, and the development of views of afterlife in Judaism (9–64).

19   See Bruce Chilton, *Abraham's Curse: Child Sacrifice in the Legacies of the West* (New York: Doubleday, 2008), 71–140 and 171–95.

20   For a particularly incisive treatment of this issue, see Eyal Regev, "The Hellenization of the Hasmoneans Revisited: The Archaeological Evidence," *Advances in Anthropology* 7 (2017): 175–96.

21   Plutarch, *Alexander* 2.2–3.3. Plutarch gives various versions of the claim in order, as Christopher Pelling says, to remain "detached and noncommittal"; Christopher Pelling, *Plutarch and History: Eighteen Studies* (London: Duckworth, 2002), 380. For the Maccabean appropriation of Hellenistic conceptions of kingship, see Vasile Babota, "Alexander Jannaeus as High Priest and King: Struggling between Jewish and Hellenistic Concepts of Rule," *Religions* 11, no. 40 (2020): 1–16.

22   Josephus, *Apion* 2.16 §§ 164–67. The growing Hellenization of the Maccabees is brilliantly traced by means of their choice of Greek names by Tal Ilan, "The Greek Names of the Hasmoneans," *Jewish Quarterly Review* 78, nos. 1–2 (1987): 1–20. Geza Vermes describes the increasingly royal pretensions of the Maccabees, until Alexander Yannai came to describe himself simply as "King Alexander" on his coins; Vermes, *True Herod*, 27–31.

23   Ever solicitous of their place in history, the Maccabees even recorded their agreement with Alexander Balas (1 Macc 10:18–21). He falsely claimed to be the son of Antiochus IV and enjoyed Roman and Ptolemaic backing as well as Maccabean cooperation; his reign was short, contested, and divisive for his realms. The Maccabees, however, enjoyed long-term gain from his action.

24   Josephus sometimes gives his name as "Antipas," a shortened form. But because his grandson—the Herodian ruler of Galilee in the time of Jesus—went by the shortened name, for purposes of historical discussion, it seems best to maintain the distinction between the two forms, even if that consistency is not maintained by the primary sources. In his article, Babota traces the increasing reliance of the Maccabees on mercenary forces to Hellenistic patterns of governance; Babota, "Alexander Jannaeus," 1–16.

25   The impact of Cyrus and the ironically productive influence of the Babylonian exile in the emergence of the Bible are well described in David M. Carr,

Holy Resilience: The Bible's Traumatic Origins (New Haven: Yale University Press, 2014), 67–90, 128–40.

26 A fine early discussion of the development of the Essenes is available in Jerome Murphy-O'Connor, "The Essenes in Palestine," *The Biblical Archaeologist* 40, no. 3 (1977): 100–124. Since that publication, links to Babylonian traditions have been uncovered; see Mladen Popović, "Physiognomic Knowledge in Qumran and Babylonia: Form, Interdisciplinarity, and Secrecy," *Dead Sea Discoveries* 13, no. 2 (2006): 150–76; and *Reading the Human Body: Physiognomics and Astrology in the Dead Sea Scrolls and Hellenistic-Early Roman Period Judaism*, Studies on the Texts of the Desert of Judea 67 (Leiden: Brill, 2007). Although the scrolls at Qumran evidently stem from the Judean phase of the movement, they refer and allude to the earlier establishment of Essene theology, and its relationship to Babylonian traditions was quite complex, involving an openness to a distinctive cosmology. Cf. Kenneth Atkinson and Jodi Magness, "Josephus's Essenes and the Qumran Community," *Journal of Biblical Literature* 129, no. 2 (2010): 317–42.

27 See Bruce Chilton, *Redeeming Time: The Wisdom of Ancient Jewish and Christian Festal Calendars* (Peabody, MA: Hendrickson, 2002).

28 With its Babylonian names of months. In fact, the traditional calendar is known as "luni-solar." The reason for that is that Passover is calculated from the first new moon after the spring equinox of the sun. But once the clock is started, it proceeds on a monthly rhythm that follows the phases of the moon. See Lawrence H. Schiffman, "From Observation to Calculation: The Development of the Rabbinic Lunar Calendar," in *Living the Lunar Calendar*, ed. Ben-Dov Jonathan, Wayne Horowitz, and John M. Steele (Oakville: Oxbow Books, 2012), 231–44.

29 Documented in the Qumran text called *Miḳtsat maʿaśe ha-Torah*; see John Kampen and Moshe Bernstein, *Reading 4QMMT: New Perspectives on Qumran Law and History*, Symposium Series 2 (Atlanta: Scholars Press, 1994).

30 Secondary literature on the Essenes is enormous, and controversy since the discovery of the Dead Sea Scrolls in 1947 has not abated. A particularly fraught question is whether the people of Qumran were Essenes. Among recent discussions, the most productive in my judgment is that of Albert Baumgarten, "Who Cares and Why Does It Matter? Qumran and the Essenes, Once Again," *Dead Sea Discoveries* 11, no. 2 (2004): 174–90. He concludes that it cannot be ascertained whether "one group was an offshoot of the other" (Baumgarten, 189) but that they represent responses "to the same cultural context and its dilemmas" (Baumgarten, 188). The designation "Essene" seems to me to be a description of a wider movement that did not control the temple or fully endorse its

administration and sought its cohesion in the company of angels. The *yachad* at Qumran leaves the richest record of one such Essene community, and the fact that its library included works by those far outside the movement suggests that its members understood themselves as the vanguard of a larger tendency. See James C. VanderKam, *The Dead Sea Scrolls Today* (Grand Rapids: Eerdmans, 2010). Michael O. Wise argues for a first-century BCE dating for the "Teacher of Righteousness," without denying the earlier roots of the movements involved; see "Dating the Teacher of Righteousness and the Floruit of His Movement," *Journal of Biblical Literature* 122, no. 1 (2003): 53–87.

31 The *War Scroll* (as it is commonly known in a shortened title) is available in translation with other major texts from Qumran in Michael O. Wise, Martin G. Abegg, and Edward M. Cook, *The Dead Sea Scrolls: A New Translation* (New York: HarperCollins, 2005).

32 Which of them is particularly in mind by means of the designation is a matter of such controversy that an aggregate usage has been suggested; see Timothy H. Lim, "The Wicked Priests of the Groningen Hypothesis," *Journal of Biblical Literature* 112, no. 3 (1993): 415–25. That appears plausible to me, but of the group, John Hyrcanus was obviously outstanding.

33 Some of the clans of Esau are enumerated in Genesis 36:15–19. For an excellent survey of the evidence, see Yigal Levin, "The Formation of Idumean Identity," *Aram* 27, nos. 1–2 (2015): 187–202. The range of data tells against the hypothesis of Nikos Kokkinos, *The Herodian Dynasty: Origins, Role in Society and Eclipse*, Journal for the Study of the Pseudepigrapha Supplement Series 30 (Sheffield, UK: Sheffield Academic Press, 1998), which maintains that Antipater was a Phoenician by descent. But because the Maccabees engaged even Herod's father and grandfather (Josephus, *Antiquities* 14 §§ 8–10), the Judaism of the family is evident, as is their rootedness in the military nomadism of the Idumeans. See the brilliant article by David J. Bryan, "The Herodians: A Case of Disputed Identity: A Review Article of Nikos Kokkinos, *The Herodian Dynasty*," *Tyndale Bulletin* 53, no. 2 (2002): 223–38. Ancient views of the Idumeans in terms of an ethnos (including but by no means restricted to affiliation with Phoenecia) are analyzed by Michal Marciak in "Hellenistic-Roman Idumea in Light of Greek and Latin Non-Jewish Authors," *Klio: Beiträge zur alten Geschichte* 100, no. 3 (2018): 877–910. For inscriptional evidence of the Idumean clan structure within an eclectic economic environment, see Tania Notarius, "The Syntax of Clan Names in Aramaic Ostraca from Idumea," *Maarav* 22, nos. 1–2 (2018): 21–43.

34 See Josephus, *Jewish War* 1 § 181. This passage also indicates that "Arabia" for Josephus could be synonymous with Nabataea. At a later stage, Antipater even entrusted his children to the king when he was engaged in battle.

See John F. Healey, *The Religion of the Nabataeans: A Conspectus*, Religions in the Graeco-Roman World 136 (Leiden: Brill, 2001).

35 The claim by the Herodian court historian Nicholas of Damascus that Herod descended from the Jews of Babylonia (Josephus, *Antiquities* 14 § 9) seems as untenable as it is propagandistic; Bryan, "Herodians," 227. That is also Josephus's view, although by the time he wrote his *Antiquities*, he was touting his own priestly pedigree (as an alleged Maccabean) over that of the Herodians (16 §§ 184–87). For the same reason, Antipater's courage in battle is dismissed in *Antiquities* (14 § 8) as deriving from his character as a *stasiastês* ("fomenter of sedition"). Given the period of the Maccabean conversion of Idumea and Antipater's service to the conquerors, Herod himself is well described by Peter Richardson as "a third-generation Jew"; *Herod: King of the Jews and Friend of the Romans*, Studies in the Personalities of the New Testament (Columbia: University of South Carolina Press, 1996), xiii. His grandfather, another Antipas, served the Maccabean Alexander Jannaeus (*Antiquities* 14 § 10). Generally speaking, the Herodian dynasty maintained their status within Judaism even as they accommodated to the culture of Hellenism; see Eyal Regev, "Herod's Jewish Ideology Facing Romanization: On Intermarriage, Ritual Baths, and Speeches," *Jewish Quarterly Review* 100, no. 2 (2010): 197–222.

36 Gaulanitis (also spelled "Gaulonitis"), the precursor of what is now called Golan Heights, at various times included part or all of Trachonitis and Auranitis to the east. For this reason, I use the term for this region of the Herodian realm, even though its borders proved elastic (as indeed do those of the Golan Heights today).

37 See Josephus, *Jewish War* 1 § 63; Josephus, *Antiquities* 13 §§ 257–58. The latter passage makes these conquests the occasion of insisting that the Idumeans keep the covenant of circumcision.

38 See Samuel Rocca, *The Army of Herod the Great*, Men at Arms 443 (Oxford: Osprey, 2008). For the prominence of Idumean mercenaries, see Dorothy J. Thompson Crawford, "The Idumaeans of Memphis and the Ptolemaic 'Politeumata,'" in *Atti del XVII Congresso internazionale di papirologia: Napoli, 19–26 maggio 1983*, ed. M. Manfredi (Napoli: Centro internazionale per lo studio dei papiri ercolanesi, 1984), 3:1069–75.

39 See Doron Mendels, "A Note on the Tradition of Antiochus IV's Death," *Israel Exploration Journal* 31, nos. 1–2 (1981): 53–56.

40 See 1 Maccabees 8:23–28; Josephus, *Antiquities* 12 §§ 417–19; and Menahem Stern, "The Treaty between Judaea and Rome in 161 BCE," *Zion* 51 (1986): 3–28.

41 See Görge K. Hasselhoff and Meret Strothmann, eds., *"Religio licita?": Rom und die Juden*, Studia Judaica 84 (Berlin: de Gruyter, 2017). The first essay, "Rom und die Juden—ein Kategorienfehler?" (13–54), by Benedikt

Eckhardt, problematizes the application of *religio licita* as if it were an established legal category from the outset. In response, one reviewer emphasizes that "Romans categorized *Iudaei* essentially on an ethnic basis"; Arco den Heijer, review of *"Religio licita?" Rom und die Juden*, ed. Görge K. Hasselhoff and Meret Strothmann, *Bryn Mawr Classical Review* 11, no. 42 (2017), http://bmcr.brynmawr.edu/2017/2017-11-42.html.

42   See Robert G. Hall, "Epispasm and the Dating of Ancient Jewish Writings," *Journal for the Study of the Pseudepigrapha* 2 (1988): 71–86; and Sander L. Gilman, "Decircumcision: The First Aesthetic Surgery," *Modern Judaism* 17, no. 3 (1997): 201–10.

43   See Bezalel Bar-Kochva, *Judas Maccabeus: The Jewish Struggle against the Seleucids* (Cambridge: Cambridge University Press, 1989), which deals with the military context of Hellenistic armies and offers well-informed estimates of the size of forces during the period.

44   See Menahem Haran, *Temples and Temple-Service in Ancient Israel: An Inquiry into Biblical Cult Phenomena and the Historical Setting of the Priestly School* (Winona Lake, IN: Eisenbrauns, 1995), 165–74, 210–29.

45   Josephus, *Jewish War* 1 §§ 88–89, 96–98; Josephus, *Antiquities* 13 §§ 372–73, §§ 380–83. In the course of expanding the narrative in the *Antiquities*, Josephus related an incident concerning John Hyrcanus, the father of Alexander Jannaeus and grandfather of Hyrcanus II (see 13 § 292), when objectors claimed that his mother had been a captive under Antiochus Epiphanes. The point of the charge was that Hyrcanus's unknown paternity disqualified him from serving as a priest. A fine recent article by Tal Ilan and Vered Noam argues that Josephus applied a story about Jannaeus (Talmud Bavli Qiddushin 66a) to his father, Hyrcanus (*Antiquities* 13 §§ 289–97); "Remnants of a Pharisaic Apologetic Source in Josephus and the Babylonian Talmud," in *Tradition, Transmission and Transformation from Second Temple Literature through Judaism and Christianity in Late Antiquity: Proceedings of the Thirteenth International Symposium of the Orion Center for the Study of the Dead Sea Scrolls and Associated Literature*, Studies on the Texts of the Desert of Judah 113, ed. Menahem Kister, Hillel I. Newman, Michael Segal and Ruth A. Clements (Leiden: Brill, 2015), 112–33. They also argue convincingly that the story in the Talmud accurately reflects conflicted Pharisaic opinion in regard to Maccabean rule and that Josephus anachronistically inserts Sadducean views into his version of the story.

46   Josephus, *Jewish War* 1 §§ 110–12; Josephus, *Antiquities* 13 §§ 408–15.

47   See Josephus, *Jewish War* 1 §§ 107–9; and Josephus, *Antiquities* 13 §§ 407–8. Even at this early point, Josephus mentions Hyrcanus's reputation for being lazy, which his mother—the ambitious Alexandra—saw as an advantage. Josephus concedes she was an effective ruler, largely owing to a reputation of piety that made her a welcome departure from her

husband. Yet Josephus criticizes her as overly dependent on the Pharisees to the extent that they effectively ruled; this represents prejudice in regard to Alexandra and an anachronistic evaluation of the Pharisees; Josephus, *Jewish War* 1 §§ 110–12; Josephus, *Antiquities* 13 §§ 408–15. Steve Mason has shown, correcting the views of Hölscher, Schwartz, and Sanders, that Josephus's membership of a "priestly elite" put him constitutionally at odds with the Pharisees; "Josephus' Pharisees: The Narratives," in *In Quest of the Historical Pharisees*, ed. Jacob Neusner and Bruce Chilton (Waco: Baylor University Press, 2007), 3–40, especially 10, 12, 21, 37. She was not the first person to be deceived by Hyrcanus's apparent lack of ambition. The armed dispute with Aristobulus is described in Josephus, *Jewish War* 1 §§ 117–30; Josephus, *Antiquities* 13 § 422 to 15 § 33.

48 Josephus, *Jewish War* 1 §§ 123–27; Josephus, *Antiquities* 14 §§ 4–33. This was the occasion when Antipater left his children with Aretas, the Nabataean king. Aretas dispatched fifty thousand troops according to Josephus, who would have tipped the balance definitively but for the opportunistic intervention of Scaurus (in exchange for a bribe), the Roman officer serving under Pompey.

49 Josephus, *Jewish War* 1 §§ 131–58; Josephus, *Antiquities* 14 §§ 34–79. These two works in aggregate set out the tortuous path that led to Roman occupation of Jerusalem and Judea. The bribery was not crude but always an at least implicit issue. Indeed, Aristobulus had already bribed Scaurus, the officer of Pompey, in order to escape from Aretas (see Josephus, *Jewish War* 1 § 128; Josephus, *Antiquities* 14 §§ 30–33). In the latter passage, Josephus also states that Hyrcanus attempted a counteroffer.

50 For this scene and the military campaign that follows, see Josephus, *Jewish War* 1 §§ 131–51; and Josephus, *Antiquities* 14 §§ 34–71. Aristobulus's odd conduct, which vacillated between appeasing Pompey and resisting him, is described in detail.

51 Numbers varied over time but are estimated as tightly as possible in Thomas Fischer, *Army of the Roman Emperors*, trans. M. C. Bishop (Havertown, PA: Casemate, 2019), xxii–xxxix.

52 Josephus describes the scene in *Antiquities* 14 §§ 72–73, effectively serving as a propagandist for Rome by describing Pompey as full of reverence. Writing earlier in Josephus, *Jewish War* 1 §§ 152–53, Josephus is less fulsome in his praise for Pompey.

53 See, for example, Ta'anit 4:8, 68d, in the Talmud Yerushalmi, and Genesis Rabbah 63:7; and Mireille Hadas-Lebel, *Jerusalem against Rome*, Interdisciplinary Studies in Culture and Religion, trans. Robyn Fréchet (Leuven: Peeters, 2006).

54 See Josephus, *Jewish War* 1 § 153; Josephus, *Antiquities* 14 § 73. For the display of Aristobulus and his family in Rome (less one son, who escaped), see *Jewish War* 1 §§ 157–58; and *Antiquities* 14 § 79.

Chapter 2: Herod's Debut

1   In correspondence with his friend Atticus, where the term is not one of
approval, since he also calls Pompey *traductor ad plebem* in the same sentence;
Cicero, *Letter to Atticus* 2.9. Cicero was also aware of the moniker "great"
without taking it too seriously (1.16). This attitude helps explain Cicero's failure to work effectively with Pompey; see Manfred Fuhrman, *Cicero and the
Roman Republic*, trans. W. E. Yuill (Oxford: Blackwell, 1992), 71–88; and
Anthony Everitt, *Cicero: The Life and Times of Rome's Greatest Politician* (New
York: Random House, 2001), 202–21. Still, even Cicero's sarcasm marked
an improvement on Pompey's earlier nickname: "adolescent butcher"; see
D. R. Shackleton Baily, ed. and trans., *Valerius Maximus, Memorable Doings
and Sayings: Books 6–9*, Loeb Classical Library 493 (Cambridge, MA: Har-
vard University Press, 2000), 6.2.8. He had earned that cognomen because
of his earlier campaigns on behalf of the dictator Sulla and his associates.
Sulla himself gave him the status of "the Great."

2   Pompey capitalized on the situation and crucified six thousand rebel slaves
on the road between Rome and Capua, the starting point of the revolt; see
Appian, *Civil Wars* 1.120.

3   See Olga Tellegen Couperus, *A Short History of Roman Law* (London: Routledge, 2003), 31–32.

4   The death in 54 BCE of Julia, Pompey's wife and Caesar's daughter, had
taken away another mediating influence.

5   Plutarch, *Caesar* 49. In this account, Cleopatra concealed herself in bed
linen (*strômatodesmos*) so that she could be delivered to the general without
being seen by hostile forces or personal enemies. The death of Pompey is
celebrated in Psalms of Solomon 2:25–31: "He failed to recognize that it is
God who is great" (v. 29); see Nadav Sharon, *Judea under Roman Domination: The First Generation of Statelessness and Its Legacy*, Early Judaism and Its
Literature (Atlanta: SBL Press, 2017), 116–17.

6   Josephus uses the term "Arab" for troops who affiliated with him that were
not identical with the Judean/Idumean forces that Antipater led into battle;
Josephus, *Jewish War* 1 § 187; Josephus, *Antiquities* 14 §§ 128–29. The
latter passage also distinguishes those from "Arabia" from those from Syria,
much as in *War* 1 § 188. Controversy over the word is well conveyed by
Fred M. Donner's review of *The Arabs in Antiquity*, by Jan Retsö, *Journal
of Near Eastern Studies* 66, no. 4 (2007): 312–16; and Jan Retsö, *The Arabs
in Antiquity: Their History from the Assyrians to the Umayyads* (London:
Routledge, 2003). In this particular usage by Josephus, Retsö's definition in
terms of a warrior community finds some support.

7   The fact that he did so in the name of Hyrcanus suggests that Antipater
was aware that his own status within Judaism would not readily have been

recognized, owing to his Idumean ancestry. See Josephus, *Antiquities* 14 § 131, although not his more condensed account in *Jewish War* 1 § 190. *Antiquities* 14 § 138 even records the claim by Strabo of Cappadocia that Hyrcanus invaded Egypt with Antipater. But it does not seem to me that Josephus endorses the contention. See the detailed treatment offered by Luciano Canfora, "Caesar Saved by the Jews," in *Julius Caesar: The People's Dictator*, trans. Marian Hill and Kevin Windle (Edinburgh: Edinburgh University Press, 2007), 209–17; and the useful comparison of the *War* and *Antiquities* in this regard by Sharon, *Judea under Roman Domination*, 119–24.

8 See Chilton, *Resurrection Logic*, 15–20.

9 During this relationship, Cleopatra married yet another younger brother, Ptolemy XIV, who died quickly enough to make way for her ambition to put Caesarion on the throne of Egypt. Josephus claimed that she hastened her new husband's death by poisoning him; *Antiquities* 14 § 89. For Josephus, Cleopatra was a lawless figure, and his charges should be taken with caution. See Margaret M. Miles, ed., *Cleopatra: A Sphinx Revisited* (Berkeley: University of California Press, 2011). Still, the charge that she poisoned Ptolemy XIV has proved irresistible; see Stacy Schiff, *Cleopatra: A Life* (New York: Little, Brown, 2010), 134.

10 Josephus, *Jewish War* 1 §§ 184–85. Scipio, the Roman commander in Antioch and Pompey's father-in-law, beheaded Antigonus's brother Alexander, also in support of Pompey.

11 Josephus takes delight in the contrast the scene enables him to draw between Antigonus and Antipater; *Jewish War* 1 §§ 193–200; *Antiquities* 14 §§ 140–44. In the latter (and longer) account, Antigonus and Antipater are both more articulate, and Hyrcanus occupies more attention. Additional sources came to Josephus's attention, but unfortunately, he misapplied some of them to the story of Hyrcanus; see Claude Eilers, "Forgery, Dishonesty, and Incompetence in Josephus' 'Acta': The Decree of Athens (*AJ* 14. 149–155)," *Zeitschrift für Papyrologie und Epigraphik* 166 (2008): 211–17. A deeper issue is why Josephus, who denigrates Hyrcanus in *Jewish War*, elevates his standing in *Antiquities*. By the time he came to write the later work, the Herodian dynasty was in eclipse, and Josephus was looking for different heroes of the past on whom to model his own prospects. His strategic and narrative shift is described in the epilogue.

12 Antigonus's ill-judged accusation of profiteering against Antipater and Antipater's grand gesture are detailed in Josephus, *Jewish War* 1 §§ 195–98.

13 Josephus, *Jewish War* 1 §§ 282–85; Josephus, *Antiquities* 14 §§ 381–85. On the way to Rome, Herod also made magnificent progress through Alexandria, where he was fêted by Cleopatra; *Jewish War* 1 § 279; *Antiquities* 14 §§ 375–76. For the symbolism of the diadem see Ido Noy, "Head

Decoration Representations on Hasmonean and Herodian Coins," *Israel Numismatic Research* 8 (2013): 39–54 (with plates).

14   Josephus, *Antiquities* 14 § 194; and Sharon, *Judea under Roman Domination*, 126–29. Sharon's further argument (pp. 260–80), that the title also implies a role for Hyrcanus in the Diaspora, strikes me as in accord with events at the time.

15   *Epitropos* in Josephus's Greek; *Jewish War* 1 §§ 199–200; *Antiquities* 14 §§ 143–44. In both accounts, authorization to repair the walls of Jerusalem is involved. Typically, Josephus credits this decision to Hyrcanus's intercession in *Antiquities*, while in *Jewish War* only Antipater is in view. Anachronistically, Josephus even calls Jerusalem the *patris* ("homeland") of Antipater, which could only be said accurately of later Herodians.

16   Judaic practice required the circumcision of males on the eighth day of life (Gen 17:9–12). Antipater, Phasael, and Herod had lived under the Maccabean regime in Idumea, and Antipater's father had already served Alexander Jannaeus (Josephus, *Antiquities* 14 §§ 9–10). But perhaps a scruple in regard to the timing of his own circumcision encouraged Antipater to use his sons (both of whom had been circumcised on the eighth day of life) for governance in Judea and Galilee. Even given the generosity of his character, it is difficult to account for his decision on other grounds, although his own preference for his native Idumea is implicit in his allocation of regions of governance.

17   See Sharon, *Judea under Roman Domination*, 280–311. An earlier article by Solomon Zeitlin remains useful: "The Political Synedrion and the Religious Sanhedrin," *Jewish Quarterly Review* 36, no. 2 (1945): 109–40.

18   Gabinius, the proconsul of Syria, finalized the arrangement in 57 BCE. Josephus makes his administration sound radical (Josephus, *Antiquities* 14 §§ 90–91). It is much more likely that he regularized the ad hoc headquarters of conquest and occupation and followed customary practice. See B. Kanael, "The Partition of Judea by Gabinius," *Israel Exploration Journal* 7, no. 2 (1957): 98–106.

19   King Josiah's authorization of this practice is reported in 2 Kings 23:1–30. For an introduction to this involved topic of inquiry, see Brian Neil Peterson, "The Deuteronomistic History since Martin Noth," in *The Authors of the Deuteronomistic History: Locating a Tradition in Ancient Israel* (Minneapolis: Augsburg Fortress, 2014), 7–36.

20   The moment of the "discovery" of the authoritative Moses is depicted as under the reign of Josiah in 2 Kings 22:8–13. The scene probably reflects the Deuteronomic program that began under Josiah and matured during the exile. For the related issue of the practice of human sacrifice, see Chilton, *Abraham's Curse*, 17–68.

21   See Robert Hayward, "The Jewish Temple of Leontopolis: A Reconsideration," *Journal of Jewish Studies* 33 (1981): 429–43.

22 See Bezalel Porten, *Archives from Elephantine: The Life of an Ancient Jewish Military Colony* (Berkeley: University of California Press, 1968). From Elephantine comes the curious case law of a woman divorcing her husband; see David Instone Brewer, "Jewish Women Divorcing Their Husbands in Early Judaism: The Background to Papyrus Se'elim 13," *Harvard Theological Review* 92, no. 3 (1999): 349–57. The curiosity, however, might only be apparent; see Adiel Schremer, "Divorce in Papyrus Se'elim Once Again: A Reply to Tal Ilan," *Harvard Theological Review* 91, no. 2 (1998): 193–202.

23 See A. I. Baumgarten, "The Zadokite Priests at Qumran: A Reconsideration," *Dead Sea Discoveries* 4, no. 2 (1997): 137–56.

24 See Bargil Pixner, "The History of the 'Essene Gate' Area," *Zeitschrift des Deutschen Palästina-Vereins* 105 (1989): 96–104. Pixner identifies the building of the remains as Herodian but claims Essene presence in Jerusalem prior to that time as well as Herod's favoritism toward them. There is no reason to suppose, however, that Herod innovated where they should enter the city and the temple. Out of a similar consideration, I assess with some caution the argument of Shimon Gibson, who severely criticizes Pixner by way of arguing that Essenes were not resident in Jerusalem and that the Essene Gate "led directly into the property of the place of Herod the Great and the later praetorium"; see Shimon Gibson, "The Trial of Jesus at the Jerusalem Praetorium: New Archaeological Evidence," in *The World of Jesus and the Early Church: Identity and Interpretation in Early Communities of Faith*, ed. Craig A. Evans (Peabody, MA: Hendrickson, 2011), 97–118, especially 116. The former assertion is more plausible than the latter, yet whether the Essenes resided in their own neighborhood and/or enjoyed the hospitality of sympathizers, their presence in Jerusalem remains quite conceivable. That issue and the identity of the gate's builder are beside the main point—that a gate was associated with the Essenes.

25 Indeed, even the number of seats is uncertain. Was it twenty-three or seventy-one? The sources go their separate ways, and the finesse eventually developed of imagining a "Lesser Sanhedrin" and a "Great Sanhedrin," or a "religious" and "political" Sanhedrin; see Zeitlin, "Political Synedrion," 109–40. Such expedients are to be treated warily and have not carried far into critical discussion. Rabbinic literature of a later period attributed more power, coherent structure, and consistency to the institution because they projected rabbinic power on to the Sanhedrin. In fact, it is not clear that their predecessors, the Pharisees, ever truly dominated the system in any case, other than in rabbinic imagination. A brief but very effective analysis is available in Michael S. Berger, *Rabbinic Authority* (New York: Oxford University Press, 1998), 40–51; this may be supplemented by Isaiah M. Gafni, "Sanhedrin," in *The Oxford Encyclopedia of the Bible and Law*, Oxford Encyclopedias of the Bible 1, ed. Brent A. Strawn (Oxford: Oxford

University Press, 2017), http://www.oxfordbiblicalstudies.com/article/opr/
t526/. (URL inactive.)

26 See Josephus, *Jewish War* 1 § 110; and Josephus, *Antiquities* 13 § 408,
where the emphasis on being accurate in observing tradition is echoed in
Paul's description of his own devotion as a Pharisee in Philippians 3:5 and
Galatians 1:14.

27 Jannaeus's drinking is featured in Josephus, *Jewish War* 1 § 97; and Josephus, *Antiquities* 13 § 398. In addition, Josephus claims in *Antiquities* 13
§§ 372–73 (although not in *Jewish War*) that Pharisees doubted his paternity, which would have excluded him from high priestly service. But that
is exactly the scenario of an onslaught on the legitimacy of John Hyrcanus,
the father of Alexander Jannaeus; see Josephus, *Antiquities* 13 §§ 288–98.
In that case, a sage named Eleazar makes the charge, not the Pharisees,
although they arouse John Hyrcanus's ire by not demanding the death
penalty for this lèse-majesté. As sometimes happens, Josephus conflates
John Hyrcanus and Alexander Jannaeus. He also pictures the Pharisees as
an influential group from their beginnings. I doubt that and see the Roman
sunhedrion as their pedestal of real—although still contested—power until
the destruction of the Second Temple in 70 CE. Josephus deals with Sadducees, Pharisees, and Essenes under the Maccabees as if they were just as he
found them under the Herodians a century later.

28 Surprisingly, some historians still describe what he did in this way. They are
identified and effectively refuted in Jeffrey Rubenstein, "The Sadducees and the
Water Libation," *Jewish Quarterly Review* 84, no. 4 (1994): 417–44. Rubenstein opens the way to see Alexander Jannaeus as operating within a view of
purity unlike the Pharisees', but a view of purity nonetheless. The most relevant
rabbinic sources include Mishnah Sukkot 4:8 and Talmud Bavli Sukkot 48b.

29 We will encounter many examples of this, and Josephus remarks that festivals
were occasions for outbreaks of popular revolt; Josephus, *Jewish War* 1 § 88.

30 Josephus, *Antiquities* 13 §§ 372–80; cf. Josephus, *Jewish War* 1 §§ 88–89,
97–98. The fact that Josephus uses the same number as those crucified by
Pompey at the end of the Third Servile War (the Spartacus revolt, see note 2
in this chapter) makes the number sound suspicious.

31 See Avodah Zarah in the Talmud Yerushalmi 1.2, 39 c (cf. Shir ha-Shirim
Rabbah 1) and Sanhedrin 21b; and Shabbat 56b in the Talmud Bavli, all
brilliantly handled in Ron Naiweld, "Use of Rabbinic Traditions about
Rome in the Babylonian Talmud," *Revue de l'histoire des religions* 233, no. 2
(2016): 255–85, especially 272–77. He goes on to detail the rabbinic link
between Esau/Edom and Rome in a helpful way.

32 The issue of his age at the time of his appointment—and therefore of his
chronology—has been complicated by the statement in Josephus, *Antiquities* 14 § 158 that Herod was only fifteen years old when Antipater made

him the *stratêgos* of Galilee. In a comprehensive treatment, Nadav Sharon shows that Josephus at this point followed the flattering portrayal of Nicholas of Damascus, Herod's courtier and biographer; see "Herod's Age When Appointed Strategos of Galilee: Scribal Error or Literary Motif?," *Biblica* 95, no. 1 (2014): 49–63. Herod liked to pass himself off as younger than he was through much of his life, and Nicholas's flattery presented Herod as a young military hero, along the lines of David, Pompey, and Octavian. Sharon also suggests (following Abraham Schalit) that Herod harbored messianic pretensions (60–62). Although that seems eminently possible, as will become apparent, I do not see that as an overt aspect of Nicholas's portrayal. In any case, if Herod was born in 74 BCE, he was twenty-seven at the time of his appointment: young but scarcely callow.

33 For a description, see Stewart Perowne, *The Life and Times of Herod the Great* (London: Arrow, 1960), 49, who follows the aggregations of references in Josephus developed by A. H. M. Jones, *The Herods of Judaea* (Oxford: Clarendon, 1938). See Josephus, *Jewish War* 1 §§ 429–30. A counterproposal appears in Aryeh Kasher (with Eliezer Witztum), *King Herod: A Persecuted Persecutor: A Case Study in Psychohistory and Psychobiography* (Berlin: De Gruyter, 2007), 305. The chief datum for this assertion, however, comes from near the end of Herod's life, when he is depicted as jealous of his son Alexander in physical and athletic terms (so Josephus, *Antiquities* 16 §§ 246–47, 305–6). Indeed, by this stage, Herod was dyeing his hair (*Antiquities* 16 §§ 233).

34 Occasions that will occupy our attention in due course.

35 See Loren R. Spielman, "Playing Roman in Jerusalem: Jewish Attitudes towards Sport and Spectacle during the Second Temple Period," in *Jews in the Gym: Judaism, Sports, and Athletics*, Studies in Jewish Civilization, ed. Leonard J. Greenspoon (West Lafayette, IN: Purdue University Press, 2012), 1–24, which deals comprehensively and critically with the classic point of departure, Josephus, *Antiquities* 15 §§ 267–79.

36 See Josephus, *Jewish War* 1 § 429, where Josephus credits Herod with hunting down forty animals in a single day.

37 See M. C. Bishop, "Cavalry Equipment of the Roman Army in the First Century A.D.," in *Military Equipment and the Identity of Roman Soldiers: Proceedings of the Fourth Roman Military Equipment Conference*, British Archaeological Report International Series 394, ed. J. C. Coulston (Oxford: BAR, 1988), 67–195. He also shows from archaeological evidence that the Roman saddle evolved to the point that the framework that underpinned the seat was shaped from copper or copper-alloy horns (79–81, 88–89, 91–93, 104–5, 107, 127–28).

38 This Galilean devotion to God's kingdom and refusal of Roman dominion are well described in Richard A. Horsley and John S. Hanson, *Bandits,*

Prophets, and Messiahs: Popular Movements in the Time of Jesus (Harrisburg: Trinity, 1999). As the following note will indicate, controversy in regard to Horsley's position has been almost as severe as in regard to Hezekiah's. But allowing for a certain anachronism in attributing modern economic motives to ancient figures, I have found Horsley's model helpful. In particular, however, claims of socioeconomic distress in Galilee do not appear to have been well founded; see Morten Hørning Jensen, "Rural Galilee and Rapid Changes: An Investigation of the Socio-economic Dynamics and Developments in Roman Galilee," *Biblica* 93, no. 1 (2012): 43–67.

39　The predicament has been classically described by Richard A. Horsley in *Jesus and the Spiral of Violence: Popular Resistance in Roman Palestine* (Minneapolis: Fortress, 1993). See also his recent book, *Jesus and the Politics of Roman Palestine* (Columbia: University of South Carolina Press, 2014), as well as Douglas E. Oakman, "Power and Imperium," in *The Political Aims of Jesus* (Minneapolis: Augsburg Fortress, 2012), 45–78. Horsley and Oakman considerably refine the earlier study of S. G. F. Brandon, *Jesus and the Zealots: A Study of the Political Factor in Primitive Christianity* (Manchester: Manchester University Press, 1967). Unfortunately, in an otherwise nuanced analysis, Brandon used the term "Zealot" rather loosely in his title. The same mistake, without the nuance, characterizes Reza Aslan, *Zealot: The Life and Times of Jesus of Nazareth* (New York: Random House, 2013). Such efforts would benefit from a careful consideration of Ernst Bammel, "The Revolution Theory from Reimarus to Brandon," in *Jesus and the Politics of His Day*, ed. Ernst Bammel and C. F. D. Moule (Cambridge: Cambridge University Press, 1984); otherwise the risk is of repeating clichés again and again. In a convincing refutation of the reconstruction of E. P Sanders, J. D. Choi shows the deep influence of the social situation on Jesus's theology in *Jesus' Teaching on Repentance*, International Studies in Formative Judaism and Christianity (Binghamton: Global Publications, 2000). A balanced appraisal of continuing research is offered in Morten H. Jensen, "Climate, Droughts, Wars, and Famines in Galilee as a Background for Understanding the Historical Jesus," *Journal of Biblical Literature* 131, no. 2 (2012): 307–24; and David A. Fiensy, "The Nature of the Galilean Economy in the Late Second Temple Period: The Sociological–Archaeological Debate," in *Christian Origins and the Ancient Economy* (Cambridge: James Clarke, 2014), 81–97. Sharon has offered a critical appraisal of Horsley's approach, coming to the conclusion that Josephus and Nicholas of Damascus used the term *lêstês* of criminals, and sometimes pejoratively of rebels; *Judea under Roman Domination*, 361–77. Linguistically, that would seem to be the case, but although Josephus does not deploy the type of "social bandit" that Horsley does, the type remains helpful.

40 In this context, Josephus described Herod as "by nature activist" (*Jewish War* 1 § 204) or "of noble purpose" (*Antiquities* 14 § 159). The source used by Josephus at this point appears to be Nicholas of Damascus; see Sharon, *Judea under Roman Domination*, 24–26.

41 Sextus's descent and political and military relationship to Julius Caesar, especially in regard to his appointment in Syria, is described with citations of primary sources by Luciano Canfora, *Julius Caesar: The Life and Times of the People's Dictator*, trans. Marian Hill and Kevin Windle (Berkeley: University of California Press, 2007), 221–22.

42 See Josephus, *Jewish War* 1 §§ 204–7; and Josephus, *Antiquities* 14 §§ 158–62.

43 For the organization of Hezekiah's insurgency, see J. Spencer Kennard, "Judas of Galilee and His Clan," *Jewish Quarterly Review* 36, no. 3 (1946): 281–86. Owing to his guerilla tactics and loose organization (which could result in a local supplementation of his forces as well as local willingness to conceal his partisans), a larger force than his was required to defeat him. Even with that advantage, Herod's success was stellar in this case.

44 A key feature of Roman formations was the capacity to bunch troops when they were attacked and spread them in offensive formations; Michael J. Taylor, "Roman Infantry Tactics in the Mid-Republic: A Reassessment," *Historia: Zeitschrift für Alte Geschichte* 63, no. 3 (2014): 301–22.

45 See Josephus, *Jewish War* 1 §§ 204–7; and Josephus, *Antiquities* 14 §§ 159–62. Josephus's report is not detailed at this point, since gratuitous cruelty is involved, but the depth of the enmity between Herodians and the family of Hezekiah is manifest; see Kennard, "Judas of Galilee," 281–86. Herod's tactics were so fearsome, his later campaign in Arbela led to martyrdoms, as described in the next chapter.

46 On the equipment used during this period, see Thomas Fischer, "Costumes, Weapons, and Equipment of the Army from Original Archaeological Finds," in *Army of the Roman Emperors*, trans. M. C. Bishop (Havertown, PA: Casemate, 2019), 116–17, where helmets in the shape of Phrygian caps are discussed.

47 Josephus, *Jewish War* 1 § 205; Josephus, *Antiquities* 14 § 160.

48 Josephus remarked that "it is impossible for prosperity to escape envy," a perspective he applied to himself implicitly and to Herod in particular; see *Jewish War* 1 §§ 208–9. Josephus depicts Hyrcanus as the principal source of envy, but the events he goes on to describe show just how deep and broad it was. By the time he came to write *Antiquities*, Josephus portrays Hyrcanus as a great supporter of Antipater and his family and attributes any animosity to his court and public opinion; *Antiquities* 14 §§ 162–69.

49 See Josephus, *Jewish War* 1 §§ 208–11. The issue of the Sanhedrin is specifically mentioned in Josephus, *Antiquities* 14 §§ 167–69. Shemaiah is later

named as Herod's most articulate opponent on the Sanhedrin (*Antiquities* 14 §§ 172–74), and his Pharisaic pedigree is given in 15 §§ 3–4.

50 This was the slogan that Hezekiah's son Judas would use; see Josephus, *Antiquities* 1 § 23; and Sharon, *Judea under Roman Domination*, 361–77.

51 The maneuvers are detailed in Josephus, *Jewish War* 1 §§ 210–15, and Josephus, *Antiquities* 14 §§ 168–84, along with the events described from this point. See Adam Kolman Marshak, *The Many Faces of Herod the Great* (Grand Rapids: Eerdmans, 2015), 82.

52 The account of the trial in Josephus's *Antiquities* (14 §§ 168–84) and *Jewish War* (1 §§ 204–15) is to some extent incorporated within the Talmud Bavli in tractate Sanhedrin 19a–b; see Richard Kalmin, *The Talmud's Narratives and Their Historical Context*, S. Mark Taper Imprint in Jewish Studies (Oakland: University of California Press, 2014), 24–28.

53 Josephus, *Jewish War* 1 § 211 takes the former line, *Antiquities* 14 § 177 the latter. Although Josephus is quite capable of contradicting himself, in this case, it seems to me that he describes Hyrcanus's disposition in *Jewish War* and his official actions in *Antiquities*. He even says that Hyrcanus "loved" Herod in *Jewish War*, a dubious statement but obviously an affective one. Nadav Sharon attributes differences between *Jewish War* and *Antiquities* in this case to Josephus's greater reliance on Nicholas of Damascus in the former work; "The Trial of Herod," in Sharon, *Judea under Roman Domination*, 379–89.

54 So Josephus, *Antiquities* 14 § 170.

Chapter 3: King Herod

1 See Dio Cassius, *Roman History* 47.26–28. Dio Cassius depicts Alchaudonius "the Arabian" as mediating the arrangement with the Parthians. Strabo describes him as king of a group of nomads near the Euphrates; Strabo, *Geography* 2.10. Alchaudonius (Al-Khaidaun) had once supported the Romans, but then he turned against Crassus at Carrhae. See Jerry Knoblet, *Herod the Great* (Lanham, MD: University Press of America, 2005), 33–34; Perowne, *Life and Times of Herod*, 48; Jones, *Herods of Judaea*, 31–32; and Josephus, *Antiquities* 14 §§ 268–69.

2 Suetonius, *Caesar* 84.

3 Those funds were always vulnerable, however. In a famous case, Cicero defended a Roman governor named Flaccus because he seized the funds; see Cicero, *Pro Flacco*, in *Cicero, Orations: In Catilinam 1–4. Pro Murena. Pro Sulla. Pro Flacco*, Loeb Classical Library 324, trans. C. MacDonald (Cambridge, MA: Harvard University Press, 1976). Because they were collected by a group that did not recognize the gods of Rome, such funds were always tempting. For Julius Caesar's indulgent practice in regard to taxation and finance, see Sharon, *Judea under Roman Domination*, 126–36.

4 Josephus, *Jewish War* 1 §§ 220–22; and Josephus, *Antiquities* 14 §§ 271–76. In the latter telling, Josephus makes Hyrcanus the source of the makeup payment, although Antipater is still identified as the mediator. Both passages mention that Herod was the quickest to collect tribute, earning the reward of Cassius's friendship.

5 Josephus, *Antiquities* 14 § 272. Josephus, *Jewish War* 1 §§ 218–19, is not as specific in regard to the payment to Cassius.

6 Josephus, *Jewish War* 1 § 222; and Josephus, *Antiquities* 14 § 276.

7 Adam Kolman Marshak suggests that Hyrcanus *ordered* Antipater to act in support of Malichus, arguing that Josephus portrays Antipater as nobler than he was; "Rise of the Idumeans: Ethnicity and Politics in Herod's Judea," in *Jewish Identity and Politics between the Maccabees and Bar Kokhba: Groups, Normativity, and Rituals,* Journal for the Study of Judaism Supplement Series 155, ed. Benedikt Eckhardt (Leiden: Brill, 2012), 117–28, esp. 121–25. This portrayal of events is dependent on theoretical models of "monarchal systems of government," which would make Hyrcanus a powerful actor, but overt stances of the kind Marshak supposes seem uncharacteristic of Hyrcanus. Similarly, his conclusion (Marshak, 119) that Malichus was, like Herod, an Idumean (but of Nabataean descent) seems forced.

8 For the plot and its execution, see Josephus, *Jewish War* 1 §§ 225–28; and Josephus, *Antiquities* 14 §§ 277–84.

9 Josephus, *Antiquities* 14 § 281 (cf. the much briefer reference in Josephus, *Jewish War* 1 § 226).

10 When Augustus died, it was rumored he had been poisoned by the drug. See Tacitus, *Annals* 1.5; and Jonathan A. Edlow, "The Case of the Wide-Eyed Boy," in *The Deadly Dinner Party: And Other Medical Detective Stories* (New Haven: Yale University Press, 2009), 116–28.

11 Josephus relates Phasael's key role in assassinating Malichus in *Jewish War* 1 §§ 227–28. He then shifts focus to Herod in his relations to Cassius as the plot matures (§§ 229–32). In Josephus, *Antiquities* 14 §§ 283–93, Phasael's deeper wisdom, compared to his brother, is depicted.

12 Josephus, *Antiquities* 14 §§ 291–93; Josephus, *Jewish War* 1 §§ 233–35. Throughout, Josephus attributes many schemes to Malichus beyond the assassination of Antipater.

13 See C. Jacob Butera and Matthew A. Sears, "The Camps of Brutus and Cassius at Philippi, 42 B.C.," *Hesperia: The Journal of the American School of Classical Studies at Athens* 86, no. 2 (2017): 359–77; and Alain M. Gowing, "Appian and Cassius' Speech before Philippi ('Bella Civilia' 4.90–100)," *Phoenix* 44, no. 2 (1990): 158–81. Cassius committed suicide because he anticipated defeat at Antony's hands, and on the next engagement, Brutus took the same route when the victory of Antony and Octavian became inevitable.

14 Josephus, *Jewish War* 1 §§ 240–41; Josephus, *Antiquities* 14 §§ 297–300. See Regev, "Herod's Jewish Ideology," 197–222. In regard to Mariamme's age at the time of her marriage, see Tal Ilan, *Jewish Women in Greco-Roman Palestine: An Inquiry into Image and Status*, Texte und Studien zum Antiken Judentum 44 (Tübingen: Mohr, 1995), 68.

15 Josephus, *Jewish War* 1 § 242; Josephus, *Antiquities* 14 §§ 301–3.

16 For Antigonus's evolving strategy at this stage, see Josephus, *Jewish War* 1 §§ 195–96 (and Josephus, *Antiquities* 14 §§ 140–42); 1 §§ 239–40 (and *Antiquities* 14 §§ 297–99); and 1 §§ 248–50 (and *Antiquities* 14 §§ 330–33). Josephus does not spell out the shifts of allegiance and the basis of Antigonus's appeal, but they are latent in the description overall.

17 Known conventionally as the Second Triumvirate, to distinguish it from the triumvirate of Pompey, Julius Caesar, and Crassus.

18 Josephus, *Jewish War* 1 §§ 243–47; Josephus, *Antiquities* 14 §§ 324–29. Josephus gives a pragmatic account of the transfer of power, based on the account of Nicholas of Damascus. Probably as a result of the latter's bias, Herod now appears as the senior partner to his older brother.

19 Plutarch, *Antony* 26. Cleopatra's gesture amounted to a royal trope; see Wendy A. Cheshire, "Aphrodite Cleopatra," *Journal of the American Research Center in Egypt* 43 (2007): 151–91.

20 So also Plutarch, *Antony* 26; see Bruce Chilton, *Rabbi Paul: An Intellectual Biography* (New York: Doubleday, 2005), 6–8.

21 And according to Plutarch in *Antony*, 28, not the only one. He portrays the Roman general as thoroughly corrupted by Cleopatra and the flesh pots of Egypt. In my view, however, we should correct for the mill of rumor, both ancient and modern, and credit Antony and Cleopatra with a daring stratagem that their physical pleasures reinforced. To see them as intelligent people who became slaves to lust is Augustan propaganda (and because it is Augustan, enduring propaganda). In any case, as the epilogue indicates, Antony's behavior seems consistent with or without the influence of Cleopatra.

22 Josephus describes the onslaught of Jerusalem in particular in *Jewish War* 1 §§ 250–53; and *Antiquities* 14 §§ 330–39.

23 Josephus attempts to exculpate Antigonus in *Jewish War* 1 §§ 248–49 by attributing the offer to Lysanias, a friendly (and also pro-Parthian) tetrarch who ruled a region called Chalcis (among other names), north of Galilee. Why Lysanias should be so generous on behalf of Antigonus is not explained. In any case, in *Jewish War* 1 § 257 and *Antiquities* 14 §§ 331–32, § 343, Josephus admits that Antigonus himself made the offer. In the latter case, Josephus tries to soften the implicit corruption by pointing out that Antigonus never followed through on the payment. Perhaps so, but it was not for want of trying. For the complex balance of power between Rome and Parthia, see Jason M. Schlude and J. Andrew Overman, "Herod the

Great: A Near Eastern Case Study in Roman-Parthian Politics," in *Arsacids, Romans and Local Elites: Cross-Cultural Interactions of the Parthian Empire*, ed. Jason M. Schlude and Benjamin B. Rubin (Oxford: Oxbow Books, 2017), 93–110.

24 In this regard, see the remarkably succinct and incisive presentation of Eleanor Goltz Huzar, "Parthia Invicta," in *Mark Antony: A Biography* (Minneapolis: University of Minnesota Press, 1978), 169–84.

25 Josephus, *Jewish War* 1 §§ 250–54; Josephus, *Antiquities* 14 §§ 332–39.

26 Josephus, *Jewish War* 1 §§ 254–55; Josephus, *Antiquities* 14 §§ 340–41.

27 Josephus, *Jewish War* 1 § 255; Josephus, *Antiquities* 14 § 342. This agreement shows up Hyrcanus's ambition, a partiality toward Parthia, and utter ineptitude.

28 His frightful end, despite his determined efforts to negotiate with the satrap Barzaphranes on behalf of Hyrcanus and himself even after they were imprisoned, is related in Josephus, *Jewish War* 1 §§ 255–60, 272; and Josephus, *Antiquities* 14 §§ 342–48, 367–69.

29 See Vesta Sarkhosh Curtis, Elizabeth J. Pendleton, Michael Alram, and Touraj Daryaee, eds., *The Parthian and Early Sasanian Empires: Adaptation and Expansion* (Oxford: Oxbow, 2016). Ironically, Rome finally defeated the Sassanids as an empire based in Constantinople, only to be defeated a few years later by forces under the Caliph Umar at Yarmuk in 636 CE; see Chilton, *Abraham's Curse*, 183–84.

30 Josephus, *Jewish War* 1 § 270; Josephus, *Antiquities* 14 § 366.

31 The two passages cited in n. 30 are echoed in similar (and much later) statements by Julius Africanus and Syncellus; see the note of Ralph Marcus in *Josephus*, vol. 7, *Jewish Antiquities, Books XII–XIV*, Loeb Classical Library 365 (Cambridge, MA: Harvard University Press, 1986), 641 n. "f." On this occasion, however, Josephus does not call attention to the existence of two different accounts, as he does in the case of Phasael's death, where he either died outright from his fall or was killed by a physician under the direction of Antigonus. See Josephus, *Jewish War* 1 §§ 271–72; and Josephus, *Antiquities* 14 §§ 367–69.

32 See Josephus, *Jewish War* 1 § 273. The implications for Rome are beautifully brought out in Schlude and Overman, "Herod the Great," 93–110.

33 Details of the escape and its timing are provided in Josephus, *Antiquities* 14 §§ 352–60; and Josephus, *Jewish War* 1 §§ 263–67.

34 See R. M. Rattenbury, "An Ancient Armoured Force," *Classical Review* 56, no. 3 (1942): 113–16. The tactical advantage of the two configurations combined is well described by Susan P. Mattern-Parkes, "The Defeat of Crassus and the Just War," *Classical World* 96, no. 4 (2003): 387–96.

35 Even in retreat, the "Parthian shot," when the rider swiveled on his mount to let an arrow fly while continuing to control the animal in its rapid flight,

was a famous and feared tactic; see M. Rostovtzeff, "The Parthian Shot," *American Journal of Archaeology* 47, no. 2 (1943): 174–87.

36 With a total height of over two thousand feet but only a few hundred feet above the level ground, the hill had a rounded top at the time, which Josephus describes as a breast shape after Herod built his complex there. See Josephus, *Jewish War* 1 §§ 419–21; and Josephus, *Antiquities* 14 § 360. As a result of various predations, the top is now shaped like a cone, although the splendor of Herod's design is still plain; see Barbara Mary Denise Bergin, "Herodium: Herod's Innovative Masterpiece," *Cultural and Religious Studies* 5, no. 6 (2017): 360–70. Josephus refers to the installation both by its Latin name (*Jewish War* 1 § 265) and as Herodias, the Greek equivalent (*Antiquities* 14 § 360). The tactics Herod deployed may be inferred from Josephus's description of the site and from Herod's familiarity with the highly flexible formation, the manipular cohort, which easily permitted division in retreat as well as the rapid formation of a wedge-shaped attack force in the case of assault; see Michael J. Taylor, "Visual Evidence for Roman Infantry Tactics," *Memoirs of the American Academy in Rome* 59, no. 6 (2014): 103–20.

37 Josephus, *Jewish War* 1 §§ 274–78; Josephus, *Antiquities* 14 §§ 370–75. The surrender of Aretas III to Roman rule in 62 BCE had deprived Antipater's family of a helpful, independent ally. The king by the time of Herod's retreat was Malchus I; see Duane W. Roller, *Cleopatra: A Biography* (Oxford: Oxford University Press, 2010), 86. Leaders in both Judea and Nabataea evidently attempted to find room to maneuver between the two great powers of the time.

38 Josephus intimates that he also refused her sexual favors, but that says more about Josephus's view of Cleopatra than the facts of the case. See *Jewish War* 1 § 279; and *Antiquities* 14 §§ 375–76. Later in the narrative, Josephus claims overtly that Cleopatra attempted to seduce Herod. By then, however, Cleopatra and Antony were mutually and irrevocably bound together, and A. H. M. Jones is right to attribute such claims to Herod's own proclivity to exaggerate. Although Jones puts the case too strongly when he states that Cleopatra would not have "wasted her charms on a client king of no political importance," he does have a point; *Herods of Judaea*, 51. Jones's interpretation engages very closely with the text of Josephus, although he leaves it to the reader to follow along without the benefit of bibliography or notes. Still, a tenacious reader can learn a great deal from him.

39 Josephus, *Jewish War* 1 §§ 282–85; Josephus, *Antiquities* 14 §§ 381–89.

40 For this reason, the diadem would feature prominently among Herod's coins; see D. T. Ariel, "The Coins of Herod the Great in the Context of the Augustan Empire," in *Herod and Augustus: Papers Presented at the*

IJS Conference, 21st–23rd June 2005, IJS Studies in Judaica 6, ed.
D. M. Jacobson and N. Kokkinos (Leiden: Brill, 2009), 113–26, 425–27;
David Jacobson, "Herod the Great's Royal Monogram," *Israel Numismatic Research* 9 (2014): 95–101; and Noy, "Head Decoration," 39–54 (with plates). Episodes such as Herod's appearance in Rome have naturally resulted in the estimate that his Judaism was purely a convenience. But dealing with Rome required concessions from every Jewish ruler who cooperated with them, and I agree with Vermes that Herod's religious orientation, however compromised, was not spurious; see *True Herod*, 46.

41 His actual title, *socius et amicus populi Romani* ("associate and friend of the Roman people"), conveys the dependent status that the modern term *client king* expresses; see Erich S. Gruen, "Herod, Rome, and the Diaspora," in *The Construct of Identity in Hellenistic Judaism: Essays on Early Jewish Literature and History* (Berlin: De Gruyter, 2016), 383–96, especially 384. The colonialist resonance of the term *client* means that *client king* should be used with caution to make clear the military and personal relationships that the Romans formalized when they named a king. With that in mind, I am less reticent than Gruen is to accept usage of the modern term. Antony and Octavian skillfully used the institution as extensions of their personal power and encouraged coordination among their clients; see David Jacobson, "Three Roman Client Kings: Herod of Judaea, Archelaus of Cappadocia and Juba of Mauretania," *Palestine Exploration Quarterly* 133 (2001): 22–38.

42 In the way of Roman practice at the time, Ventidius and Silo, his subordinate, had sought gain from Antigonus. When Herod returned in 39 BCE with his newly minted authorization from Antony (and a message from his agent, Dellius), they backed Herod as instructed. See Josephus, *Jewish War* 1 §§ 288–92; and Josephus, *Antiquities* 14 §§ 392–95.

43 Still, Josephus's claim that "all Galilee" backed him (*Jewish War* 1 §§ 291–92; *Antiquities* 14 § 395) is a manifest exaggeration, since he qualifies what he says with the phrase "apart from a few." The program of propaganda he pursued (and to some extent inherited from Nicholas of Damascus) did not completely obliterate a sense of reality.

44 The sequence of the campaign is set out in Josephus, *Jewish War* 1 §§ 292–96; and Josephus, *Antiquities* 14 §§ 396–400.

45 See Josephus, *Antiquities* 14 § 403, where Antigonus even makes the claim to the Roman commander Silo.

46 See Kenneth Atkinson, "Herod the Great, Sosius, and the Siege of Jerusalem (37 B.C.E.) in Psalm of Solomon 17," *Novum Testamentum* 38, no. 4 (1996): 313–22. Pharisaic opinion did not coalesce around the concept of a Davidic messiah until the second century CE, but there were precedents for the concept centuries earlier, and resistance to the Herod's status as king did

not require a formally messianic counterargument. Pharisaic resistance to Herod is well described in Horsley, "Conflict with the Scribes and Pharisees," in Horsley, *Jesus and the Politics of Roman Palestine*, 128–53. He refers in particular to Pollio and Shemaiah as criticizing Herod over Hezekiah's execution (Horsley, 131), citing Josephus, *Antiquities* 14 §§ 172–76; 15 §§ 3–4. A much later tradition in the Talmud Bavli (Baba Batra 3b–4a) refers to Herod slaying rabbis who interpreted Deuteronomy 17:15 (which prohibits the appointment of a foreigner as king) against him. See Yonatan Feintuch, "External Appearance versus Internal Truth: The Aggadah of Herod in Bavli Bava Batra," *Association of Jewish Studies Review* 35, no. 1 (2011): 85–104; and Jeffrey L. Rubenstein, "King Herod in Ardashir's Court: The Rabbinic Story of Herod (B. Bava Batra 3b–4a) in Light of Persian Sources," *Association of Jewish Studies Review* 38, no. 2 (2014): 249–74. The grisly events of the siege itself are recounted in Josephus, *Jewish War* 1 §§ 294–303, 345–53; and Josephus, *Antiquities* 14 §§ 397–412, 468–81. The reason for the break in both narratives is that Herod's campaigns outside Jerusalem while the Romans under Silo wintered.

47 Josephus, *Jewish War* 1 §§ 302–3; Josephus, *Antiquities* 14 §§ 411–13. This proved to be a massive, bloody campaign; I here give the most famous example of Herod's improvisational cruelty.

48 Josephus, *Jewish War* 1 §§ 309–13; Josephus, *Antiquities* 14 §§ 420–30. The passage is clearly modeled after 2 Maccabees 7 and serves to illustrate the motivation of Herod's enemies. Indeed, the story can be told for or against Herod and seems imperfectly turned into Herodian propaganda in *Jewish War*. Even the skills of Nicholas of Damascus, Josephus's most immediate source, cannot get away from the fact that the typology of 2 Maccabees puts Herod in the role of Antiochus Epiphanes. For that reason, it seems to me the initial source of the story was not Nicholas but that Nicholas attempted to turn opposition propaganda to his own purposes. Josephus seems to correct even further on Herod's behalf in the *Antiquities*, but his efforts also fail to ennoble Herod's behavior. Helen K. Bond observes the discordant note struck by the story; "Josephus on Herod's Domestic Intrigue in the 'Jewish War,'" *Journal for the Study of Judaism in the Persian, Hellenistic, and Roman Period* 43, no. 3 (2012): 295–314, 298n7.

49 Josephus, *Jewish War* 1 §§ 320–22; Josephus, *Antiquities* 14 §§ 436–47.

50 Josephus, *Jewish War* 1 §§ 323–30; Josephus, *Antiquities* 14 §§ 448–53.

51 Josephus, *Jewish War* 1 §§ 331–33; Josephus, *Antiquities* 14 §§ 454–55.

52 Josephus, *Jewish War* 1 §§ 333–39; Josephus, *Antiquities* 14 §§ 456–61.

53 This scene, one of several of Herod's fortunate escapes, is recounted in Josephus, *Jewish War* 1 §§ 340–41; and Josephus, *Antiquities* 14 §§ 462–63.

54 Josephus, *Jewish War* 1 §§ 342–46; Josephus, *Antiquities* 14 §§ 464–69.

55 Josephus, *Jewish War* 1 § 352; Josephus, *Antiquities* 14 § 480.

56 Josephus, *Jewish War* 1 § 353; Josephus, *Antiquities* 14 § 481.

57 Dio Cassius, *Roman History* 49.22.6, discussed contextually in Sverre Bøe, *Cross-Bearing in Luke*, Wissenschaftliche Untersuchungen zum Neuen Testament 278 (Tübingen: Mohr Siebeck, 2010), 61–63. This section of the *History* also makes clear Antony's difficulties in dealing with Parthia, the main enemy.

58 Of a relatively low denomination, however, since Tyrian Silver coinage continued to be used during the Maccabean and Herodian periods; see David Jacobson, "Herodian Bronze and Tyrian Silver Coinage," *Zeitschrift des Deutschen Palästina-Vereins* 130 (2014): 138–54.

Chapter 4: Mariamme

1 The coins also feature a helmet, likely a reference to Herod's own equipment for war; see Catharine Lorber, "The Iconographic Program of the Year 3 Coinage of Herod the Great," *American Journal of Numismatics* 25, no. 1 (2013): 127–69. Although I agree with her that Herod incorporated classical themes in his coins deliberately (e.g., the ivy leaves dear to both Dionysus and Antony), that incorporation was well underway during the period of Maccabean minting; see Regev, "Hellenization," 175–96, especially 182–88. Her argument that Herod wished to identify himself with the god Dionysus strikes me as exaggerated. Even his ambition had some limits. In any case, David Jacobson has answered Lorber's argument (as well as her chronology) in "Herod the Great, Augustus Caesar and Herod's 'Year 3' Coins," *Strata* 33 (2015): 89–118.

2 Jones finds Herod's motivation "obscure"; Jones, *Herods of Judaea*, 52–53. But dedicated dynasty building explains his actions adequately. Hyrcanus's return was the seal that he had conquered both Jerusalem and Mariamme, a connection that Josephus himself makes in *Jewish War* 1 § 344. He also portrays Herod as self-conscious in regard to his own claim to kingship in bringing Hyrcanus back; *Antiquities* 15 §§ 11–20. But at this point, it is more Josephus than Herod who dwells on Herod's nonroyal pedigree; *Antiquities* 14 §§ 487–91. By the time Josephus came to write the *Antiquities*, as we shall see in the epilogue, he cast himself as the plausible heir of a Maccabean lineage that had only been removed from power temporarily in the shape of the interloper Herod.

3 Josephus, *Antiquities* 15 §§ 22, 34, 39–41, 56; Wilker, *Für Rom*, 218–19, 319–20, 368. Interestingly, the Mishnah turns Ananel into an Egyptian (Parah 3:5). Herod subsequently demoted Ananel and promoted him again, depending on the political winds. Ralph Marcus cites Joseph Klausner's suggestion that Herod wished to "discredit" the Maccabean lineage by this act; see *Josephus: Jewish Antiquities, Books XV–XVII* (Cambridge, MA:

Harvard University Press, 1990), 13. But in the context of the repatriation of Hyrcanus and the deployment of Ananel (whose name may also be rendered as Chananel) as a political shuttlecock, this reading attributes to Herod's program a greater coherence than it really had as a priestly strategy.

4 Josephus, *Antiquities* 15 §§ 3–4, where Josephus also claims that Shemaiah called for Herod to be accepted in Jerusalem during the siege; cf. also 14 §§ 172–76. From the opening of book 15 of the *Antiquities*, Herod's purge of the Sanhedrin and the aristocracy is described. Here Josephus also mentions Pollion, Shemaiah's teacher.

5 Josephus, *Jewish War* 1 §§ 435–36. A third son died in Rome, where he was educated (along with Alexander and Aristobulus). Even before they lived together, Mariamme had intervened to prevent Herod from traveling with Phasael and Hyrcanus with the emissaries of Pacorus; Josephus, *Jewish War* 1 § 262.

6 Antony and Cleopatra wisely did not solemnize their wedding, since to do so would have announced that Antony was a bigamist (in that he was still married to Octavian's sister). In addition, Cleopatra as a foreigner was not a qualified wife for the Romans. Sheila L. Ager contributed a brilliant analysis that casts appropriate doubt on a formal wedding between Antony and Cleopatra, perhaps, however, without adequately recognizing the public force of their association in power; "Marriage or Mirage? The Phantom Wedding of Cleopatra and Antony," *Classical Philology* 108, no. 2 (2013): 139–55. Their mutual governance and Antony's gift to his wife (legal or otherwise) of lands in Syria were major events in 37 CE. Herod's politics of marriage (legal albeit polygamous) might have echoed Antony's behavior as well as his confidence (indicated by Josephus, *Jewish War* 1 § 344) that he was about to take Jerusalem.

7 See Dio Cassius, *Roman History* 49.41.6; 50.3.5; and the comprehensive discussion of Caesarion in Michael Gray-Fow, "What to Do with Caesarion," *Greece & Rome* 61, no. 1 (2014): 38–67, especially 55–56.

8 Subject to deep controversy from the time that Octavian appropriated the will illegally, it has been a matter of contention in ancient and modern sources since Plutarch's *Antony* 58.2–4. For a deft treatment of the affair in context, see Huzar, "Breaking with Octavian," in *Mark Antony*, 185–208.

9 These negotiations are detailed in a narrative in Josephus, *Jewish War* 1 §§ 360–63; and Josephus, *Antiquities* 15 §§ 79, 88, 92–120.

10 Josephus maintains that Alexandra even took the initiative in plotting with Cleopatra just after the appointment of Ananel; Josephus, *Antiquities* 15 §§ 23–24. Mariamme's request is narrated in *Antiquities* 15 §§ 31–38, in the midst of Josephus's account of Alexandra's ceaseless machinations.

11 See the comprehensive treatment of this insult by Benedikt Eckhardt, "'An Idumean, That Is, a Half-Jew': Hasmoneans and Herodians between

Ancestry and Merit," in Eckhardt, *Jewish Identity*, 91–115; and Josephus, *Antiquities* 14 § 403.

12 She might even have thought of herself in the role of Salomé Alexandra, who took over as regent of the Maccabean throne after the death of her husband, Alexander Jannaeus. In that role, Mariamme could offer advancement to her brother and secure the high priesthood for her own family line, quite apart from Herod's relatives. She was much younger than Herod, and such an ambition would have been reasonable.

13 Josephus, *Antiquities* 15 §§ 23–30. The intermediary in this bizarre affair was Dellius, who ultimately deserted Antony before the battle of Actium according to Dio Cassius, *Roman History* 49.39. Although Josephus does not say so, he appears in this case to have been acting in the service of Cleopatra.

14 For Herod's action and Alexandra's response, see Josephus, *Antiquities* 15 §§ 31–41.

15 Josephus, *Antiquities* 15 §§ 42–52.

16 See Ehud Netzer, *The Architecture of Herod, the Great Builder* (Tübingen: Mohr Siebeck, 2006).

17 For the archeology and interpretation of the site, see Regev, "Hellenization," 175–96.

18 In 35 BCE, as Josephus relates in *Antiquities* 15 §§ 53–56. References to the intrigue involved become much sparer in Josephus's *Jewish War* at this stage (see 1 § 437). Monika Bernett comments on the bizarre arrangement of having the high priest swim with underlings of the house; "Herrschaft und Repräsentation under den Herodiern," *Zeitschrift des Deutschen Palästina-Vereins* 127, no. 1 (2011): 74–105, especially 99–100. Her comparison is with Roman and Hellenistic court practice, but Herod in some ways continued to conduct himself as if his house were a military camp.

19 Indeed, Herod seems to have calculated the assassination to inflict the maximum harm on Alexandra, who lost her son at her own house party. Although Josephus claims that a fear of Cleopatra made him spare Alexandra (*Antiquities* 15 § 48), her extreme reaction to her son's drowning (*Antiquities* 15 §§ 57–59) shows that Herod knew exactly how to inflict the most pain on her.

20 The episode is set out in Josephus, *Antiquities* 15 §§ 62–87; and Josephus, *Jewish War* 1 §§ 438–44. The maneuvering in the absence of Herod was intense, and it seems Alexandra very much hoped that Antony would weaken, depose, or even kill her son-in-law. Herod's sister Salomé took the opportunity to dispose of her husband, Joseph, by endorsing Herod's suspicions that he had been intimate with Mariamme. Salomé also emerged as Mariamme's principal enemy within the court at this stage. The account in *Jewish War* 1 §§ 438–44 has been read (e.g., by Ralph Marcus and Allen

Wikgren in their edition of the *Antiquities* passage on pp. 42–43) to mean that Herod put Mariamme to death at that point. If so, that would be an instance of Josephus's "evident anachronisms." But at this point, I think that Josephus's attempt to condense has got the better of him. For this reason, in regard to Mariamme, I prefer the *Antiquities* as a source.

21 See Simon Goldhill, "The Art of Reception: J. W. Waterhouse and the Painting of Desire in Victorian Britain," in *Victorian Culture and Classical Antiquity: Art, Opera, Fiction, and the Proclamation of Modernity* (Princeton, NJ: Princeton University Press, 2011), 23–64, especially 45–52. Goldhill offers a convincing account of how Waterhouse both oversimplifies the image of Mariamme and calls attention to what he oversimplifies. For a survey, see Maurice J. Valency, *The Tragedies of Herod and Mariamne* (New York: AMS Press, 1966).

22 Josephus, *Antiquities* 15 §§ 96–103. For the interplay between the presentation of Nicholas of Damascus, on which Josephus relies, and Herod's own literary efforts, see Tal Ilan, "King David, King Herod and Nicolaus of Damascus," *Jewish Studies Quarterly* 5, no. 3 (1998): 95–240; and Mark Toher, "Nicolaus and Herod in the 'Antiquitates Judaicae,'" *Harvard Studies in Classical Philology* 101 (2003): 427–47.

23 Josephus, *Antiquities* 15 §§ 108–20.

24 See Revital Ken-Tor, Amotz Agnon, Yehouda Enzel, Mordecae Stein, Shmuel Marco, and Jorg F. W. Negendank, "High-Resolution Geological Record of Historic Earthquakes in the Dead Sea Basin," *Palestine Exploration Quarterly* 106, no. B2 (2001): 2221–34. The pairing is made by Josephus, *Antiquities* 15 §§ 121–22.

25 The background and course of the battle are brilliantly described in Carsten Hjort Lange, "The Battle of Actium: A Reconsideration," *Classical Quarterly* 61, no. 2 (2011): 608–23, on the basis of Plutarch, Dio Cassius, and other sources. Lange, however, attributes the debacle to Cleopatra's "panic" (Lange, 620), following Dio Cassius (*Roman History* 50.33.1–2), compounded by Antony's "indefensible error" (Lange, 621; cf. Plutarch, *Antony* 66.4–5; 68.2–3). More likely, first Cleopatra and then Antony, confronting the likelihood of defeat at sea, made the calculation that preserving the navy by means of retreat took precedence over supporting even their amassed troops. Crucially, they had already stowed sails for this eventuality, which Lange acknowledges was an unusual measure prior to battle (616).

26 She resorted to a series of desperate stratagems, not all of them fully cogent or put into effect with a commitment to success; the situation after Actium became so confused that even the details of Caesarion's death are unknown. See Gray-Fow, "What to Do with Caesarion," 38–67, 56–65.

27 Josephus, *Antiquities* 15 §§ 121–60. In this section, as in Josephus, *Jewish War* 1 §§ 364–85, Josephus treats the term *Arab* as interchangeable with *Nabataean*. Both accounts also lay the blame for the initial defeat on

insubordination: Herod (and Josephus) alleged that the thinning of formations in pursuit of the foe was the fault of his soldiers' overconfidence, not his order. That rashness permitted Athenion to wreak his havoc. I take this to be Herodian propaganda, which Josephus expands in the version of Herod's speech in the *Antiquities*, sharpening the critique of all opponents.

28 Josephus gives alternative accounts of the legal proceeding, based on Herod's own memoir and on contemporary opinion; *Antiquities* 15 §§ 161–82. They differ on the degree of Hyrcanus's guilt, on Alexandra's complicity in dealings with the Nabataeans, and on the role of the Sanhedrin.

29 The separation of Herod's birth family from his mother-in-law and Mariamme is set out in Josephus, *Antiquities* 15 §§ 183–86.

30 Herod's approach and Octavian's response are detailed in Josephus, *Jewish War* 1 §§ 386–400; and Josephus, *Antiquities* 15 §§ 187–201.

31 See Josephus, *Jewish War* 1 § 390; cf. Josephus, *Antiquities* 15 § 193.

32 As Jones, *Herods of Judaea*, 59, observes.

33 A pattern, of course, that was later repeated in the crucifixion of Jesus, but in that case, at the order of the Roman administrator of the time; see Josephus, *Antiquities* 15 § 173.

34 See David M. Jacobson, "King Herod's 'Heroic' Public Image," *Revue Biblique* 95, no. 3 (1988): 386–403. He poses the striking question, "Could not the depiction of a ceremony of homage to the Dioscuri evident on this coin issue also have hinted at the adoration that Herod fervently desired but which was denied him by the Jews?" (Jacobson, 403). Association with both horsemanship and seamanship makes the thought appealing, but the motif of the conical cap and the star is so widespread that Jacobson's suggestion seems unlikely, intriguing though it is.

35 See Josephus, *Jewish War* 2 § 439; 5 §§ 162–71.

36 My student Francis Karagodins has pointed out to me the similarity with Cicero, *Pro Caelio* §§ 57–67.

37 Josephus, *Antiquities* 15 §§ 202–39. The corresponding passage in *Jewish War* is so compressed that its chronology becomes unclear (1 §§ 431–44). Josephus's usage of Nicholas's history is not consistent. And sometimes, he and Nicholas do not agree on the portrayal of characters. In Josephus's telling, Mariamme was arrogant; in Nicholas's telling, she was noble. Geza Vermes reads *Antiquities* 15 §§ 227–29 to make execution hinge on a repetition of the earlier narrative of Herod's departure, when he put the hapless Joseph in charge of Mariamme, with Soaimos taking the place of Joseph. But the similarity is more the result of Josephus's narrative device than the events; cf. Vermes, *True Herod*, 59.

38 See John Granger Cook, *Crucifixion in the Mediterranean World*, Wissenschaftliche Untersuchungen zum Neuen Testament 327 (Tübingen: Mohr Siebeck, 2019), 3–4, 315–16n36.

39 See the Talmud Bavli, Baba Batra 3b–4a. For a helpful treatment, see Fein-
     tuch, "External Appearance," 85–104. Herod's unstable but vicious state
     after he had Mariamme executed is described in *Antiquities* 15 §§ 240–66.

40 Josephus, *Antiquities* 15 §§ 267–76. By this point, Costobar had been
     divorced by Salomé, which Josephus notes was not in accord with the laws
     of Judaism; Josephus also recounts how the Pharisees involved, followers of
     "Baba" (commonly thought to be the Baba ben Buta of Talmudic litera-
     ture), had backed Antigonus against Herod.

41 By inclusive count, we would say they happened every four years. For
     the evolution of these games in Jerusalem and later Caesarea, see Joseph
     Patrich, "Herod's Hippodrome-Stadium at Caesarea and the Games
     Conducted Therein," in *What Athens Has to Do with Jerusalem: Essays on
     Classical, Jewish, and Early Christian Art and Archaeology in Honor of Gideon
     Foerster*, Interdisciplinary Studies in Ancient Culture and Religion 1, ed.
     Leonard V. Rutgers (Leuven: Peeters, 2002), 29–68; Josephus, *Antiqui-
     ties* 15 §§ 267–76. This initiative was such a violation of ancestral practice
     that Josephus describes it as one reason for the disaster that was to follow
     Herod's reign. Josephus explains the initiative on the basis of the killing of
     so many in Hyrcanus's family (*Antiquities* 15 §§ 267). If the narrative were
     placed later, Octavian's acclamation as Augustus in 27 BCE might be taken
     as an incentive. But after that date, Herod played on the name of Augustus
     in Greek (*Sebastos*), and the games moved to places where contention was
     greatly reduced. I agree with Patrich, therefore, that a date prior to 27 BCE
     is preferable; see Zeev Weiss, *Public Spectacles in Roman and Late Antique
     Palestine* (Cambridge, MA: Harvard University Press, 2014), 14; and Peter
     Richardson and Amy Marie Fisher, *Herod: King of the Jews and Friend of the
     Romans*, Routledge Ancient Biographies (London: Routledge, 2018), 25.
     The last work cited is a second edition of Richardson's 1996 book, with a
     good discussion of the chronological challenges in reading Josephus and the
     secondary literature (Richardson and Fisher, 19–30). As in his case, I have
     adjusted dates to accord with the analysis as it develops. Patrich has conve-
     niently assembled the evidence in "Herodian Entertainment Structures," in
     Jacobson and Kokkinos, *Herod and Augustus*, 181–213, settling on a date of
     28 BCE.

42 The source within the *Antiquities* (15 §§ 267–98; cf. Ralph Marcus,
     Josephus, 127) reflects the hostility to Herod's actions during this period
     as a form of corruption. The expense of his excesses is emphasized, and
     the source of his wealth has remained a question, since the overall level of
     taxation he imposed seems to have been reasonable. Jones, *Herods of Judaea*,
     87–92, plausibly suggests a combination of taxing commercial transactions
     and taking proceeds from royally sponsored operations such as mining. To
     that should be added income from his magnificent buildings.

43 Josephus, *Antiquities* 15 §§ 289–91.

44 For a remarkably lucid treatment, see J. S. Richardson, "Princeps, 29–12 BC," in *Augustan Rome 44 BC to AD 14: The Restoration of the Republic and the Establishment of the Empire*, The Edinburgh History of Ancient Rome (Edinburgh: Edinburgh University Press, 2012), 80–134.

45 See Andrea M. Berlin, "Herod the Tastemaker," *Near Eastern Archaeology* 77, no. 2 (2014): 108–19.

46 See Shimon Gibson and Ron E. Tappy, "Samaria and Sebaste," in *Archaeology in the "Land of Tells and Ruins": A History of Excavations in the Holy Land Inspired by the Photographs and Accounts of Leo Boer*, ed. Bart Wagemakers (Oxford: Oxbow, 2014), 60–87; David M. Jacobson, "Herod the Great Shows His True Colors," *Near Eastern Archaeology* 64, no. 3 (2001): 100–104, 110–12; and Bieke Mahieu, "The Foundation Year of Samaria-Sebaste and its Chronological Implications," *Ancient Society* 38 (2008): 183–96.

47 Josephus, *Antiquities* 15 §§ 299–316.

48 Josephus, *Antiquities* 15 §§ 317–25. He names the new wife in *Antiquities* 18 § 136; and *Jewish War* 1 § 562. Here I will not detail all Herod's ten marriages, only those that proved key within events and/or provided heirs who were crucial in the Herodian project. Richardson and Fisher, *Herod* (2018), 31, offer a clear and well-researched family tree.

49 See Ehud Netzer, "Greater Herodium," *Qedem* 13 (1981): 1, 3–147.

50 See Joseph Patrich, "Urban Space in Caesarea Maritima, Israel," in *Urban Centers and Rural Contexts in Late Antiquity*, ed. Thomas S. Burns and John W. Eadie (East Lansing: Michigan State University Press, 2001), 77–110; Josephus, *Antiquities* 15 §§ 331–41; and Josephus, *Jewish War* 1 §§ 408–15.

51 See Barbara Burrell, "Herod's Caesarea on Sebastos: Urban Structures and Influences," in Jacobson and Kokkinos, *Herod and Augustus*, 217–33. For an informed discussion of the dating of the erection of Caesarea Maritima, see Daniel R. Schwartz's review of *Herod: King of the Jews and Friend of the Romans*, by Peter Richardson, *Jewish Quarterly Review* 87, nos. 3–4 (1998): 348–55, esp. 350–51. Despite the contention involved and Josephus's use of both 40 BCE and 37 BCE as the beginning of Herod's regnal years, 22 BCE appears to be the scholarly consensus for the commencement of building.

52 Josephus deals with this encounter and its consequences in *Antiquities* 15 §§ 354–69. His statement that Herod was, in effect, the third most important person in the Roman Empire (§ 361) is no doubt exaggerated and probably derives from Herod's own propaganda at the hands of Nicholas of Damascus.

53 Josephus, *Antiquities* 15 §§ 342–53.

54 So Josephus, *Antiquities* 16 §§ 1–5. For an excellent treatment of slavery in Roman practice, see Noel Lenski, "Violence and the Roman Slave," in *The Topography of Violence in the Greco-Roman World*, ed. Werner Riess and Garrett G. Fagan (Ann Arbor: University of Michigan Press, 2016), 275–96.

55 By Josephus, for example, in the last passage cited, which indicates a broadening of the principle expressed in Exodus 21:7–11.

56 In *Jewish War* 1 § 483, Josephus locates the region on the east side of the Jordan River, in effect Perea; cf. *Antiquities* 15 §§ 362.

57 Josephus, *Antiquities* 15 §§ 363–64.

58 Josephus, *Antiquities* 15 §§ 365–70. As in the earlier case, Josephus mentions Pollion too. Vermes wrongly generalizes the exception to construe the Pharisees as exempted as a whole; *True Herod*, 50. He also appears to think of Pollion and Shemaiah as the same person.

59 So Josephus, *Antiquities* 15 §§ 365–79. This and related actions are treated by Solomon Zeitlin, "Herod: A Malevolent Maniac," *Jewish Quarterly Review* 54, no. 1 (1963): 1–27; and Horsley, "Conflict with the Scribes and Pharisees," 128–53, 131. An alternative seam of explanation in regard to the Essenes has posited that since Herod persecuted Pharisees, he must have been even more vindictive in relation to Essenes; so Charles T. Fritsch, "Herod the Great and the Qumran Community," *Journal of Biblical Literature* 74, no. 3 (1955): 173–81. Jodi Magness has taken this approach as a line of investigation in order to explain the pattern of habitation at Qumran; see Jodi Magness, "The Chronology of the Settlement at Qumran in the Herodian Period," *Dead Sea Discoveries* 2, no. 1 (1995): 58–65; and Dennis Mizzi and Jodi Magness, "Was Qumran Abandoned at the End of the First Century BCE?," *Journal of Biblical Literature* 135, no. 2 (2016): 301–20. Yet the stance of Baba Batra 3b–4a makes the killing of the Pharisees a matter of principle, since they interpreted Deuteronomy 17:15 against Herod. The Essenes, however, because they only expected true theocracy after divine intervention, could sit more loosely to the government in power, especially if it did not embrace priestly pretensions. This may explain why someone like Menahem the Essene could envisage Herodian rule. Essene fatalism is described by Josephus in *Antiquities* 18 §§ 18–22; and *Jewish War* 2 §§ 119–61. Shemaiah's orientation is also described as fatalistic; see *Antiquities* 14 §§ 172–76. Herod seems to have been happy to embrace acquiescence to his rule as prophetic support. In sorting out differences among Essenes, Pharisees, and Sadducees along the lines of how they treated free will in relation to fate, Josephus no doubt attempts to package these groups more neatly as philosophical schools than is reasonable. But eschatological predeterminism indeed seems to have been an Essene trait.

60 Josephus, *Antiquities* 17 §§ 41–51, 58–60, all in a flashback to the time of the loyalty oath. Less obvious is why any Pharisee would endorse Pheroras

over Herod. The latter's marriage with Mariamme might provide the key; in that case, Herod's attempt to found a hybrid dynasty was at the center of his contention with the Pharisees.

61 See David Jacobson, "The Jerusalem Temple of Herod the Great," in *The World of the Herods: Volume 1 of the International Conference "The World of the Herods and Nabataeans" Held at the British Museum, 17–19 April 2001*, Oriens et Occidens 14, ed. Nikos Kokkinos (Stuttgart: Steiner, 2007), 145–76. Josephus quotes Herod at the time work had begun in *Antiquities* 15 § 387: "Now since I rule by God's will, and a long peace persists and prosperity of wealth and huge revenues, and above all since the Romans—through whose benevolence all acknowledge their mastery—are friends, I shall try to set right the lapse occasion by the want and subjection of the former time and by this act of piety give full return to God for all I have obtained of this kingdom." Cf. the wider passage §§ 380–425. In a fine article, Regev makes this passage a centerpiece of Herod's political and religious project; see Regev, "Herod's Jewish Ideology," 213–14. The scale of the building involved is detailed by James H. Charlesworth, who points out that the largest stones in the temple platform weighed 570 tons, while those used in the pyramids weighed no more than 70 tons; "Jesus and the Temple," in *Jesus and the Temple: Textual and Archaeological Explorations* (Minneapolis: Augsburg Fortress, 2014), 146–48.

62 Samuel Rocca makes a strong case that the eagle was not specifically Roman but reflected Herod's absorption of fashion in the Hellenistic East; "The Source of Herod's Eagle on the Façade of the Temple: Eastern Hellenistic or Roman," *Mediterraneo Antico* 21, nos. 1–2 (2018): 449–75.

63 See Philo of Alexandria, *Embassy to Gaius* §§ 157, 291. According to Josephus, *Against Apion* 2 §§ 77–78, the expense was assumed by Jews as a whole; cf. Josephus, *Jewish War* 2 § 197.

64 Josephus, *Antiquities* 16 §§ 6–7.

65 Josephus, *Antiquities* 16 §§ 12–65. This remarkable passage also portrays Herod as reinforcing the rights of Jews outside his lands and includes an eloquent address by Nicholas of Damascus in support of those rights. Even allowing for propagandistic intent, the account shows Herod's ambition to be the king for Jews within the Roman Empire, not only of Judea.

66 He refers proudly to his good health in Josephus, *Antiquities* 16 § 134; and his prowess is vaunted in Josephus, *Jewish War* 1 §§ 429–30, complete with the claim that once he bagged forty wild animals in a single hunt.

67 See Josephus, *Antiquities* 16 §§ 66–77 (and earlier, §§ 6–11). Josephus lays principal blame for the friction on Herod's sister Salomé, but the actions and attitudes of his sons gave her more than enough to work with in her intrigue.

68 Josephus, *Antiquities* 15 §§ 366–67.

69 See Josephus, *Antiquities* 16 §§ 78–90.

70 Josephus, *Antiquities* 16 §§ 90–129. Josephus, *Jewish War* 1 §§ 452–54, puts this meeting in Rome; cf. also *Antiquities* 16 § 106. In the last passage, Alexander appeals to his father by pointing out that he must never have intended his sons harm, since "no one who undertakes to kill someone brings him to a sanctuary or temple." Rome is identified as the locum in that sense in a fascinating appeal to a religious practice that is evidently not specifically Judaic.

71 See Josephus, *Antiquities* 16 §§ 190–93.

72 See Shaun Tougher, "The Aesthetics of Castration: The Beauty of Roman Eunuchs," in *Castration and Culture in the Middle Ages*, ed. Tracy Larissa (Rochester, NY: Boydell & Brewer, 2013), 48–72; and Walter Stevenson, "The Rise of Eunuchs in Greco-Roman Antiquity," *Journal of the History of Sexuality* 5, no. 4 (1995): 495–511. Both these cases make it very clear that Roman culture resisted and yet adapted to the identity of the eunuch.

73 Josephus, *Antiquities* 16 §§ 235–70.

74 Josephus, *Antiquities* 16 §§ 229–34. Sexual scandal was by now characteristic of Herod's court. His brother Pheroras, infatuated with a slave, preferred to marry her rather than the king's daughter Salampsio. After Herod thought Pheroras's ardor had worn off, he tried to convince him to marry Cypros, another daughter. That arrangement also failed (Josephus, *Antiquities* 16 §§ 194–200). In any case, Herod's penchant for the marriage of near relatives, although agreeable to Hellenistic and Roman royal practice, was in obvious contradiction of the Torah (see Lev 18:1–18).

75 Josephus, *Antiquities* 16 §§ 271–77.

76 Josephus, *Antiquities* 16 §§ 278–99, 333–55. In regard to Syllaeus, see Nada Al-Rawabdeh, "About the Nabataean Minister Syllaeus from New Silver Coins," *Mediterranean Archaeology and Archaeometry* 15, no. 1 (2015): 73–82.

77 Josephus, *Antiquities* 16 § 291.

78 Josephus, *Antiquities* 16 §§ 356–94.

79 Josephus's description of the symptoms (in *Antiquities* 17 §§ 146–48, 168–72) makes a condition known since the nineteenth century as Fournier's gangrene seem a possible diagnosis. For a treatment of how Josephus weaves moral judgment into medical symptoms, see David J. Ladouceur, "The Death of Herod the Great," *Classical Philology* 76, no. 1 (1981): 25–34. His grandson, Agrippa I, died at a much earlier age with similar symptoms; Herod's ceaseless activity had perhaps prolonged his life considerably. See Jan V. Hirschman, Peter Richardson, Ross S. Kraemer, and Philip A. Mackowiak, "Death of an Arabian Jew," *Archives of Internal Medicine* 164, no. 8 (2004): 833–41.

80 Josephus, *Antiquities* 17 §§ 151–67. See note 62.

81 Attempts have been pursued to adjust the chronology of Herod to permit Matthew 2:16–18 to be accurate as written; see Andrew E. Steinmann, "When Did Herod the Great Reign?," *Novum Testamentum* 51, no. 1 (2009): 1–29. For an answer to what seems to be involved special pleading with reference to subsequent discussion, see Sharon, *Judea under Roman Domination*, 391–96. This incident is more plausibly dated during the tenure of Archelaus; its context is treated in the next chapter. The opposite move is to date Jesus's birth earlier than is plausible, as in the first edition of Richardson, *Herod*, xx. (I might note that the conditions of the pandemic during 2020–21 prevented me from consulting the different editions at the same time.) Vermes wisely discounts any effort to perpetuate the image of Herod the Great as "the Ivan the Terrible of antiquity," but his dismissal of the story as "fictional or twisted" is not convincing; see *True Herod*, 41–43.

82 Josephus, *Antiquities* 17 §§ 89–132.

83 Josephus, *Antiquities* 17 §§ 133–48, 182–92.

Chapter 5: Archelaus

1 See Josephus, *Jewish War* 1 §§ 650–60; and Josephus, *Antiquities* 17 §§ 177–81. In the latter passage, Josephus speaks of Herod's lack of humanity at the end of his life.

2 See Josephus, *Jewish War* 1 §§ 661–69; and Josephus, *Antiquities* 17 §§ 182–95.

3 See Josephus, *Jewish War* 1 §§ 670–73; and Josephus, *Antiquities* 17 §§ 196–99.

4 So Josephus, *Antiquities* 17 § 21.

5 Josephus, *Jewish War* 1 §§ 668–73; and Josephus, *Antiquities* 17 §§ 193–99.

6 Macrobius, *Saturnalia* 2.4.11. Diogenes Laertius somewhat similarly reports that Diogenes of Sinope, "noticing that in Megara the sheep were protected with leather skins, but the boys went without them . . . said, 'It's better to be a Megarian's ram (*krion*) than his son (*huion*)'"; see Pamela Mensch, trans., *Lives of Eminent Philosophers, Diogenes Laertius*, ed. James Miller (New York: Oxford University Press, 2018), 6.41. In a comparable way, Augustus played on words as well as on the reputation of Jews for abhorring pork.

7 See Josephus, *Jewish War* 1 §§ 562. His half brother, born of Mariamme II and named Herod, has also been attributed the name Philip, on the basis of Mark 6:17; so, for example, Louis H. Feldman, *Josephus: Jewish Antiquities, Books XVIII–XIX*, Loeb Classical Library 433 (Josephus IX) (Cambridge, MA: Harvard University Press, 1992), 93 (who miscites the Markan passage). But Josephus at this point simply calls this brother "Herod" (Josephus,

Antiquities 18 §§ 135–36). This is a real contradiction, not a simple confusion of names, as will be discussed at the point of the scandal of Antipas's decision to marry his brother Philip's wife.

8   Josephus, *Jewish War* 1 §§ 664, 667–69; 2 §§ 93–97, 167–68; Josephus, *Antiquities* 17 §§ 188–89; 18 §§ 318–20.

9   Josephus, *Antiquities* 17 §§ 80, 146. It is for this reason, I think, that Josephus calls Philip the "genuine brother" of Archelaus (*Antiquities* 17 § 189). They did not have the same mother, but they had maintained a common front in the hostile environment of Herod's court near the time of his death.

10 Beautifully described by Josephus in *Jewish War* 2 §§ 1–13; and *Antiquities* 17 §§ 200–218.

11 Josephus, *Jewish War* 2 § 4. Written closer in time to when the temple stood than the *Antiquities*, this account refers to sacrifice continuing in the midst of the entire confrontation.

12 Josephus, *Antiquities* 17 §§ 206–18; Josephus, *Jewish War* 2 §§ 1–13.

13 A cohort was a group of six centuries, each commanded by a centurion. Tribunes commanded cohorts; see Fischer, *Army of the Roman Emperors*, xxiii. This was an instance in which the Herodian military organization mimicked that of Rome.

14 Josephus, *Antiquities* 17 §§ 216.

15 See Josephus, *Antiquities* 13 §§ 372–80; cf. Josephus, *Jewish War* 1 §§ 88–89, 97–98; and the description in chapter 2.

16 The *oikoumenê*, or "inhabited world," as subjects of the Roman Empire came to call that expansive hegemony. The term later came to refer to "ecumenical" Christianity, but that usage was an adaptation of the earlier imperial sense of the word. Cf. Byron R. McCane, "Simply Irresistible: Augustus, Herod, and the Empire," *Journal of Biblical Literature* 127, no. 4 (2008): 725–35.

17 See Josephus, *Antiquities* 17 §§ 217–18; cf. Josephus, *Jewish War* 2 §§ 12–13; and the vivid description of Jones, *Herods of Judaea*, 156–58.

18 Described in Josephus, *Jewish War* 2 §§ 16–19; and Josephus, *Antiquities* 17 §§ 221–23.

19 Josephus, *Antiquities* 17 §§ 250–68. Josephus artfully intercalates events, and they are restored to a critical chronology here.

20 Josephus, *Antiquities* 17 §§ 224–49; Josephus, *Jewish War* 2 §§ 20–38. Even Malthaké is said to support Antipas against Archelaus in *Jewish War* 2 § 21, and both accounts also put Nicholas's brother on Antipas's side. The issue of Archelaus's character, which at times appears mysterious, seems embedded from the outset. His failures were clearly not entirely of his own making because revolutionary conditions after Herod's death were beyond his power to control—and perhaps greater than any living member of the

dynasty could have mastered—but he exacerbated the challenges he faced and provoked the dislike of people who should have remained loyal to him. Antipas, Salomé, Malthaké, and Nicholas's brother Ptolemy no doubt all had personal agendas, but their common antipathy to Archelaus suggests that the better people knew him, the less they trusted him.

21　Josephus, *Antiquities* 17 §§ 252–53. Josephus portrays Sabinus's actions as those of a representative gone rogue, but it seems clear that he believed he acted on Augustus's behalf. As the imperial system emerged, the emperor could increasingly support more than one set of tactics at once, to see which would best profit him. The issue of Archelaus's accession clearly tested the limits of Augustus's loyalty to the Herodian dynasty, and the emperor seems to have explored the possibilities of exploiting Archelaus's weaknesses.

22　Josephus, *Antiquities* 17 §§ 269–77. Josephus says that the same Achiab had prevented Herod's attempt at suicide at the end of his life (*Antiquities* 17 §§ 182–84), and he remarks on what a striking figure Simon was (Josephus, *Jewish War* 2 §§ 57–59) in his organization of a criminal force.

23　Tacitus, *Histories* 5.9.2: "At Herod's death, without waiting for imperial decision, a certain Simon usurped the title of king. He was dealt with by the governor of Syria, Quinctilius Varus, while the Jews were divided up into three kingdoms ruled by Herod's sons." The complexity of Tacitus's attitude is explored in Erich S. Gruen, "Tacitus and the Defamation of the Jews," in *The Construct of Identity in Hellenistic Judaism: Essays on Early Jewish Literature and History* (Berlin: De Gruyter, 2016), 265–80. He dates the *Histories* between 105 and 110 CE (Gruen, 268).

24　Josephus, *Antiquities* 17 §§ 278–84.

25　Josephus, *Antiquities* 17 §§ 285–98. Estimates of legionary size and strength are available in Fischer, *Army of the Roman Emperors*, xxiii.

26　The account involves a unique conception of what it meant for Jesus to be raised from the dead, detailed in Chilton, *Resurrection Logic*, 140–43.

27　The wills are nicely detailed in Peter Richardson, *Herod: King of the Jews and Friend of the Romans*, Personalities of the New Testament (Minneapolis: Fortress, 1999), 32–36.

28　Josephus, *Antiquities* 17 §§ 299–316.

29　See Josephus, *Antiquities* 14 §§ 168–77; Josephus, *Jewish War* 2 §§ 204–12 (discussed in chapter 2); and *Antiquities* 17 §§ 151–67 (discussed in chapter 4).

30　The Sadducees' name as it consistently appears in Josephus and the New Testament invokes their claim that their families derived from Zadok, the sole scion of priestly legitimacy according to Ezekiel 40:45–46; 43:18–19; 44:15–27; 48:10–12. The overlap with Essene theology is evident and has led to the claim that the Sadducees should be associated with the library at Qumran; see Norman Golb, *Who Wrote the Dead Sea Scrolls? The Search for the Secret of Qumran* (New York: Touchstone, 1996). Such views, similar to those of Karl Heinrich Rengstorf in *Hirbet Qumran und die Bibliotheck vom Toten Meer*, Studia Delitzschiana 5 (Stuttgart: Kohlhammer, 1960), have been considerably nuanced by Lawrence H. Schiffman in *Reclaiming the Dead Sea Scrolls: The History of Judaism, the Background of Christianity, the Lost Library of Qumran* (Philadelphia: Jewish Publication Society of America, 1994). For an extremely helpful survey, see *The Dead Sea Scrolls in Scholarly Perspective: A History of Research*, Studies on the Texts of the Desert of Judah 99, ed. Devorah Dimant (Leiden: Brill, 2012). On my reading, Schiffman offers the most satisfying account of the origins of the library at Qumran, within an Essene group with Sadducean connections. In any case, the emergence of the Sadducees as power players in the political turmoil surrounding Archelaus presupposes their earlier existence (perhaps from the second century BCE; cf. Avot of Rabbi Natan 5:2) and their capacity to appeal beyond their own ranks with an argument for legitimacy. In his treatment of Josephus's presentation of the Sadducees, Steve Mason points out that they were attached to their rule as an "aristocracy" allegedly authorized by Moses rather than a monarchy; see Josephus, *Antiquities* 4 § 233; and Mason, "Chief Priests, Sadducees, Pharisees, and Sanhedrin in Luke-Acts and Josephus," in *Josephus, Judea, and Christian Origins: Methods and Categories*, ed. Michael W. Helfield (Peabody, MA: Hendrickson, 2009), 329–73. The delegation described in *Antiquities* 17 is sent by the nation and backed by eight thousand of the Judeans in Rome in order to seek "auton-omy" (§§ 299–300) rather than monarchy (§ 314). As a political faction, embodying an approach that Josephus himself would embrace, the Saddu-cees crystallize at this moment. Josephus even sees its seeds in the preference of Antipas over Archelaus, saying that the relatives of the two claimants were motivated by a hatred of Archelaus and the conviction that it would be better to have a Roman governor than a king, or at least Antipas rather than the overweening Archelaus (*Antiquities* 17 § 227).

31 Josephus, *Antiquities* 17 §§ 317–23.

32 This is the suggestion of William Milwitzky, "Antipas (Herod Antipas)," in *The Jewish Encyclopedia*, vol. 1, ed. Isidore Singer (New York: Funk and Wagnalls, 1901), 638–39.

33 Josephus, *Jewish War* 1 §§ 562, 602, 646, 668; 2 § 14. According to the first passage, Philip's brother was named Herod, although Mariamme II had also given birth to a son by that name. Mariamme's son was struck out of the royal will as a result of a plot of poisoning that involved Mariamme II herself (1 §§ 599–600).

34 By the estimate of Josephus, six hundred talents for Archelaus a year, two hundred for Antipas, and one hundred for Philip, with Salomé netting sixty talents a year. See Josephus, *Antiquities* 17 §§ 318–23; and Josephus,

Jewish War 2 §§ 93–100 (the latter of which supplies the figure for Philip, reducing the income of Archelaus to four hundred talents).

35 Josephus, *Antiquities* 17 §§ 324–38; Josephus, *Jewish War* 2 §§ 101–10. The claimed descent from Mariamme I is cited by Josephus as exciting crowds even in Rome (*Antiquities* 17 §§ 330–31). The account in *Antiquities* portrays Augustus as interrogating the false Alexander directly, while in Josephus, *Jewish War* 2 §§ 105–10, it is the freedman Celadus who cross-examines him and offers clemency. This contradicts the statement in *Antiquities* 17 § 332 that Celadus had been deceived.

36 Other descendants after his sons also took up the name of Herod, so that confusion characterizes both ancient and modern sources. It is an interesting difficulty to this day. Historians routinely distinguish one pope named Pius from the others, disambiguate one king named Henry from his predecessors and successors, and manage to keep their Vladimirs straight; when it comes to "Herod," however, patience with amalgamation persists.

37 See Karsten Dahmen, "With Rome in Mind? Case Studies in the Coinage of Client Kings," in *Kingdoms and Principalities in the Roman Near East*, ed. Ted Kaizer and Margherita Facella (Stuttgart: Steiner, 2010), 99–112; and John Francis Wilson, *Caesarea Philippi: Banias, the Lost City of Pan* (London: Tauris, 2004), 197–98.

38 See Josephus, *Jewish War* 2 §§ 114–16; and Josephus, *Antiquities* 17 §§ 339–41. The marital politics of Herod are nicely described by Regev, "Herod's Jewish Ideology," 197–222. He also details how at this period (that is, prior to the second century CE), Judaic ancestry was reckoned as a rule in patrilinear rather than matrilinear terms.

39 Beautifully explained by Brian Schultz, "Jesus as Archelaus in the Parable of the Pounds (Lk. 19:11–27)," *Novum Testamentum* 49, no. 2 (2007): 105–27. On the founding, archaeology, and subsequent history of Archelaïs, see Adam Zertal and Shay Bar, *The Mannasseh Hill Country Survey*, vol. 5, *The Middle Jordan Valley, from Wadi Fasael to Wadi 'Aujah*, Culture and History of the Ancient Near East 21.5, trans. Amitsia Halevi, ed. John Tressman (Leiden: Brill, 2019), 54, 68, 79, 317–18, 587, based on the observations of Pliny, *Natural History* 13.9.44; and Josephus, *Antiquities* 18 § 31. For further discussion, see Wilker, *Für Rom*, 74.

40 Josephus, *Antiquities* 17 §§ 342–55.

41 Josephus, *Antiquities* 17 § 340.

42 This results in modern attempts to lengthen Herod the Great's life and reign such as in Steinmann, "When Did Herod the Great Reign?," 1–29. But Jesus seems clearly to have been born after the death of Herod the Great, if Luke's notice in 3:23 of Jesus being around thirty years old has any merit. Josephus is quite categorical that Herod the Great ruled thirty-four years from the time of Antigonus's death (in 37 BCE) or thirty-seven years

from the time he was made king by the Romans (in 40 CE). See Josephus, *Jewish War* 1 § 665; and Josephus, *Antiquities* 17 § 191. Just as the Synoptic Gospels can call Antipas Herod, and with some reason in view of Antipas's coins, so the assignment to Archelaus of the name Herod is scarcely a stretch. In addition, the messianic paranoia attributed to this "Herod" is much more consistent with the situation of Archelaus's reign as described by Josephus than with that of Herod the Great's reign. Herod's paranoia had more to do with the Pharisees and members of his own family than with the emergence of popular leaders.

43 A cliché defines insanity as doing the same thing over and over again while expecting different results. In my view, that is better seen as stupidity, a likely source of Archelaus's difficulties.

44 The method of this source is described in a uniquely Matthean passage (13:52): "For this reason every letterer studied for the kingdom of the heavens is like a man who is a householder, who puts out from his treasure new and old." The centrality of this approach within the Matthew program is described by David Orton, *The Understanding Scribe: Matthew and the Apocalyptic Ideal*, Library of New Testament Studies 25 (London: Bloomsbury, 1997).

45 The rising of stars and other astrological occurrences were omens of significant events (Josephus, *Jewish War* 6 § 289; Jubilees 8:3; 12:17; cf. Testament of Levi 18:3; Testament of Judah 24:1; Babylonian Talmud Shabbat 156a; Babylonian Talmud Rosh Hashanah 11b). Astrological images were sometimes used to describe important eschatological figures (cf. 1 En 106:2, 10; *Liber Antiquitatum Biblicarum* 21:3). In 2 CE, the likely year of Jesus's birth if he died age thirty in 32 CE (cf. Luke 3:23), astronomical regressions show an alignment of Mars and Saturn during the autumn. The precise connection with Judean Bethlehem features as a scriptural aspect of Matthew's source. For further dates connected with Jesus, see Bruce Chilton, *Rabbi Jesus: An Intimate Biography* (New York: Doubleday, 2000), xiii–xvi.

46 The situation is comparable to that of the Essenes, whose background is so veiled in the *Habakkuk Pesher* by the interest in connections to Scripture that their history remains a matter of great dispute. The issue of whether the community at Qumran is to be associated with the Essenes, for example, produced legal proceedings to a criminal level; see John Leland, "Top Court Champions Freedom to Annoy," *New York Times*, May 13, 2014, https://tinyurl.com/a6wdrkym.

47 Josephus, *Antiquities* 17 § 344.

48 Commissions were theoretically low, but the opportunity for corruption was endemic, in both the level of taxes charged and the opportunities to engage in moneylending. See Edgar Kiser and Danielle Kane, "The Perils of Privatization: How the Characteristics of Principals Affected Tax Farming in

the Roman Republic and Empire," *Social Science History* 31, no. 2 (2007): 191–212; and Fritz Herrenbrück, *Jesus und die Zöllner: Histoirische und neutestamentlich-exegetische Untersuchungen*, Wissenschaftliche Untersuchungen zum Neuen Testament 41 (Tübingen: Mohr-Siebeck, 1990).

49 See 2 Samuel 24:1–17; and 1 Chronicles 21:1–17. This resistance helps account for the odd statement in Luke 2:1 that the "inhabited world" (*oikoumenê*) was to be taxed. The Syrian provenience of Luke, which put the whole area under the Roman legate, best explains the usage.

50 Josephus, *Antiquities* 18 §§ 1–28.

51 His name as given in Josephus, *Jewish War* 2 § 118; Josephus, *Antiquities* 18 § 4 refines the designation as the *Gaulanitês*, from the east side of the Sea of Galilee.

52 Tacitus, *Annals* 1.61.

53 Josephus, *Jewish War* 2 §§ 167–68; Josephus, *Antiquities* 18 §§ 28, 106–8.

54 See Wilson, *Caesarea Philippi*; Fred Strickert, "The Founding of Bethsaida-Julias: Evidence from the Coins of Philip," *Shofar* 13, no. 4 (1995): 40–51; and Morten Hørning Jensen, *Herod Antipas in Galilee: The Literary and Archaeological Sources on the Reign of Herod Antipas and Its Socio-economic Impact on Galilee*, Wissenschaftliche Untersuchungen zum Neuen Testament 213 (Tübingen: Mohr, 2010), 199.

55 See Jonathan Marshall, *Jesus, Patrons, and Benefactors: Roman Palestine and the Gospel of Luke* (Eugene: Wipf and Stock, 2015), 112–18, with a comparison to the Judaic enclave cultures in Gamla and Bethsaida.

Chapter 6: Antipas, Herodias, and Philip

1 Josephus, *Antiquities* 17 §§ 271–72, 286–89; in Josephus, *Jewish War* 2 §§ 66–71, Varus's son is not mentioned, only his friend Gaius.

2 See Anna Iamim, "The Missing Building(s) at Sepphoris," *Israel Exploration Journal* 66, no. 1 (2016): 96–113; as well as the still valuable article by James F. Strange, "Recent Discoveries at Sepphoris and Their Relevance for Biblical Research," *Neotestamentica* 34, no. 1 (2000): 125–41. The degree of urbanization involved is a matter of judgment, and the first-century and fourth-century remains of the city evidently need to be distinguished; see Eric M. Meyers, Ehud Netzer, and Carol L. Meyers, "Sepphoris: 'Ornament of All Galilee,'" *Biblical Archaeologist* 49, no. 1 (1986): 4–19.

3 See Zeev Weiss, "Josephus and Archaeology on the Cities of Galilee," in *Making History: Josephus and Historical Method*, Supplements to the *Journal for the Study of Judaism* 110, ed. Zuleika Rodgers (Leiden: Brill, 2007), 385–414; Josephus, *Antiquities* 18 §§ 27–28; and Josephus, *Jewish War* 2 § 168. Livia's name later became Julia, so the Perean city is known as both Livias and Julias; Wilson, *Caesarea Philippi*, 18–21.

4 See Elise A. Friedland, *The Roman Marble Sculptures from the Sanctuary of Pan at Caesarea Philippi/Panias (Israel)*, American Schools of Oriental Research Archaeological Reports 17 (Boston: American Schools of Oriental Research, 2012).

5 See Jensen, *Herod Antipas in Galilee*, 204.

6 See A. Kindler, "A Coin of Herod Philip—the Earliest Portrait of a Herodian Ruler," *Israel Exploration Journal* 21, nos. 2–3 (1971): 161–63. The significance of this change in comparison with the policy of Herod the Great is well developed by Ulrich Hübner, "Die Münzprägung Herodes' des Grossen (40/37–4 v. Chr.)," in *Macht Des Geldes—Macht Der Bilder: Kolloquium Zur Ikonographie Auf Munzen Im Ostmediterranen Raum in Hellenistisch-Romischer Zeit*, Abhandlungen ses Deutschen Palästina-Vereins 42, ed. Anne Lykke (Wiesbaden: Harrassowitz, 2013), 93–122.

7 Josephus, *Antiquities* 17 §§ 318–23; and Josephus, *Jewish War* 2 §§ 93–100 (the latter of which supplies the figure for Philip).

8 In either case, of course, the so-called sea was a freshwater lake; see R. Steven Notley, "The Sea of Galilee: Development of an Early Christian Toponym," *Journal of Biblical Literature* 128, no. 1 (2009): 183–88. Although I appreciate Notley's survey, I do not think all instances of the usage of the "Sea of Galilee" can be derived from Isaiah 8:23, as applied in Matthew 4:15.

9 Her original name was Livia, but on his death, Augustus had her adopted into the Julian clan, so the city bore the name of Julia, which was appended to Bethsaida. This has caused confusion as to the identity of the honorand, evident in Wilson, *Caesarea Philippi*, 18–21; and even Josephus, *Antiquities* 18 § 28. That problem is neatly sorted out in Strickert, "Founding of Bethsaida-Julias," 40–51. I have had to disagree with his conclusion in regard to dating (30 CE), however, since I do not agree that the date of a coin needs to be seen as signaling the chronology of the city's founding. For further helpful background and discussion, see R. Steven Notley, "Et-Tell Is Not Bethsaida," *Near Eastern Archaeology* 70, no. 4 (2007): 220–30. Controversy over the precise siting of the city is likely to continue for some time.

10 He had died of illness the year prior to Herod's death (cf. Josephus, *Jewish War* 1 §§ 578–81), during a period when Herod at last attempted a reconciliation.

11 Josephus, *Antiquities* 17 § 287. Earlier, Augustus had toyed with the idea of supplanting the fractious Nabataean leadership by adding Nabataea to Herod's portfolio but thought better of it in view of Herod's instability at the end of his life (*Antiquities* 16 §§ 353–55). Aretas had every reason, then, to placate the Romans and to rejoice in the eventual removal of Archelaus. According to Josephus, even Aretas's alliance with the Romans

was motivated by his hatred of Herod, and his troops indulged in pillaging and burning for this reason; Josephus, *Antiquities* 17 §§ 287–90. Varus himself, however, was no kinder when it came to Emmaus (see § 291).

12 Josephus, *Antiquities* 18 § 109. Later events would show to what extent this was a marriage of convenience as well as of state. Unfortunately, Josephus does name the wife and only refers to the marriage having lasted a long period by the time it came apart. That would place the union early in Antipas's tenure, while Augustus was still alive. The death of Augustus, we shall see, opened up new prospects for Antipas to curry favor with Tiberius; the marriage with Aretas's daughter fell victim to his new campaign for advancement. Nikos Kokkinos suggests that her name was Phasaelis and places the marriage even earlier than Antipas's assumption of power as tetrarch; Kokkinos, *Herodian Dynasty*, 230–33. In my opinion, Antipas's position at that time was too unstable to make such a marriage plausible, but it *is* clear that he must have married her near the start of his effective rule, say around 11 CE. She would then have been married to Antipas for a decade at the time of his liaison with Herodias; Josephus says in the passage cited that the marriage had been contracted a long time (*khronon êdê polun*) before.

13 See Jensen, *Herod Antipas in Galilee*, 210–11. Controversy over how to restore the wording does not reduce the importance of the fact of the inscription.

14 Josephus, *Jewish War* 2 § 168; Josephus, *Antiquities* 18 §§ 36–38. For a sober assessment of Antipas's impact on Galilee, see Morten Hørning Jensen, "Political History in Galilee from the First Century BCE to the End of Second Century CE," in *Galilee in the Late Second Temple and Mishnaic Periods*, vol. 1, *Life, Culture, and Society*, ed. David A. Fiensy and James Riley Strange (Minneapolis: Fortress, 2014), 51–77.

15 See Morten Hørning Jensen, "Purity and Politics in Herod Antipas's Galilee: The Case for Religious Motivation," *Journal for the Study of the Historical Jesus* 11 (2013): 3–34; see also Jensen, *Herod Antipas in Galilee*, 135–49.

16 See Lee Levine, "R. Simeon B. Yoḥai and the Purification of Tiberias: History and Tradition," *Hebrew Union College Annual* 49 (1978): 143–85.

17 See Chilton, *Rabbi Jesus*, 91–93; Chilton, *Mary Magdalene: A Biography* (New York: Doubleday, 2005), 35–37; and Josephus, *Antiquities* 18 §§ 36–38.

18 Josephus, *Jewish War* 1 §§ 552, 557; Josephus, *Antiquities* 17 §§ 12–14.

19 Josephus, *Jewish War* 1 § 600; Josephus, *Antiquities* 17 § 78.

20 See Bruce Rosenstock, "Incest, Nakedness, and Holiness: Biblical Israel at the Limits of Culture," *Jewish Studies Quarterly* 16, no. 4 (2009): 333–62; and Leviticus 18, 20. Levirate marriage (Deut 25:5–6), in the case that a married man died childless, was beside the point.

21 Josephus himself undertook to destroy the images, he claims, during the war with Rome; *Life* §§ 64–69.

22 Josephus, *Antiquities* 18 §§ 109–10.

23 As Christine Saulnier has observed, this relation had to have been solidified by the time Herod Agrippa was invited to join Antipas and Herodias in Tiberias in 24 CE. This implies that the marriage is much earlier than some scholars have proposed, which accords with the period of the foundation of the Tiberias in 19 CE. See "Herode Antipas et Jean le Baptiste: Quelques remarques sur les confusions chronologiques de Flavius Josèphe," *Revue Biblique* 91 (1984): 362–76, 365–68.

24 Josephus, *Antiquities* 17 §§ 340–41.

25 See Birgit van der Lans, "The Politics of Exclusion: Expulsions of Jews and Others from Rome," in *People under Power: Early Jewish and Christian Responses to the Roman Power Empire*, ed. Michael Labahn and Outi Lehtipuu (Amsterdam: Amsterdam University Press, 2015), 33–78. The key texts are Tacitus, *Annals* 2.85; Suetonius, *Tiberius* 36.1; and Josephus, *Antiquities* 18 §§ 81–84. As van der Lans points out (36), Josephus's assertion that four thousand people were expelled seems "hardly credible." More likely, a transfer of soldiers is the issue, out of concern that they had fallen under the influence of proselytism; see Max Radin, *The Jews among the Greeks and Romans* (Philadelphia: Jewish Publication Society of America, 1915), 306–13. Josephus's attempt to assign blame to a single charlatan draws Radin's memorable observation (306) that among the ancient sources, "Josephus is probably the nearest in time to the events he is describing, but also the most remote in comprehension"; although the formulation is splendid, the implication of naivete requires adjustment in the direction of Josephus's political posturing.

26 See Josephus, *Antiquities* 18 §§ 109–13. Because that quarrel ultimately led to battle, some scholars have dated the marriage with Herodias far too late. In fact, there was a considerable delay between the start of hostility and open war. Josephus's famous report about John in *Antiquities* 18 §§ 116–19 is a flashback, related to explain the opinion among "some Jews" that the defeat of Antipas's army at the hands of Aretas, the king of Nabataea, was divine retribution for his treatment of John the Baptist (*Antiquities* 18 § 116). Josephus says that Aretas made this "the beginning of enmity," but really, Antipas picked the fight with his former ally when he schemed with Herodias. That is scarcely a chronological account, as F. F. Bruce recognized long ago; cf. *New Testament History* (Garden City, NY: Doubleday, 1972), 28, 30–31. Open battle with Aretas only commenced after Philip's death in 34 CE, by which time some of Philip's troops joined Antipas, only to betray him (cf. *Antiquities* 18 §§ 113–15). Indeed, the punitive mission of Vitellius against Aretas was only aborted as a result of Tiberius's death

in 37 CE (*Antiquities* 18 §§ 115, 120–25). A critical reading of Josephus
suggests that John should no longer be dated by means of the Synoptic
chronology, whose usage as a catechetical instrument makes it an unreliable historical tool. (The idea of a single-year ministry of Jesus, frequently
repeated, is nothing other than a confusion of the duration of events with
the period of instruction for those who were taught on the basis of the
Synoptic Gospels.) Rather, John was put to death in 21 CE, well before
Jesus came to public prominence, during a period when Herod Antipas was
emboldened by his recent foundation of Tiberias as well as his marriage
to the ever-ambitious Herodias, once his brother's wife. My chronology is
comparable to Saulnier's ("Herode Antipas," 365–66), although in my view,
she does not give sufficient weight to the *Senatus consultum* of 19 CE, which
gave Antipas an opportunity to portray himself to Tiberius as a ruler who
did not let being a Jew get in the way of being a Roman.

27 See Joan E. Taylor, *The Immerser: John the Baptist within Second Temple
Judaism*, Studying the Historical Jesus (Grand Rapids: Eerdmans, 1997);
Bruce Chilton, "Yochanan the Purifier and His Immersion," *Toronto Journal
of Theology* 14, no. 2 (1998): 197–212; and Chilton, "John the Purifier: His
Immersion and His Death," *Teologiese Studies* 57, nos. 1–2 (2001): 247–67.
An attempt has recently been made to argue that John's aim was "atonement" rather than "purification"; see Eyal Regev, "Washing, Repentance,
and Atonement in Early Christian Baptism and Qumranic Purification
Liturgies," *Journal for the Study of the Jesus Movement in Its Jewish Setting* 3
(2016): 33–60, especially 43–47, concluding that "John drew on this *association* of immersion in water as an act of purification, but did not baptize to
purify the immersed person from defilement." In addition to the question
as to whether this distinction would have been obvious to those who came
to John, the treatment does not seem to devote adequate attention to the
importance of the Spirit both before and after John; see Chilton, *Jesus'
Baptism and Jesus' Healing: His Personal Practice of Spirituality* (Harrisburg:
Trinity Press International, 1998).

28 Although Josephus does not enter into specifics, he portrays Antipas as
fearing that John would lead an opposition to him, and he gives the details
of Antipas's abortive divorce from Aretas's daughter in order to marry Herodias in the context of a description of John's death (*Antiquities* 18 §§ 109–
12). The relationship between the Gospels and Josephus on this point
might be described as a dovetail; see Robert L. Webb, "John the Baptist
and His Relationship to Jesus," in *Studying the Historical Jesus: Evaluations
of the State of Current Research*, New Testament Tools and Studies 19, ed.
Bruce Chilton and C. A. Evans (Leiden: Brill, 1994), 179–229, esp. 209. For
the view that the sources are independent, see Ross S. Kraemer, "Implicating
Herodias and Her Daughter in the Death of John the Baptizer: A (Christian)

Theological Strategy?," *Journal of Biblical Literature* 125, no. 2 (2006): 321–49.

29   Josephus, *Antiquities* 18 §§ 33–35, 177.

30   See the specification of Philip as the spurned husband in Mark 6:18–29; and Matthew 14:3–12. Josephus demurs, portraying Herodias as the wife of Herod II (as scholars have come to call the son of Mariamme II; Josephus, *Antiquities* 18 §§ 109–10). In this, Josephus assumes that the marriage between Herod II and Herodias as planned by Herod the Great was consummated and endured, despite Herod II's later fall from favor. In an attempt to resolve the issue, Herod II has often been called Herod Philip by scholars, an expedient rejected as illusory by Kokkinos, *Herodian Dynasty*, 223, 233, 266. In this regard, see Kraemer, "Implicating Herodias," 321–49, especially 333 and n. 26. Yet Kokkinos has argued that Herodias married first Herod II and then Philip the tetrarch prior to her marriage to Antipas; see *Herodian Dynasty*, 264–71. As Kraemer points out, however, this forces Kokkinos to date John's death sometime *after* the death of Philip in 34 CE, since Antipas was making a play for his brother's estate on this reconstruction. But if Antipas's motive was simple ambition, there is no reason to make him wait for Philip's death. It is notable, however, that even after Philip's death, some of his troops deliberately turned against Antipas in battle (*Antiquities* 18 § 114), suggesting that they repaid one form of treachery with another. All in all, the Gospels' identification of Philip as Herodias's husband prior to Antipas should not be summarily dismissed. This is still the reflex of Wilker, *Für Rom*, 25–26, although in other ways, she finds confluence between Josephus and the New Testament. On the other hand, Josephus's statement that Philip died without children (*Antiquities* 18 § 108) suggests that he did not father Herodias's daughter. Presumably, the young lady came from Herodias's marriage with Herod II, as Josephus indicates.

31   Josephus, *Antiquities* 18 §§ 116–19.

32   Josephus in *Antiquities* 18 §§ 136–37, unlike the Gospels, names the daughter as Salomé and refers to her father as Herod II. But then, as if to complicate matters, he says this Salomé married Philip and then went on to marry the son of Agrippa I's brother, named Aristobulus, bearing three sons. As Kraemer ("Implicating Herodias," 329) points out, however, Aristobulus struck a coin with his wife, Salomé, in 54 CE; the delay in time between Philip's death and her bearing children to Aristobulus makes it appear unlikely the same Salomé is at issue. Kokkinos (*Herodian Dynasty*, 237, 305) seems wise not to credit the claim of a marriage between Philip and Herodias's daughter Salomé. Chiefly as a consequence of Oscar Wilde's play, Salomé is among the most famous women associated with the Bible, although she is not named biblically and is evanescent in historical terms.

33 See Kraemer, "Implicating Herodias," who on p. 337 refers to the story of
Lucius Quinctius Flaminius, who beheaded a condemned man at a dinner
party because a courtesan said she had never seen a person have his head
cut off. He was expelled from the Senate in 184 BCE, and the story was
repeated until the first century and has been cited often. Kraemer's position
apparently derives from that of the present writer in *Rabbi Jesus*, 61–63,
that the song and dance were not necessary (which is why Luke 3:19–20
actually eliminates them).

34 Joanna plays a central role in the reconstruction of Jesus's movement by
Marianne Sawicki, "Magdalenes and Tiberiennes: City Women in the
Entourage of Jesus," in *Transformative Encounters: Jesus and Women Re-
viewed*, Biblical Interpretation 43, ed. Ingrid R. Kitzberger (Leiden: Brill,
2000), 181–202. See also Wilker, *Für Rom*, 117, 266 (cf. also 323), also
mentioning Manaen in Acts 13:1. As Sean Freyne points out, Sawicki portrays
a more uniformly upper-class group than is plausible; see "Archaeology and
the Historical Jesus," in *Jesus and Archaeology*, ed. James H. Charlesworth
(Grand Rapids: Eerdmans, 2006), 64–83, 81–83. On the other hand,
Freyne's own attempt to explain the reference to Joanna and Chuza as
"a Lukan retrojection" (82) seems facile, although in what follows, I agree
with his view of a sympathetic portrayal of Herodians within Luke and
Luke's sources.

35 His role in Jesus's movement is discussed in Chilton, *Rabbi Jesus*, 111–13,
120–21, 255–56. Since the publication of that work, the German monograph by Bernd Kollmann has appeared in English; see *Joseph Barnabas: His
Life and Legacy*, trans. Miranda Henry (Collegeville, MN: Liturgical Press,
2004). His conclusions may find support in recent archaeological work; see
Philip H. Young, "The Cypriot Aphrodite Cult: Paphos, Rantidi, and Saint
Barnabas," *Journal of Near Eastern Studies* 64, no. 1 (2005): 23–44.

36 See the book of Esther in the Hebrew Bible, for example, and Judith in
the Apocrypha, as well as the sober assessment of Morten Hørning Jensen,
"Herod Antipas in Galilee: Friend or Foe of the Historical Jesus?," *Journal
for the Study of the Historical Jesus* 5, no. 1 (2007): 7–32.

37 Josephus, *Antiquities* 18 §§ 143–46.

38 Tacitus, *Annals* 4.3.

39 Tacitus portrays Sejanus as responsible in an elaborate plot of poisoning
(*Annals* 4.8–11) but acknowledges that rumors to that effect had grown
luxuriantly by his time. Tiberius's continuing association with Sejanus
makes the portrayal seem unlikely. Tiberius's strategy of governance and
his mythological attachment to the story of the Dioscuri are brilliantly
detailed in Edward Champlin, "Tiberius and the Heavenly Twins," *Journal
of Roman Studies* 101 (2011): 73–99. Daniel R. Schwartz attempts to argue
against the portrayal of the impact of Drusus's death by Josephus, seeing it

as a "romantic" exaggeration of a source; *Agrippa I: The Last King of Judaea,* Texte und Studien zum antiken Judentum 23 (Tübingen: Mohr, 1990), 46. Speaking in purely pragmatic terms, however, it seems evident that the loss of Drusus's protection carried consequences.

40 Josephus, *Antiquities* 18 §§ 147–49. Josephus recounts the letter written by Agrippa's wife to Herodias, detailing his desperate psychological state. I doubt much was necessary to convince Herodias and Antipas, however, that by coming to the aid of Agrippa, they would both preserve Herodian honor and ingratiate themselves with Tiberius and his court. Josephus's description does not allow for a lapse of ten years prior to Agrippa's appointment to Tiberias, as David M. Jacobson posits in *Agrippa II: The Last of the Herods,* Routledge Ancient Biographies (London: Routledge, 2019). Dating the appointment in 34 CE does not allow time for Agrippa's movements between that time and his return to Rome; it would also coincide with the end of Philip's life, an inauspicious moment for Antipas to bring Agrippa out of his Idumean exile.

41 See the masterful article by H. W. Bird, "L. Aelius Seianus and His Political Significance," *Latomus* 28, no. 1 (1969): 61–98. Bird credits Tacitus's claim that Sejanus arranged to have Drusus poisoned (66–67). He rightly points out that Sejanus's divorced wife, Apicata, is the linchpin of evidence to this effect. He dents my skepticism of the claim without quite removing it; Bird's own skepticism surfaces again on p. 90. In this regard, I am more in accord with Edward Champlin, "Seianus Augustus," *Chiron: Mitteilungen der Kommission für alte Geschichte* 42 (2012): 378–81.

42 Suetonius, *Tiberius* 43–45.

43 See Cicero, *Pro Flacco* 60–69. For the background of Pilate's appointment, see Chilton, *Rabbi Jesus,* 207–12. For a precise delineation of the political considerations, see H. W. Bird, "L. Aelius Seianus: Further Observations," *Latomus* 29, no. 4 (1970): 1046–50; and in general terms, Eusebius, *Ecclesiastical History* 2.5.6–7.

44 See Josephus, *Jewish War* 2 §§ 169–74; and Josephus, *Antiquities* 18 §§ 55–59. My reference to them as shields derives from the treatment in Philo's *Embassy to Gaius* (see the next note) and a convincing argument that Josephus here exaggerates the sacrilege for rhetorical reasons; see Jason von Ehrenkrook, "Sculpture, Space and the Poetics of Idolatry in Josephus' *Bellum Judaicum,*" *Journal for the Study of Judaism* 39 (2008): 170–91. Additional support for Ehrenkrook might be found in Josephus's silence in regard to the delegation to Rome, which derives from Philo. On the other hand, Philo for rhetorical reasons downplays the offense of the shields; see Helen K. Bond, who attempts to date the episode Philo refers to after Sejanus's fall; *Pontius Pilate in History and Interpretation,* Society of New Testament Studies Monograph Series 100 (Cambridge: Cambridge University

Press, 1998), 24–48. If, as she says, at issue were "decorative shields set up
in honour of the Emperor" (41) near both the temple and the Herodian
palace, that would explain the two accounts, with Philo minimizing the
offense (in the description and the placement in the Herodian palace) and
Josephus exaggerating it (by the reference to an image of Caesar and the
explicit idolatry involved).

45   Philo, *Embassy to Gaius* §§ 299–308, 301. Jensen, *Herod Antipas in Galilee*,
106–9, provides a good discussion, but I differ from his later dating of the
incident. Josephus refers to a period of time between this outrage
and the incident of confiscating temple funds in order to build an aqueduct
in Josephus, *Jewish War* 2 § 175 (treated below). Another issue is whether
Philo is recounting the same incident as Josephus's report or an additional
provocation. In *Rabbi Jesus* (210–12), I treated them as variant reports of
the same incident, and that reading still seems to be the most critical, since
otherwise, Pilate would have repeated a provocation with the knowledge he
would likely be reversed yet again. This problem is exacerbated by Helen K.
Bond, who attempts to date the episode Philo refers to after Sejanus's fall;
see Bond, *Pontius Pilate*, 24–48, 45–46. That would have been exactly the
wrong time for Pilate to inflame Judean and Herodian opinion against himself. The problem of multiplying such incidents also weakens the treatment
of Wilker, *Für Rom*, 93–105.

46   Specifically, the *simpulum* (a ladle) and *lituus* (a staff for augury); see
David M. Jacobson, "Coins of the First Century Roman Governors of
Judaea and Their Motifs," *Electrum* 26 (2019): 73–96, especially 81–82,
88–89; Joan E. Taylor, "Pontius Pilate and the Imperial Cult in Roman
Judaea," *New Testament Studies* 52, no. 4 (2006): 555–82, especially 557–
59; and David E. Graves, "The Pilate Ring and Roman Religion," *Near
East Archaeological Society Bulletin* 64 (2019): 1–20. Helen K. Bond offers
a more benign portrayal of Pilate's choice of symbols while acknowledg-
ing how unusual they were and that their issuance appears to have ceased
after the year 32 CE, a date whose significance will appear later; "The
Coins of Pontius Pilate: Part of an Attempt to Provoke the People or
to Integrate them into the Empire?," *Journal for the Study of Judaism in
the Persian, Hellenistic, and Roman Period* 7, no. 3 (1996): 241–62. To a
significant extent, she is correcting against the view that Sejanus wanted
Pilate to stir up a revolt in Judea, and in that regard, I can only agree.
Sejanus and Pilate were not anti-Semitic to the point that they wished
Rome to pay a price for their prejudice.

47   Jensen, *Herod Antipas in Galilee*, 206; David Hendin, *A Guide to Biblical
Coins* (New York: Amphora, 1996), 511a.

48   The Galilean roots of "Q" are manifest; see John S. Kloppenborg, "Q, Bethsaida, Capernaum," in *Q in Context*, vol. 2, *Social Setting and Archaeological*

Background, Bonner biblische Beiträge 173, ed. Markus Tiwald (Göttingen: Vandenhoeck & Ruprecht, 2015), 61–81. The central saying that concerns Kloppenborg, Luke 10:13–15, nonetheless assumes that the messengers of Jesus after the resurrection had not been accepted in Galilean centers, which implies that they collected their Mishnah elsewhere, in Jerusalem, the only other attested point of gathering at this stage.

49   For this and a still valuable treatment of the entire question, see Joseph B. Tyson, "Jesus and Herod Antipas," *Journal of Biblical Literature* 79, no. 2 (1960): 239–46.

50   These events are traced in further detail in Chilton, *Rabbi Jesus,* 150–73.

51   See the extent of Josephus's treatment of John, *Antiquities* 18 §§ 116–19, as compared to that of Jesus, *Antiquities* 18 §§ 63–64. In the latter case, a major literature has dealt with the issue of whether the *testamonium Flavianum* (as it is called) is an addition to or (as I would argue) a supplemented version of a more modest description of Jesus; see Alice Whealey, "The *Testamonium Flavianum,*" in *A Companion to Josephus,* Blackwell Companions to the Ancient World, ed. Honora Howell Chapman and Zuleika Rodgers (Oxford: Wiley, 2016), 345–55. No matter how the issue is resolved, it is clear that Josephus thought John the Baptist was far more important than Jesus, although that to an extent reflects a Judean bias as distinct from a Galilean one.

52   Chilton, *Rabbi Jesus,* 174–96.

53   See Josephus, *Antiquities* 18 §§ 312–13; and Exodus 30:11–16.

54   A good synthesis of historical and archaeological analysis is available in Jensen, "Rural Galilee," 43–67. I concur with the thesis of the economic stability of Herodian rule and its capacity to encourage growth, with the observation that the layers of taxation were vexing.

55   See Bruce Chilton, "A Coin of Three Realms: Matthew 17:24–27," in *The Bible in Three Dimensions: Essays in Celebration of Forty Years of Biblical Studies in the University of Sheffield,* Journal for the Study of the Old Testament Supplement 87, ed. D. J. A. Clines, S. E. Fowl, and S. E. Porter (Sheffield, UK: JSOT, 1990), 269–82; and A. G. Van Aarde, "A Silver Coin in the Mouth of a Fish (Matthew 17:24–27)—a Miracle of Nature, Ecology, Economy and the Politics of Holiness," *Neotestamentica* 27, no. 1 (1993): 1–25.

56   Josephus, *Jewish War* 2 §§ 175–77; Josephus, *Antiquities* 18 §§ 60–62. Pilate's building of an aqueduct brought water in from fifty miles away and was evidently costly as well as beneficial to Jerusalem and the operation of the temple. Without being describable as humane, Pilate was an effective governor from the point of view of Rome. It is interesting that Josephus's reference to Jesus (albeit glossed in Christian interests) appears immediately after the presentation of this incident in *Antiquities* 18 §§ 63–64.

Wilker, *Für Rom*, 106–8, refers to critical discussion but on balance argues against the connection between Luke and Josephus that other scholars have supported.

57 Described with reference to other primary texts and critical discussion in Chilton, *Rabbi Jesus*, 213–30. As indicated there, this analysis depends on earlier work: Cecil Roth, "The Cleansing of the Temple and Zechariah xiv 21," *Novum Testamentum* 4, no. 3 (1960): 174–81; Victor Eppstein, "The Historicity of the Gospel Account of the Cleansing of the Temple," *Zeitschrift für die neutestamentliche Wissenschaft* 55 (1964): 42–58; Chilton, *Temple of Jesus*; Bernhard Lang, *Sacred Games: A History of Christian Worship* (New Haven: Yale University Press, 1997); and now see Eyal Regev, "The Trial of Jesus and the Temple: Sadducean and Roman Perspectives," in *Soundings in the Religion of Jesus: Perspectives and Methods in Jewish and Christian Scholarship*, ed. Bruce Chilton, Anthony Le Donne, and Jacob Neusner (Minneapolis: Augsburg Fortress, 2012), 97–108. The perspective is taken up, albeit without detail, in Charlesworth, "Jesus and the Temple," 145–81.

58 See Dio Cassius, *Roman History* 58.9–12; the collation with other evidence in Chilton, *Rabbi Jesus*, 197–212, 231–47; and the sensitive and sensible treatment by Ann Boddington, "Sejanus: Whose Conspiracy?," *American Journal of Philology* 84, no. 1 (1963): 1–16.

59 See Antony Hostein, "Monnaie et *damnatio memoriae*: Problèmes méthod-ologiques (Ier-IVe siècle après J.-C.)," *Cahiers Du Centre Gustave Glotz* 15 (2004): 219–36.

60 The high priest was required, for example, to petition the prefect for the robes used at great feasts, since they were kept in the Antonia fortress. The arrangement was justified by concerns for security but amounted to an indignity. See Josephus's description of the garments and their significance in *Antiquities* 3 §§ 151–87, 214–18, and of the policy in regard their custody in 15 §§ 403–9 and 18 §§ 90–95; 20 § 12. As he explains, Hyrcanus and Herod had initiated a practice of safekeeping for the vestments, which then passed to the Roman prefect after the failure of Archelaus's governance. From that point until 36 CE, when Vitellius removed Pilate and released the vestments, they were in effect held hostage.

61 An incident fully discussed in Wilker, *Für Rom*, 108–30. See also Fernando Bermejo-Rubio and Christopher B. Zeichmann, "Where Were the Romans and What Did They Know? Military and Intelligence as a Probable Factor in Jesus of Nazareth's Fate," *Scripta Classica Israelica* 38 (2019): 83–115, a skillful discussion of Roman sources (although sadly maladroit in dealing with texts of the New Testament). Shimon Gibson argues that the *praetorium* where the Romans dealt with Jesus was adjacent to the Herodian residence; see "Trial of Jesus," 97–118. Although he accepts the authenticity

of the ossuary of Caiaphas (99–100n11), however, he does not consider the implications that the site involved would have been used by prominent people such as Joseph of Arimathea; see Chilton, *Rabbi Jesus*, 248–89. Similarly, he does not confront the difficulty of securely managing a crucifixion from any location in Jerusalem but the Antonia.

62 Josephus, *Antiquities* 18 §§ 150–54. Josephus locates the incident at Tyre. It seems very clear that Antipas also accused Agrippa of accepting bribes, because that is precisely what he did when under the protection of Flaccus. Flaccus's dates as legate make it possible to date this event in 33 CE.

63 Josephus, *Antiquities* 18 §§ 106–8.

64 The image has recently been identified by Jean-Philippe Fontanille and Aaron J. Kogon, "Two New Symbols on a Coin of Herod Antipas," *Israel Numismatic Research* 10 (2015): 129–36. They see the association with the imperial cult but also point out that "Antipas is not known to have fostered the imperia cult in Galilee" (133). That, however, did not prevent Antipas from using a symbol to ingratiate himself with Rome without advertising its significance locally.

65 Josephus, *Antiquities* 18 §§ 85–89. This incident suggests that Pilate's cruelty went beyond Sejanan policy and loyalty to Tiberius, even as Josephus gives free rein to his own prejudice against the Samaritans.

66 Josephus, *Antiquities* 18 §§ 88–89. In regard to the vestments, see *Antiquities* 15 §§ 404–9; 18 §§ 90–95; and note 60. Later tradition, with a degree of plausibility, has Pilate commit suicide under compulsion; cf. Eusebius, *Ecclesiastical History* 2.7.1.

67 Suetonius, *Vitellius* 2; Josephus, *Antiquities* 18 §§ 96–105.

68 Josephus, *Antiquities* 18 §§ 151–60.

69 Josephus, *Jewish War* 2 § 178; Josephus, *Antiquities* 18 § 126.

70 Josephus, *Antiquities* 18 §§ 161–67. See the helpful discussion of the complex financial arrangements and confusing chronology in Schwartz, *Agrippa I*, 4–11, 49–53.

71 Josephus, *Antiquities* 18 §§ 166, 188.

72 Josephus, *Antiquities* 18 §§ 168–204, even by Josephan standards, a long and digressive account. Schwartz suggests that Agrippa got off relatively lightly either because Tiberius saw him as a plausible heir of Philip's territory or because the Praetorian prefect, "like Agrippa, was waiting for Tiberius to die"; Schwartz, *Agrippa I*, 54–55. By multiplying possible scenarios in this way, Schwartz takes away from his criticism of Josephus's sources, although he is largely successful in his attempt to explain varying attitudes and expansions within the narrative source critically.

73 Josephus, *Antiquities* 18 §§ 113–15.

74 Josephus, *Antiquities* 18 §§ 120–23.

Chapter 7: Agrippa I

1 Josephus, *Antiquities* 18 §§ 206–24; Philo, *Embassy to Gaius* §§ 24, 33–38; Philo, *Flaccus* §§ 12–15.

2 Josephus, *Antiquities* 18 § 237; Josephus, *Jewish War* 2 § 181. In regard to the revenue involved, see *Jewish War* 2 §§ 93–100; and (more importantly, as mentioned in the last chapter) *Antiquities* 18 §§ 106–8. In this regard, see especially Philo, *Flaccus* § 25. The monies set aside by Tiberius that might have gone Antipas's way instead made Agrippa financially whole at the intervention of his protector Caligula.

3 Josephus, *Antiquities* 18 §§ 166–67.

4 Josephus, *Antiquities* 18 §§ 123–24.

5 Philo, *Flaccus* §§ 26–35. See also Wilker, *Für Rom*, 333–53.

6 Philo, *Flaccus* §§ 36–96. As a description of ancient anti-Semitism, Philo's text remains a classic.

7 For discussion, see Seth Schwartz, "Were the Ancient Jews a Nation?," in *Early Judaism: New Insights and Scholarship*, ed. Frederick E. Greenspahn (New York: New York University Press, 2018), 71–96. As Schwartz points out, this remains a living issue. In chapter 1, we have seen how during the Maccabean period, Judea established its special relationship with the Romans.

8 Philo, *Flaccus* §§ 102–91. Philo ends his treatise with a triumphant statement of how God protects "the Judean people" (*to Ioudaiôn ethnos*).

9 A direct comparison to Sejanus opens Philo's treatise; Philo, *Flaccus* § 1. Appointed after Sejanus's fall but a partisan of Tiberius, according to Philo, Flaccus was pushed to persecute the Judeans because the leading Egyptians of the city convinced him he would ingratiate himself with Caligula by means of the policy; *Flaccus* §§ 16–24.

10 This move is comparable to Tiberius's dispatch of Piso to challenge Germanicus in Syria; see D. C. A. Shotter, "Cnaeus Calpurnius Piso, Legate of Syria," *Historia: Zeitschrift für Alte Geschichte* 23, no. 2 (1974): 229–45.

11 Philo, *Flaccus* §§ 44–53.

12 Philo, *Embassy to Gaius* §§ 132–37. Philo's attitude toward the emperor clearly evolved; in *Flaccus*, he is not yet the implacable enemy of the Jews portrayed in *Embassy to Gaius*.

13 Suetonius, *Gaius Caligula* 11.1, 50.1–52.1.

14 Philo's transliteration is faulty, appearing as "*Marin*," but he does not appear to have been at home in Semitic languages; *Flaccus* §§ 36–39, especially 39. Because Philo portrays the episode as insulting Agrippa (§ 40), apparently the new king was still in Alexandria at the time.

15 See Schwartz, *Agrippa I*, 75–77; and Josephus, *Antiquities* 19 § 277.

16 Josephus, *Antiquities* 19 §§ 292–96. Basic requirements of the Nazirite vow are set out in Numbers 6; see Jacob Neusner, Bruce Chilton, and Baruch A. Levine, "The Nazirite," in *Torah Revealed, Torah Fulfilled: Scriptural Laws in Formative Judaism and Earliest Christianity* (London: T&T Clark, 2008), 43–75. The timing of these events involves a change of Josephus's chronology. Here I follow the suggestion of Schwartz, *Agrippa I*, 55–57, on the basis of his source-critical analysis (11–17). On the other hand, Schwartz, in my view, dates the appointment of Simon (*Antiquities* 19 §§ 297–99) too early, because that was accomplished under Agrippa's sole authority as king of Judea in 41 CE. Only then could he remove Theophilus, who had been appointed by Vitellius (who continued in post until 39 CE), and replace him with Simon.

17 See Wilson, *Caesarea Philippi*, 24.

18 See Jensen, *Herod Antipas in Galilee*, 201.

19 Josephus puts the blame for this ambition on Herodias; see Josephus, *Antiquities* 18 §§ 240–46. As is by now plain, however, Herodias and Antipas had nurtured the same ambition since the time of their marriage. In this section of his work, Josephus stresses the providential rise of Agrippa (see §§ 238–39), against which Herodias is portrayed as an ambitious but ultimately helpless foil and Antipas as a pliant ruler and a weak man. It is of interest that Philo also portrays Agrippa in providential terms (Philo, *Flaccus* §§103–4) and indeed makes providence a principal theme of both *Flaccus* and *Embassy to Gaius*.

20 See Shotter, "Cnaeus Calpurnius Piso," 229–45, for a balanced and contextually sensitive appraisal.

21 Suetonius, *Gaius Caligula* 10.2.

22 See Josephus, *Antiquities* 18 §§ 247–55. In Josephus, *Jewish War* 2 § 183, the place of exile is given as Spain, a location that Daniel Schwartz surmises has been corrected in *Antiquities*; *Agrippa I*, 5. Vermes has surmised that Caligula also ordered him killed; see Vermes, *True Herod*, 130. It is no insult to today's Lyon, a magnificent city, to observe that exile to ancient Lyons was punishment enough for the ambitious Antipas.

23 See Y. Meshorer, *A Treasury of Jewish Coins from the Persian Period to Bar Kokhba* (Jerusalem: Ben-Zvi, 2001), 94–95 # 11; Hendin, *Guide to Biblical Coins*, 1241; and J. Meyshan, "The Coinage of Agrippa the First," *Israel Exploration Journal* 4, nos. 3–4 (1954): 186–200. Allen Kerkeslager develops an argument that involves the possibility of Agrippa arranging for the minting of coins prior to his departure from Rome; see "Agrippa and the Mourning Rites for Drusilla in Alexandria," *Journal for the Study of Judaism in the Persian, Hellenistic, and Roman Period* 37, no. 3 (2006): 367–400, especially 376–78. In his fascinating reconstruction, Flaccus was reacting to Judean resistance to the funeral images of Drusilla, Caligula's sister.

24 Even after he inherited all his grandfather's lands, Agrippa I used Tiberias as a place to welcome royalty; see Josephus, *Antiquities* 19 §§ 338–42, where the Syrian governor objects to this independent meeting with kings there.

25 Suetonius, *Gaius Caligula* 19.1–3; 32.1; Dio Cassius, *Roman History* 59.17. See Marc Kleijwegt, "Caligula's 'Triumph' at Baiae," *Mnemosyne* 47, no. 5 (1994): 652–71; and, more generally, Aloys Winterling, *Caligula: A Biography*, trans. Deborah Lucas Schneider, Glenn W. Most, and Paul Psionos (Berkeley: University of California Press, 2011).

26 Suetonius, *Gaius Caligula* 22.

27 Deuteronomy 6:4 and Isaiah 45:5–7 were recited frequently in various forms and permutations.

28 Josephus, *Antiquities* 18 §§ 257–59.

29 See Josephus, *Against Apion* 2 §§ 2–144.

30 Philo, *Embassy to Gaius* §§ 200–202.

31 Philo, *Embassy to Gaius* §§ 203–8; Josephus, *Antiquities* 18 §§ 257–61. See Schwartz, *Agrippa I*, 77–89, who is inclined to see greater political wisdom than I am in Caligula's decision. He also prefers to foreground the incident at Yavneh so as to dismiss the controversy in Alexandria as a cause; in my reading, the two situations are linked by a cognate concern.

32 Tacitus, *Histories* 5.9; Josephus, *Antiquities* 18 §§ 261–88; Josephus, *Jewish War* 2 §§ 184–203.

33 See Josephus, *Antiquities* 18 §§ 289–301. Philo depicts the scene quite differently, claiming that Agrippa fainted dead away when he heard during an interview what Caligula planned and wrote to him only on his recovery at home; *Embassy to Gaius* §§ 261–333. Within Philo's narrative, fainting spells abound whenever the proposed statue comes up in Judean hearing (cf. §§ 222–53). For a treatment of the contrasting accounts that attempts a reconciliation, see John Curran, "*Philorhomaioi*: The Herods between Rome and Jerusalem," *Journal for the Study of Judaism in the Persian, Hellenistic, and Roman Period* 45, nos. 4–5 (2014): 493–522, especially 504. Although Josephus echoes Esther 7 in the dynamics of the dinner, his lead has largely been followed in the secondary literature, yet in a matter of such importance, Philo's account of a letter is plausible, and Philo was near the scene while Josephus was not. According to Josephus, Agrippa even decided not to ask for additional territory, as he might have. If so, the reticence was good politics, because Agrippa's aim was for the crown of Judea by this stage, and he followed a course calculated to achieve that aim. See Wilker, *Für Rom*, 131–43.

34 Josephus, *Antiquities* 18 §§ 302–4.

35 Philo, *Embassy to Gaius* §§ 337–48; cf. Tacitus, *History* 9.2; Tacitus, *Annals* 12.54.

36 Josephus, *Antiquities* 19 § 81; Vincent M. Scramuzza, *The Emperor Claudius* (Cambridge, MA: Harvard University Press, 1949), 51.

37   Philo, *Embassy to Gaius* §§ 334–35.

38   See Tosefta Sotah 13.6; Yerushalmi Sotah 9.12 24d; Bavli Sotah 33a; the scholion to Megillat Ta'anit; and the discussion in Amran Tropper, *Simeon the Righteous in Rabbinic Literature: A Legend Reinvented*, Ancient Judaism and Christianity 84 (Leiden: Brill, 2013), 209–11.

39   See Tropper's brilliant chapter "Simeon the Righteous and the Narcissistic Nazirite," in Tropper, *Simeon the Righteous*, 81–112. The relevant passages are Yerushalmi Nedarim 1, 1 36d; Nazir 1, 7 51c; Bavli Nedarim 9b–10a; and Nazir 4b. Throughout his study, Tropper emphasizes that Simeon is set in so many different periods that a biographical treatment is out of the question. Although the vow was marked by asceticism, many people abstained from wine and meat even without taking the vow (Bavli Baba Batra 60b; Shabbat 139a).

40   See Neusner, Chilton, and Levine, "Nazirite," 43–75, and the account of Hegesippus, which Eusebius reports; see *Ecclesiastical History* 2.23.1–19. For an account of the meeting, including its date, see Chilton, *Rabbi Paul*, 131–46, 268.

41   For the roots of the practice, see Eliezer Diamond, "An Israelite Self-Offering in the Priestly Code: A New Perspective on the Nazirite," *Jewish Quarterly Review* 88, nos. 1–2 (1997): 1–18.

42   See Chilton, *Rabbi Jesus*, 213–30.

43   Hegesippus in Eusebius's *Ecclesiastical History* (2.23.7) accepts that this signification is Greek; James seems to be so named here because after his death, the siege of Jerusalem was successful (cf. 2.23.18). Charles C. Torrey, "James the Just, and His Name 'Oblias,'" *Journal of Biblical Literature* 63, no. 2 (1944): 93–98, despairs of making sense of the etymology and opts for an emendation to "Obadaiah." I prefer to suggest that Hegesippus is accurate in his transliteration but far-fetched in his translation. Derived from the Aramaic verb *'abal*, the term would mean "mourner," and mourning was what James was involved in when he fasted at the time of his vision of Jesus raised from the dead; see the Gospel of the Hebrews as cited by Jerome, *De viris Illustribus* 2; and Chilton, *Resurrection Logic*, 122–32.

44   See Joseph A. Fitzmyer and Daniel J. Harrington, *A Manual of Palestinian Aramaic Texts*, Biblica et Orientalia 34 (Rome: Biblical Institute Press, 1978).

45   See W. S. Vorster, "Literary Reflections on Mark 13:5–37: A Narrated Speech of Jesus," *Neotestamentica* 21, no. 2 (1987): 203–24; Wilker, *Für Rom*, 142; and David Schnasa Jacobsen, "An Apocalyptic Farewell Address (13:1–37)," in *Mark*, Fortress Biblical Preaching Commentaries (Minneapolis: Augsburg Fortress, 2014), 183–94.

46   See Kevin J. Madigan and Jon Douglas Levenson, *Resurrection: The Power of God for Christians and Jews* (New Haven: Yale University Press, 2008), 9.

47 Suetonius, *Gaius Caligula* 55–58; Josephus, *Antiquities* 19 §§ 1–126. See Winterling, "Murder on the Palatine," in Winterling, *Caligula*, 172–86.

48 Josephus, *Antiquities* 19 § 161. The popular confusion after the assassination is detailed in §§ 123–57.

49 Suetonius, *Gaius Caligula* 59; Josephus, *Antiquities* 19 §§ 190–200. Josephus's account at this point is very detailed, and he himself can scarcely have been an informant (since he was born in 37 CE). He appears to have relied upon a memoir connected with the court of Agrippa.

50 So Josephus, *Antiquities* 19 §§ 212–20. See also Suetonius, *Claudius* 2–3, 10, 33, 41–42. James Romm follows the opinion of Barbara Levick that Claudius had been "well briefed" on the assassination; Romm, *Dying Every Day: Seneca at the Court of Nero* (New York: Knopf, 2014), 17, 176. The evolving role of Agrippa I, however, suggests that no single "brief" was followed in the chaos of conflicting aims among the plotters.

51 Josephus, *Antiquities* 19 §§ 221–35. There has been some discussion whether Agrippa consistently maneuvered with Claudius as the beneficiary; see Curran, "*Philorhomaioi*," 493–522, especially 505–7. I think there can be little question that he did. After all, Agrippa had a connection with Claudius's family during his upbringing in Rome and shared a tutor with him. More importantly, the conception of client kingship that had benefited the Herodians relied on the maintenance of the Principate; see Jacobson, "Three Roman Client Kings," 22–38. It is true that Josephus in *Jewish War* (2 §§ 206–13) portrays Agrippa as being in touch with both the Senate and Agrippa, but I do not think that it took a long process to see him "gravitating toward Claudius," as Curran puts the matter (505). Indeed, Agrippa's frame of mind is summarized in a single sentence (in § 206) that is far shorter than the Josephan norm, where Agrippa confidently assesses that Claudius must prevail. The one who dithered was Claudius himself. Where Josephus must obviously be corrected, however, is in failing to embed Agrippa's actions within the wider nexus of machinations at the court and in the Senate, which must largely remain a matter for inference.

52 Josephus, *Antiquities* 19 §§ 236–73. For Agrippa's earlier connection with Claudius, see *Antiquities* 18 § 165.

53 Dio Cassius, *Roman History* 60.8.2–3.

54 Josephus, *Antiquities* 19 §§ 274–77; Josephus, *Jewish War* 2 §§ 214–17. Although Aristobulus had played a key role in dealing with Petronius over Caligula's edict, Agrippa had not forgotten that Aristobulus had accused him of bribery to Flaccus in Syria; see *Antiquities* 18 §§ 151–54.

55 Josephus, *Jewish War* 2 § 221. From the point of view of spelling, I follow the lead of Josephus, *Antiquities* 20 § 104.

56 See Andreas J. M. Kropp, "Crowning the Emperor: An Unorthodox Image of Claudius, Agrippa I and Herod of Chalkis," *Syria* 90 (2013): 377–89;

Théodore Reinach and George Francis Hill, *Jewish Coins*, trans. Mary Hill (London: Lawrence and Bullen, 1903), 36; and Frederick W. Madden, *Coins of the Jews, International Numismata Orientalia 7* (London: Trübner, 1881), 136–37. Kropp associates the coin with Josephus, *Antiquities* 19 § 274. In my opinion, the coin is a stylized representation of the speeches Agrippa and Herod gave before the Senate; Dio Cassius, *Roman History* 60.8.3. One reason Agrippa used only his own name was that his brother Herod had also been named a king and naturally used that designation. Still, Agrippa was quite clear that he was the "great" king, which helps explain why Josephus calls him "Agrippa the great."

57 Josephus, still operating on the basis of an Agrippan court memoir, portrays Claudius's actions in this regard as a victory for the new king and describes Claudian policy as a global breakthrough; see *Antiquities* 19 §§ 278–92. He does not mention an expulsion of Jews from Rome in 41 CE, referred to later. See the fine discussion of Schwartz, *Agrippa I*, 94–106, which corrects Josephus on the basis of other evidence.

58 Suetonius, *Claudius* 25.4; Acts 18:2. Suetonius here uses the spelling "Chrestus," a slave's name by which Romans often designated Jesus. For discussion, see Schwartz, *Agrippa I*, 94–96; and Leonard Victor Rutgers, "Roman Policy towards the Jews: Expulsions from the City of Rome during the First Century C.E.," *Classical Antiquity* 13, no. 1 (1994): 56–74, especially 65–66. I quite agree with Rutgers that, taken on its own, Suetonius's reference is difficult to see as having anything to do with the followers of Jesus, and Dio Cassius, *Roman History* 60.6.6, takes us no further. But Agrippa's policy, as directed against some of Jesus's followers (discussed later), indicates what direction Claudius followed. The date on which he acted (and how many times) is uncertain, although the period involved is between 41 CE and 49 CE. See Dixon Slingerland, "Suetonius *Claudius* 25.4, Acts 18, and Paulus Orosius's *Historiarum Adversum Paganos Libri VII*: Dating the Claudian Expulsion(s) of Roman Jews," *Jewish Quarterly Review* 83, nos. 1–2 (1992): 127–44; and more recently, Wilker, *Für Rom*, 365–68.

59 Josephus, *Antiquities* 19 §§ 293–96. As mentioned earlier (note 16), I agree with Schwartz, *Agrippa I*, 55–57, 69, and therefore have to disagree with Wilker, *Für Rom*, 148–49, that the deposit of Agrippa's golden chain is to be dated earlier. This triumphant entry into the temple had long been prepared.

60 As David Goodblatt successfully argues, this was the faction Agrippa aligned himself with rather than with the Pharisees; see "Agrippa I and Palestinian Judaism in the First Century," *Jewish History* 2, no. 1 (1987): 7–32, especially 9, 15. In the process, Goodblatt also explains how Josephus refers to the "common" Judaism of the time (as keeping *ta patria*). This

elegant, historically pointed description (8–10) anticipates the recourse of E. P. Sanders to a conception of common Judaism in *Judaism: Practice and Belief* (London: SCM, 1992). Wilker, *Für Rom*, 164–78, discusses the alliances that brought Agrippa to execute James, the son of Zebedee.

61   Mark gives the Aramaic as *Boanerges*, a plausible Greek transliteration of the Aramaic phrase *beney regesh*, in which *regesh* is better rendered as "tumult" than as "thunder." I appreciate the suggestion of John T. Root, who points out that the gamma in the Greek might here have been rendered an Aramaic ayin; "*Boanerges*, Sons of Thunder (Mark 3:17)," *Journal of Biblical Literature* 100, no. 1 (1981): 94–95. Yet if so, the meaning is much the same, and *regesh* is far more frequently found. I do not agree with Root that the term is Hebraic rather than Aramaic. For a general treatment of Acts 12:1–17, see Craig S. Keener, *Acts: New Cambridge Bible Commentaries* (Cambridge: Cambridge University Press, 2020), 314–22. Keener takes a better and more critical account of Josephus than do most commentaries, but I disagree with his characterization of Agrippa as a "nationalist." Rather, as Daniel Schwartz argues, Agrippa went after the same kind of apocalyptists that Claudius had expelled from Rome; *Agrippa I*, 119–24.

62   See James M. Robinson, Paul Hoffmann, John S. Kloppenborg, eds., *The Critical Edition of Q: Synopsis Including the Gospels of Matthew and Luke, Mark and Thomas with English, German, and French Translations of Q and Thomas: Hermeneia* (Minneapolis: Fortress, 2000).

63   See Chilton, *Rabbi Paul*, 131–41, 268. For the additional and later meeting (without Paul, reflected in vv. 20–29), see pp. 168–70. See also Chilton, "James and the (Christian) Pharisees," in *When Judaism and Christianity Began: Essays in Memory of Anthony J. Saldarini I. Christianity in the Beginning*, Supplements to the Journal for the Study of Judaism 85, ed. Alan J. Avery-Peck, Daniel Harrington, and Jacob Neusner (Leiden: Brill, 2004), 19–47.

64   For a detailed and, in my opinion, convincing explanation of the story in Acts as a paschal Haggadah, see Christian Grappe's "Traces de motifs haggadiques dans le récit de libération merveilleuse de prison de Pierre en Actes 12," in *Haggadah in Early Judaism and the New Testament*, Wissenschaftliche Untersuchungen zum Neuen Testament, ed. Roger David Aus (Tübingen: Mohr Siebeck, 2021), 335–57. He attributes the source involved to Jerusalem and suggests that the account of Agrippa's death in vv. 20–23 is a Haggadah inspired by the prince of Tyre in Ezekiel 26:1–28:16. That textual reference is well established, but I would see it as an organic whole within the paschal Haggadah; the pharaonic element is enhanced by means of the prophecy against the prince of Tyre. All this is part of a prophetic source, rooted in Jerusalem, that is reflected in Acts; see Chilton, *Resurrection Logic*, 157–68.

65   By this stage, although not completed, the renovated Herodian structure was making a huge profit, representing a source of revenue comparable to some tetrarchies; see Hayim Lapin, "Feeding the Jerusalem Temple: Cult, Hinterland, and Economy in First-Century Palestine," *Journal of Ancient Judaism* 8, no. 3 (2017): 410–53. This sophisticated treatment, by means of modeling, acknowledges the degrees of uncertainty involved but coordinates environmental, economic, and cultural considerations with literary, historical, and archaeological evidence. My estimates have been coordinated with Lapin's throughout this volume on the understanding that estimation is all that can be offered at this stage. The wealth that flowed into Agrippa is mentioned by Josephus, *Jewish War* 2 §§ 218–19.

66   Josephus, *Antiquities* 19 §§ 297–311.

67   Marshall, *Jesus, Patrons, and Benefactors*, 164–65.

68   Josephus, *Antiquities* 19 §§ 332–34. Schwartz, *Agrippa I*, 124–34, discusses the issues entangled in Agrippa's background. The previous section of *Antiquities* 19 (§§ 312–31) instances the bias toward Agrippa in an account whose details could easily be framed to portray him differently.

69   An aspect emphasized in discussion subsequent to the exceptional analysis of Schwartz, *Agrippa I*, 157–71; cf. Vermes, *True Herod*, 135; and Jacobson, *Agrippa II*, 21–24. Jacobson wisely suggests that Josephus exaggerates Agrippa's piety, but it may be the case that his reputation in that regard grew during his lifetime because it was in his interest to burnish his image. Wilker, *Für Rom*, 238–40, is right to call attention to the difficulty of assuring that Agrippa I is in view rather than Agrippa II, but the balance of probability in my view lies with the former.

70   Josephus, *Antiquities* 19 §§ 326–27.

71   See Josephus, *Antiquities* 19 §§ 294–95, and the discussion in Wilker, *Für Rom*, 179–87.

72   See Josephus, *Antiquities* 19 §§ 335–37.

73   See Josephus, *Antiquities* 19 §§ 338–44.

74   Josephus, *Antiquities* 19 §§ 345–52. An owl was also featured in the story of Agrippa's providential ascent in *Antiquities* 18 §§ 195, 200. The linking figure could be the slave Thaumastus (§§ 192–94), who might also have been involved in the panegyric source of Josephus's narrative regarding Agrippa.

75   See, for example, Saiidy Hasham, Paolo Matteucci, Paul R. W. Stanley, and Nick B. Hart, "Necrotising Fasciitis," *British Medical Journal* 330, no. 7495 (April 9, 2005), 830–33. Schwartz, *Agrippa I*, 217–18, explores other possibilities, all of them—as he rightly insists—quite tentative.

76   See Matthew 11:20–24 and Luke 10:12–15, part of a later addition to the source known as "Q," a collection of Jesus's sayings that assumed the role of his Mishnah. A comparison between Acts' account and Josephus's is available in Keener, *Acts*, 322–26.

77 Josephus, *Antiquities* 20 § 1.

78 Josephus, *Antiquities* 19 §§ 360–63. Daniel Schwartz deals very helpfully with Claudius's considerations; *Agrippa I*, 149–56. But in addition to the tendency toward imperial centralization, in my view, the local response to Agrippa I's death should also be taken into account.

79 Josephus, *Antiquities* 19 §§ 354–59.

80 Josephus, *Antiquities* 20 § 2.

81 These incidents, related in Josephus, *Antiquities* 20 §§ 2–5, 97–99, and Acts 5:36, reveal the mounting violence in and around Judea. Ben Witherington suggests that Fadus beheaded Theudas rather than crucify him "to avoid having another messianic martyr on his hands"; *New Testament History: A Narrative Account* (Grand Rapids: Baker, 2001), chap. 11. More probably, Theudas was beheaded on the field of battle in the most efficient way possible. By bringing the corpse back to Jerusalem, the Romans displayed their power by a method commensurate with crucifixion.

82 As Frank Russell points out, procurators in Judea had troops at their disposal, but not regular Roman soldiers. The result, predictably, was that these locally recruited ancillary units permitted their hostility to Jews and Judaism to spill out into their official duties; see "Roman Counterinsurgency Policy and Practice in Judea," *Brill's Companion to Insurgency and Terrorism in the Ancient Mediterranean*, Brill's Companions to Classical Studies, Warfare in the Ancient Mediterranean World 1, ed. Timothy Howe and Lee L. Brice (Leiden: Brill, 2015), 248–81, especially 252–53.

83 Josephus, *Antiquities* 19 §§ 363–66.

84 Josephus, *Antiquities* 20 §§ 6–16. For an informative discussion of this and other cases, see Paul McKechnie, "Judean Embassies and Cases before Roman Emperors, AD 44–66," *Journal of Theological Studies* 56, no. 2 (2005): 339–61, especially 342–44.

85 Josephus, *Antiquities* 20 § 102.

86 Josephus, *Antiquities* 20 § 101.

87 Josephus, *Antiquities* 20 §§ 49–53. Her practice of the Nazirite vow is attested in the Mishnah (Nazir 3:6); see Heinrich Graetz, "Zeit der anwesenheit der adiabenischen Königin in Jerusalem und der Apostel Paulus," *Monatsschrift für Geschichte und Wissenschaft des Judentums* 26, no. 6 (1877): 241–55.

88 See Josephus, *Antiquities* 20 §§ 34–48.

89 Josephus, *Jewish War* 2 § 221; Josephus, *Antiquities* 20 §§ 103–4. Herod of Chalcis owed his success to Agrippa I, and when his brother died, he arranged for the assassination of Silas, Agrippa's general who had well and truly fallen out of favor (see *Antiquities* 19 §§ 317–25, 353). Although this signaled a play for power, he seems never to have been considered seriously by Claudius to replace Agrippa I in political terms.

90 Josephus, *Jewish War* 2 §§ 223–27. The description in Josephus, *Antiquities* 20 §§ 105–12, is less sonorous.

91 Josephus, *Antiquities* 20 §§ 113–17; Josephus, *Jewish War* 2 §§ 228–31.

92 Josephus, *Antiquities* 20 §§ 118–24; Josephus, *Jewish War* 2 §§ 232–39.

93 Josephus, *Antiquities* 20 § 124; Tacitus, *Annals* 12.54.

94 Josephus, *Jewish War* 2 §§ 239–46; Josephus, *Antiquities* 20 §§ 125–36. McKechnie, "Judean Embassies," 345–49, gives a fine discussion of this episode. He rightly points out how extensive a reversal of both Cumanus and Quadratus was involved.

95 Josephus, *Jewish War* 2 §§ 247, 252; and Josephus, *Antiquities* 20 §§ 134–38. In the shuffling of responsibilities, Agrippa II lost Chalcis, which came under Nero to Herod of Chalcis's son, called Aristobulus of Chalcis. This Aristobulus functioned as a thoroughly Roman official.

Chapter 8: Bereniké and Agrippa II

1 Josephus, *Antiquities* 18 § 136, as discussed in chapter 6 in relation to Antipas and the Gospels. Oscar Wilde's play had many precedents; see William Chester Jordan, "Salome in the Middle Ages," *Jewish History* 26, nos. 1–2 (2012): 5–15; Jane C. Long, "Dangerous Women: Observations on the Feast of Herod in Florentine Art of the Early Renaissance," *Renaissance Quarterly* 66, no. 4 (2013): 1153–205; and John Stokes, "*Salomé*: Symbolism, Decadence, and Censorship," in *Discovering Literature* (London: British Library, 2014), https://tinyurl.com/yyo7of5c. Wilde's play, with unforgettable and deeply influential illustrations by Aubrey Beardsley, is widely available in the 1904 edition from Melmoth in London.

2 See Josephus, *Antiquities* 19 §§ 276–77, 354–57; and, in addition to the last chapter, Klaus-Stefan Krieger, "Berenike, die Schwester König Agrippas II., bei Flavius Josephus," *Journal for the Study of Judaism in the Persian, Hellenistic, and Roman Period* 28, no. 1 (1997): 1–11.

3 Josephus, *Jewish War* 2 § 223; Josephus, *Antiquities* 20 § 104. His appointment to Philip's former tetrarchy is covered in *Jewish War* 2 §§ 247, 252; and *Antiquities* 20 § 138. The latter move enabled the advancement of Herod of Chalcis's son Aristobulus not only to Chalcis itself but to the kingdom of Lesser Armenia. See Wilker, *Für Rom*, 35–36.

4 See Josephus, *Antiquities* 20 §§ 15–16. Wilker, *Für Rom*, 205–90, discusses the importance of the influence involved.

5 Josephus, *Antiquities* 20 §§ 137–44. Josephus also provides an elaborate tale of Felix's seduction of Drusilla by means of an imposter magician and the tragic note that Drusilla bore a son named Agrippa, with whom she perished when Vesuvius erupted in 79 CE. David M. Jacobson argues that Agrippa II "strongly disapproved of Felix's liaison," but this is an argument

from silence, based on a lack of evidence of his contact with Felix; Jacobson, *Agrippa II*, 36–37.

6 Jacobson, "Coins," 73–96, especially 86–87. This is an extremely perceptive treatment, although I disagree with the characterization that Felix was concerned only "to feather his own nest and throw his weight around." This view is an amalgam of Tacitus (*History* 5.9) and Acts (24:26) and does not allow that even greedy people might harbor lofty ambitions. Like Herod the Great, Felix tried to marry his way into a priestly prestige. Wilker, *Für Rom*, 49–67, skillfully sets out the marital policies of the Herodians, attempting (in my view, unsuccessfully) to reconcile their sexual politics with their commitment to Judaism.

7 Juvenal, *Satire* 6.155–58, in *Juvenal and Perseus*, Loeb Classical Library 91, ed. and trans. Susanna Morton Braund (Cambridge, MA: Harvard University Press, 2004), with adjustments of the translation. On the difficulties of dating, see pp. 18–20.

8 Josephus, *Antiquities* 20 §§ 145–47. Indeed, all Agrippa I's daughters are depicted as exhibiting a tendency toward serial polygamy, and Josephus shows neither the indulgence nor the tact he displays toward other Herodians. As Krieger, "Berenike," points out (3–7), Josephus evaluates Bereniké positively in *Jewish War* but is critical of her in the *Antiquities*. The key to the change is for Krieger disclosed in the *Life* (§§ 343, 355) when she is identified as the protector of Josephus's opponent Justus (7–8). To this I would add that once Bereniké's prospective marriage to Titus ended with his death, Josephus could only think of a possible restoration of the temple in terms that did not include the old Maccabean inheritance. By portraying Bereniké as having polluted that possibility, the way was open for his own appeal for the stability offered by a priestly aristocracy that operated independently of the Maccabees but in coordination with Rome. That aristocracy had been critical of both Agrippa II and Bereniké; see Daniel R. Schwartz, "*Kata Touton ton Kairon*; Josephus' Source on Agrippa II," *Jewish Quarterly Review* 72 (1982): 241–68. David M. Jacobson has recently suggested that Agrippa II's homosexuality stands in the background of the relationship; *Agrippa II*, 127. However, the basis of the assertion (in *Antiquities* 17 §§ 30–31, a reference to his friendship with Philip son of Jacimos) is slight. Still, it is a factor worth reflecting on, and a similar thought has crossed my mind in regard to Philip, Antipas's brother.

9 See Annelise Freisenbruch, "Little Cleopatra: A Jewish Princess and the First Ladies of the Flavian Dynasty," in *Caesar's Wives: Sex, Power, and Politics in the Roman Empire* (New York: Free Press, 2010), 133–54. The marital adventures of Agrippa's daughters are nicely summarized by Wilker, *Für Rom*, 32–33. It seems to me, however, that Josephus does not permit the precise and late dating of Bereniké's marriage to Polemo to 63 CE.

10 See Chilton, *Mary Magdalene*, 138–49.

11 Suetonius, *Claudius* 43–46; Josephus, *Antiquities* 20 §§ 148–57.

12 Josephus, *Antiquities* 20 §§ 158–59.

13 Josephus, *Jewish War* 2 §§ 253–57; Josephus, *Antiquities* 20 §§ 160–66. The fraught politics between Felix and the high priests are described in McKechnie, "Judean Embassies," 339–61, especially 349–50. As McKechnie points out, the case of Eleazar, son of Dinaeus, illustrates the mounting tension between the high priests and Roman rulers.

14 Josephus, *Antiquities* 20 § 166.

15 Josephus, *Antiquities* 20 §§ 167–72; see Craig A. Evans, "Josephus on John the Baptist and Other Jewish Prophets of Deliverance," in *The Historical Jesus in Context*, ed. Amy-Jill Levine, Dale C. Allison, and John Dominic Crossan (Princeton, NJ: Princeton University Press, 2006), 55–63; and Richard A. Horsley, "'Like One of the Prophets of Old': Two Types of Popular Prophets at the Time of Jesus," *Catholic Biblical Quarterly* 47, no. 3 (1985): 435–63, especially 458–59.

16 Josephus, *Antiquities* 20 §§ 179–81.

17 For the setting and Paul's strategy, see Chilton, *Rabbi Paul*, 222–45.

18 A description of James derives from this period (Eusebius, *History of the Church* 2.23.4–6): "Holy from his mother's womb, he did not drink wine or strong drink, nor did he eat meat; a razor did not mount his head; he did not anoint himself with oil, and he did not make use of a bath. He alone was fitted to go into the Sanctuary, for he did not wear wool but linen. He used to enter alone into the Temple, because he did not wear wool but linen, and he entered along into the Temple." Eusebius here quotes Hegesippus, the first Church historian (from the second century). The only element in this description that is implausible is the suggestion that James could enter the sanctuary, which was a high priestly prerogative. For a historical assessment of James, see, for example, Bruce Chilton and Craig A. Evans, eds., *James the Just and Christian Origins*, Supplements to *Novum Testamentum* 98 (Leiden: Brill, 1999); a full bibliography is available in Chilton, "James, the Brother of Jesus," *Oxford Online Bibliographies*, 2017, https://tinyurl.com/y3pytr4v.

19 See Josephus, *Jewish War* 5 §§ 193–94; and John J. Rousseau and Rami Arav, *Jesus and His World: An Archaeological and Cultural Dictionary* (Minneapolis: Fortress, 1995), 312–13.

20 His name is only mentioned first in Acts 23:26 in his letter to Felix. This delay and the fact that Paul explains his legal status twice to Claudius Lysias (Acts 21:39; 22:23–29) is a clear indication that Luke has divided up a single source related to the proceedings against Paul, introducing some duplications and splices in the process; see Dean P. Béchard, "The Disputed Case against Paul: A Redaction-Critical Analysis of Acts 21:27–22:29," *Catholic*

Biblical Quarterly 65, no. 2 (2003): 232–50. I have noted Luke's tendency to do the same with other material (see, e.g., Chilton, *Rabbi Paul*, 303–4). The observation is crucial to understanding Luke's narrative technique and to identifying his sources. In the present case, I note that the Gospel of Luke already indicates that there was a link between Jesus's movement and the Herodian court (see Luke 8:3). As in that case, I believe the likely conduit for such materials was Barnabas, a former property owner in Jerusalem (Acts 4:36–37) with long and deep connections to Jesus's movement, which included Paul's nephew (see Acts 23:16); see Chilton, *Rabbi Jesus*, 111–15, 123, 255–58. For further discussion, see Wilker, *Für Rom*, 256–82.

21 As I have argued elsewhere, this speech—which includes a Resurrection narrative—derives from a prophetic source associated with Jerusalem; see Chilton, *Resurrection Logic*, 157–62.

22 See John J. Kilgallen, "Paul before Agrippa (Acts 26, 2–23): Some Considerations," *Biblica* 69, no. 2 (1988): 170–95, especially 172–73.

23 See Kilgallen, 173; and McKechnie, "Judean Embassies," 339–61, especially 360. The usage of Josephus shows that Ananias was referred to as high priest well after the end of his time in office, which was between his appointment by Herod of Chalcis in 47 or 48 CE (Josephus, *Antiquities* 20 § 103) and Agrippa II's appointment of Ishmael in 59 CE (*Antiquities* 20 § 179); nonetheless, Ananias is called high priest in *Antiquities* 20 § 205, where his growing influence is noted; cf. Josephus, *Jewish War* 2 §§ 243, 409, 426, 429, 441–42.

24 The preferred term for followers of Jesus within rabbinic literature is *Notzerim*. The present term, *Nazoraioi*, alluded to Jesus's upbringing in Nazareth, to the practice of the Nazirite vow by some of his followers, and to the meaning of the verb *natzar*, which refers to "keeping" unapproved practices. The words *Notzerim*, *Nazoreans*, and *Nazirites* are not spelled the same, but they are entangled. The corresponding term preferred in Mark's Gospel, *Nazarene*, also participates in the entanglement, with a preference to the field of meaning associated with *Nazirite*. See Chilton, *Mary Magdalene*, 23–24, 169–70.

25 Josephus, *Jewish War* 2 §§ 266–70; Josephus, *Antiquities* 20 §§ 173–78. In a fine article, Frederick E. Brenk and Filippo Canali De Rossi sort out many of the difficulties concerning Felix and attempt to counteract his negative reputation. In so doing, however, I think they underestimate the impact of his action in Caesarea; see "The 'Notorious' Felix, Procurator of Judaea, and His Many Wives (Acts 23–24)," *Biblica* 82, no. 3 (2001): 410–17. For this episode, see McKechnie, "Judean Embassies," 339–61, especially 353–55. As Brenk and De Rossi point out, however, in any case, Felix was more successful than his successors, and Josephus even reports that he escaped any punishment except for removal (*Antiquities* 20 §§ 182–84). In the last

passage cited, Josephus can be understood to mean that Festus was sent even before Felix was removed from office. The result is continued discussion of their precise chronology as procurators.

26 Josephus, *Antiquities* 20 §§ 185–88; Josephus, *Jewish War* 2 § 271.

27 As discussed in chapter 7.

28 A prophetic interest lies behind Paul's speech in chapter 26. Its account of how Paul was commissioned by the risen Jesus (vv. 8–20) likely emerged from a prophetic circle in Antioch, much as Acts 9:1–22 arose in Damascus and Acts 22:3–21 from Jerusalem. See Chilton, *Resurrection Logic*, 157–62. Here again, Luke splices sources together, relying on the philo-Herodian account for the characterization of Agrippa II, which of course makes no mention of any charge of incestuous relations between him and his sister. By comparison, Josephus is much more prurient.

29 Josephus, *Antiquities* 20 § 190.

30 Josephus, *Antiquities* 20 § 179.

31 Josephus, *Antiquities* 20 §§ 189–96. Again, McKechnie offers a good account of the case; McKechnie, "Judean Embassies," 356–58. Only at the close of his article do I have to disagree with him, when he concludes that Nero "would have ruled in favour of the Jerusalem priests" in the case against Paul (McKechnie, 361). By that time, the case itself was no longer cogent, and the priestly factions were in disarray. Acts closes with Paul in what might be described as loose custody (see Acts 28:16), and that seems plausible until his death during Nero's pogrom in 64 CE.

32 Josephus, *Antiquities* 20 §§ 197–200; Eusebius, *Ecclesiastical History* 2.23.

33 During his graduate seminar in 1971, the late Raymond Brown referred in my hearing to the relationship between the families as being of the tenor of "the Hatfields and the McCoys." A more compelling consideration for Ananus, however, was the opportunity to eliminate a leader who encouraged lay sacrifice (in the shape of the Nazirite vow) and who had been associated with the apostle Paul. Ananias, after all, remained a great influence on the scene in Jerusalem. Relations among the high priestly families are described in E. Mary Smallwood, "High Priests and Politics in Roman Palestine," *Journal of Theological Studies* 13, no. 1 (1962): 14–34. Her characterization of their politics is disputed in Richard A. Horsley, "High Priests and the Politics of Roman Palestine: A Contextual Analysis of the Evidence in Josephus," *Journal for the Study of Judaism in the Persian, Hellenistic, and Roman Period* 17, no. 1 (1986): 23–55. Rather than being rebellious themselves, Horsley portrays the high priests as wishing to "control the rebellion until they could come to an accommodation with the Romans" (55). I would not disagree; after all, that is the attitude of Josephus in his *Life*. That accommodation, however, involved allowing for sacred autonomy.

34 See Eusebius, *History of the Church* 2.23.19. Hegesippus also portrays the execution vividly in this chapter, in terms that echo the death of Stephen in Acts 7:54–60.

35 Josephus, *Antiquities* 20 §§ 201–4.

36 Josephus, *Antiquities* 20 §§ 211–12. The new name, of course, did not survive the *damnatio memoriae* pronounced upon Nero in 68 CE; see Jacobson, *Agrippa II*, 48.

37 Josephus, *Antiquities* 20 §§ 211–23. This is beautifully described, in comparison to Herod the Great's positive impact on the Jerusalem economy by means of his program of extending the temple, in Joseph Geiger, "Rome and Jerusalem: Public Building and the Economy," in Jacobson and Kokkinos, *Herod and Augustus*, 157–69. When Vermes claims that "Agrippa II was greatly devoted to his Jewish subjects and looked after their wellbeing," he does not keep this contrast in mind; see Vermes, *True Herod*, 139. In terms of expenditure, Agrippa II's primary devotion was clearly to Rome; after that came Judaism and Bereniké, in an order that would bear discussion. In this regard, see Jacobson, *Agrippa II*, 51–52. Because Jacobson has correctly captured Agrippa II's attitude during this period, however, I cannot concur with him that he agreed to Bereniké's marriage to Polemo as late as 63 CE (47), an estimate he apparently derived from Wilker, *Für Rom*, 32–33.

38 See Tacitus, *Annals* 15.37–44; and Chilton, *Rabbi Paul*, 250–52.

39 Josephus, *Antiquities* 20 §§ 252–58.

40 See, for example, his use of the term *aristokratia* at the close of his list of the high priests of Israel; Josephus, *Antiquities* 20 §§ 224–51. We will see how this reflects his own political philosophy. See Wilker, *Für Rom*, 44, 75. My approach to this question develops the suggestion made in Chilton, "Joseph Bar Matthias's Vision," 69–87.

41 Josephus, *Jewish War* 2 §§ 277–308. His account in the *Antiquities* ends with Florus, since he had already told the story of the war in his earlier work.

42 Josephus, *Jewish War* 2 § 309. Jacobson, *Agrippa II*, 29, makes Agrippa II's later speech in Jerusalem the moment at which he became "unstuck." In my view, it was the belatedness of his intervention that was more his error. Above all, however, Agrippa II's loyalty lay more with Rome than with his people, a flaw in a Herodian at any time, which became fatal because it was obvious.

43 Josephus, *Jewish War* 2 §§ 310–14; and the description in Wilker, *Für Rom*, 64–66. She also describes the speech of Agrippa II on pp. 394–97, in my opinion attributing more piety to him than is warranted.

44 Josephus, *Jewish War* 2 §§ 315–29.

45 Josephus, *Jewish War* 2 §§ 330–32.

46 Josephus, *Jewish War* 2 §§ 333–41.

47 Josephus, *Jewish War* 2 §§ 342–404. The speech is clearly written, well thought out, and a triumph of sycophancy. At the same time, I do not know of a better or more moving summary of the extent and overwhelming force of the Roman Empire. There is no reasonable doubt of Josephus's sincerity on this point and every reason to suppose that Agrippa II truly did share the opinion, even if he did not speak the words as Josephus wrote them. Still, the prediction that the Roman would consign the Holy City to flames in the event of war (§ 397) is an example of *vaticinium ex eventu*. For a good discussion, see Jacobson, *Agrippa II*, 60–66.

48 Josephus, *Jewish War* 2 §§ 391–94.

49 Josephus, *Jewish War* 2 § 344.

50 Josephus, *Jewish War* 2 §§ 405–7. I observe that Josephus does not name the capital here, referring simply to Agrippa's "kingdom." He attempted to blunt the irony of how blatantly Agrippa was choosing sides.

51 Josephus, *Jewish War* 2 §§ 408–10. The centrality of this practice within the settlement with Rome is a matter of agreement between Josephus and Philo, although they disagree on a practical matter. Philo says the emperor bore the expense (*Embassy to Gaius* §§ 157, 317), while Josephus claims that Judea paid (*Against Apion* 2 § 77)

52 Josephus, *Jewish War* 2 §§ 411–56.

53 Josephus, *Jewish War* 2 §§ 457–80.

54 Josephus, *Jewish War* 2 §§ 487–98.

55 Josephus, *Jewish War* 2 §§ 281–483.

56 Josephus, *Jewish War* 2 §§ 499–558. Throughout this section of his narrative, Josephus provides a detailed account that is interesting in tactical terms; only pivotal moments of the war are indicated here.

57 Josephus, *Jewish War* 2 §§ 559–94. While in his *Life* §§ 28–29, Josephus portrays his aim as conciliating the populace with the realities of Roman power, his account of his purpose is more accurately described in *Jewish War* 2 §§ 569–84 as military. Similarly, he claims in *Jewish War* (2 § 575) to have had John of Gischala under his control until John turned greedy (§§ 585–94; see also §§ 599, 614–31), while in *Life* (§§ 45, 189–99), he complains that John freelanced for his own interests and undermined Josephus from the outset. In both cases, the power of hindsight is on display. Whichever source is consulted, it is clear that Josephus hated John more than he hated the Romans and that he loved his life more than he hated the two of them combined. In any case, the consensus for the revolt seems unmistakable among those whom Josephus ostensibly led; see Josephus, *Jewish War* 3 §§ 9–28.

58 Josephus, *Jewish War* 2 §§ 595–613. The town is named after its principal product, salted fish, in Greek. In Aramaic, it was known as *Magdala'*.

59 Josephus, *Jewish War* 2 §§ 632–46.

60 Josephus, *Jewish War* 3 §§ 1–3, 29–34, 59–69, 110–28. Josephus's digressive panegyric on Roman military organization (§§ 70–109) is valuable for its content and the attitude it reveals.

61 Josephus, *Jewish War* 3 §§ 110–14, 129–40. Josephus even claims that he already foresaw defeat but urged a course of moderation to Jerusalem because he wished to avoid disloyalty by personally surrendering to the Romans (§§ 136–40). His own account of his thought of flight from Jotapata (§§ 193–206) makes such claims appear transparently self-serving.

62 Josephus, *Jewish War* 3 §§ 141–391, especially 350–54. In Josephus's conception, Latin *fortuna* (*tukhê* in Josephus's Greek) and the Septuagint's *pronoia* operated together to make the Roman victory a providential necessity; for an analysis along these lines, see Nicole Kelley, "The Cosmopolitan Expression of Josephus's Prophetic Perspective in the 'Jewish War,'" *Harvard Theological Review* 97, no. 3 (2004): 257–74. She provides an incisive analysis of the presentations of the closing events of the siege at Jotapata and the more famous siege at Masada. Josephus's detailed description of the sieges and the tactics deployed on both sides remains convincing (apart from sporadic claims of Roman discomfiture and Josephan heroism), however self-interested and theologically argumentative. Still, when he claims that all Jerusalem went into mourning at the report of his death (*Jewish War* 3 § 436), the effect is comic.

63 Josephus, *Jewish War* 3 §§ 392–408. For an attempt to identify the scriptural background of Josephus's alleged prophecy, see Roger David Aus, "Isaiah 10:34 and the 'Ambiguous Oracle' in Josephus, *Bellum Judaicum* 6.312–313 (Part One)," *Review of Rabbinic Judaism* 21, no. 2 (2018): 151–75; and "Isaiah 10:34 and the 'Ambiguous Oracle' in Josephus, *Bellum Judaicum* 6.312–313 (Part Two)," *Review of Rabbinic Judaism* 22, no. 1 (2019): 1–30.

64 See Tacitus, *History* 1.10, 2.1, 5.13; and Suetonius, *Life of Vespasian* 4.

65 See Tacitus, *History* 5.13; and the discussion in Warren Carter, *Matthew and Empire: Initial Explorations* (Harrisburg: Trinity Press International, 2001), 23–34. It is notable that Tacitus refers to the oracles as *ambages*, while Josephus uses the Greek *amphiboles* in *Jewish War* 6 § 312. Tacitus also attributes healings to Vespasian, with some neatly rationalistic commentary worthy of Plutarch, while Josephus recounts an exorcism in Vespasian's presence and his own by a sage named Eleazar in *Antiquities* 8 §§ 46–49.

66 Talmud Bavli Gittin 56b and comparable texts, ably discussed in Anthony J. Saldarini, "Johanan be Zakkai's Escape from Jerusalem: Origin and Development of a Rabbinic Story," *Journal for the Study of Judaism in the Persian, Hellenistic, and Roman Period* 6, no. 2 (1975): 189–204.

67 See the quoted principle of Yochanan in Avot de Rabbi Natan 4, which cited Hosea 6:6: "I desire mercy rather than sacrifice." It is of interest that

Yochanan was contemporary with the emergence of the Gospel of Matthew (see Matthew 9:13; 12:7).

68   The edict of Caligula had inspired the approach along apocalyptic lines; now it reached full fruition. Silas or Silvanus was an apostolic agent for James (Acts 15:27, 30–33), who also had a role in composing letters with apocalyptic content: 1 Thessalonians (1:1) and 1 Peter (5:12); see Chilton, *Resurrection Logic*, 139–40, 160–61. He likely composed Mark 13 in its substantially final form.

69   He and other former associates of James appear to have escaped from Jerusalem, as did much of the population; see Josephus, *Jewish War* 5 §§ 420–23. Craig Koester has made a good argument that patristic reference to a flight to Pella should be understood in this context; "The Origin and Significance of the Flight to Pella Tradition," *Catholic Biblical Quarterly* 51, no. 1 (1989): 90–106.

70   Josephus, *Jewish War* 3 §§ 396–98, 408, 485. He also claims that Titus took pity on the inhabitants of Magdala (§ 501), although at the end of the battle, Vespasian consigned huge numbers to death and slavery, with Agrippa II's cooperation (§§ 532–42, especially 462–542). This day (September 26, 67 CE) likely saw the end of Mary Magdalene's life; see Chilton, *Mary Magdalene*, 90–92. Josephus also credits Titus with tenderness toward the inhabitants of Gischala (§§ 92, 117–20).

71   Josephus, *Jewish War* 3 §§ 443–47.

72   Josephus, *Life* §§ 349–56. The figure involved was Justus, against whom Josephus develops a long argument. After the war, Justus and Josephus competed for the honor of being more philo-Roman than the other, bringing credit to neither. But the harangue is interesting for the way it relates to the description of the campaign against Tiberias in Josephus, *Jewish War* 3 §§ 445–61.

73   Josephus, *Jewish War* 4 §§ 1–53, 62–83. After this, Josephus relates the campaign against Gischala, which gives him occasion to settle accounts with another competitor, John of Gischala (§§ 84–120).

74   Josephus, *Jewish War* 4 §§ 121–365.

75   Josephus, *Jewish War* 4 §§ 318–25, 387–88, 503–44, 556–84. On Vespasian, see §§ 366–77. The description that follows of Zealot predations in Jerusalem (§§ 378–409) is classic; see Richard A. Horsley, "The Zealots: Their Origin, Relationships and Importance in the Jewish Revolt," *Novum Testamentum* 28, no. 2 (1986): 159–92. Josephus gives Vespasian's confidence as a reason for his delay in pressing the siege of Jerusalem; a more urgent concern for him was maintaining a huge army in the field as various generals jockeyed for position to succeed Nero.

76   Josephus, *Jewish War* 4 §§ 486–502 (cf. §§ 545–55, 585–91, 630–55). But Vespasian had been preparing the final siege of Jerusalem since § 410 according to this account.

77 Josephus, *Jewish War* 4 §§ 592–621. Josephus also places his own liberation at this time (see §§ 622–29), all as part of Vespasian's appreciation of those who played a role in the "providence" (*pronoia*) that had brought him to the cusp of power. By this stage, the author had earned the name under which he appears in library catalogs: Flavius Josephus, since he was the virtual property of the Flavian house. That was a new identity for Joseph bar Mattiya, as he had been known by his family, the priesthood, and the revolutionaries.

78 Josephus, *Jewish War* 4 §§ 656–63.

79 Josephus, *Jewish War* 5 §§ 39–46. By contrast, Josephus describes the deadly internecine divisions within Jerusalem and even God's providential opposition to the resistance in §§ 1–39.

80 Josephus, *Jewish War* 5 §§ 114, 362–423. Josephus attributes to himself much the same kind of speech he had attributed to Agrippa II in *Jewish War* 2 §§ 342–404.

81 Josephus, *Jewish War* 5 §§ 447–51, especially 455–56. Throughout this section of *Jewish War*, Josephus details the campaign, the geography, the architecture of Jerusalem and the temple, and the Roman tactics and the tactical methods of the resisters in loving, ghastly detail.

82 Josephus, *Jewish War* 5 §§ 261–65. Josephus calls Titus "Caesar" in this account as well as in the next vignette mentioned here.

83 Josephus, *Jewish War* 5 §§ 541–47.

84 Josephus, *Jewish War* 6 §§ 33–53, 93–113.

85 Josephus, *Jewish War* 6 §§ 164–68, 177–92, 228.

86 Josephus, *Jewish War* 6 §§ 241, 249–66, 281–84. This alleged magnanimity on Titus's part is famously contradicted by the later Christian historian Sulpicius Severus; *Chronicle* 2.30. If correct, however, the counterassertion by Sulpicius Severus is only true by luck, since it anachronistically attributes to Titus an opposition to both Judaism and Christianity.

87 Josephus, *Jewish War* 3 § 446. This resolve is expressed in the midst of the Galilean campaign, in close association with Titus's action in support of his father. After the destruction of the temple, Vespasian also ordered that the temple in Leontopolis should be destroyed (*Jewish War* 7 §§ 420–36). Little doubt of his purpose exists, except in Josephus's estimate.

88 Josephus, *Jewish War* 6 §§ 310–15. Cf. Aus, "Isaiah 10:34," parts 1 and 2.

89 Josephus, *Jewish War* 6 §§ 411–12.

90 Josephus, *Jewish War* 6 § 316.

91 Josephus, *Jewish War* 7 §§ 23–39.

92 Josephus, *Jewish War* 7 §§ 100–115.

93 See Tacitus, *Histories* 2.2; and Wilson, *Caesarea Philippi*, 33–37.

94 Dio Cassius, *Roman History* 65.15.3–5; cf. Suetonius, *Titus* 7.7; and Quintilian, *Orator's Education* 4.1.19.

95 Jacob Maltiel-Gerstenfeld, "A Portrait Coin of Berenice, Sister of Agrippa II?," *Israel Numismatic Journal* 4 (1980): 25–26. A literature has grown around the issue of when Bereniké left Rome and returned and even whether she did return; see Arthur Keaveney and John Madden, "Berenice at Rome," *Museum Helveticum* 60, no. 1 (2003): 39–43. As they acknowledge, they and other scholars have largely followed the remarkable study of John A. Crook, "Titus and Berenice," *American Journal of Philology* 72, no. 2 (1951): 162–75. While I agree with them that Crook pressed the estimate of Bereniké's influence too far, they seem to me to read against the grain of Quintilian and Dio Cassius as well as Josephus in minimizing her role.

96 Josephus, *Jewish War* 5 § 19.

97 Josephus, *Jewish War* 5 § 334.

98 Josephus, *Antiquities* 20 §§ 143–44. Josephus promised a fuller account, but none is known. Titus's brief reign and death are treated in Suetonius, *Titus* 7–10; and Brian W. Jones, *The Emperor Titus* (New York: St. Martin's, 1984).

99 Because Josephus took to passing on salacious gossip of incestuous relations between Agrippa II and Bereniké, it has been argued that they (or at least Agrippa) had died by the time Josephus wrote the *Antiquities* in 93 CE. A good, responsible argument has been offered by Wilker, *Für Rom*, 43, 462–64. But Kokkinos has maintained on inscriptional evidence that because an officer named Archieus served under Agrippa II and then Trajan (whose reign began in 98 CE), a later death for Agrippa II must be inferred; *Herodian Dynasty*, 397. Kokkinos's argument has been refuted by Rudolf Haensch on the grounds that a continuous military career of such a length is likely not at issue; see "The Contributions of Inscriptions to Our Knowledge of the Herodian Dynasty," *Scripta Classica Israelica* 33 (2014): 99–116, especially 110. Although Haensch's reservations are notable, it remains probable that Agrippa survived later into the century. After all, Josephus changed his attitude toward him by the time he came to write his *Life* (see, e.g., §§ 361–67). In *Agrippa II*, Jacobson attempts to date Agrippa's death on the basis of numismatic evidence, but that only provides a *terminus post quem* (in this case 95 CE) and is sensitive to the possibility of the future discovery of later coins.

100 Dahmen, "With Rome in Mind?," 99–112, especially 109–10.

Epilogue: The Herodian Caesura within the Politics of Empire

1 Such an evaluation was fulsomely articulated at the end of the nineteenth century. Albert Réville's précis of the Herodian achievement would seem outlandish to anyone not familiar with the simple facts of the case. See

"Les Hérodes et le rêve hérodien," *Revue de l'histoire des religions* 28 (1893): 283–301, especially 283: "Un élément perturbateur, interrompant le déroulement logique de l'histoire du peuple d'Israël au dernier siècle avant notre ère et pendant le premier qui la commence; une série d'efforts vigoureux, systématiquement poursuivis sans jamais aboutir qu'à des résultats partiels et temporaires; quelque chose de brilliant et de somber à la fois; de quoi fournir la matière d'une douzaine de tragédies historiques; des éclipses et des retours de fortune également inattendus; le plus singulier mélange de diplomatie raffinée et de passions barbares, d'énergie indomptable et de lâches faiblesses; une énigme enfin dont la solution pique la curiosité des historiens:—tel est l'ensemble de faits aggloméré autour de ce nom d'Hérode qu se détache avec un étrange relief sur le fond lugubre des derniers temps de la nation juive." Although Réville's style is not readily translated into English, his summary might be rendered as: "A disruptive component, interrupting the logical unfolding of the history of the people of Israel during the first century before the Common Era and the following century; a series of efforts in force, systematically pursued but reaching only partial and temporary results; brilliant and somber at the same time; sufficient to furnish material for a dozen historical tragedies; equally unexpected collapses and rebounds of fortune; the most singular mix of refined diplomacy and barbaric passion, of unconquerable energy and base weaknesses; a mystery, in the end, whose solution arouses historians' curiosity—such are the aggregate facts around the name Herod, which stands in strange relief against the dismal background of the final period of the Jewish nation." The close of this précis shows that a view of the Herodians as aberrant travels easily with a conception of "the Jewish nation" as a spent force.

2 F. E. Romer, "A Case of Client-Kingship," *American Journal of Philology* 106, no. 1 (1985): 75–100; see also Jacobson, "Three Roman Client Kings," 22–38; and Michael Alexander Speidel, "Early Roman Rule in Commagene," in *Heer und Herrschaft im Römischen Reich der Hohen Kaiserzeit* (Stuttgart: Franz Steiner, 2009), 563–80. Romer and Jacobson skillfully untangle the accounts in Josephus, *Jewish War* and *Antiquities*; Tacitus, *Histories* and *Annals*; Suetonius, *Lives*; and Dio Cassius, *Roman History*. In this epilogue, I will not comment in detail on ancient sources. At the same time, the epilogue does not set out a summary of results but refers back to the discussion in the body of the book, indicating the appropriate chapter and providing only selective citations in the course of commenting on the political impact and legacy of the Herodians.

3 See Josephus, *Jewish War* 1 § 446; 2 §§ 114–16; Josephus, *Antiquities* 17 §§ 339–41; and the discussion in chapters 5 and 6.

4 See Josephus, *Antiquities* 16 §§ 90–129, 261–69; Josephus, *Jewish War* 1 §§ 455–56; and the discussion in chapter 4. Josephus makes Archelaus's

purpose and effect clear, although the order in which his different kinds of intervention occurred seems to have suffered from a recourse to differing sources.

5   So Josephus, *Antiquities* 16 §§ 325–60. As Josephus indicates, by this stage, Herod imagined that Archelaus (and even Glaphyra) had plotted with Alexander.

6   As seen in chapter 5.

7   Josephus, *Apion* 2 §§ 164–67. He claims (§§ 164–65), "The particular differences among the customs and laws of all people are endless. For instance, some entrust the authority of government to monarchies, others to the rule of many, yet others to the populace. Our lawgiver, however, acknowledged none of these, but—as someone might say forcing an expression—pointed to a governmental 'theocracy,' attributing all power and might to God." Josephus here confuses the form of governance with its basis, in that (as we shall see) monarchies, oligarchies, democracies, and many combinations of those forms may be theocratically justified, and any appeal to divine rule must assign some instrument of its communication to people.

8   For a fine treatment, see George Heyman, "The Roman Imperial Cult," in *The Power of Sacrifice: Roman and Christian Discourses in Conflict* (Washington, DC: Catholic University of America Press, 2007), 45–94.

9   See Alison Keith, "Philosophical Currents in Flavian Literature: Introduction," *Phoenix* 72, nos. 3–4 (2018): 211–17.

10   A theme explored in Chilton, *Abraham's Curse*, 33–43.

11   See Josephus, *Jewish War* 1 §§ 193–200; Josephus, *Antiquities* 14 §§ 140–44; and the discussion in chapters 1 and 2.

12   For further discussion of this theme, see Bruce Chilton, "The Modernization of Christianity," in *Religious Foundations of Western Civilization: Judaism, Christianity, and Islam*, ed. Jacob Neusner (Nashville: Abingdon, 2006), 431–84.

13   See Josephus, *Jewish War* 1 §§ 282–85; Josephus, *Antiquities* 14 §§ 381–89; and chapters 2 and 3.

14   See Josephus, *Jewish War* 1 §§ 241, 344; Josephus, *Antiquities* 14 §§ 300, 467; and chapters 3 and 4. The centrality of the theocratic claim of the Herodian dynastic project is well explored by Wilker, *Für Rom*, although it strikes me as an overstatement to say that they were "predestined" (477) for their role of mediation with Rome and even more so to claim a religious motivation on their behalf (49–67, 475–77). Perhaps in correcting (helpfully and wisely) against the routine dismissal of the Herodians' affiliation with Judaism, Wilker attributes more piety to them as a whole than is warranted.

15   See E. P. Sanders, "The Essenes and the Dead Sea Sect I: Origins, History, Membership and Organization," in *Judaism: Practice and Belief,*

63 BCE–66 CE (Minneapolis: 1517 Media, 2016), 535–76. To call the Hasmoneans a "common enemy" (543), however, overlooks Herod's marriage to Mariamme.

16 See Josephus, *Antiquities* 15 §§ 365–79; and chapter 4.

17 See Josephus, *Jewish War* 1 §§ 110–14; Josephus, *Antiquities* 13 §§ 408–18; and chapter 1.

18 See Josephus, *Jewish War* 1 § 204; Josephus, *Antiquities* 14 § 159; and chapter 2.

19 See Josephus, *Antiquities* 15 §§ 267–79; and chapter 4.

20 See Josephus, *Jewish War* 1 §§ 648–50; Josephus, *Antiquities* 17 §§ 151–67; and chapter 4.

21 Discussed in chapter 2 with regard to Josephus's *Antiquities* 14 §§ 168–84; and *Jewish War* 1 §§ 204–15.

22 Discussed in chapter 4 with regard to Josephus, *Antiquities* 17 §§ 151–67.

23 See Josephus, *Antiquities* 17 §§ 340–41; and the discussion in chapter 5. Because Alexander and Glaphyra had had children, there was no question of a levirate marriage (Deut 25:5–10). One of them, Tigranes, became king of Armenia on Augustus's appointment. His nephew, another Tigranes, was also appointed king by Nero. Both of them wisely kept their distance from the center of the Herodian dynasty and left behind marks of their thorough assimilation into the Roman Empire in their coins; see Frank L. Kovacs, "Tigranes IV, V, and VI: New Attributions," *American Journal of Numismatics* 20 (2008): 337–50. For other Herodian relatives who enjoyed Roman preferment, see Jacobson, *Agrippa II*, 2–3.

24 See Josephus, *Jewish War* 2 §§ 80–92; Josephus, *Antiquities* 17 §§ 299–316; and the discussion in chapter 5.

25 See Josephus, *Antiquities* 18 §§ 116–19; and the discussion in chapter 6.

26 Detailed in chapter 6.

27 See Michael J. Hollerich, "Religion and Politics in the Writings of Eusebius: Reassessing the First 'Court Theologian,'" *Church History* 59, no. 3 (1990): 309–25.

28 Chapters 7 and 8 explain how the referents of the source shift over time as it evolved and also deal with related passages.

29 Eusebius emphasizes James's legitimate role as bishop; see *Ecclesiastical History* 2.1.2–5; 2.23.1, referring in the first passage to Clement's *Hupotuposeis*. The term *episkopos* means "overseer," as does *mebaqqar*, an office with a responsibility to do many of the same things that an *episkopos* was to do: to teach the Torah (even to priests) as well as the particular traditions of the community, to administer discipline, and to see to the distribution of wealth (see *Damascus Document* 13.7–8; 14.8–9, 13–14; and 1 Tim 3:1–7). Cf. Bruce Chilton, "Jesus, Levitical Purity, and the Development of Primitive Christianity," in *The Book of Leviticus: Composition and Reception*, ed. Rolf

Rendtorff and Robert A. Kugler, Vetus Testamentum Supplements 93 (Leiden: Brill, 2003), 358–82, especially 375–77.

30   Discussed in chapter 7.

31   Manaen is identified as a companion of Antipas yet belongs to a prophetic circle in Antioch; see Chilton, *Resurrection Logic*, 157–68.

32   See Romm, *Dying Every Day*, 89–92 (dealing especially with *De Clementia*).

33   See Chilton, *Abraham's Curse*, 121–24; and Éric Rebillard, "Persecution and the Limits of Religious Allegiance," in *Christians and Their Many Identities in Late Antiquity, North Africa, 200–450 CE* (Ithaca, NY: Cornell University Press, 2012), 34–60.

34   See Seneca, *De Clementia* 1.5.1; and the discussion in John K. McVay, "The Human Body as Social and Political Metaphor in Stoic Literature and Early Christian Writers," *Bulletin of the American Society of Papyrologists* 37 (2000): 135–47.

35   See Eusebius, *In Praise of Constantine* 1.6, 3.5; and Bruce Chilton, "Religion, Politics, Culture, Law, and Society: Christianity," in Neusner, *Religious Foundations*, 177–90.

36   See Sabine MacCormack, "Cicero in Late Antiquity," in *Cambridge Companion to Cicero*, ed. Catharine Steel (Cambridge: Cambridge University Press, 2013), 251–305.

37   See Philo, *Flaccus* §§ 102–91, discussed in chapter 7. For a treatment of Philo's active engagement in the philosophical tradition before him, see Maren Niehoff, "Roman Philosophy and the Jews," in *Philo of Alexandria: An Intellectual Biography* (New Haven: Yale University Press, 2018), 69–90.

38   See Josephus, *Antiquities* 18 §§ 195–202; 19 §§ 345–52.

39   See Marleen B. Flory, "Octavian and the Omen of the 'Gallina Alba,'" *Classical Journal* 84, no. 4 (1989): 343–56; M. Gwyn Morgan, "Vespasian and the Omens in Tacitus 'Histories' 2.78," *Phoenix* 501 (1996): 41–55; and Trevor S. Luke, "A Healing Touch for Empire: Vespasian's Wonders in Domitianic Rome," *Greece & Rome* 57, no. 1 (2010): 77–106.

40   So Josephus, *Jewish War* 3 §§ 399–408, discussed in chapter 8. See also 6 §§ 310–15.

41   For the role of the metaphor in the historiography of John F. Kennedy, see Richard Aldous, *Schlesinger: The Imperial Historian* (New York: Norton, 2017), 313.

42   See Suetonius, *Nero* 21.

43   Vigorously expressed in Josephus, *Jewish War* 5 § 19.

44   So Josephus, *Jewish War* 5 §§ 124–28; see the discussion in chapter 8.

45   See, for example, Targum Isaiah 1:15; Bruce Chilton, *The Isaiah Targum: Introduction, Translation, Apparatus and Notes*, Aramaic Bible 11 (Wilmington: Glazier, 1987), 3.

46 Josephus, *Jewish War* 5 §§ 60–61, where arrows miss an unprotected Titus during his reconnaissance of Jerusalem.

47 The Sadducean position under Archelaus is discussed in chapter 5; Josephus's characterization of the Sadducees as brutal appears in Josephus, *Jewish War* 2 §§ 164–66. He describes their ethos as *agriôteron*, which I take refers to a more unpleasant attitude than mere abruptness (at least in Josephus's experience), so I have sought a stronger term than "boorish," the usual rendering.

48 See Josephus in *Antiquities* 20 §§ 145–47; and the discussion in chapters 7 and 8.

49 See Steve Mason, "Of Despots, Diadems and *Diadochoi*: Josephus and Flavian Politics," in *Writing Politics in Imperial Rome*, Brill's Companions to Classical Studies, ed. W. J. Dominik, J. Garthwaite, P. A. Roche (Leiden: Brill, 2009), 323–49; and Josephus, *Jewish War* 2 §§ 90–91. Mason argues that Josephus's sustained argument for aristocracy, which extends through the *Antiquities*, applies to Roman politics. His observation, based on the awareness that Josephus is "the most prolific author from Flavian Rome" (349), is apposite, although after all, Josephus's argument is applied to Judea in particular.

50 This comes out strongly in his *Life* §§ 1–16.

51 See, for example, Josephus, *Jewish War* 2 §§ 595–613, within the discussion in chapter 8.

52 See the frequently cited edition, Carl von Clausewitz, *On War*, trans. J. J. Graham (New York: Barnes & Noble, 2004), 1 § 24 (although the aphorism appears in various forms throughout the work).

53 See Josephus, *Jewish War* 2 §§ 151–53. The heroism Josephus attributes to the Essenes during the war with Rome stands in contrast to a persistent preference to portray them as pacifists, a continuing trope of scholarship derived from Philo. See, for example, Sanders, "Essenes and the Dead Sea Sect," 544–45. A bracing corrective is offered by Steve Mason in "Essenes and Lurking Spartans in Josephus *Judean War*: From Story to History," in Rodgers, *Making History*, 219–61.

54 See Josephus, *Life* §§ 361–66; and Steve Mason, "Of Audience and Meaning: Reading Josephus's *Bellum Judaicum* in the Context of a Flavian Audience," in *Josephus and Jewish History in Flavian Rome and Beyond*, ed. Joseph Sievers and Gaia Lembi (Leiden: Brill, 2005), 71–100, especially 84–87.

55 And the prospect endured, of course, at least until the fourth century; see Honora Howell Chapman, "What Josephus Sees: The Temple of Peace and the Jerusalem Temple as Spectacle and Text," *Phoenix* 63, nos. 1–2 (2009): 107–30.

56   See Taʿanit 4:8 in the Talmud Yerushalmi and the fine treatment of Matthew V. Novenson, "Why Does R. Akiba Acclaim Bar Kokhba as Messiah?," *Journal for the Study of Judaism* 40, nos. 4–5 (2009): 551–72.

57   See Naiweld, "Use of Rabbinic Traditions," 255–85.

58   See Hayim Lapin, *Rabbis as Romans: The Rabbinic Movement in Palestine, 100–400 CE* (Oxford: Oxford University Press, 2012).

59   Mark 12:17; Matthew 22:21; Luke 20:25; discussed in chapter 6.

60   Evident in the contrast between Romans 13:1–7 and Philippians 3:20; see chapter 8.

61   Sporadically surfacing, for example, in Luke 8:3 and Acts 13:1; discussed in chapters 6 and 8.

62   See Mark 13 and its developing associations over decades, discussed in chapters 7 and 8.

63   See Bruce Chilton, "Justin and Israelite Prophecy," in *Justin Martyr and His Worlds*, ed. Sara Parvis and Paul Foster (Minneapolis: Fortress, 2007), 77–87.

64   See, for example, James Carroll, *Constantine's Sword: The Church and the Jews, a History* (Boston: Houghton Mifflin, 2001).

65   See the edition of William Haller, "The Tenure of Magistrates and Kings," in *The Works of John Milton* (New York: Columbia University Press, 1932); and the treatment of the theme in Chilton, "Modernization of Christianity," 431–81.

66   Josephus, *Jewish War* 2 § 197.

67   Well criticized by Amarta Sen, *Identity and Violence: The Illusion of Destiny*, Issues of Our Time (New York: Norton, 2006), responding to Samuel P. Huntington's *The Clash of Civilizations and the Remaking of World Order* (New York: Simon & Shuster, 1996).

BIBLIOGRAPHY OF SOURCES

ANCIENT WRITINGS HAVE been sourced from the following editions:

APPIAN

Appian, Roman History. Vol. 3, *The Civil Wars, Books 1–3.26*. Loeb
    Classical Library 4, edited by Horace White. Cambridge, MA:
    Harvard University Press, 1913.

CICERO

Cicero, Letters to Atticus. Vol. 1. Loeb Classical Library 7, edited by
    D. R. Shackleton Bailey. Cambridge, MA: Harvard University
    Press, 1999.
Cicero, Orations: In Catilinam 1–4. Pro Murena. Pro Sulla. Pro Flacco.
    Loeb Classical Library 324, edited by C. MacDonald. Cam-
    bridge, MA: Harvard University Press, 1976.
Cicero, Orations: Pro Caelio, De Provinciis Consularibis, Pro Balbo. Loeb
    Classical Library 447, edited by R. Gardner. Cambridge, MA:
    Harvard University Press, 1958.

DIO CASSIUS

Dio Cassius, Roman History. Vol. 5, *Books 46–50*. Loeb Classical
    Library 82, edited by Earnest Cary and Herbert B. Foster.
    Cambridge, MA: Harvard University Press, 1917.
Dio Cassius, Roman History. Vol. 7, *Books 56–60*. Loeb Classical
    Library 175, edited by Earnest Cary and Herbert B. Foster. Cam-
    bridge, MA: Harvard University Press, 1924.

EUSEBIUS

Eusebius, Ecclesiastical History. Vol. 1, *Books 1–5.* Loeb Classical Library 153, edited by Kirsopp Lake. Cambridge, MA: Harvard University Press, 1926.

"Tricennatsrede an Constantin" [generally known as *In Praise of Constantine*], *Eusebius Werke I.* Die Griechischen Christlichen Schriftsteller der ersten drei Jahrhunderte 7, edited by Ivar A. Heikel, 195–259. Leipzig: Hinrichs, 1902.

HEBREW BIBLE

Biblia Hebraica Stuttgartensia. Edited by K. Elliger, W. Rudolph, et al. Stuttgart: Deutsche Bibelgesellschaft, 1997.

JOSEPHUS

Josephus, Jewish Antiquities. Vol. 7, *Books 12–14.* Loeb Classical Library 365, edited by Ralph Marcus. Cambridge, MA: Harvard University Press, 1963.

Josephus, Jewish Antiquities. Vol. 8, *Books 15–17*, edited by Ralph Marcus and Allen Wikgren. Cambridge, MA: Harvard University Press, 1963.

Josephus, Jewish Antiquities. Vol. 9, *Books 18–19.* Loeb Classical Library 433, edited by Louis H. Feldman. Cambridge, MA: Harvard University Press, 1965.

Josephus, Jewish Antiquities, Book 20, General Index. Loeb Classical Library 446, edited by Louis H. Feldman. Cambridge, MA: Harvard University Press, 1965.

Josephus, The Jewish War. Vol. 1, *Books 1–3.* Loeb Classical Library 203, edited by H. St. J. Thackeray. Cambridge, MA: Harvard University Press, 1927.

Josephus, The Jewish War. Vol. 2, *Books 4–7.* Loeb Classical Library 210, edited by H. St. J. Thackeray. Cambridge, MA: Harvard University Press, 1928.

Josephus, The Life. Against Apion. Loeb Classical Library 186, edited by H. St. J. Thackeray. Cambridge, MA: Harvard University Press, 1926.

JUVENAL

Juvenal and Perseus. Loeb Classical Library 91, edited by Susanna Morton Braund. Cambridge, MA: Harvard University Press, 2004.

LIVY

Livy, History of Rome. Vol. 10, *Books 35–37*. Loeb Classical Library 301, edited by J. C. Yardley. Cambridge, MA: Harvard University Press, 2018.

MACROBIUS

Macrobius, Saturnalia. Vol. 1, *Books 1–2*. Loeb Classical Library 510, edited by Robert A. Kaster. Cambridge, MA: Harvard University Press, 2011.

Macrobius, Saturnalia. Vol. 2, *Books 3–5*. Loeb Classical Library 511, edited by Robert A. Kaster. Cambridge, MA: Harvard University Press, 2011.

MIDRASH RABBAH

Midrash rabah ha-mevo'ar. Jerusalem: Havre ha-Makhon, 1998.

MISHNAH

Mishnayoth. Edited by Philip Blackman. Gateshead, UK: Judaica, 1990.

NEW TESTAMENT

Novum Testamentum Graece. Edited by Barbara and Kurt Aland et al. Stuttgart: Deutsche Bibelgesellschaft, 2012.

PHILO

Philo, "Flaccus," Philo in Ten Volumes. Vol. 9. Loeb Classical Library 363, edited by F. H. Colson, 293–403. Cambridge, MA: Harvard University Press, 1962.

Philo, The Embassy to Gaius. Loeb Classical Library 379, edited by F. H. Colson. Cambridge, MA: Harvard University Press, 1991.

PLUTARCH

Plutarch, Lives. Vol. 7, *Demosthenes and Cicero, Alexander and Caesar.* Loeb Classical Library 99, edited by Bernadotte Perrin. Cambridge, MA: Harvard University Press, 1919.

Plutarch, Lives. Vol. 9, *Demetrius and Antony. Pyrrhus and Gaius Marius.* Loeb Classical Library 101, edited by Bernadotte Perrin. Cambridge, MA: Harvard University Press, 1920.

QUINTILIAN

Quintilian, The Orator's Education. Vol. 2, *Books 3–5.* Loeb Classical Library 125, edited by Donald A. Russell. Cambridge, MA: Harvard University Press, 2001.

SENECA

Seneca, Moral Essays. Vol. 1, *De Providentia. De Constantia. De Ira. De Clementia.* Loeb Classical Library 214, edited by John Basore. Cambridge, MA: Harvard University Press, 1928.

SEPTUAGINT

Septuaginta. Edited by Alfred Rahlfs. Stuttgart: Württembergische Bibelanstalt, 1935.

STRABO

Strabo, Geography. Vol. 1, *Books 1–2.* Loeb Classical Library 49, edited by Horace Leonard Jones. Cambridge, MA: Harvard University Press, 1917.

SUETONIUS

Suetonius, Lives of the Caesars. Vol. 2, *Claudius. Nero. Galba, Otho, and Vitellius. Vespasian. Titus, Domitian. Lives of Illustrious Men: Grammarians and Rhetoricians. Poets (Terence. Virgil. Horace. Tibullus. Persius. Lucan). Lives of Pliny the Elder and Passienus Crispus.* Loeb Classical Library 38, edited by J. C. Rolfe. Cambridge, MA: Harvard University Press, 1914.

Suetonius, Lives of the Twelve Caesars. Vol. 1, *Julius. Augustus. Tiberius. Gaius Caligula.* Loeb Classical Library 31, edited by J. C. Rolfe. Cambridge, MA: Harvard University Press, 1914.

SULPICIUS SEVERUS

Sulpicii Severi Chronica. Corpus Christianorum Series Latina 63, edited by Piergiorgio Parroni. Turnhout: Brepols, 2017.

TACITUS

Tacitus. Vol. 3, *Histories, Books 4–5; Annals, Books 1–3.* Loeb Classical Library 249, edited by Clifford H. Moore and John Jackson. Cambridge, MA: Harvard University Press, 1931.

Tacitus. Vol. 4, *Annals, Books 4–6, 11–12.* Loeb Classical Library 312, edited by John Jackson. Cambridge, MA: Harvard University Press, 1937.

TALMUD BAVLI (BABYLONIAN TALMUD)

Talmud Bavli: The Gemara, the Classic Vilna Edition. Edited by Yisroel Simcha Schorr et al. Brooklyn: Mesorah, 2006.

TALMUD YERUSHALMI (JERUSALEM TALMUD [SOMETIMES ALSO CALLED PALESTINIAN TALMUD AND TALMUD OF THE LAND OF ISRAEL])

The Jerusalem Talmud. Studia Judaica, edited by Heinrich W. Guggenheimer. Berlin: De Gruyter, 2020.

TOSEFTA

Tosefta nach den Erfurter und Wiener Handschriften. Edited by Moses Samuel Zuckermandl. Trier: Lintz, 1882.

INDEX OF HISTORICAL FIGURES

INDEX OF SCHOLARS